LEROY
HORSEMOUTH
WALLACE
GREG
ERRICO
MILLIONS
JACK
WHITE
SUSIE IBARRA
PAULI
THE
PSM
RYAN
SAWYER
JIM KELTNER

THE DRUM THING

DEIRDRE O'CALLAGHAN

THE DRUM THING

PRESTEL
Munich • London • New York

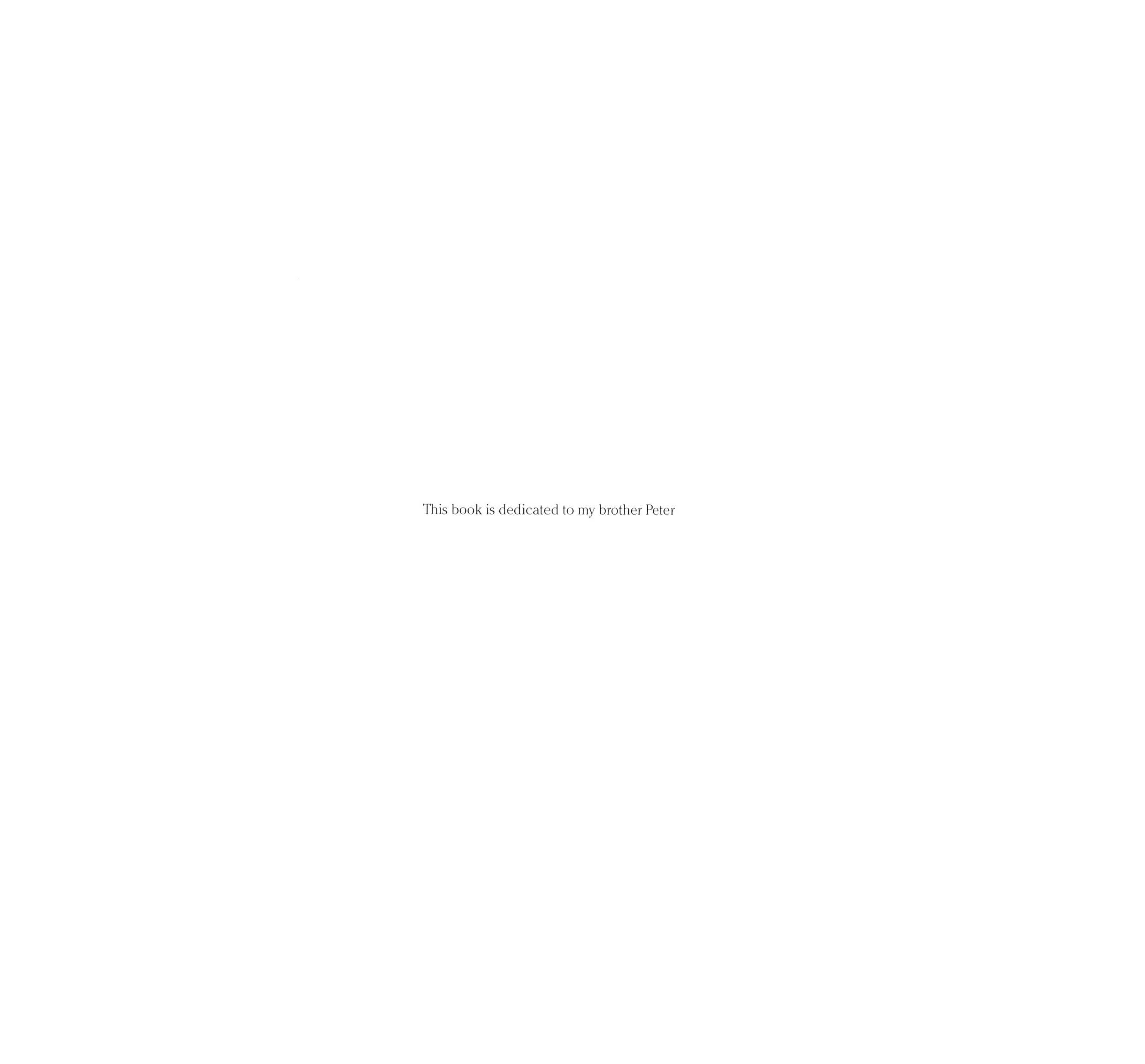

This book is dedicated to my brother Peter

CONTENTS

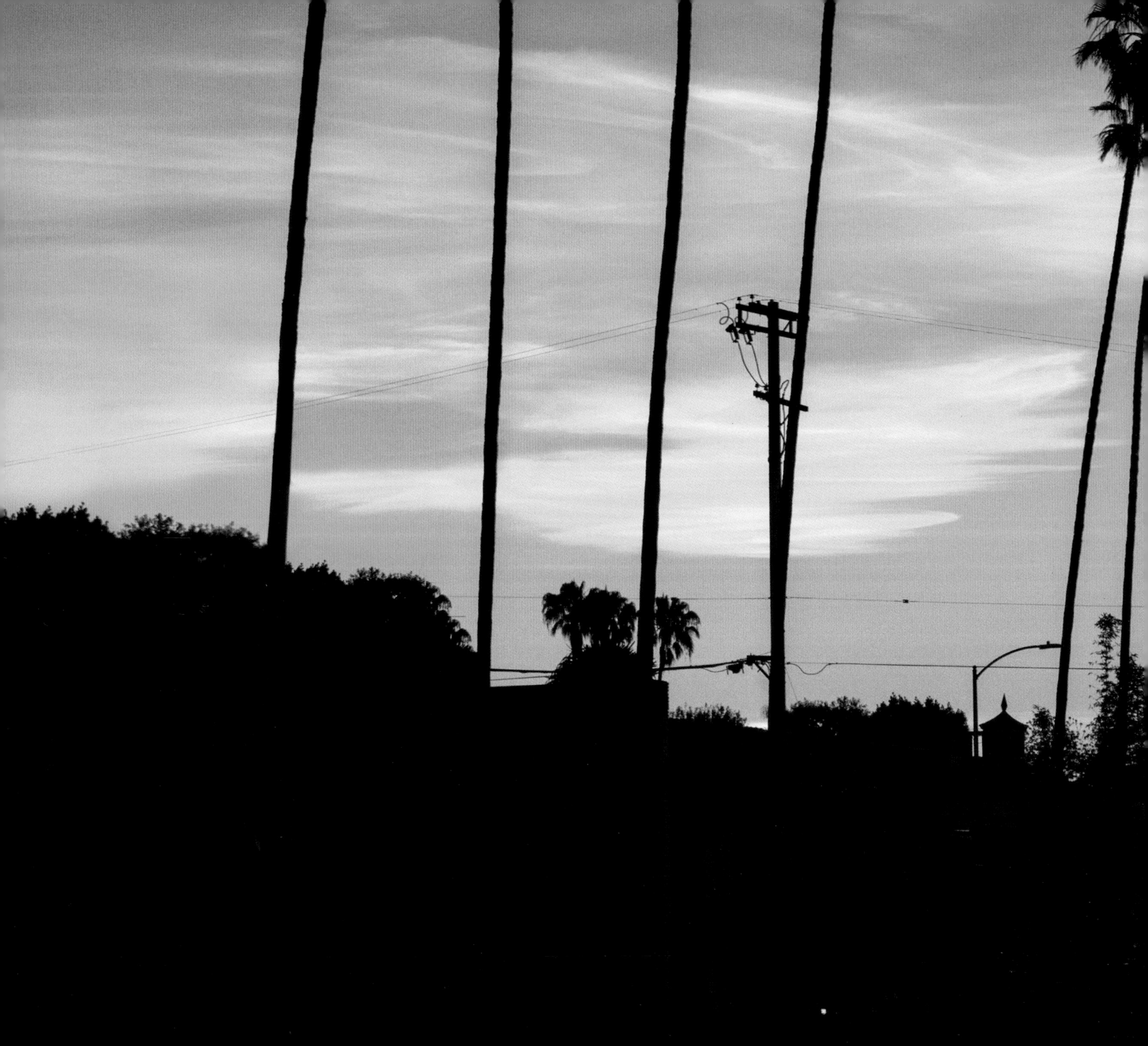

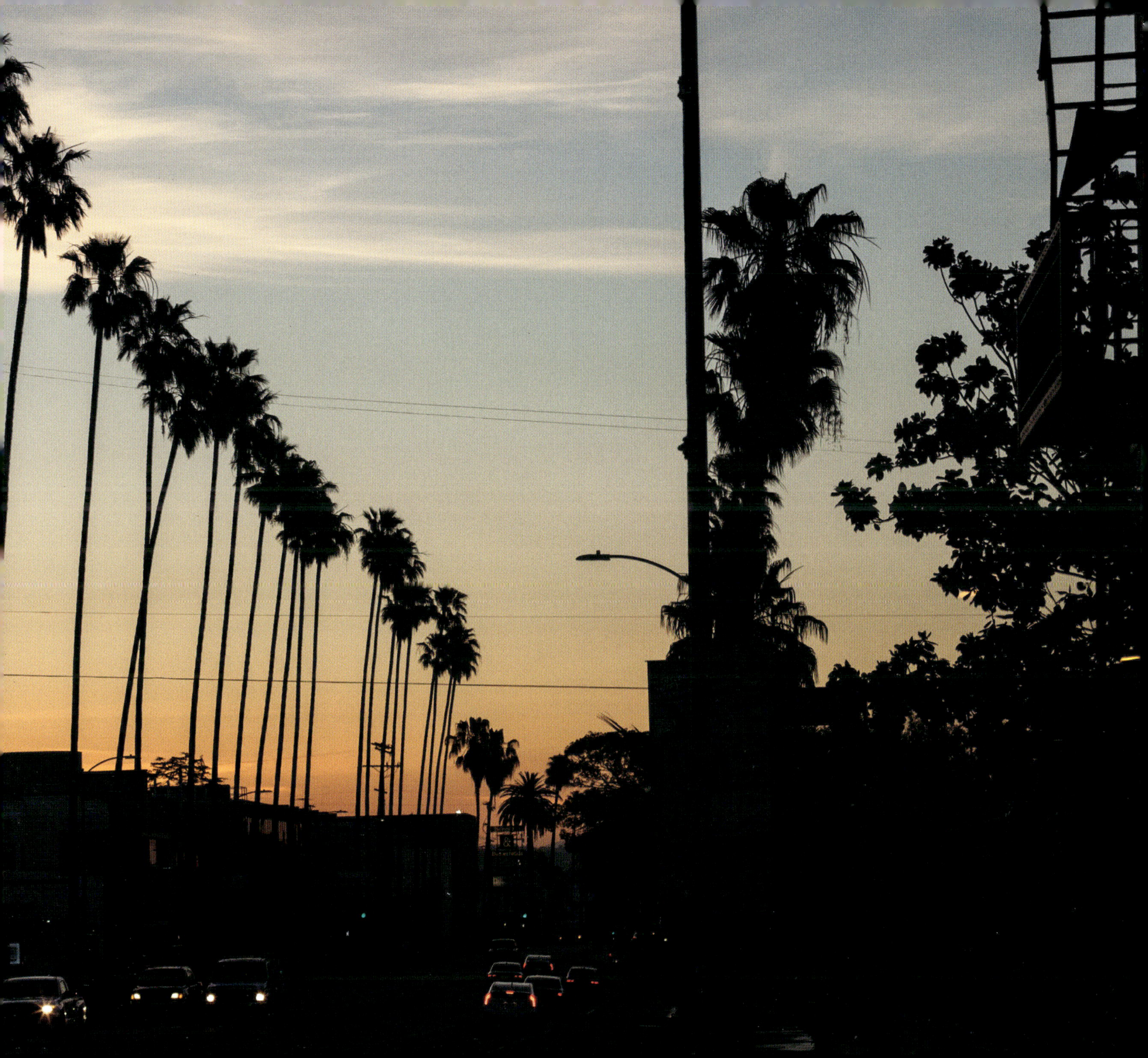

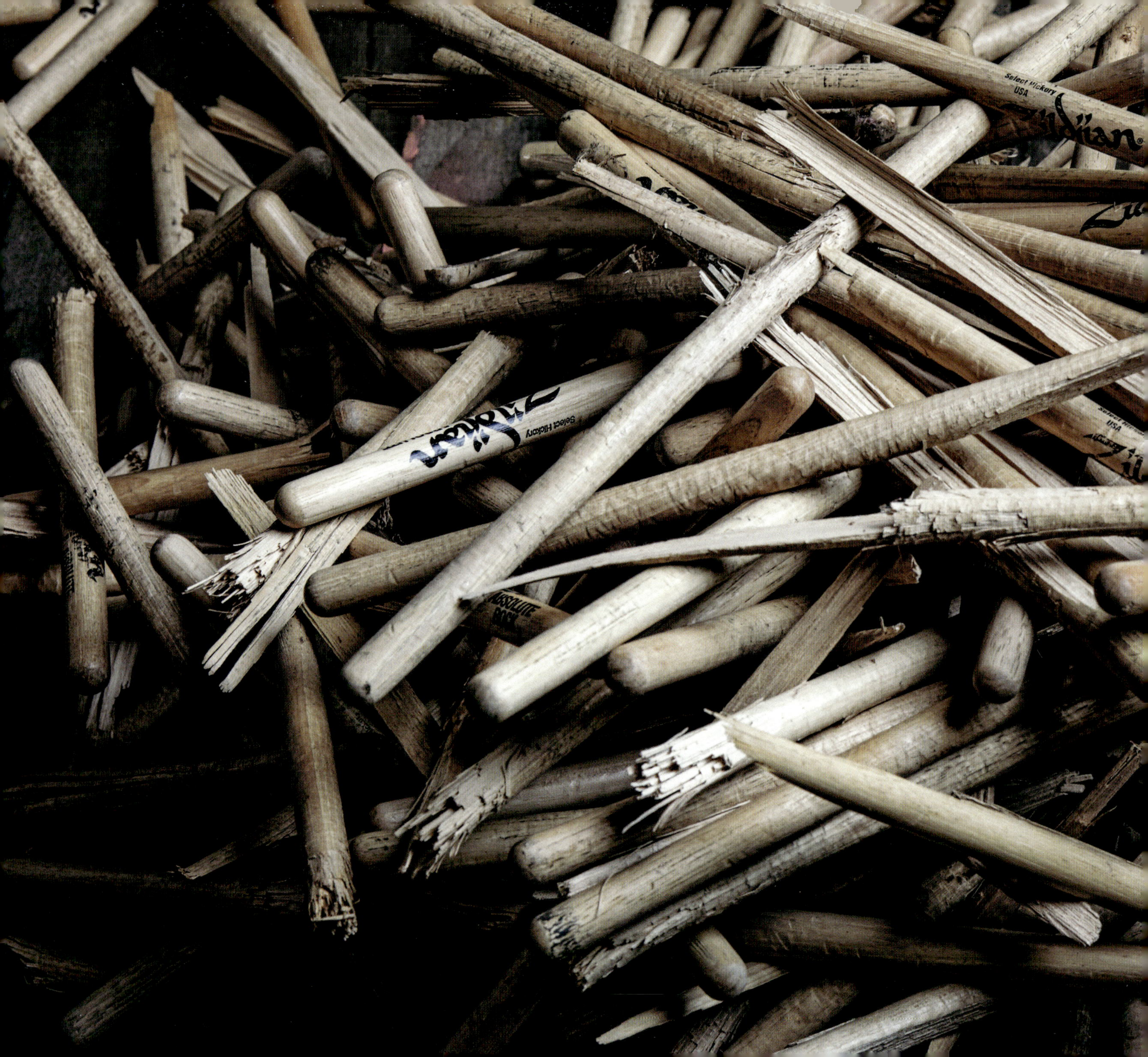
Select Hickory
USA
Zildjian
Select Hickory

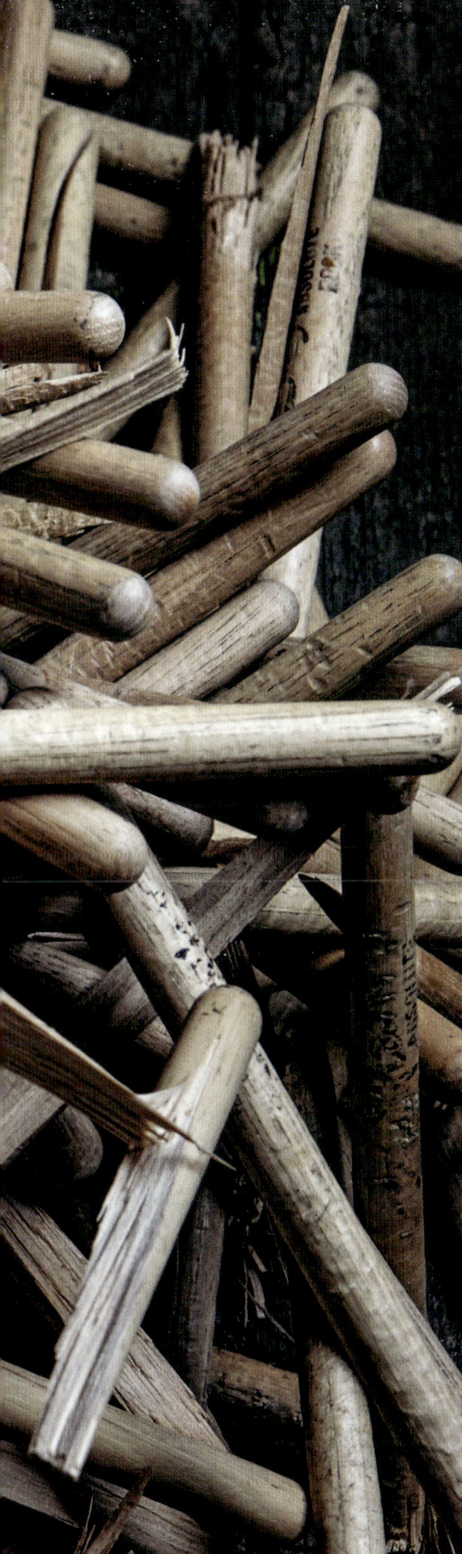

INTRODUCTION

I love the rhythm section. Drummers are underrated and underappreciated. They are the leaders even though they sit at the back. They are a band's foundation. They express the intuitive rhythm we all have inside us, connecting us to our primal instincts. They also display respect and restraint, managing time with intelligence and skill.

I grew up in Cork, Ireland, as part of a large family that loved music: reggae coming from one room, hip hop or Neil Young from another. The radio in the kitchen was always tuned to some Irish station playing god knows what. There were also programmes my father always listened to, which featured all the old Irish rebel and folk songs. To top it off, my sister, who was studying music at university, had a giant tape deck in our shared bedroom from which she played classical music, blasting out Rachmaninoff, Sibelius and Mahler at midnight. As a result, my taste in music has always been eclectic, but one constant is that I've always been drawn to the rhythm section.

Some say rhythm is medicine; drumming has been compared to an addiction, a form of meditation and a language in and of itself – a way of communicating. Playing an instrument is like storytelling, and the whole personality of a musician is translated into how they play. As a photographer, I love watching a drummer perform – the sheer physicality of playing this kind of instrument. To me drumming is almost like a dance, and the idea of capturing this energy and rhythm really appealed to me. This was something I wanted to explore by creating a book which tells drummers' stories, not only in pictures, but also in their words, to find out more about what drives them, both as musicians and as people.

I feel very privileged and honoured that all these musicians welcomed me into their homes, studios and lives so that I could document and share their stories. As I was preparing this book, I spent a few weeks in Ireland listening back through the interviews, hearing about how they got started, why they chose their instruments and the journeys their music has taken them on. Certain phrases and pauses took me back to where I had been sitting in the room and reminded me of what it felt like on the day of the interview. I hope that this book evokes those moments, not only through my pictures but through the words of the drummers themselves.

Note: The interviews and photo shoots for this book were conducted between 2011 and 2015.

Deirdre O'Callaghan

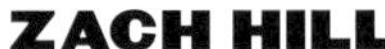

ZACH HILL

Death Grips / Hella / The I.L.Y's / Undo K From Hot. Photographed in California

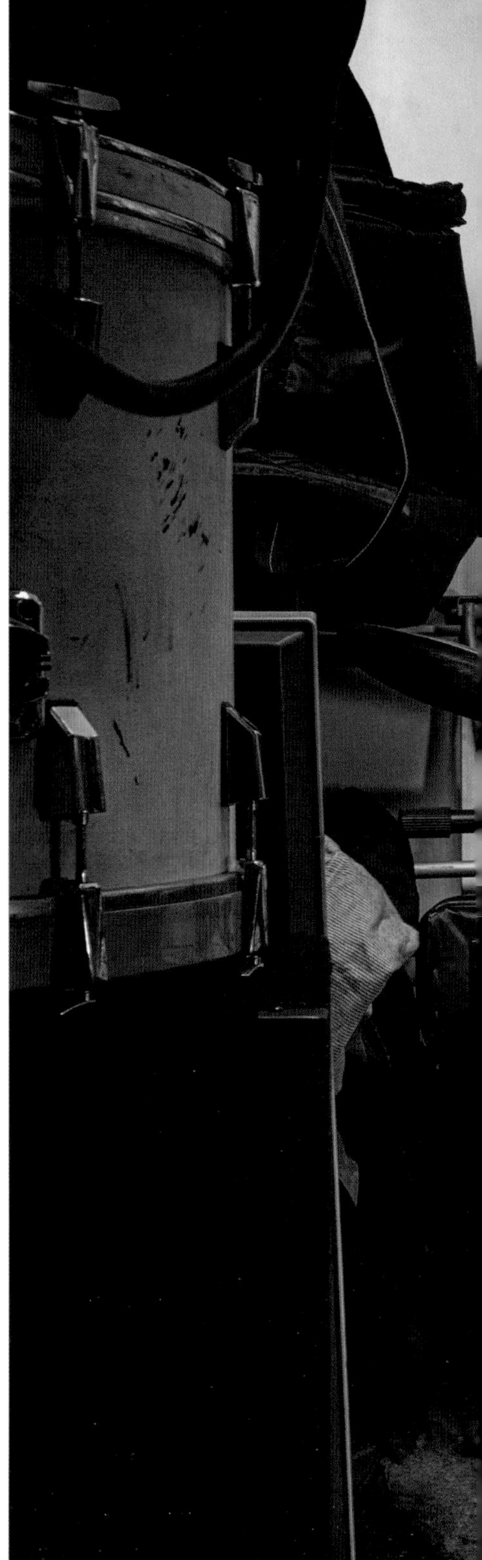

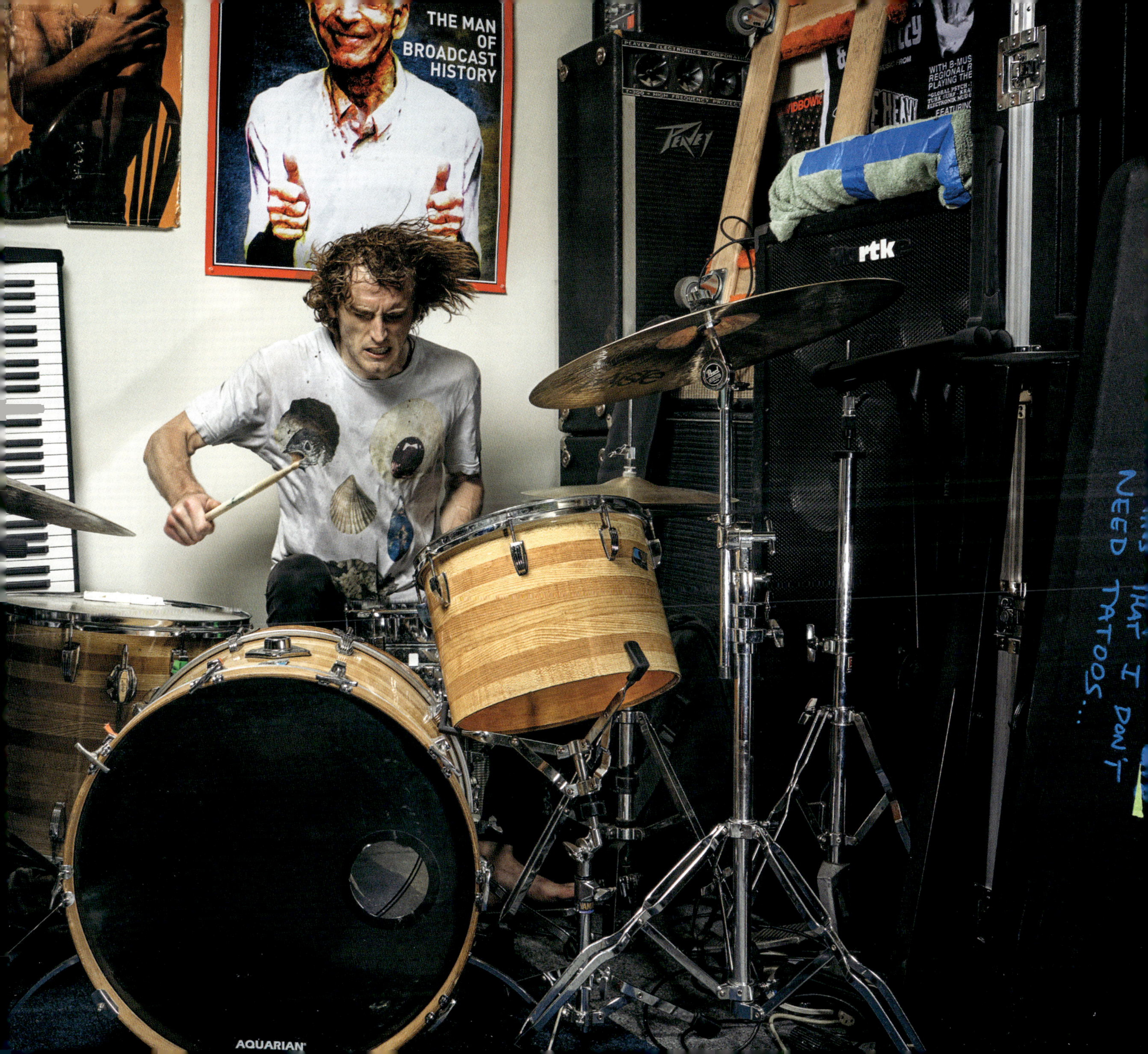
THE MAN
OF
BROADCAST
HISTORY
Peavey
rtk
NEED TATOOS...
THAT I DON'T
AQUARIAN

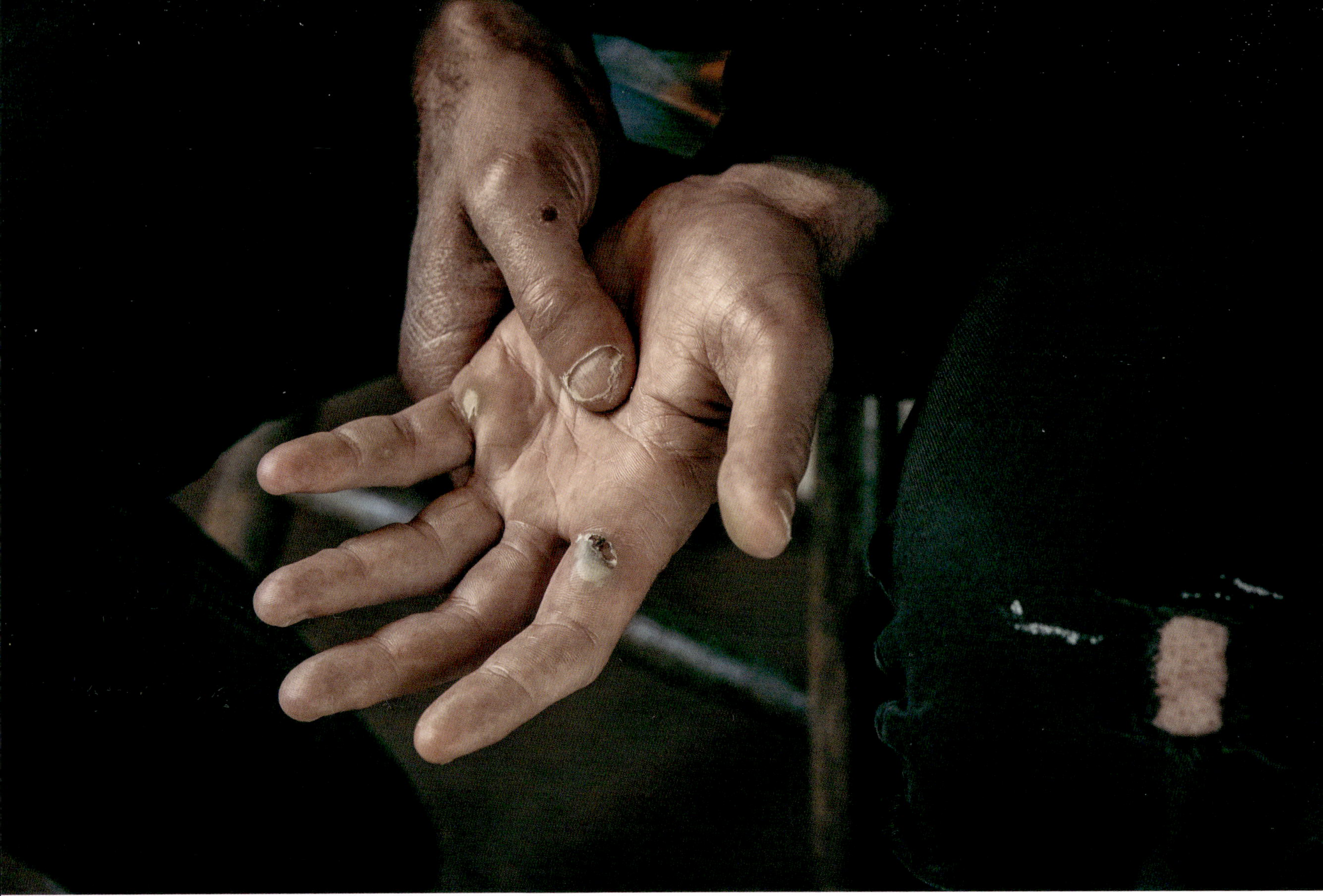

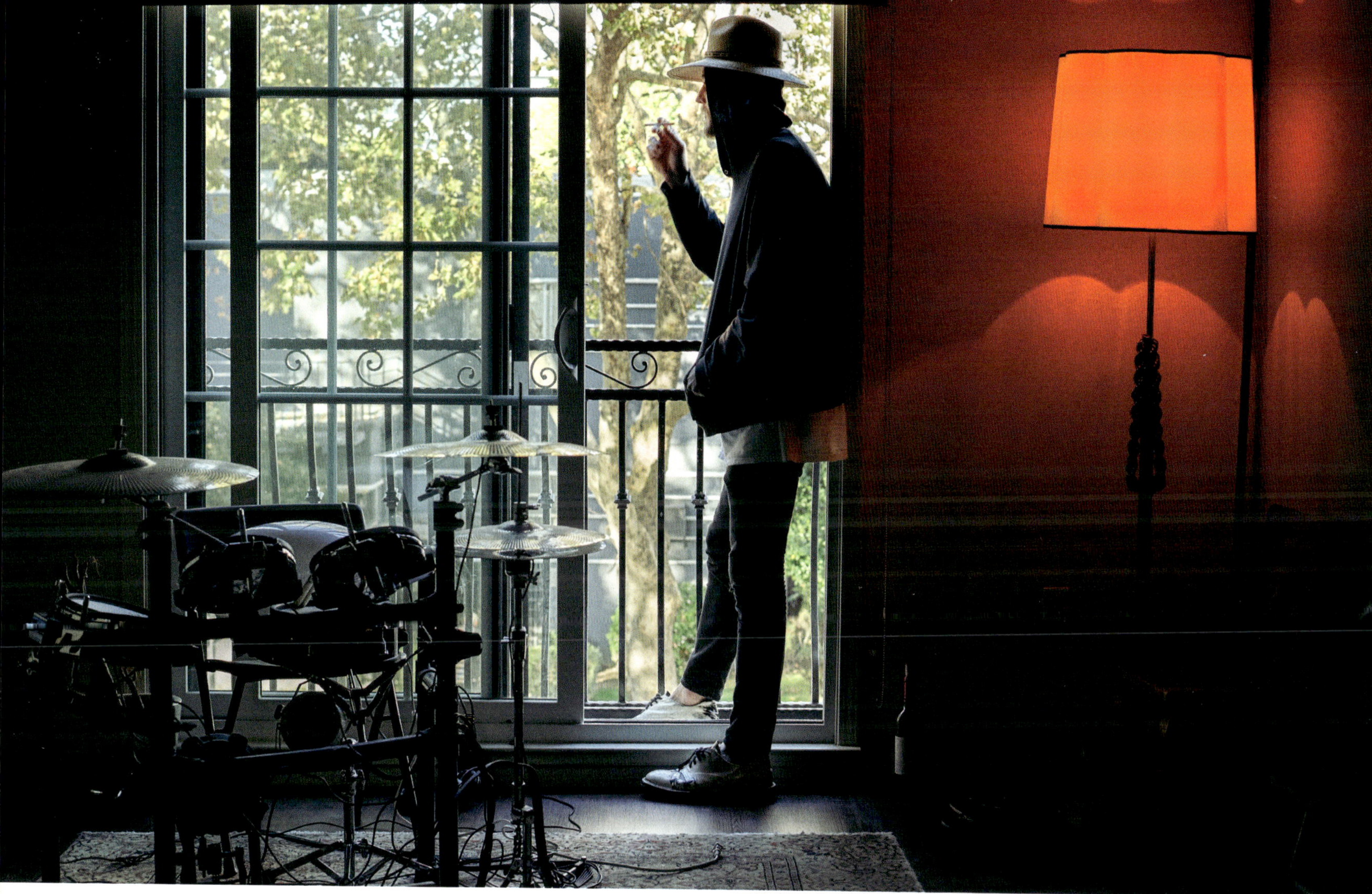

Just thinking about the universe humbles me. Thinking about space, about the ocean, about atoms – thinking about all these things inspires me. When I'm playing, my mind is clear of the things that are normally eating away at me or doing unhealthy things to my mind and my body. Playing takes me away from that. I definitely would have gone on a different path without it, one not nearly as good.

I have a hard time talking about music because I play music. It's my whole language and I play to express things that I can't verbalize. I'm slightly a masochist by nature in a lot of ways. Playing, I want it to be biting me, grating on me while I'm doing it. It's like I'm concentrating so hard that I'm not concentrating at all. I want to be overtaken when I'm playing and then that's the time in my day not to think about other things and let something else in, let my body host a different type of energy through playing the drums.

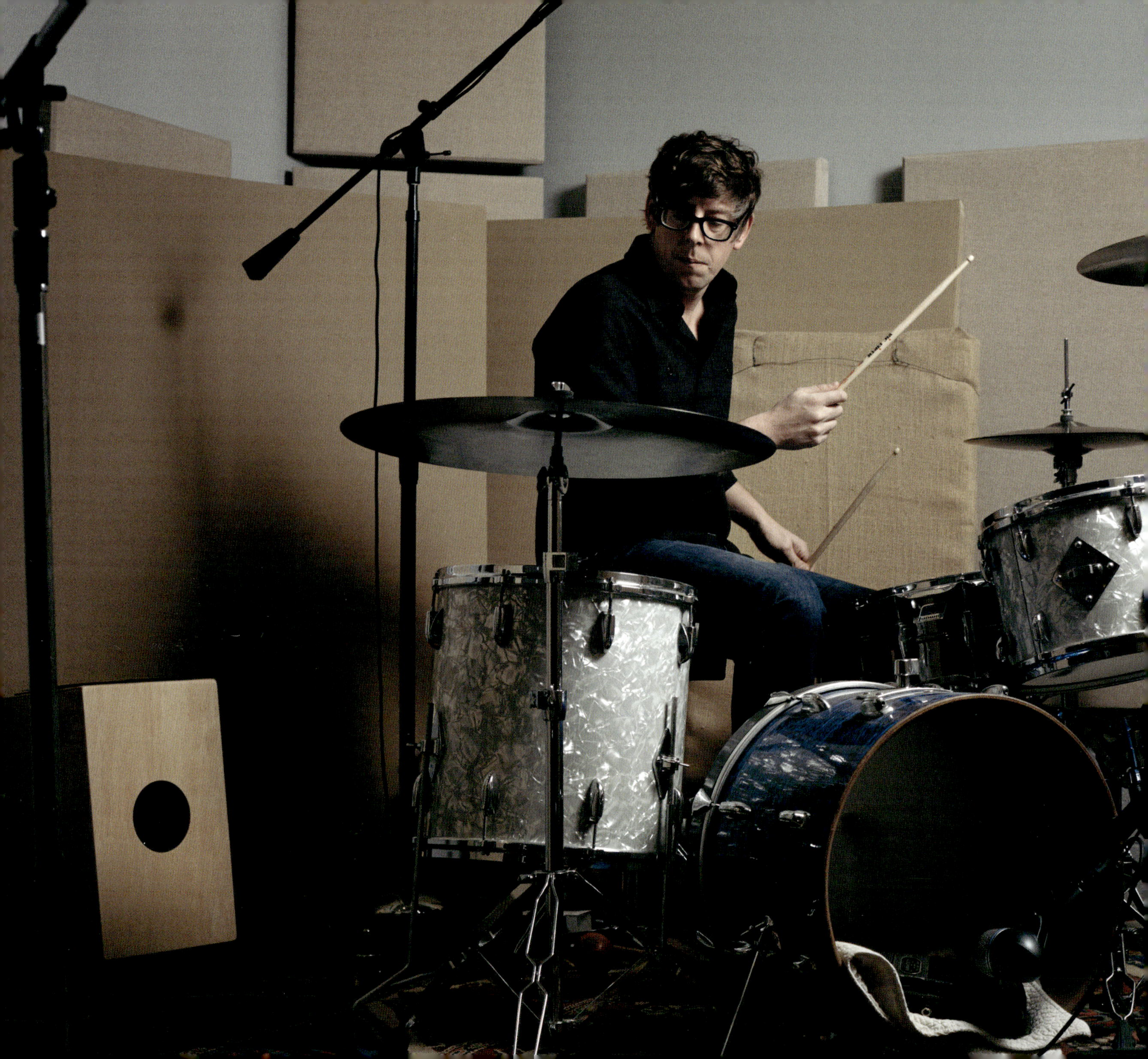

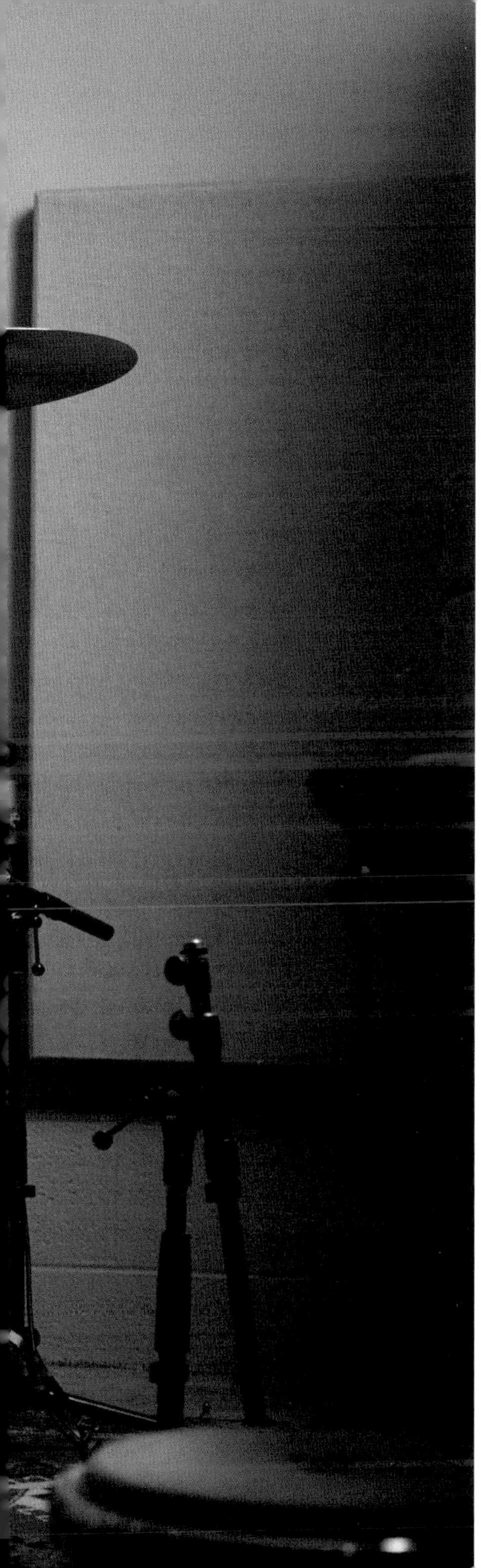

PATRICK CARNEY

The Black Keys. Photographed in his home studio, Tennessee

To me a good drummer is someone who has an unpredictability going on. Anybody has the capacity to be a great drummer; it's just about finding the right people to be a great drummer with. When I play with Dan [Auerbach, lead singer and guitarist for The Black Keys] I consider myself a good drummer, but when I play with someone I've never played with, I consider myself to be average or below. You learn how to play with certain people.

My favourite recording experience ever was in Muscle Shoals [Sound Studio]. Dan and I liked being isolated and the engineer that we hired from San Diego brought out the recording equipment. I used his old Gretsch kit. We just set up simple, minimal mics. We started from scratch and wrote fifteen songs in twelve days. We'd go to the studio and stay there until midnight. When we came out of there, for the first time ever I felt like we'd captured something completely off the top of our heads and really special. I don't think we even realized what it was until a couple of months later. There's an energy in that room – most studios are dark, but that's the darkest studio I've ever been in. There's no light in there. It's just like a cave. When I had this control room built, I wanted it to be the opposite. Because I've been working in basements my whole life, I wanted to have a view of the outside. But it works there.

The thing about drums is people take the instrument for granted. The drums are maybe the least appealing instrument to most kids, but they're the most important in making something interesting. There's nuance to the instrument that changes the entire dynamic of a song. I'm constantly thinking about drums and how they work. I'm also frustrated constantly by the instrument, which is the whole fun of it. There are endless possibilities and there are endless fills and there's endless little things. It's like golf – you can golf forever and still suck, and drumming is the same but in a good way; it keeps it interesting. That's why people golf until they're dead, because they're constantly searching to improve.

I usually take two weeks off from playing the drums [before going on tour], because then when I go back out on tour, I will have forgotten what I was doing before and I'll approach most of the parts in a slightly different way. What makes it more interesting to me is that there is constant evolution of forgetting and relearning. I'm not competitive with drumming. It's this magical, weird thing. It's the only thing in my life that's like that and I don't want to ruin it by putting too much pressure on myself.

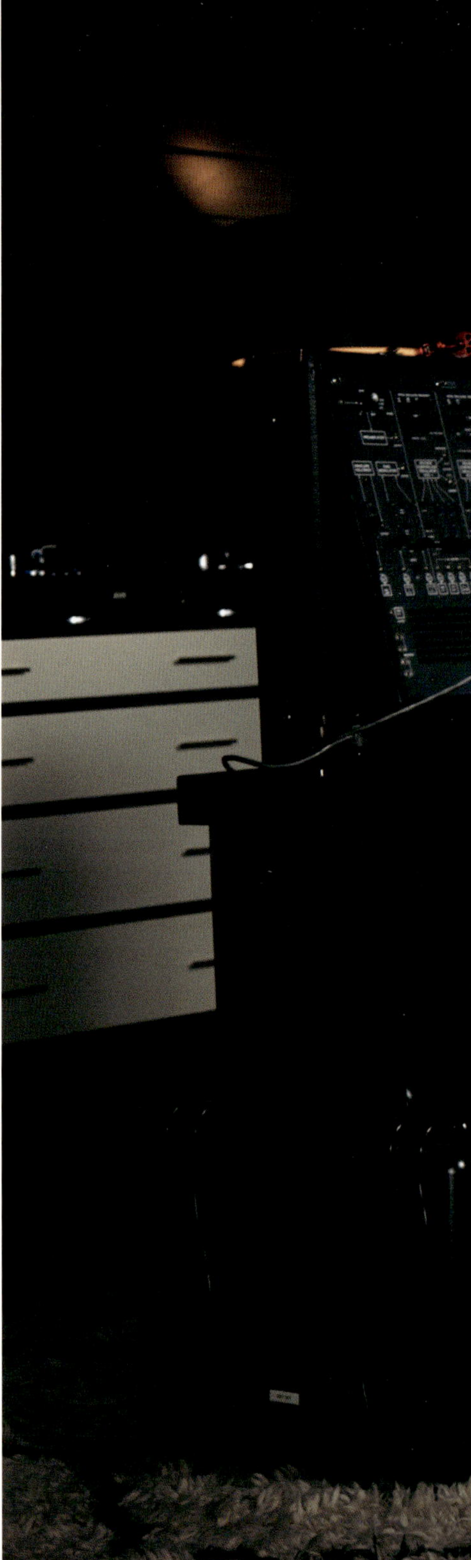

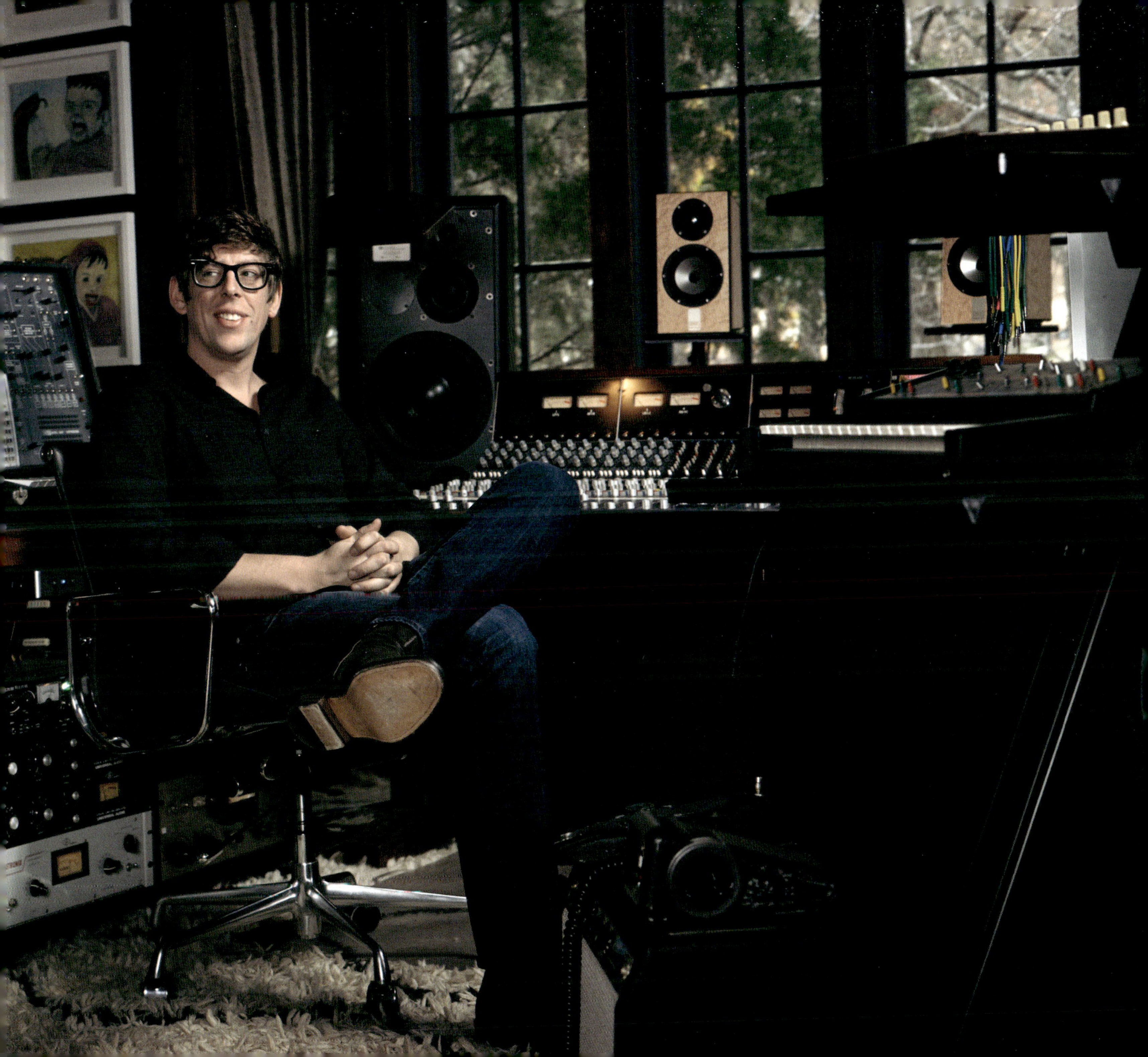

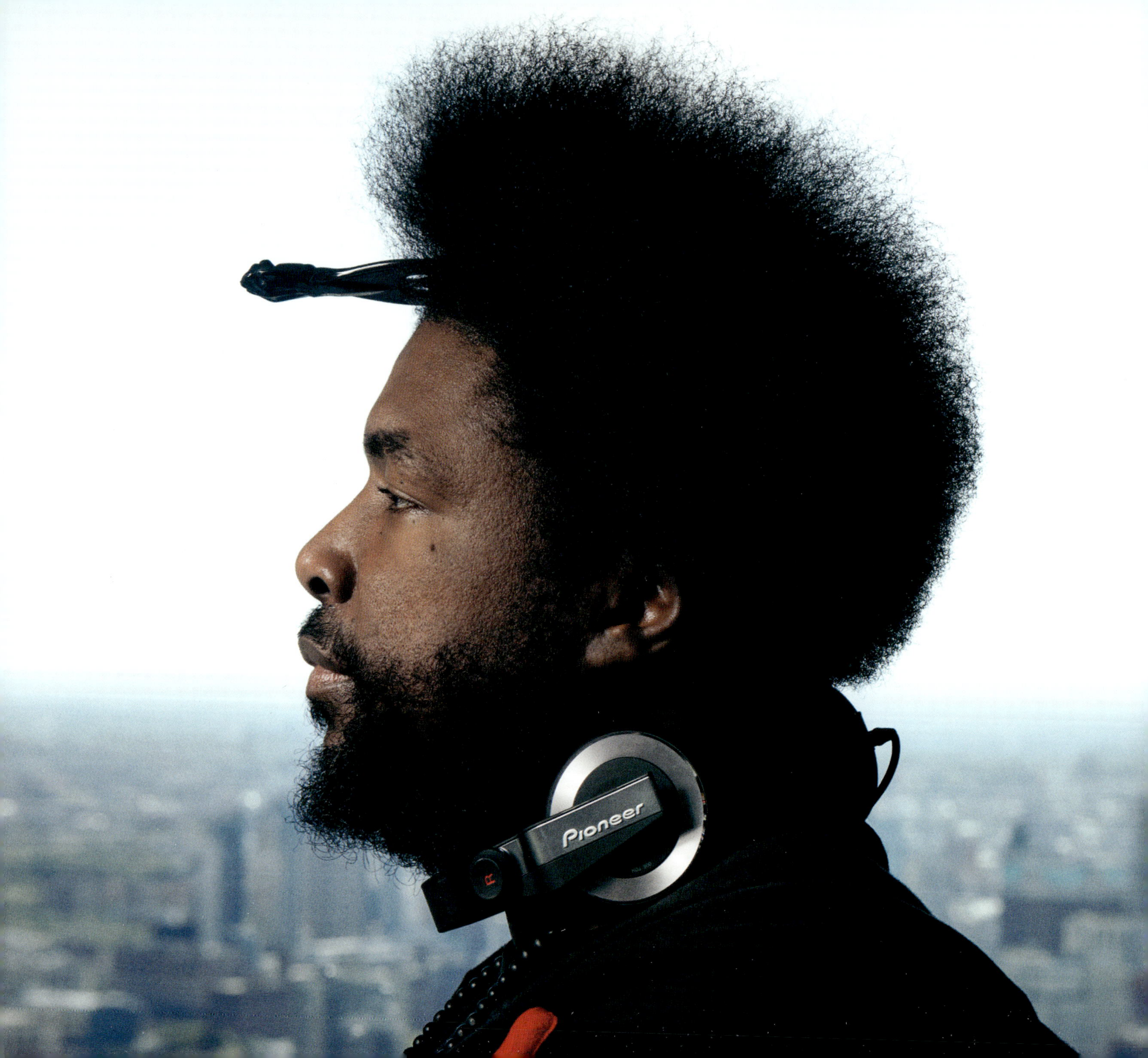
Pioneer

“I WAS LIKE SECONDS AWAY FROM HAVING A BREAKDOWN, BUT PRINCE HAD SUCH AN ELABORATE CHOCOLATE FONDUE DISPLAY THAT IT DISTRACTED ME”

AHMIR ‘QUESTLOVE’ THOMPSON

The Roots / D’Angelo / Elvis Costello / Al Green / Jay Z / *The Tonight Show starring Jimmy Fallon*. Photographed at home, New York

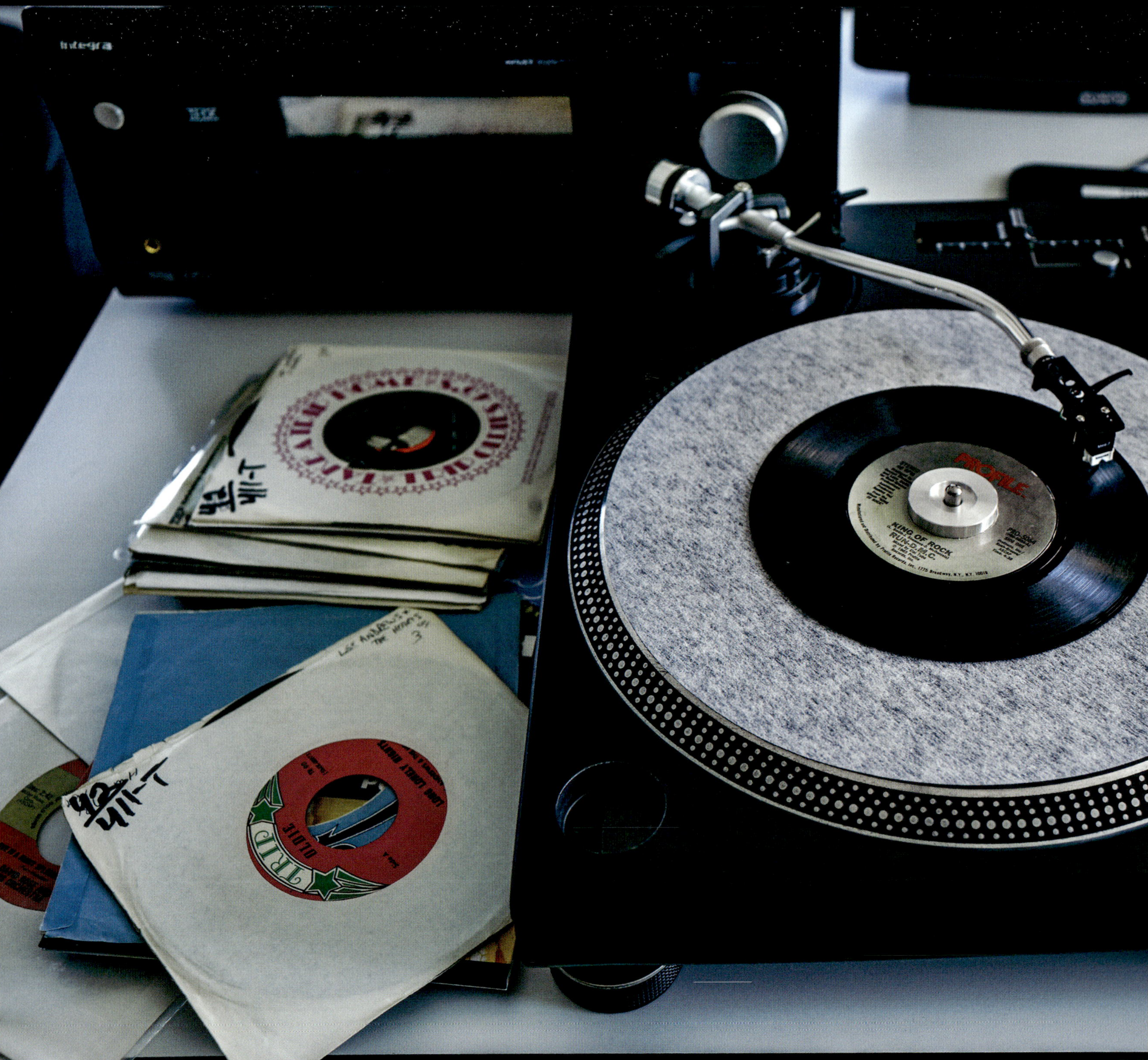
Integra
PROFILE
KING OF ROCK
RUN-D.M.C.

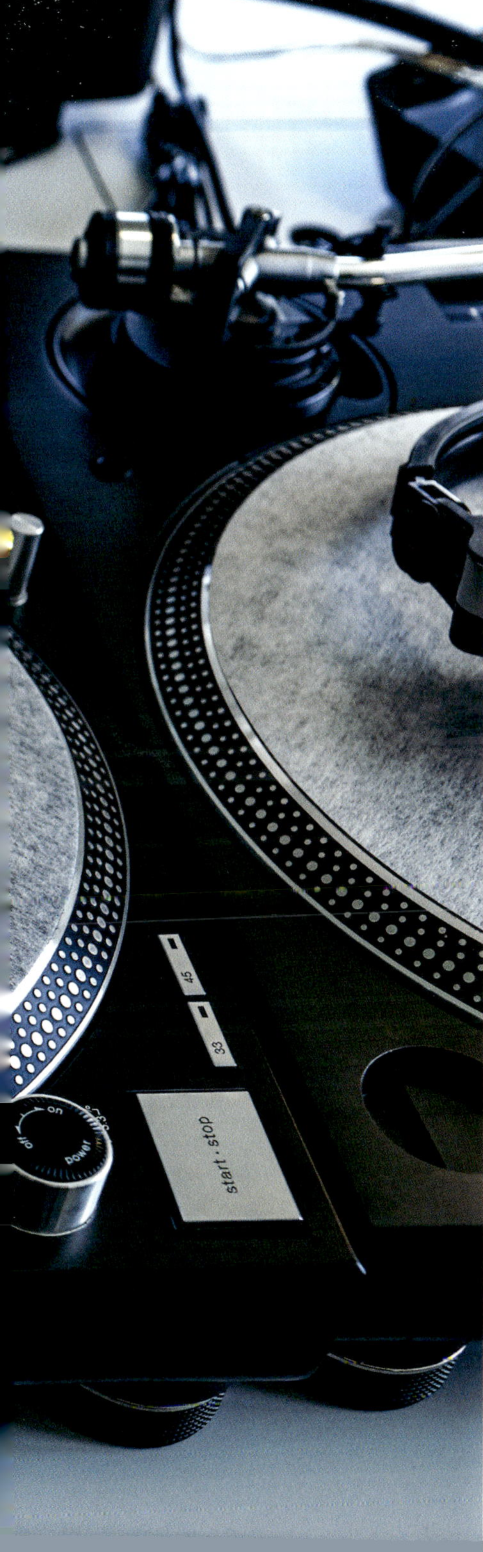

I got introduced to jazz as a punishment. I had deceived my older cousin into buying me a 45 of a song that my parents wouldn't allow me to have. I asked them for it, and they said, 'No, we don't like that song, that song is dirty, you're not getting it.' And after about three weeks of plotting and scheming, always missing the song when it was on the radio, trying to record it … It was a song called 'Juicy Fruit' by James Mtume, who was the percussionist for Miles Davis. It seems harmless by today's standards … All of Miles Davis's musicians were heavy jazz cats but in the mid-'80s they all wanted to get paid, so they all did regular pop music. This was one of his breakthrough singles and Notorious B.I.G. sampled it for his first single, 'Juicy'. But I was twelve at the time and I didn't understand double entendres. I really thought, maybe it's about a stick of gum, Juicy Fruit. Stupid me! I thought it was about candy. I didn't know it was a metaphor for sex.

One lesson I learned is that whenever I lied or did something deceitful in my family, karma would always pay me back twice and I'd always get found out, so very rarely did I ever try to go that route. So they found out, and my punishment was that I had to listen to jazz. They forced John Coltrane on me, literally. They were like, 'No more rap music, no more Prince …'. This was '83, a very important breakout year. It was the year I discovered Prince, the year I discovered The Time, the year I really discovered hip hop. I'd started buying a lot of street records, which my somewhat strict Christian household frowned upon; so to exorcise these demons I had to sit and listen to Coltrane's *My Favorite Things* at a very loud volume.

When news broke that one of the torture methods that was being used on detainees in Guantanamo was blasting music, I got a letter from a lawyer saying, 'Stop the government from using your music.' I found out that my song was one of the fifty songs they blasted 24/7. And I was just like, wow, isn't it funny: when I was a kid, something as beautiful as John Coltrane was used as punishment on me and now, some twenty years later, something as well-intentioned as The Roots' music is being used as torture. It's weird.

My highlight of all time was playing in Prince's living room. I'm on drums and Prince is on bass and Sheila E. is on percussion, Frank McComb is on piano, and the jazz singer Rachelle Ferrell is singing. And then in walks Stevie Wonder and he's at the keyboards. And I'm thinking, am I actually sitting here? Not only am I sitting here playing Stevie Wonder's music with him, but there's one point at which Prince shoots Sheila a look – and he whispers, almost like they are saying, 'Can you believe this?' So I stopped, which is weird because why would you ever want to stop that magic moment of playing with all your musical heroes in Prince's living room, having this intimate jam session? I think I was like seconds away from having a breakdown, but Prince had such an elaborate chocolate fondue display that it distracted me. I was like, wait a minute, am I really walking away from playing one of my favourite Stevie Wonder songs with all my …? Oh my god, fondue! To be in this jam session playing the songs of the people that I practised to for so many hours as a kid was very overwhelming. Very magical.

My father instilled practice in me. I didn't go outside and play; I had to come home straight from school, put in about two hours of practice every day and then do my homework and then eat, and then be in bed by ten o'clock – every night, without fail. Keeping me off the streets kept me alive because between the two households that I grew up in, and counting the thirty-plus childhood friends that I had, I'm one of three people not in jail or dead. Of the other two, I know that one went to college and has a family; the other one's struggling a little bit – but it's almost like a victory if you're not dead or in jail, that's a win.

CHRIS 'DADDY' DAVE

D'Angelo / Maxwell / Robert Glasper Experiment / Mos Def (Yasiin Bey) / Adele / Little Simz / The Drumhedz / Mary J. Blige. Photographed in California

'Time is going to be there whether you are thinking about it or not. So it's more about embracing it and having fun with it than being scared of it'

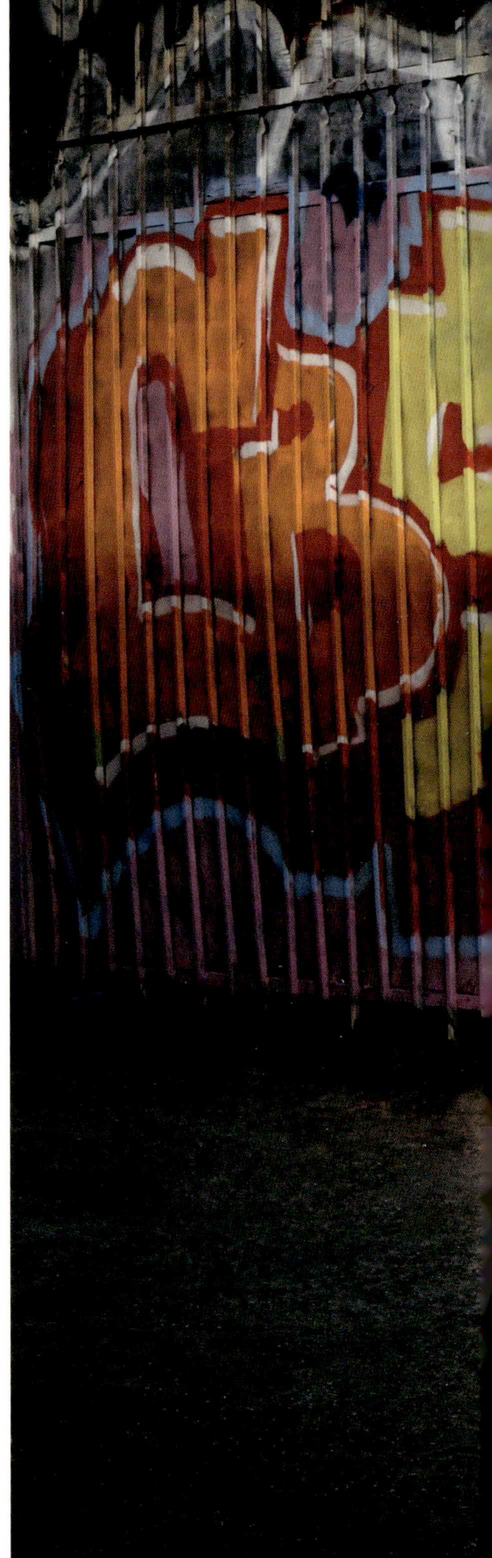

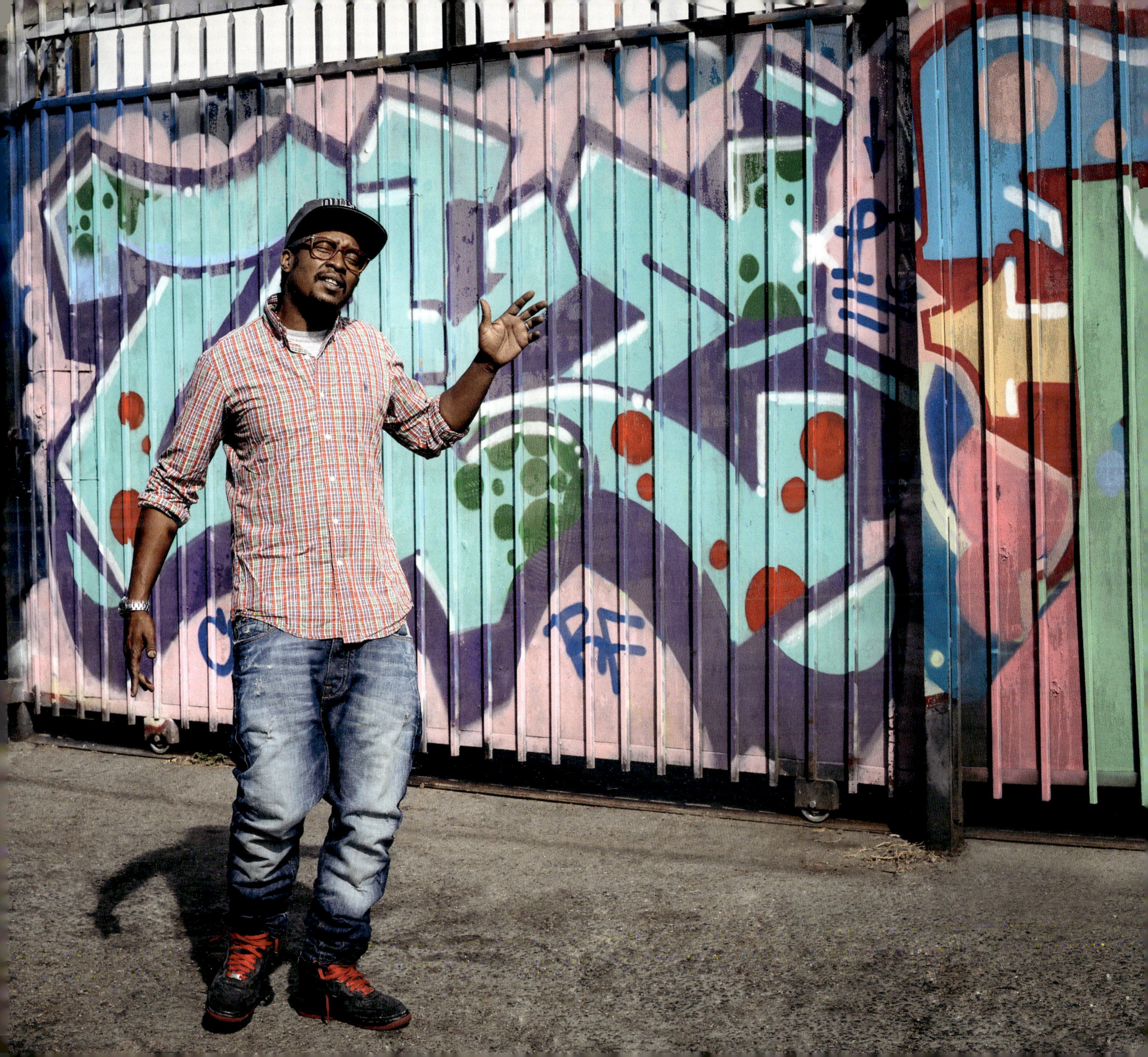

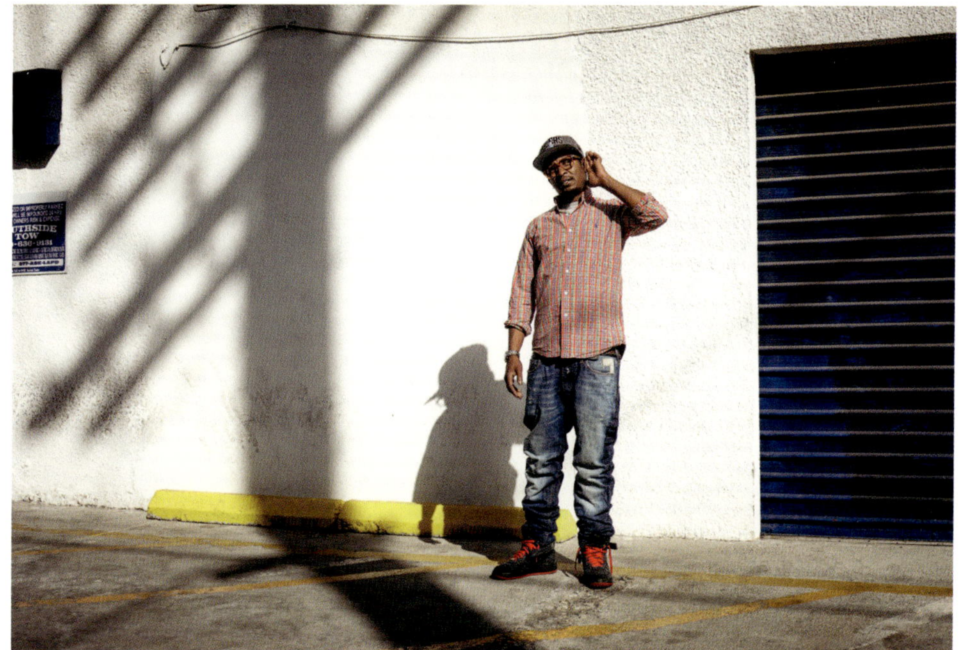

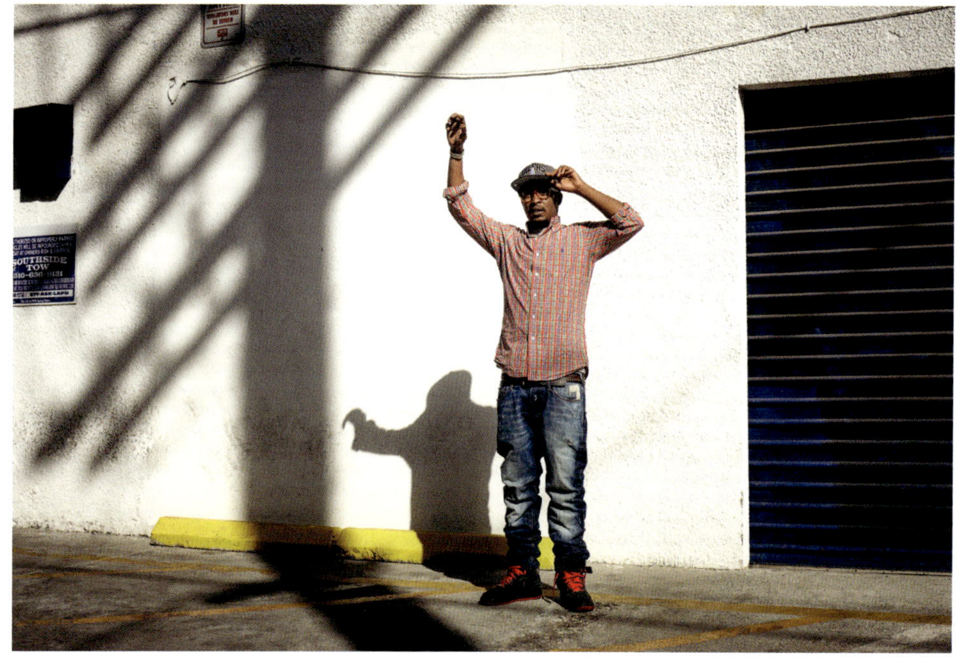
SOUTHSIDE
TOW

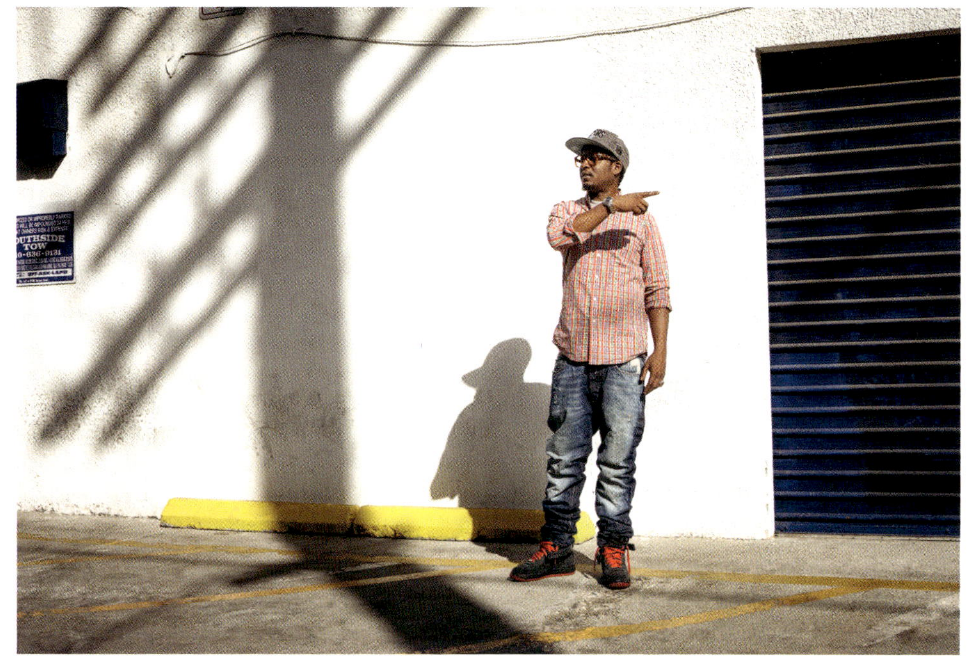
OUTHSIDE
TOW

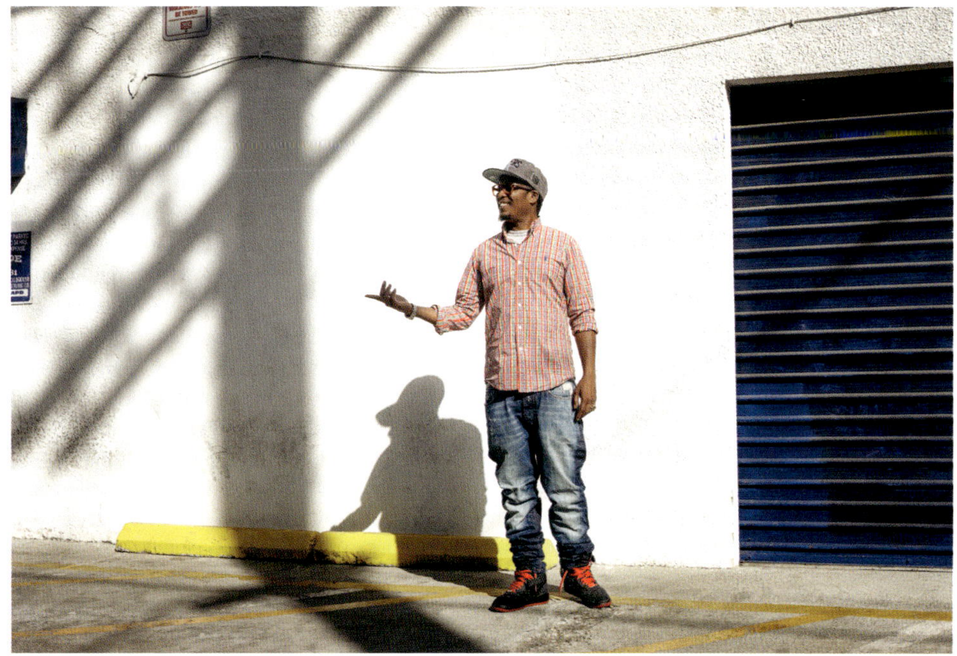

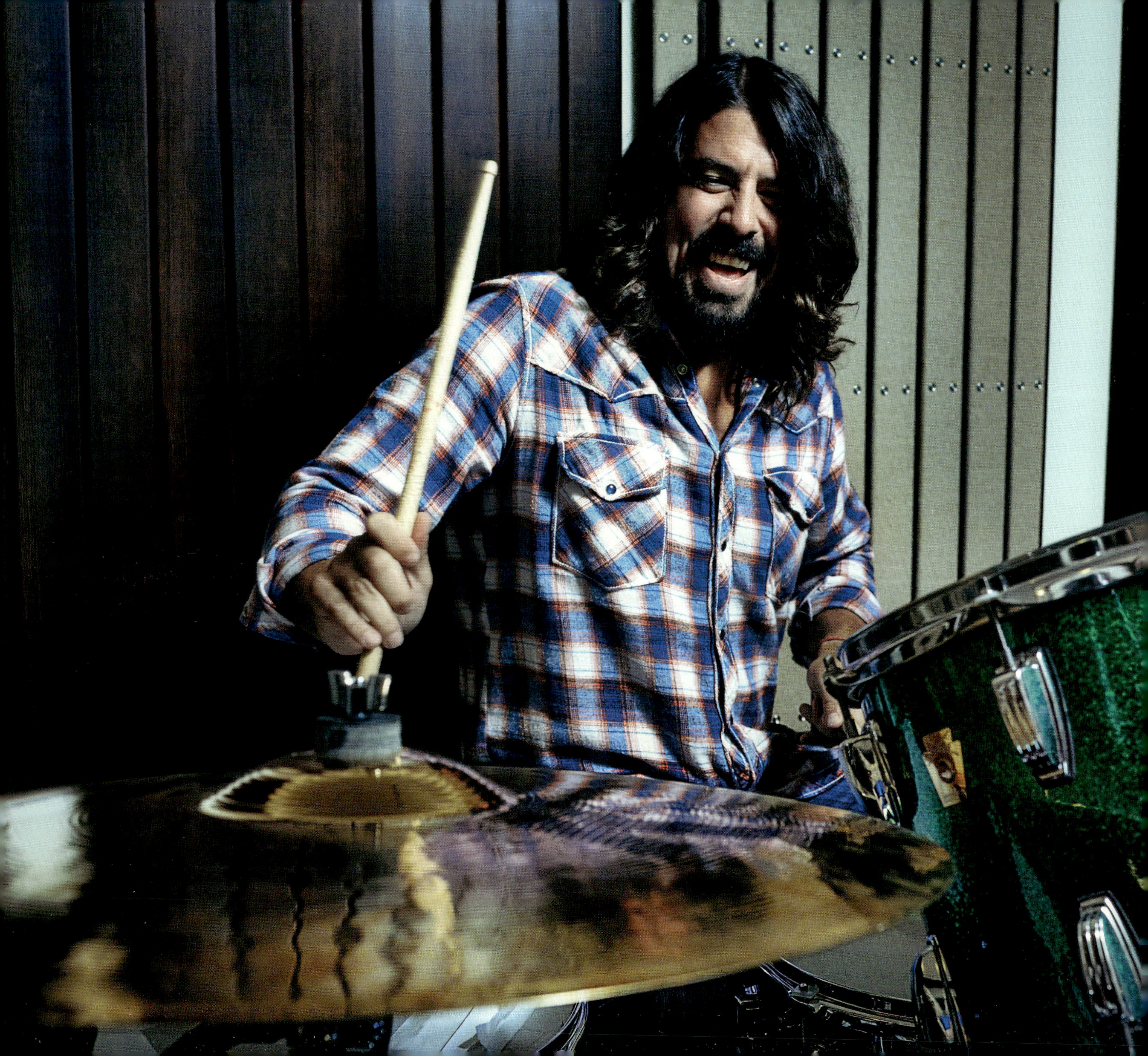

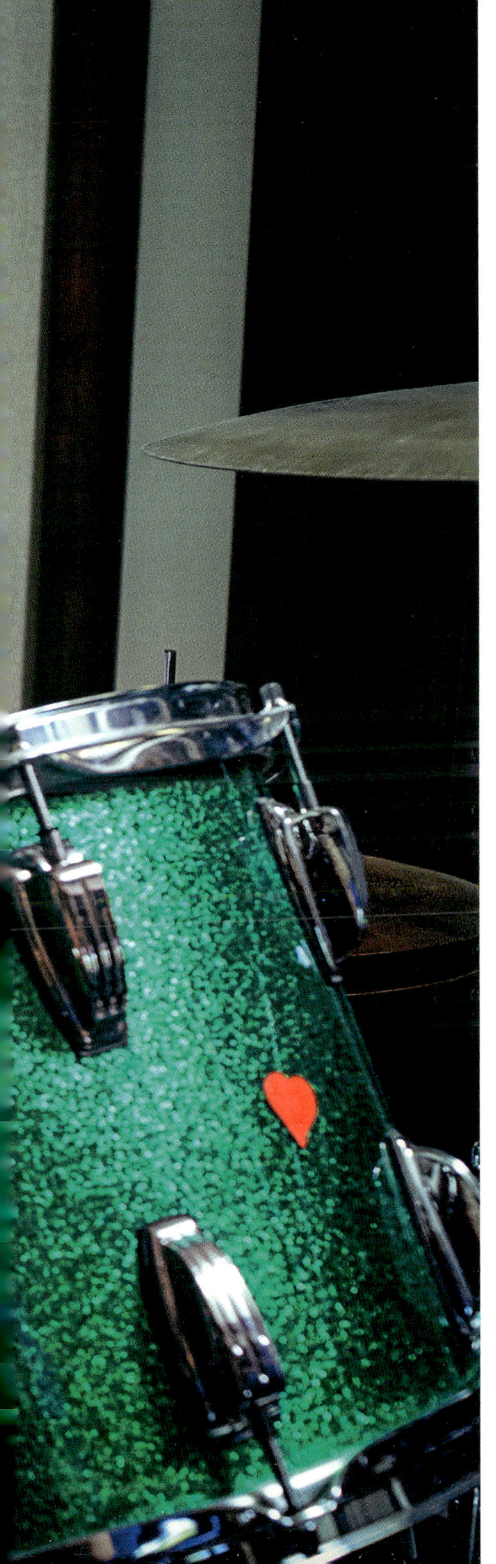

"ULTIMATELY THE REASON PEOPLE ARE SHAKING THEIR ASSES IS YOU: IT'S NOT THE LYRICS, IT'S YOUR BACKBEAT"

DAVE GROHL

Nirvana / Them Crooked Vultures. Photographed at home, California

The album that really got me interested in the drums was *2112* by Rush. I focused on the drumming and I immediately set up pillows as a drum set and tried to imitate what Neil Peart was doing. I never took lessons.

Some of my favourite drummers would be considered some of the worst drummers of all time because their tempo fluctuates so much or there is inconsistency, but it's the passion of the playing that really interests me. I can't do a drum solo. I never practise by myself. I only play the drums when there are other people to play with. I just feel like it's more musical; it's more of an interaction. It's like, I'd never really dance alone – I dance with someone else – and it's kind of the same way with drumming.

I think that it takes a certain type of person to be a drummer. It's your responsibility to make sure this thing gets off the ground, but don't expect any thanks. There is something about the altruistic nature of drumming: you're there to serve the song, you're there to get people to move. They might not really know why they're dancing, but it's you. Ultimately the reason people are shaking their asses is you: it's not the lyrics, it's your backbeat. Drummers are usually the last ones to get any credit. They're almost like the goalkeepers, they're the ones where the buck stops. Bottom line: your band is only as good as its drummer. They are your foundation or your backbone.

In Nirvana, I never got recognized. I lived this perfect existence: I was in one of the biggest bands ever, but I could walk in the front door of a Nirvana gig and no one would recognize me. It was awesome. I watched Kurt get so bummed out about not being able to walk down the street without people hassling him. I felt lucky that I didn't get that. Then I could get up there and play those great songs and watch people go bananas. It was the ideal situation.

With Them Crooked Vultures, which was with my buddy Josh from Queens of the Stone Age and John Paul Jones from Led Zeppelin, the first time we jammed together it immediately clicked. I mean, I have Zeppelin tattoos and stuff so I was obviously fucking terrified that I was playing with John Paul Jones. We started playing and I remember after a couple of minutes thinking, wow, man, I'm really grooving. This is great, I'm really in there. And then I realized that it wasn't really me, it was John Paul Jones making me sound good. His bass was making my drums sound good. And I'd never played with someone like that. I'd never had that kind of connection, like, oh, my god, he's locked on me like glue. That guy did so many sessions in the '60s. He would sit down with any number of drummers and just lock on to them and put plastic wrap around what they do. It was amazing.

I've always been kind of fascinated with the Ringo debate. Was Ringo Starr a great drummer? Of course he was a great drummer: you hear three and a half seconds of his playing and you immediately know that it's him. Was Buddy Rich the greatest drummer of all time? Of course Buddy Rich was the greatest drummer of all time. You hear three and a half seconds of his playing and you know that it's him. To me that's what it was always about. It's about establishing your sound or being able to get your personality, your sense of humour and your passion, or whatever it is, your voice, out of you, through your hands and into this instrument. It goes for any instrument. There's no wrong or right, as long as it's an accurate representation of yourself. So I would always step back from any of that technical stuff because I really didn't think that it made a difference. I like the drummers that sound like themselves no matter how technically proficient they are. That's the goal. How can you establish yourself so that what you do is so pure a signature that everyone knows it's you? Just absorb your influences but don't let anyone tell you what to do.

I can play drums with my teeth. As a kid I'd grind my teeth in a certain way. I could do super-fast drum rolls, and my back teeth are like my kicks, my front teeth are like my snares. One time I went to the dentist, and he was looking at my mouth and said, 'Do you chew a lot of ice? Your teeth are really getting ground down.' I got him to put his ear to my mouth and listen. I had a punk rock band back then and we would have a thirty-minute slot at a club downtown. My walk home from school was about thirty minutes, so I would write the set list in my head and time it out. I would perform all the songs in my mouth on the way home and think, like, okay, cool, that's the set. I'd know which songs would fit in the thirty minutes.

Kurt Cobain was also a drummer; he played the drums a little bit too. If you watch something like *Unplugged* or any live Nirvana performance, look at his mouth. He used to do the same thing. You'll see his jaw grinding back and forth because he's playing drums in his mouth as he's playing guitar. I kind of feel like we're not the only two people in the history of music to do this.

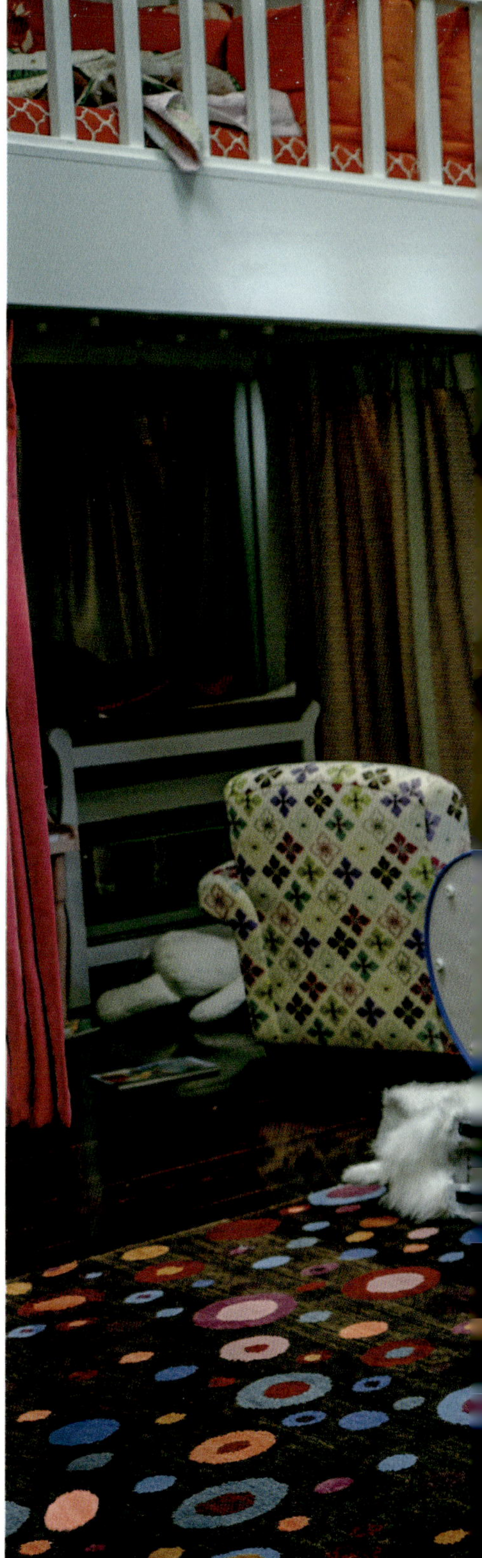

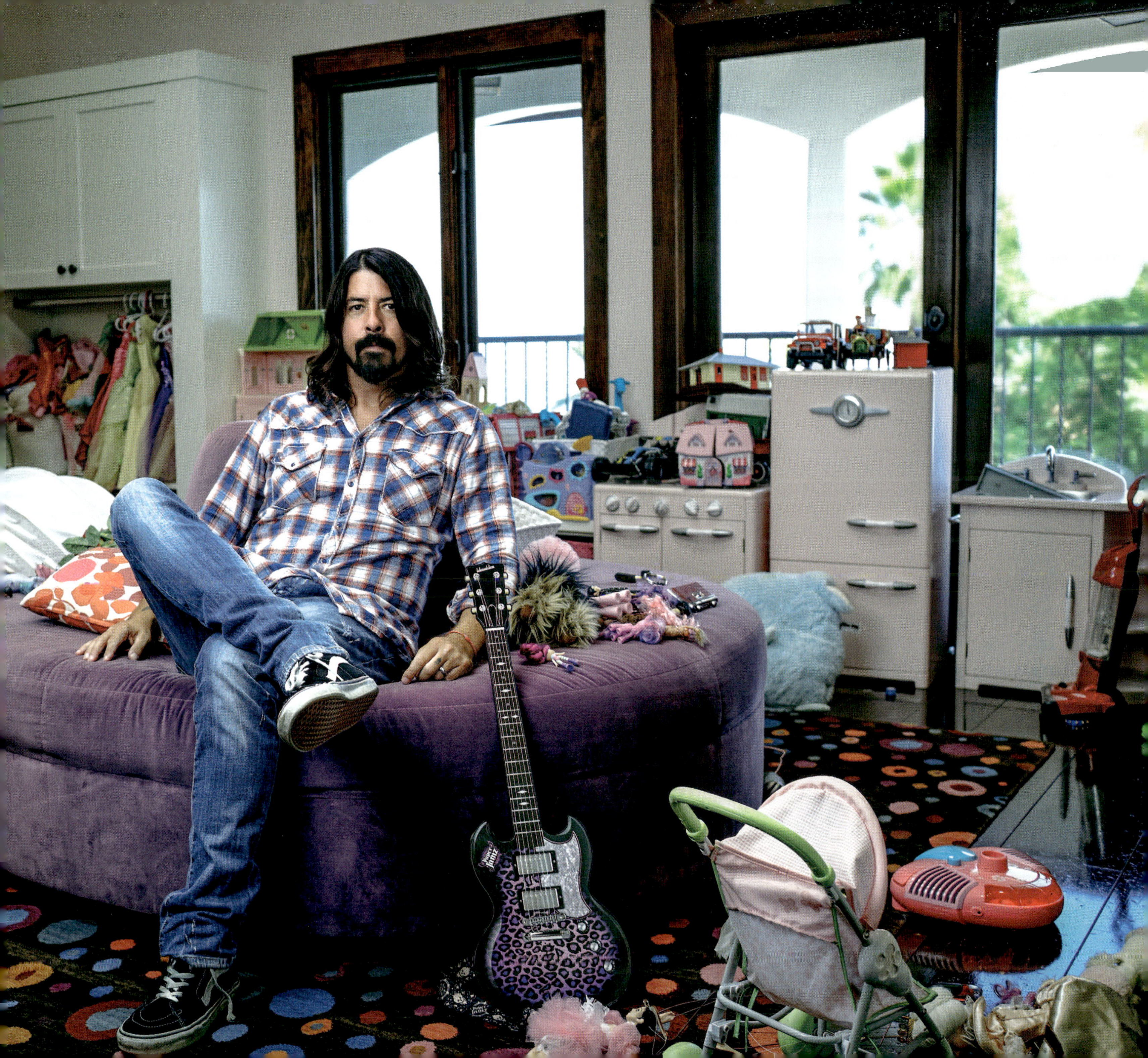

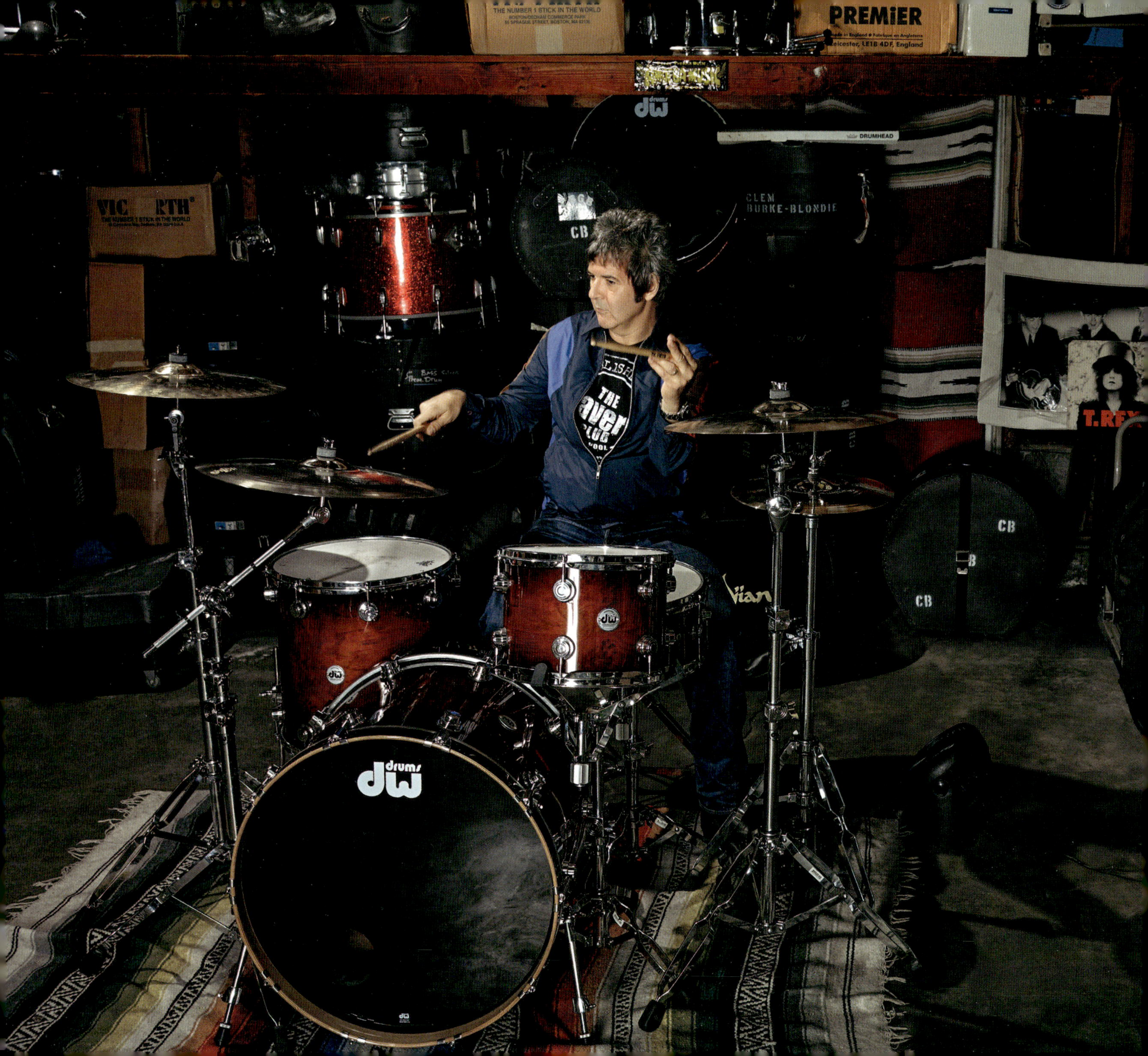
THE NUMBER 1 STICK IN THE WORLD
PREMIER
Leicester, LE18 4DF, England
DRUMHEAD
CLEM
BURKE-BLONDIE
CB
CB
CB
T.REX
dw drums

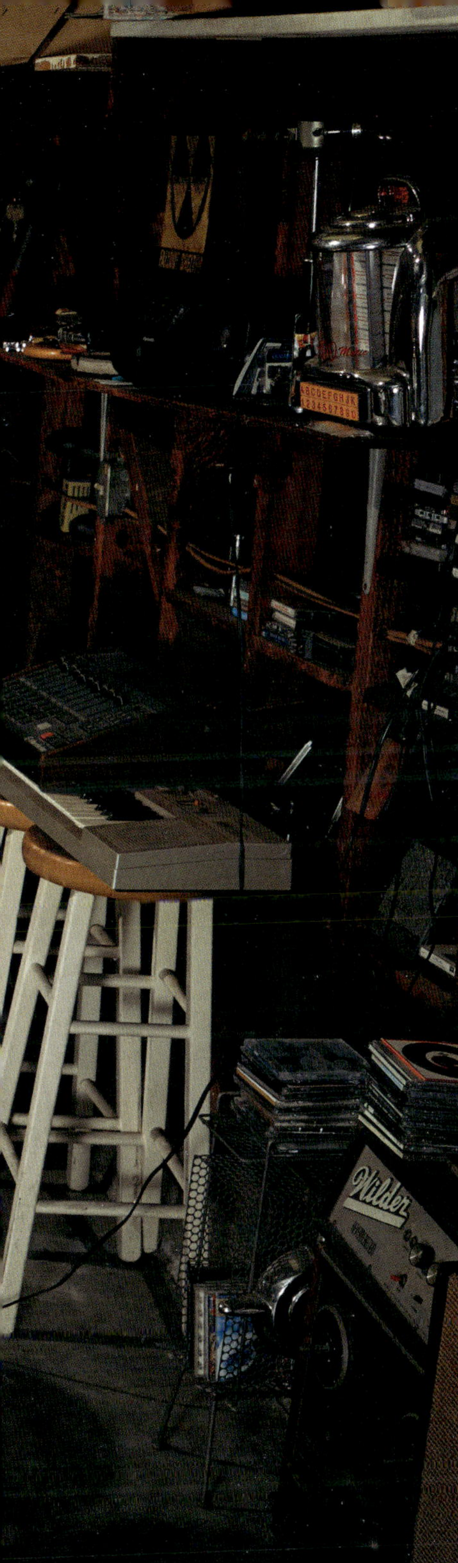

CLEM BURKE

Blondie. Photographed at home, California

David Bowie had a big impact on me musically. The first concert he did in New York at Carnegie Hall as Ziggy Stardust – turns out most people I know from the New York rock scene were at that show, including Debbie and Chris from Blondie, and Joey Ramone. That was a pivotal moment in New York. David Bowie was a major inspiration for the band, for Blondie itself: the way he really didn't restrict himself in any kind of musical idiom, constantly changing, going from soul to glam rock, to the Can and Kraftwerk influence. He was almost a template for our band in a lot of ways. For me it was always about finding somebody who was like Bowie or Mick Jagger or Elvis or Marc Bolan, and it just so happened it turned out to be Debbie. I knew I needed to connect with someone with that sort of magic.

We met Debbie at a place in New York called Club 82, at 82 East 4th Street, which was like the headquarters for glam rock. New York Dolls would play there, and Debbie and Chris had a band called The Stilettos and they would play there. I had a band called Sweet Revenge, we're talking 1974-ish; we played there. That whole scene kind of evolved into the CBGB scene, which was right around the corner on the Bowery.

Blondie's first tour, with Iggy Pop and David Bowie, was a real highlight for me. We did a six-week tour with them. It was when David was producing *The Idiot* with Iggy. We played at Max's Kansas City, two sold-out shows, and then we drove up to Canada overnight; we all slept in one bed in the RV. The next night we were in the dressing room and next thing the door opens and David Bowie and Iggy Pop walk in to introduce themselves. It set the bar, really, for how to interact with people on a tour – they were real gentlemen and they made a point of saying they were excited about us being on tour.

It was a very creative time, there was a real energy and it was very microcosmic in a way. There wasn't really anything going on outside the little scene, not too many people knew about it. If you revisit it now, some of the people that were around, the people who survived it, it is very much like going back and meeting someone you went to school with – whether it be someone from Talking Heads or someone from Television or the guys who are still alive from the New York Dolls. They and The Velvet Underground were big influences, and when I met Debbie and Chris we had a lot of common ground in the type of music we liked; there weren't really too many people around that I knew who really enjoyed that kind of music. It was a very specialized, underground type of music, and the whole sort of English scene, the New York glam rock scene is what really influenced my playing and my outlook and my performance, and how I liked to feel onstage.

JOSH FREESE

Nine Inch Nails / A Perfect Circle / Devo / The Vandals
Photographed in his home studio, California

The first music I was exposed to was big band and jazz. My father conducted the big band out at Disneyland. I would go and see him do these sets, three or four sets a day. When I was about seven or eight my uncle played me the first Van Halen record and I'll never forget it.

I didn't have a big brother so a lot of the music I got hip to was on my own, either through friends at school or from reading magazines. I would read *Modern Drummer* – the reason I got into Frank Zappa's music was I would read interviews with Chad Wackerman, Terry Bozzio and Vinnie Colaiuta and they would all say Frank Zappa was 'challenging' and talk about 'the complexities of his arrangements'. So I went out and got all of Frank Zappa's records and I became completely obsessed with them.

I was about fourteen when I started playing with Dweezil Zappa, and the bass player in the band was Frank Zappa's bass player, Scott Thunes. He was a big influence on me and is still a dear friend. He became like an older brother to me and turned me on to a lot of stuff. I was in my jazz fusion phase and I was trying to impress Scott. I remember talking to him on a break, I said, 'Hey, you want to play some jazz?' I was super naive and young. He looked at me, saying, 'Jazz? No man, you don't want to listen to jazz. You gotta get into the Ramones, Killing Joke, the Butthole Surfers.' He taught me the beauty of that stuff. I ditched the jazz fusion and I started getting into more extreme rock and roll. I was getting into the Sex Pistols, The Damned, The Replacements and all these bands. Then I got into all the punk rock from here in America: Circle Jerks and the Descendents and Fear. Some of those bands couldn't play, some of them could, but it didn't really matter if the song was good or what they were saying was something that I liked. The Circle Jerks weren't proficient musicians, but they were a great band. The same with the Sex Pistols; the same with the Ramones. Then there were bands like Fear that really could play, and they were weird, hardcore and scary and vulgar, but they were tight as hell.

These days I take little bits of all the things I liked growing up and I try not to be prejudiced. I don't have to hate jazz fusion music like I did when I was seventeen and discovered punk rock. Usually the music I lean towards admiring and listening to is in the indie field – a little bit more reckless and a little bit dirtier and maybe crazier. I like eccentric people and I like reading about them. I'd want to read about Frank Zappa and I'd want to read about Van Halen and read about my favourite drummers, not just listen to them. I wanted to know what they were thinking, what they were into, what kind of people they were, how they dressed. I was as into all that stuff as I was the music.

I went to shows when I was a kid growing up in Orange County and I befriended some famous drummers and tagged along with them. Vinnie Colaiuta, Terry Bozzio, Gregg Bissonette, they are all still friends. I took a couple of formal lessons with Gregg. My mom would drive me up to the Valley and Gregg was teaching in his garage. People still to this day say I studied with Vinnie Colaiuta. I never studied with Vinnie, but Vinnie was kind enough to take me under his wing; I've been friends with Vinnie since I was eleven or twelve. He put me on a guest list to go see him play up in LA at this jazz club, The Baked Potato. My parents made me take a nap because it was on a Sunday night, a school night. I was ten, so I was all excited. It was with Michael Landau. It was basically the Joni Mitchell backup band in 1983 or '84, they were called Dog Cheese. My parents would drive me up to the Valley, Vinnie would save a couple of seats right by the drums and I would have my mind fucking blown. I'd watch him play and I wouldn't know what the hell was going on but it was really cool.

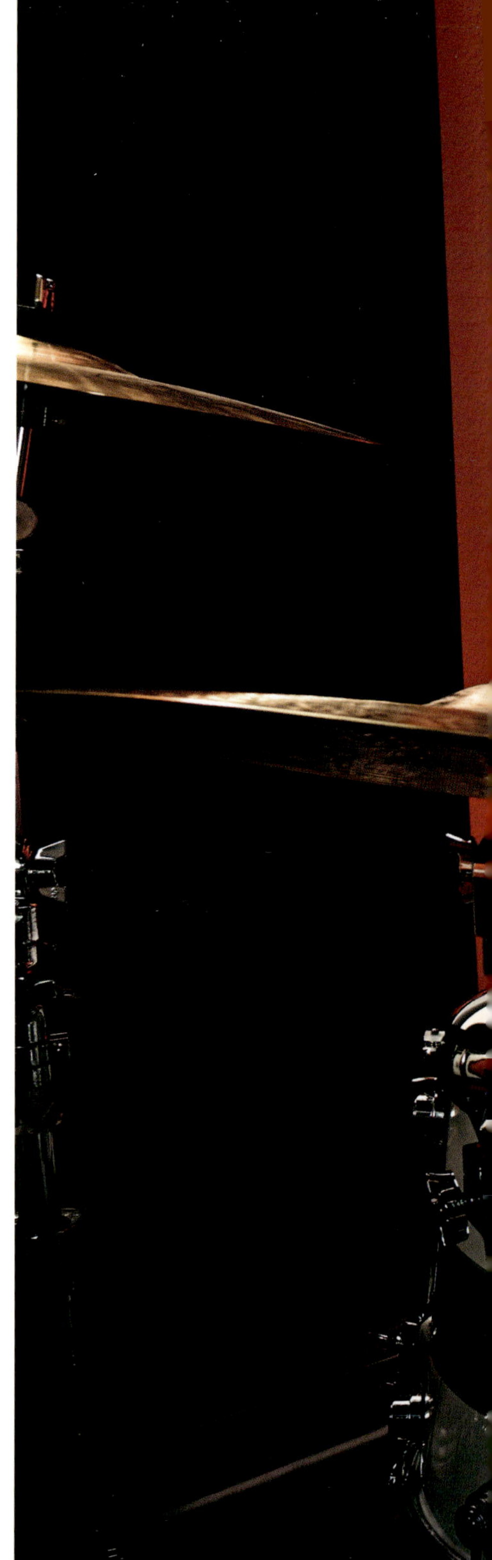

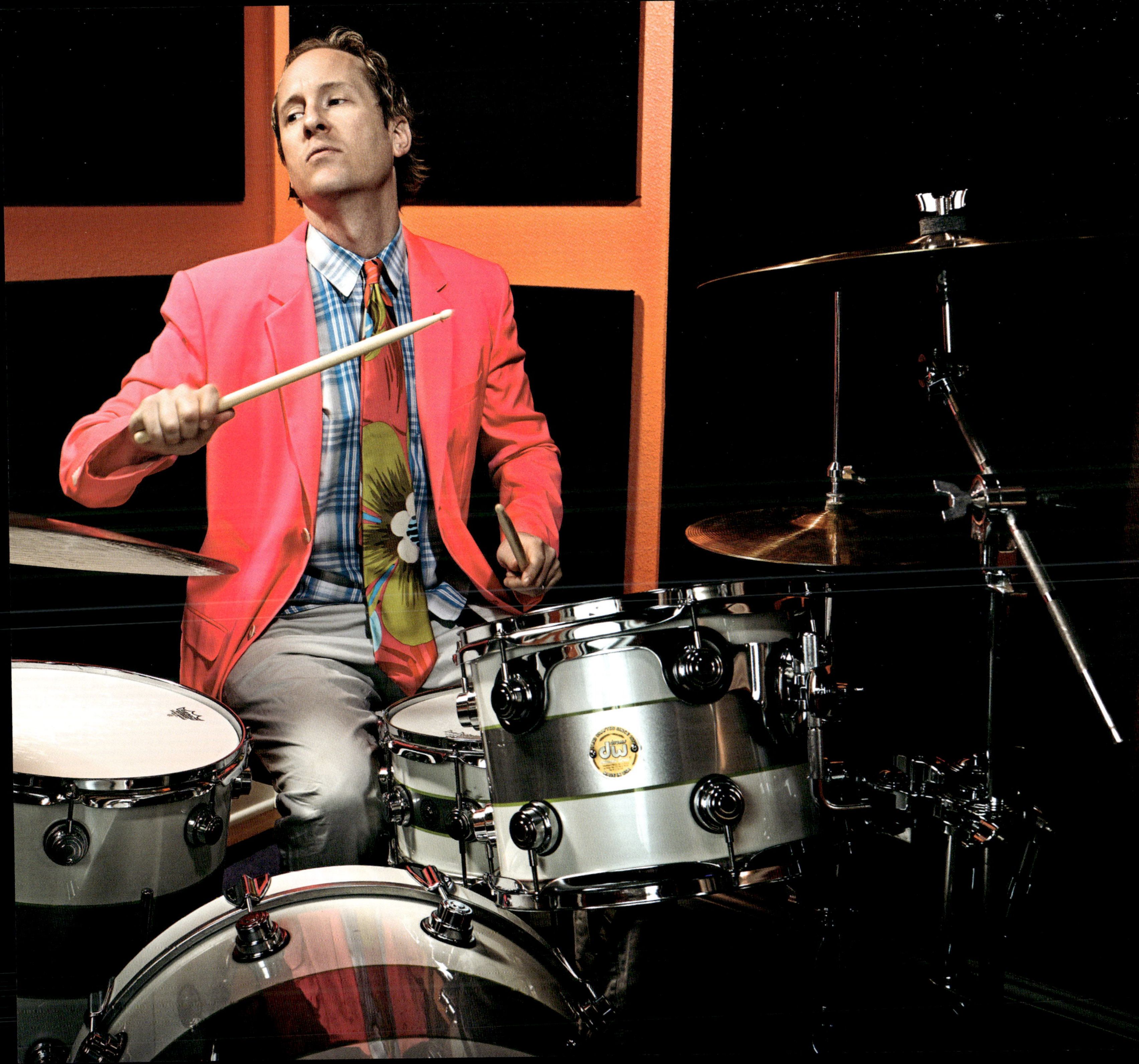

“I GOTTA GIVE PROPS TO KELTNER – HE’S GOT CUSTOM-MADE COWBOY BOOTS FOR PLAYING THE DRUMS”

MIKE D

Beastie Boys. Photographed in his home studio, California

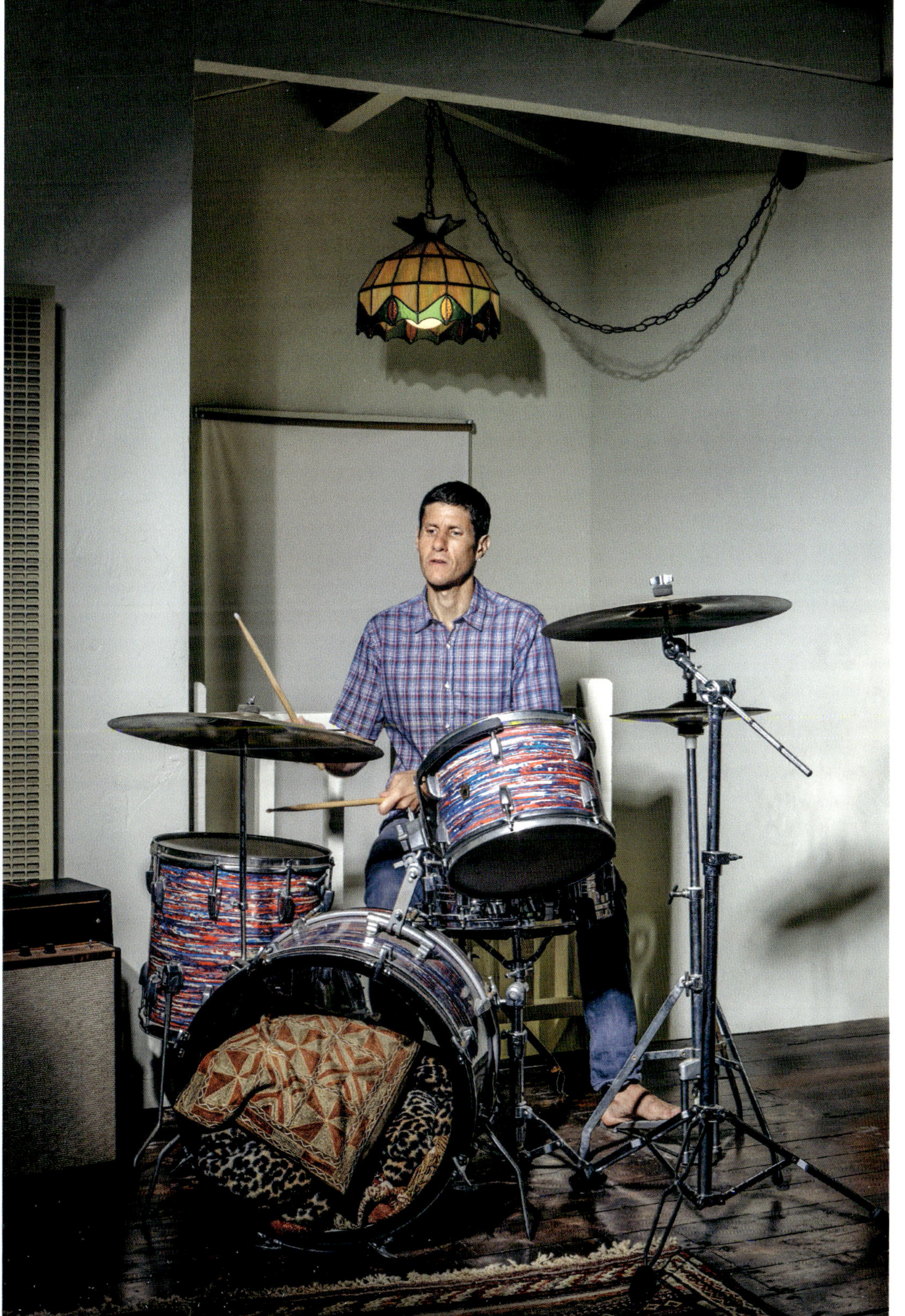

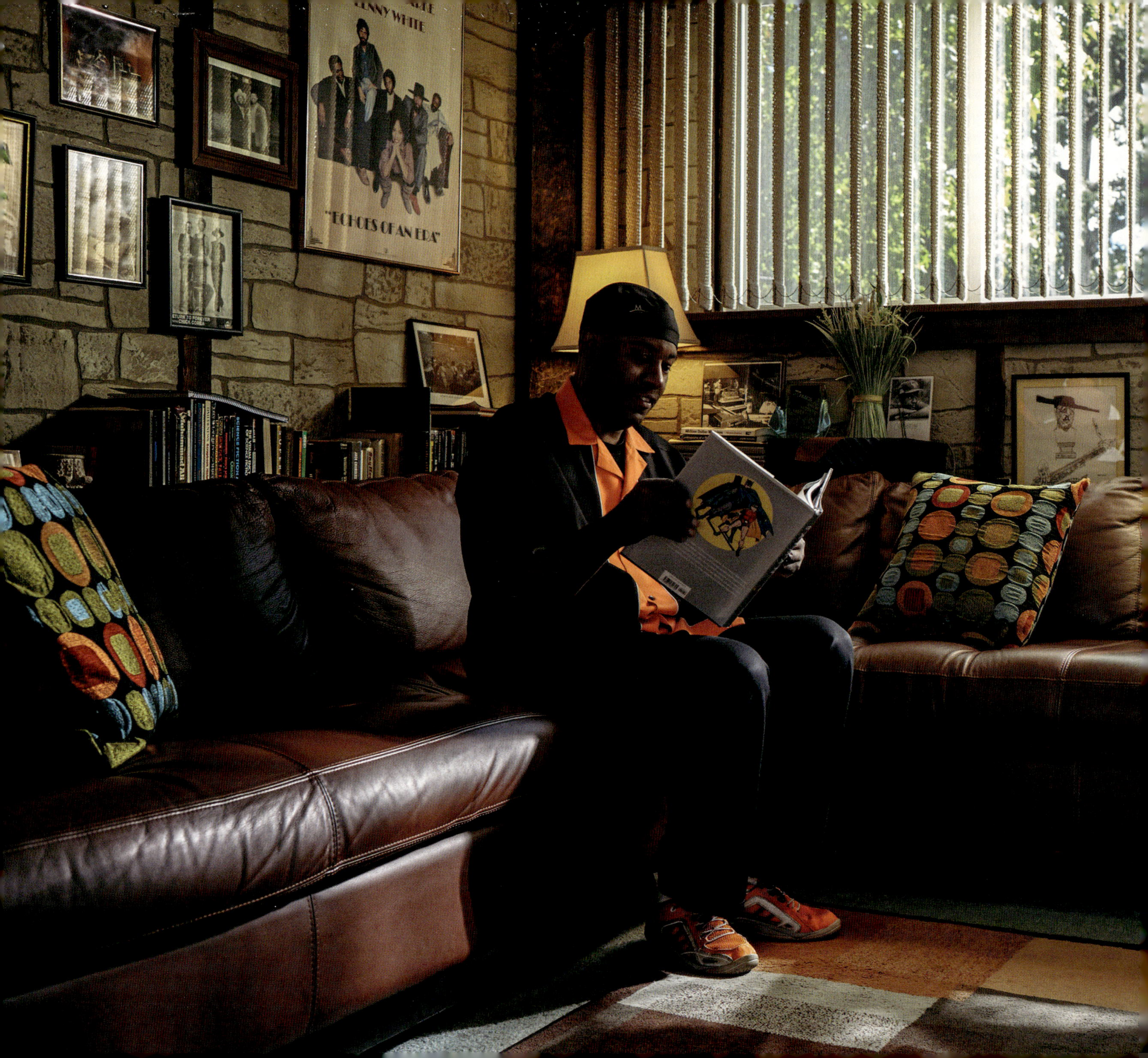
"ECHOES OF AN ERA"

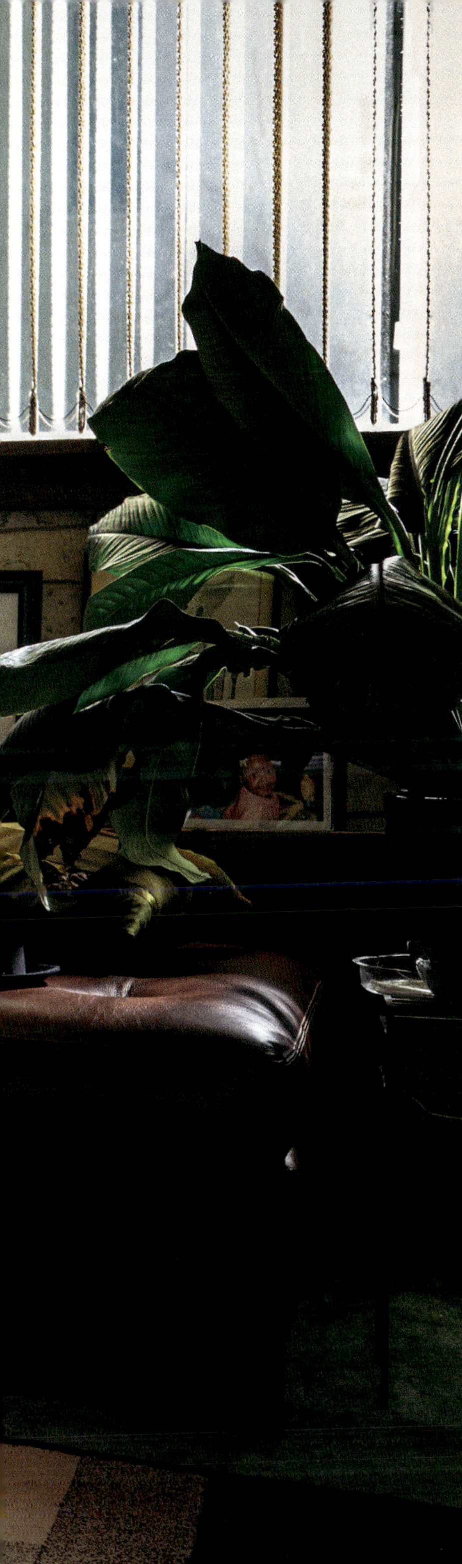

LENNY WHITE

Miles Davis / Freddie Hubbard / Return to Forever / Gato Barbieri / Jaco Pastorius
Photographed at home, New Jersey

I probably learned more from Miles Davis than anybody else. We were recording a tune called 'Miles Runs the Voodoo Down' and Miles wanted it to have a really funky beat. Tony Williams, who played with Miles, was a hero of mine, so I figured: I'm going to play like Tony and Jack DeJohnette. And I'm playing … I thought it sounded really good. Miles came up to me, he said, 'Nah, nah, nah man, you're not getting the chicken.' That was an expression to say you're not funky. So Don Alias – great person, great drummer, great percussionist – he said, 'Miles, I got a beat that we could play.' He played this real simple beat and I thought, you got to be kidding me. I knew I could have done that. I wanted to impress Miles – I never asked what he wanted. I just went out and played what I thought he wanted and it was totally the opposite of what he wanted. I wound up playing percussion on it rather than playing drums. And so when the session was over, I was pretty despondent. I was sitting over in the corner with my head in my hands. He came over and asked what was wrong. I said, 'Man, I really … I thought that ….' He said, 'Don't even worry about it, come back tomorrow, it's another day.' That's the mark of a true professional: to be able to go into a situation, ask what's wanted and do what is asked. That's the biggest thing that I learned that day. The next day I was right back into it.

There's a natural rhythm to the universe and some people are closer to that pulse, they understand things a bit better. Rhythm is something that's innate and inherent in everything, because everything vibrates, everything is frequency. Everybody has a heartbeat. Everybody knows how to walk, and when you walk there's a rhythm. All languages have a rhythm, like if you go to Italy and you hear people speak, they speak in a certain way and there's a rhythm to that. In Italy the way the language flows is because of their use of vowels. The difference between Italian and English is the emphasis is on consonants, not vowels. I listen that way and really use that in my playing. I'd ride the train a lot back and forth to school; listening to how the trains go, these rhythms – these kinds of things stay with me.

It's interesting because rhythm has taken over; with hip hop, rhythm superseded melody. The young kids would make beats, they would transfer the melodic importance of a song to the rhythmic importance of a song. And there was a very interesting change. I saw it and thought, wow! If you think about pop music, for so many years it was primarily based on melody. But it changed, especially in the '80s here in the States with hip hop, because it was just rhyming but the rhythm was great, the beat was … oh man, that beat is infectious.

What we need to be thinking about is how music is made, because that's what's different. When I came up, there were musicians making music. Now, that's not the case. Music has become a way to sell things as opposed to it being music for music's sake, and that's scary. In 1983 I bought a drum machine because I said if it's going that way, I want to know how to do this so that I won't be out of work. Fortunately it wasn't like that. I did a lot of things, produced a lot of sessions using drum machines and stuff. The issue is not what kind of music's being made, it's how it's being made. It's really important for you to understand why there's a demise and why you're losing in the battle to keep art and music alive. I read somewhere about declining empires, that their decline can be related to the debasement of their music. Every ruling empire that failed, you can look back and see that when the music went down, the empire went down. There will always be artists creating art. And there will always be people that are into commerce to the point where they'll compromise in order to get on.

STEVE JORDAN

The Verbs / The Rolling Stones / John Mayer Trio / Sonny Rollins / Eric Clapton. Photographed in New York

The first time I knew that I was going to really work at being a musician was when I was in the seventh grade and every Wednesday there would be a performance by students in the auditorium. I was in my first real band, called Mystic Funk. The bass player got complete and utter stage fright and he couldn't go on. We were playing a Donny Hathaway tune called 'The Ghetto', which is all about the bass line. So now we gotta go up onstage and play this song without the bass line. So it was the guitar, sax and drums. You kind of black out because the adrenaline is running and now you're in an impossible position: you can't not play, even though this whole thing is around the bass and there's no bass player. So we went ahead and we played, and we became the most popular guys in the school. Like, within ten minutes – we were like the nerds prior and then the most popular kids right afterwards. I thought, I don't know what's happening here but it's really weird. So that's when I thought, okay, there might be something to this.

As I always say, you really got to be on the case because it doesn't matter what the situation is, if something's not going right, they always look to the drummer first. Like, if the thing isn't happening, it's gonna be the drummer's fault. Always. So you gotta know what's going on, you gotta know, like, if the bass player is rushing, or the thing's out of groove. It's more thinking, okay, you know what's happening here, I think you're a little bit on top of me, so maybe I'll compensate and lay back a little so we can get this thing going. Or maybe we can work on this turnaround here. So you have to know, even if you're not producing and you're not the arranger; you still have to figure stuff out. It's basically your butt on the line. The arranger might not know, the producer might not know, the writer might not know, the engineer might not know. You better know.

As an engineer, as a producer, as a composer, as a player, there are a lot of hats you wear. I love being able to work with Burt Bacharach and to have him trust me. I have so many stories of the wildest, most amazing things, from working with Bootsy Collins to my friendships with Willie Weeks and Pino Palladino and getting to play with Bob Babbitt when I was a teenager. I had no idea. When I first played with Bob Babbitt I felt this thing going through my body and I thought, I know that feeling. I got chills, I got goosebumps. I didn't know he was the bass player on 'Signed, Sealed, Delivered I'm Yours' by Stevie Wonder. I didn't know he played on 'Papa was a Rollin' Stone'. I got to play with a lot of people, especially doing studio work when I was a teenager. I was in high school and I was working at Bill's Music Rentals. Bill's Music Rentals was the place for people to rehearse. I met a lot of people there, from Stevie Wonder to Roberta Flack – you name it, they all rehearsed there. They used to supply a lot of percussion instruments to Broadway. Somebody in studio A needs something and you roll in a timpani or you're maintaining the gear. It was a great experience.

Stevie Wonder was there right around *Songs in the Key of Life* – he was recording at The Hit Factory and rehearsing at Bill's. They were also at the time auditioning for drummers. Bill was trying to get me an audition but I was too young. I was still at school so I couldn't go out on the road. Once the auditions were closed they said, 'Let the kid play.' I was really into fusion at the time, and so was Stevie Wonder. We broke into this Return to Forever/Chick Corea tune, which I knew and he knew but nobody else knew. So the two of us were playing this thing and everybody was going like, whoa! It was the most incredible thing in the world. I would have to leave by a certain time to get the train to go back to the Bronx; it was like being Cinderella before the thing turns into a pumpkin.

About two months ago I was in the recording studio with Chick Corea. I told Chick that the first time Stevie Wonder and I played together we played 'Hymn of the Seventh Galaxy', and how wild it was now that I'm finally getting to play with him. Then three or four weeks ago, I flew to Los Angeles to do the Emmy Awards and Chick was playing at Catalina's and sitting in front of me is Stevie Wonder and his son. It gets crazier. So Stevie sits in and everybody's freaking out and he makes a really eloquent speech about respect and peace and love and everything. And then before he plays he says, 'I love this man very much.' He's talking about Chick. And he talked about, you know, back in 1973 or '72, he had this massive car accident in which he was almost killed. He had a contusion that put him in a coma and for two weeks it was very touch-and-go. And when he came out of the coma, the first music he heard was Chick Corea. There's a tune on *Songs in the Key of Life* called 'Contusion' – that's why he wrote it. It was his version of a fusion tune. That was the reason why he knew that music; it's the music he heard when he came out of a coma and he loved it. It was completely surreal, the whole thing, after all these years, the full circle of that story. But yes, I saw Stevie do some incredible stuff and it really made me go, okay, this is what I want to do with my life.

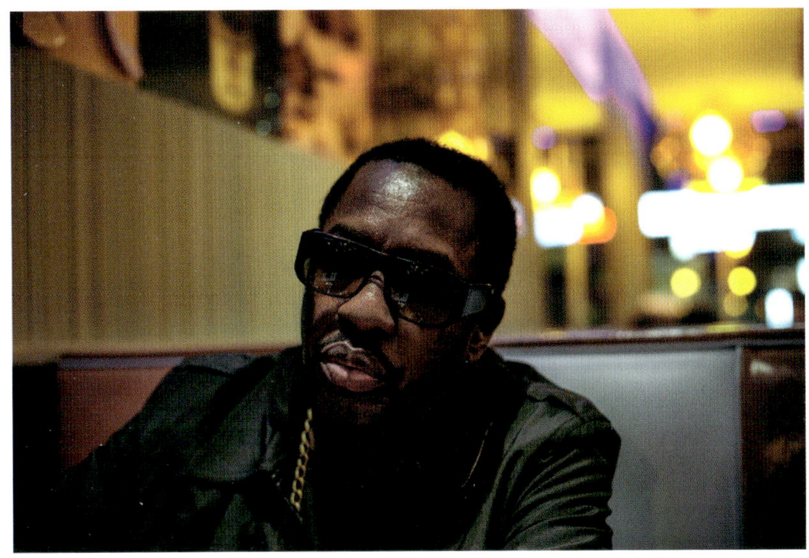
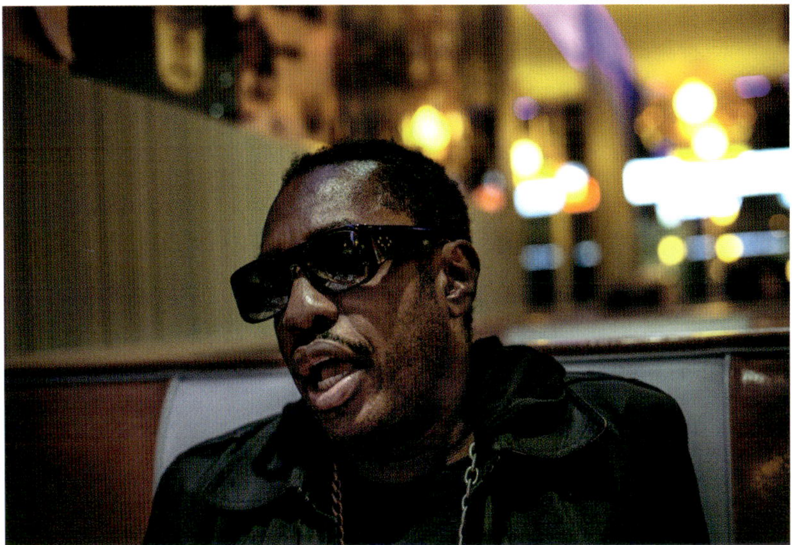
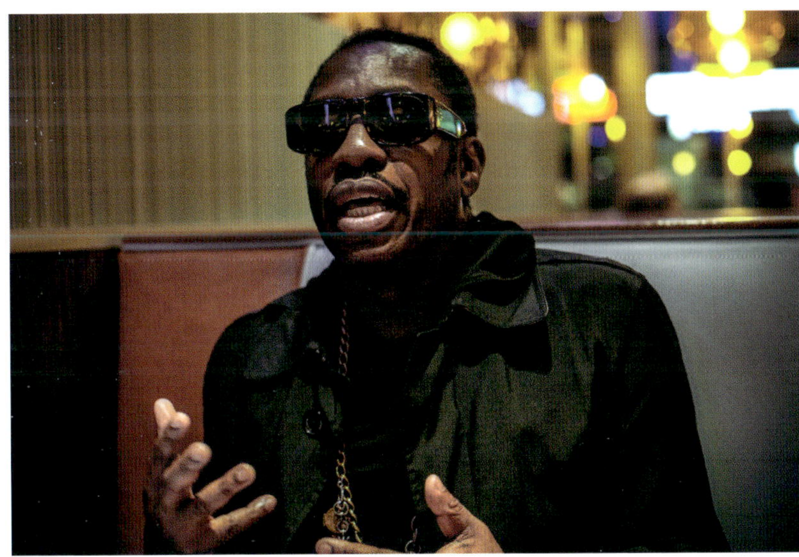
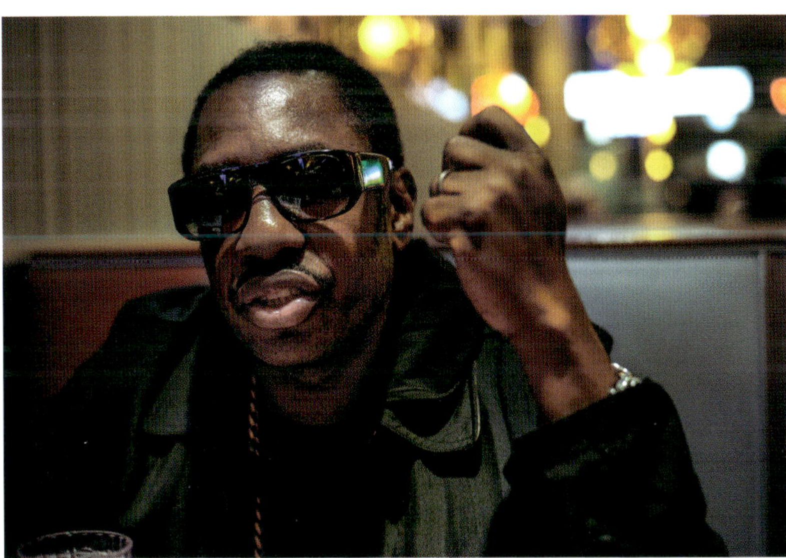

TYSHAWN SOREY

Tyshawn Sorey Trio / John Zorn / Vijay Iyer / Steve Lehman / Myra Melford
Photographed at home, New York

Somebody once told me, 'You're like a young old guy.' It was hard for me socially, growing up in an environment where everybody was doing the normal things they do when they're younger; I was always kind of like the freak in the room. I never fitted in with the social norm at any point in my life. People said, 'You're only hanging out with old people,' but I was getting information and learning, and I liked them because they were taking time out of their schedule to really show me things. I'd be on the telephone with some of these older guys for four or five hours sometimes, talking about music and talking about life and all kinds of different things. It was really nice to have those experiences coming up. That's what led me to my belief that you basically have to seek out as much information as you can in order to get better at what you're doing, because nobody's going to show it to you if you don't ask.

When I met with Milford Graves recently, he said something along the lines of: 'Man, we need to be in a situation where younger people and older musicians hang out together. Because that's not really happening now.' Milford told me if you want to get better at what you do, you need to learn from the masters. You really need to get with those people who can tell you some stories that you might not be able to get from anywhere else. It could be part of the reason why the music is suffering. Younger musicians are only playing with each other; there's never a situation where younger musicians are coming up under older musicians, and that's partly because a lot of our masters whom we've respected for a long time have left us now. There aren't really as many situations out there like there used to be, like an Art Blakey, someone who would oftentimes work with younger musicians. We don't have people like that around any more.

I think of myself as sort of an orchestrator, you know, I don't think of myself as no timekeeper – that's not really my job, I don't think. Of course it is my job in theory, but I'm not just going to sit there and do nothing to affect the music in some way. After I hear what chord or harmony is there, I see colours; I see things visually. I have what you call synaesthesia, when you see colour whenever you hear something in a particular key, or whenever you hear a certain pattern of notes – it can apply in that sense. I try to coordinate those colours in a way that makes sense to the music. So like, if I hear a certain harmony or something, maybe I want to play a certain cymbal for this and a certain way for that. Or if I'm hearing a section in a piece of music that sounds like it's a dark colour, maybe I want to approach it a little differently. I'm not just playing behind all this interesting stuff going on harmonically or melodically. I really want to know how I can make it … I don't want to say better, but how I can make it come out in the way that it should come out.

The album *Offering* is a recording of John Coltrane's quintet from 1966 from Temple University. Only around 800 people came out to the performance in a place that seats about 1,700 people. They were expecting sold-out tickets but only about half the seats were filled. It was an unforgettable concert, so they decided to put it out as a record. When I heard the live version of 'Crescent', I can't really describe it in words … it was like the music just elevated itself. Somehow I felt like I couldn't move. Pharoah Sanders comes in and the music starts getting more and more heavy. And then Coltrane comes back in, and the music goes to this whole other level. It just keeps building and building to the point Coltrane takes the horn out of his mouth and starts chanting – and that was it. That did it for me. Listening to him take the horn out because he felt he really couldn't do anything more with the horn. He had already exhausted everything he could play on that instrument, and he just starts beating his chest and chanting this beautiful-sounding chant that comes out. And you know, a lot of people thought he was crazy for doing that, but it brought out a whole other kind of emotion that I don't think was ever really captured on record or probably in all of music. It was so profound and it was so highly energetic to the point where it wasn't music anymore. I couldn't move for about thirty minutes after listening to that recording. It was a humbling experience to sit and listen to that and really think to myself as a composer, and as a performer, this is exactly what I want to give my audience. I want to make them feel they're loved and to be taken through all these different emotions. I want my audience to feel cleansed after listening to my work like I did after listening to Coltrane's. I was moved to tears by that.

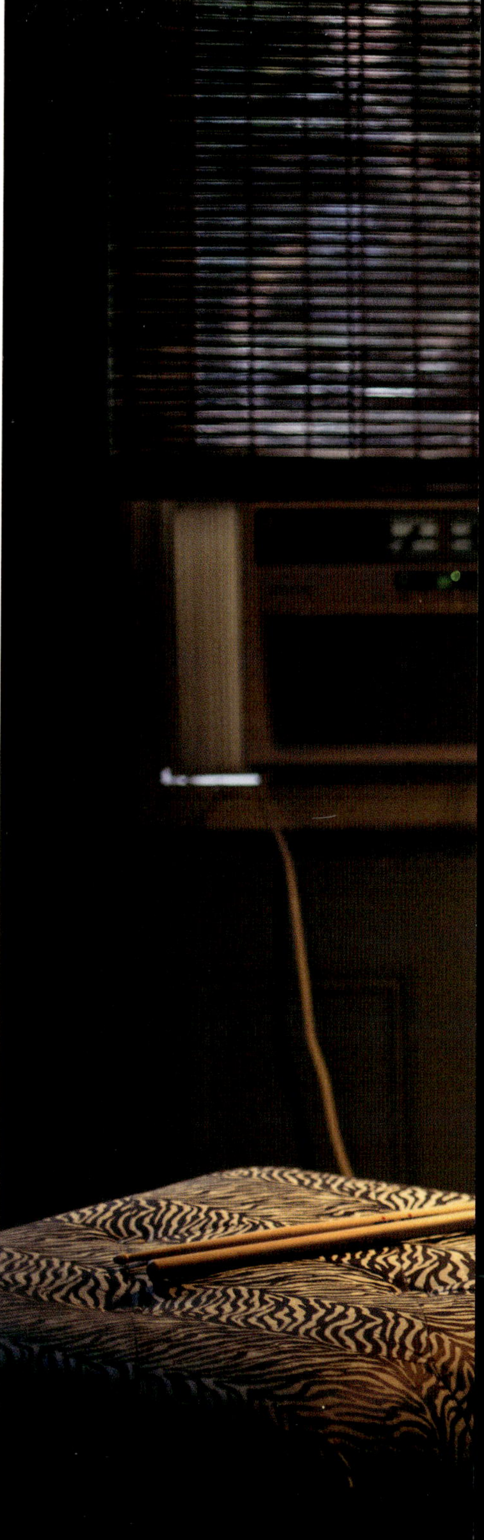

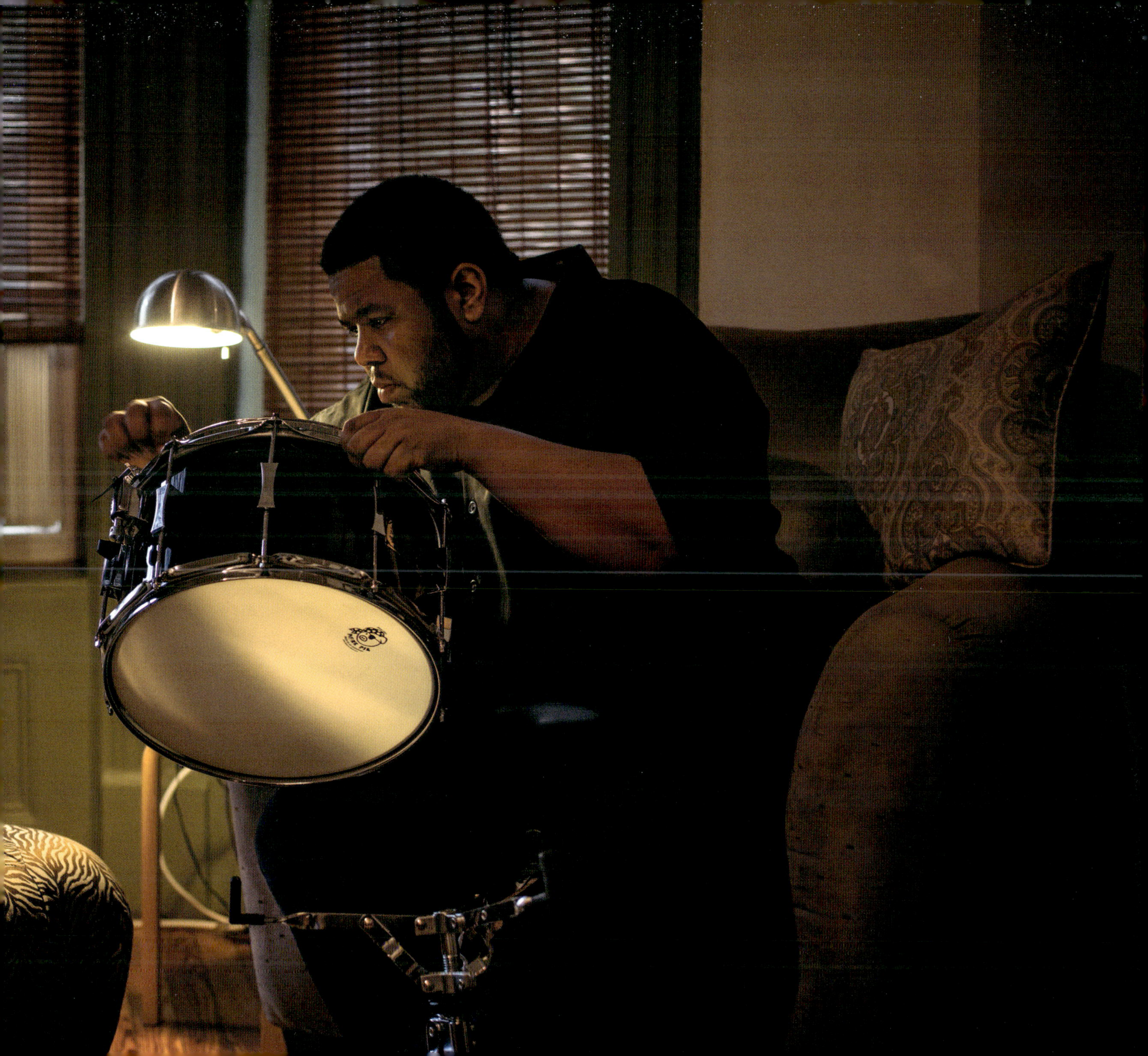

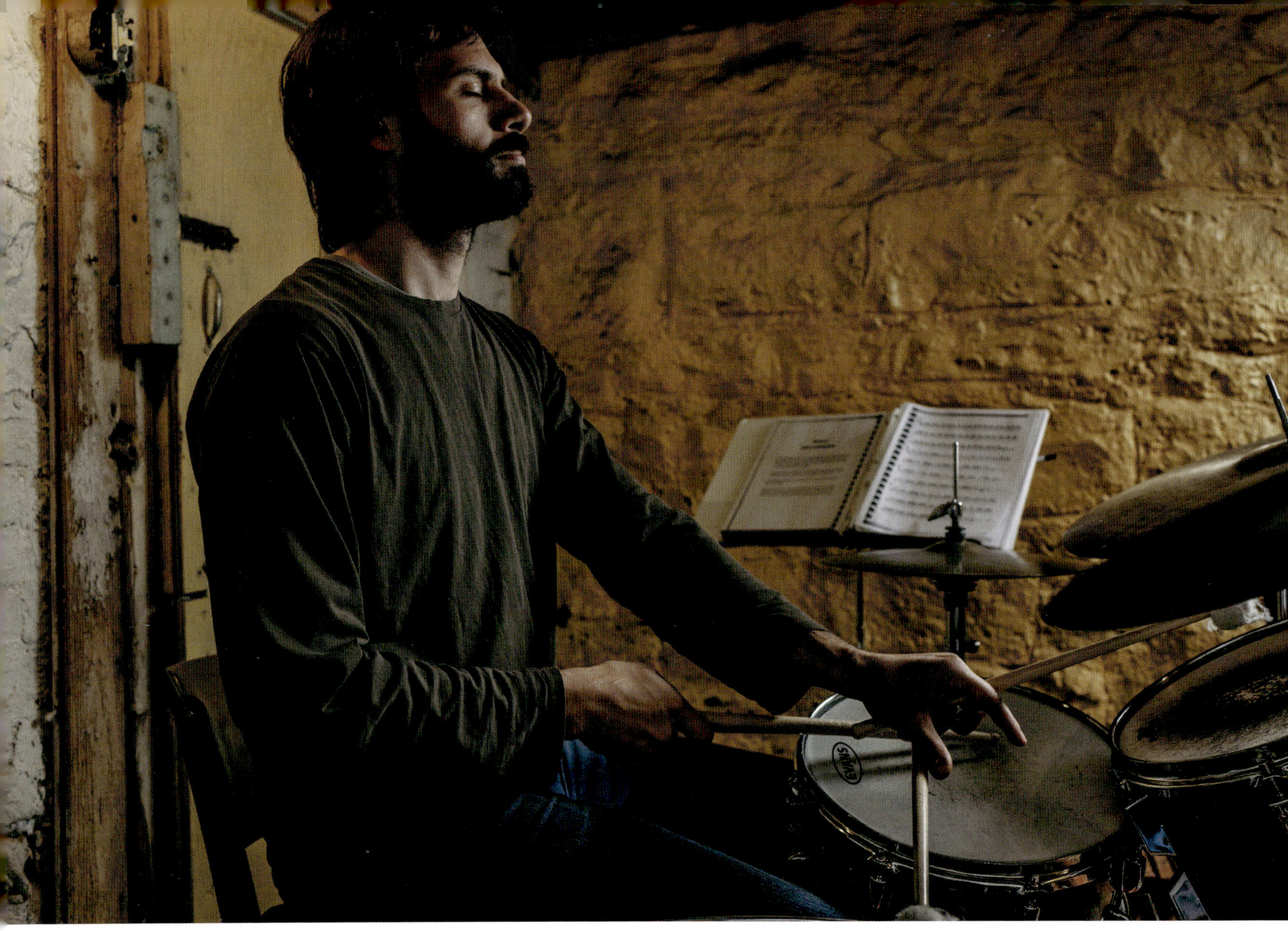
EVANS

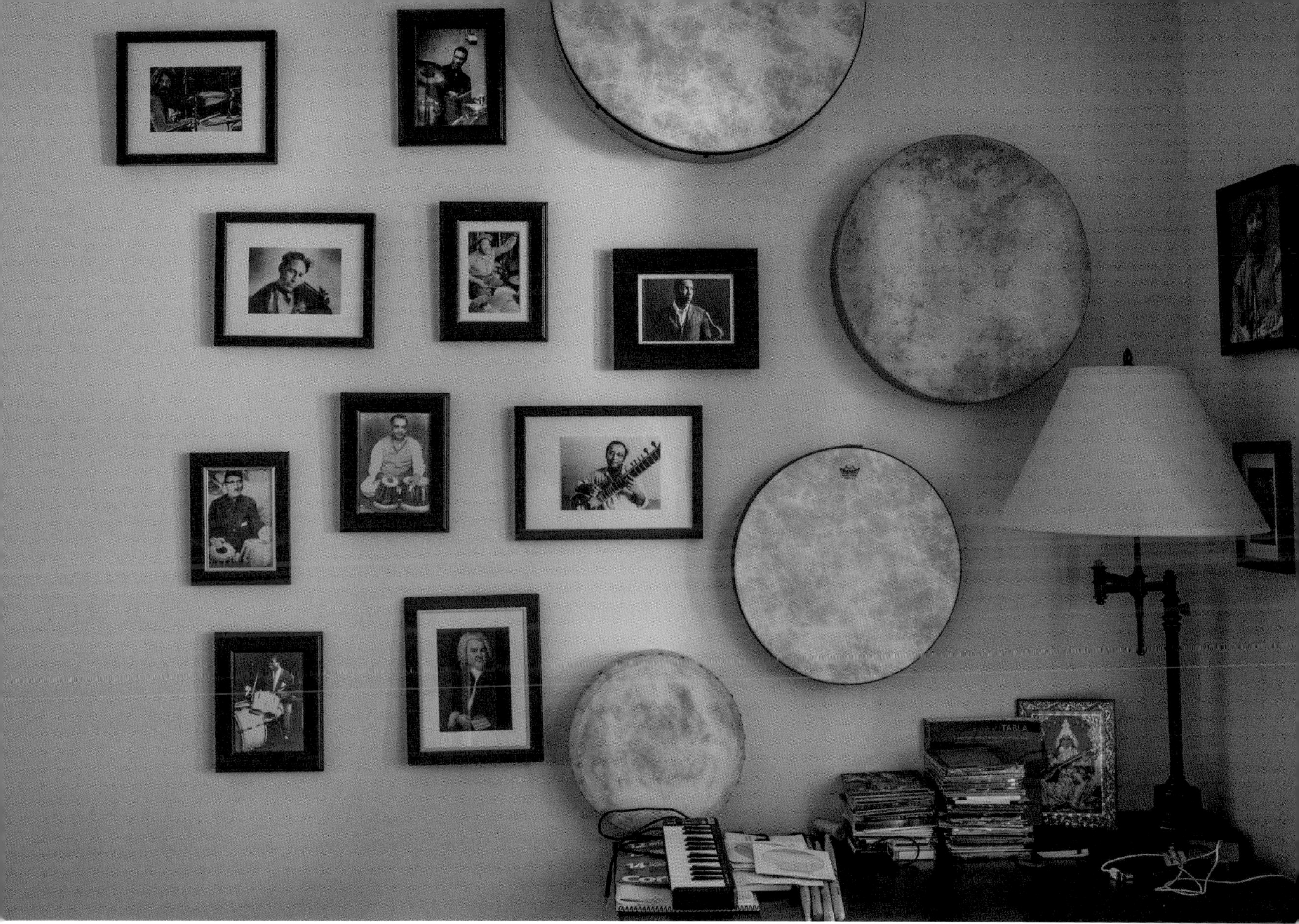

DAN WEISS

Dan Weiss Trio / Starebaby / David Binney / Miles Okazaki / Rez Abbasi
Photographed at home, New York

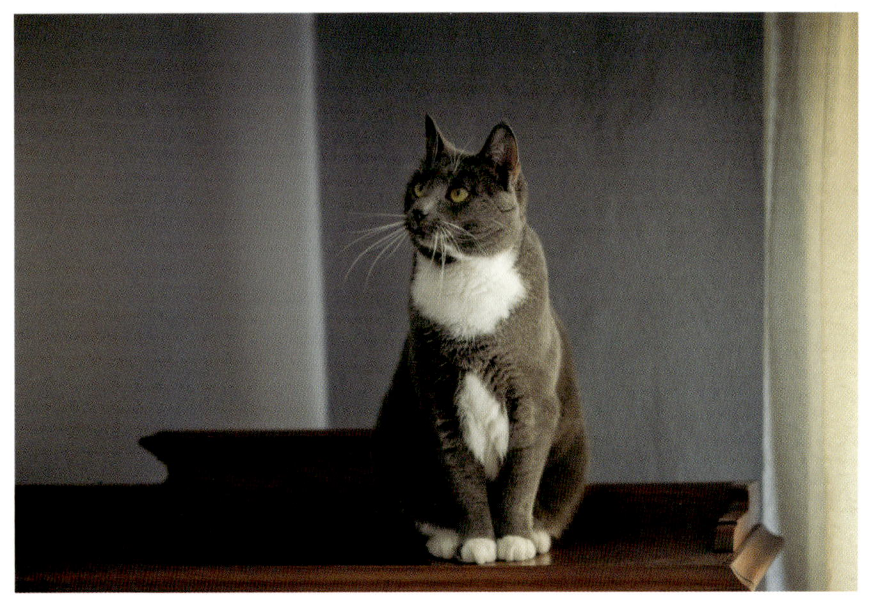

GENE CHRISMAN

The Memphis Boys Rhythm Section (Jerry Lee Lewis / The Highwaymen / Aretha Franklin / Elvis Presley / Neil Diamond)
Photographed at home, Kentucky

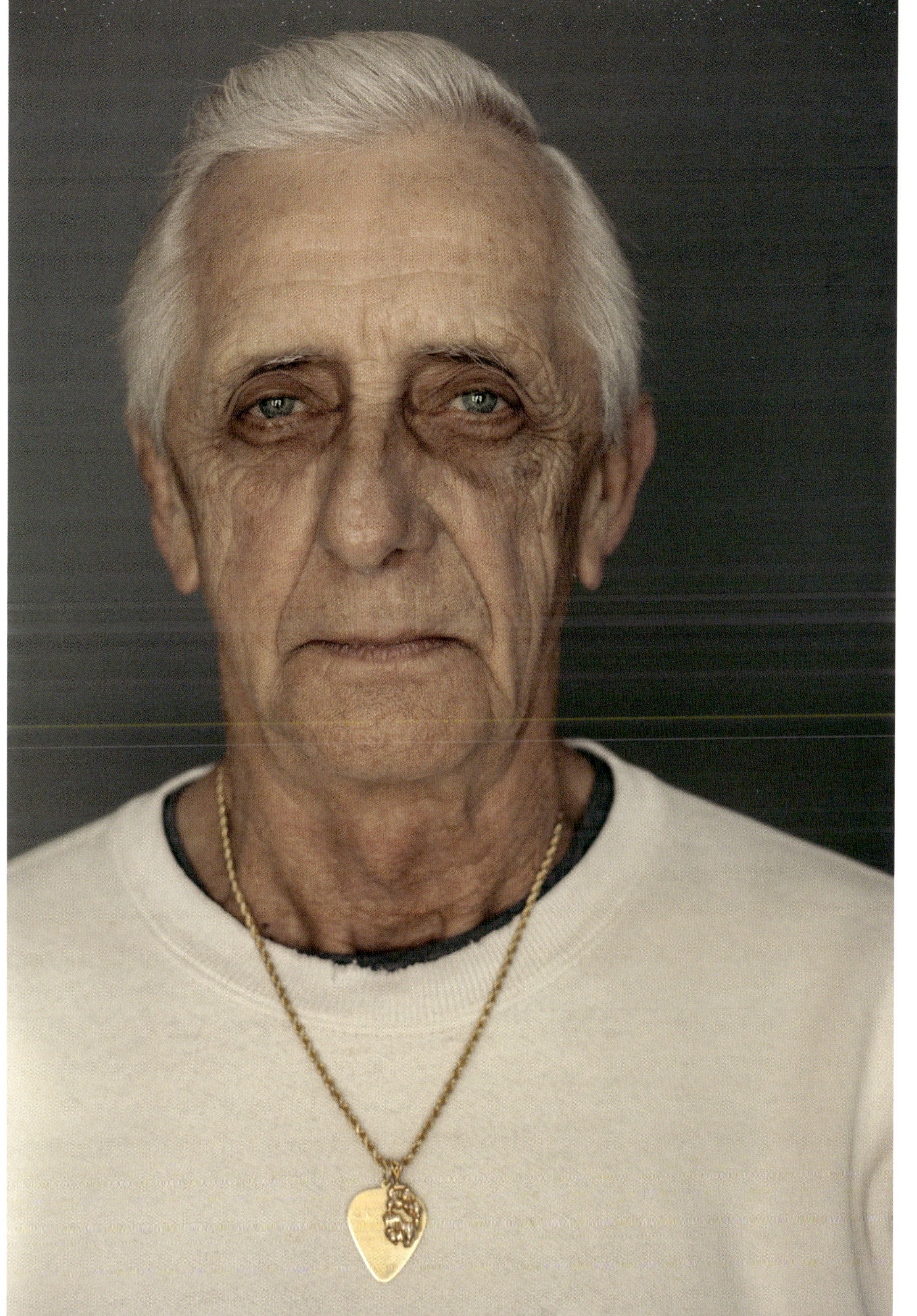

BRIAN CHIPPENDALE

Lightning Bolt / Black Pus. Photographed at home, Rhode Island

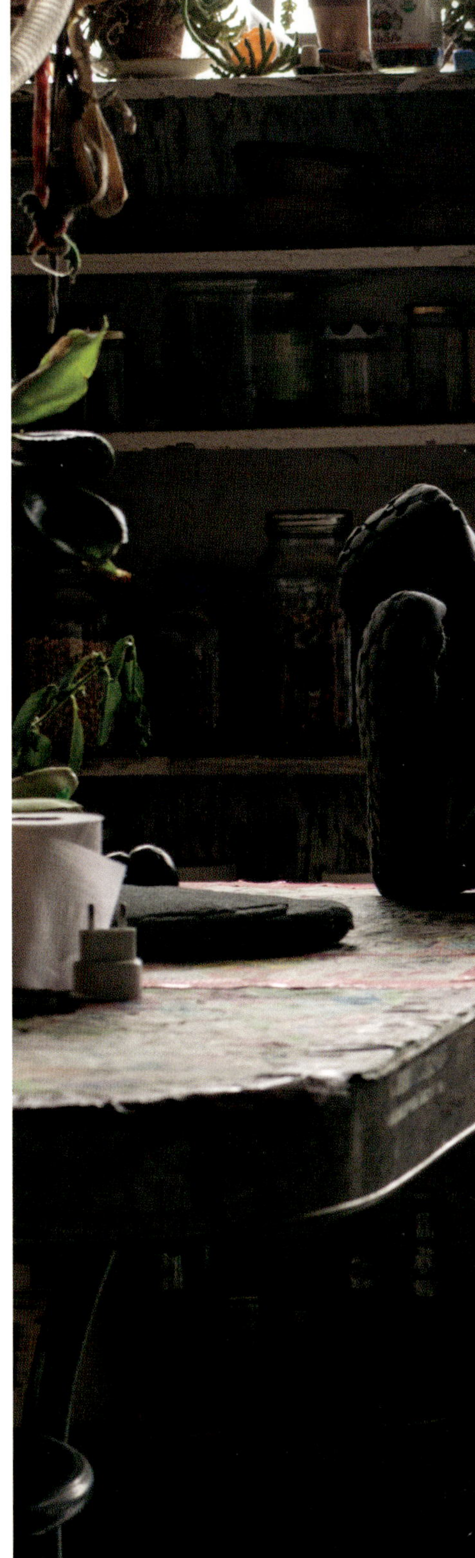

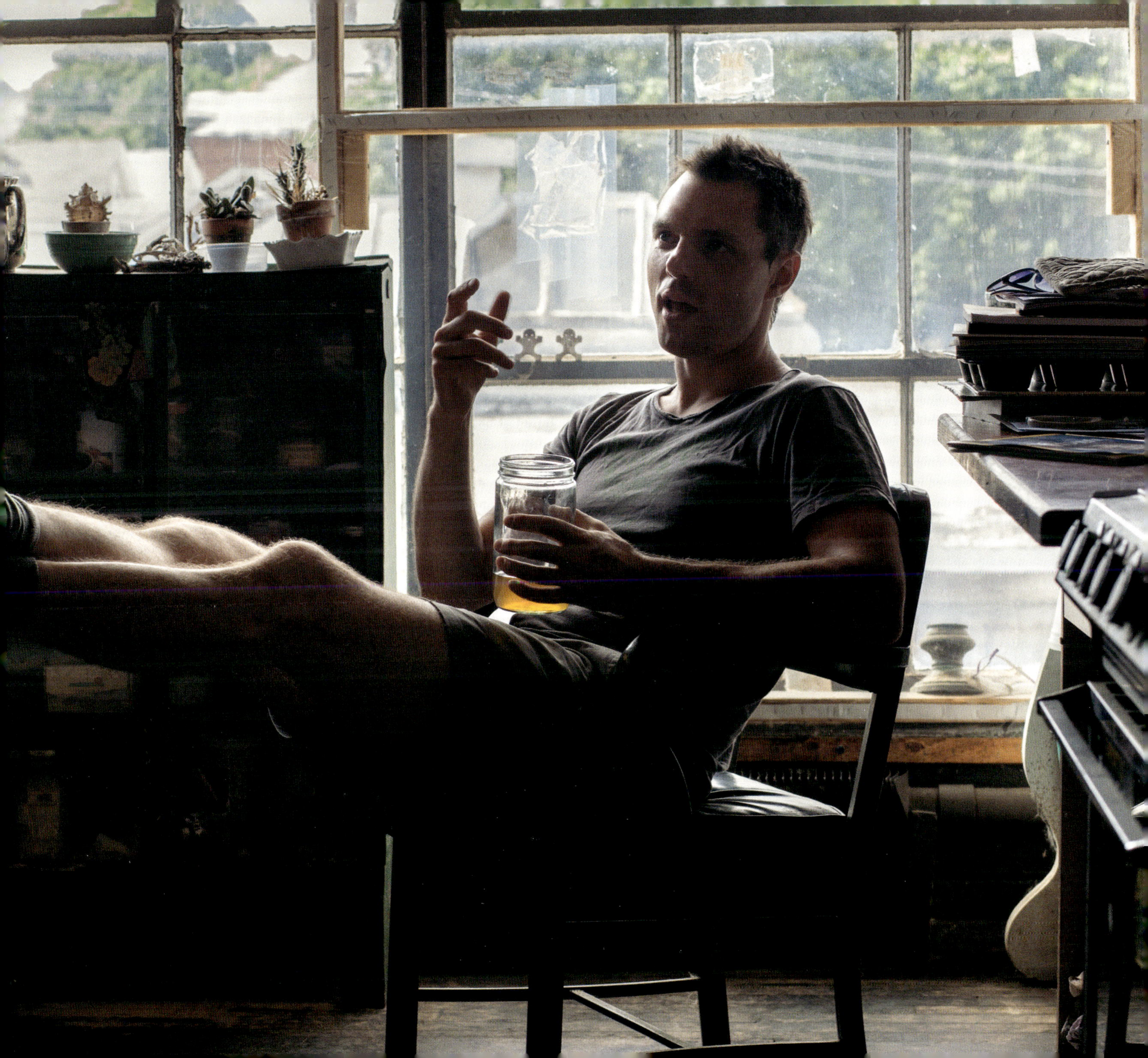

It feels like all the shows I've ever played are so crazy. Even if they're not, even if nothing's happening, in my mind they're so crazy because I'm trying to play to the edge of my ability all the time. So they're all just like blinking your eyes really fast for an hour. They all seem really intense. Some have been more intense, like playing during the summer in July in New Orleans in a storefront with no air conditioning. Or another one in Louisiana – I remember the outlet caught on fire. I think it was because it was so hot, as we were running all this gear, this fire started in the corner. I thought it would be funny to tape my mask to my head. I was like, it's so goddamn hot in here, I'm not going to take it off – and then ended up almost passing out.

Again – this was in July – we played in this little place called Flywheel in Easthampton, Massachusetts. They moved and they're bigger now. It used to be this little room. And it was us and three members of Sonic Youth and this duo from Japan called Afrirampo, two women. So basically playing with Sonic Youth in this little tiny room; it was packed and I think we played last. It was the kind of show where you walked into the room and, like, the ceiling was just dripping because it was so hot and we hadn't even started yet. We set up and I think we were on our third song and I was dying. I think I'd probably taken my mask off at that point because some of those shows I just couldn't even ... I just shove the mic in my mouth and, whatever, we just play. It doesn't matter, everyone's in pain. I was thinking, I feel like I'm swimming, I have to pee. I'm in the ocean right now. Like when you're in the ocean you just pee, so I was playing and I just started peeing. That was the only show where I peed myself. It just felt like it didn't even matter. And then I think within fifteen minutes I was laying on my rug half passed out, probably in my own pee. I've probably since slept on that rug.

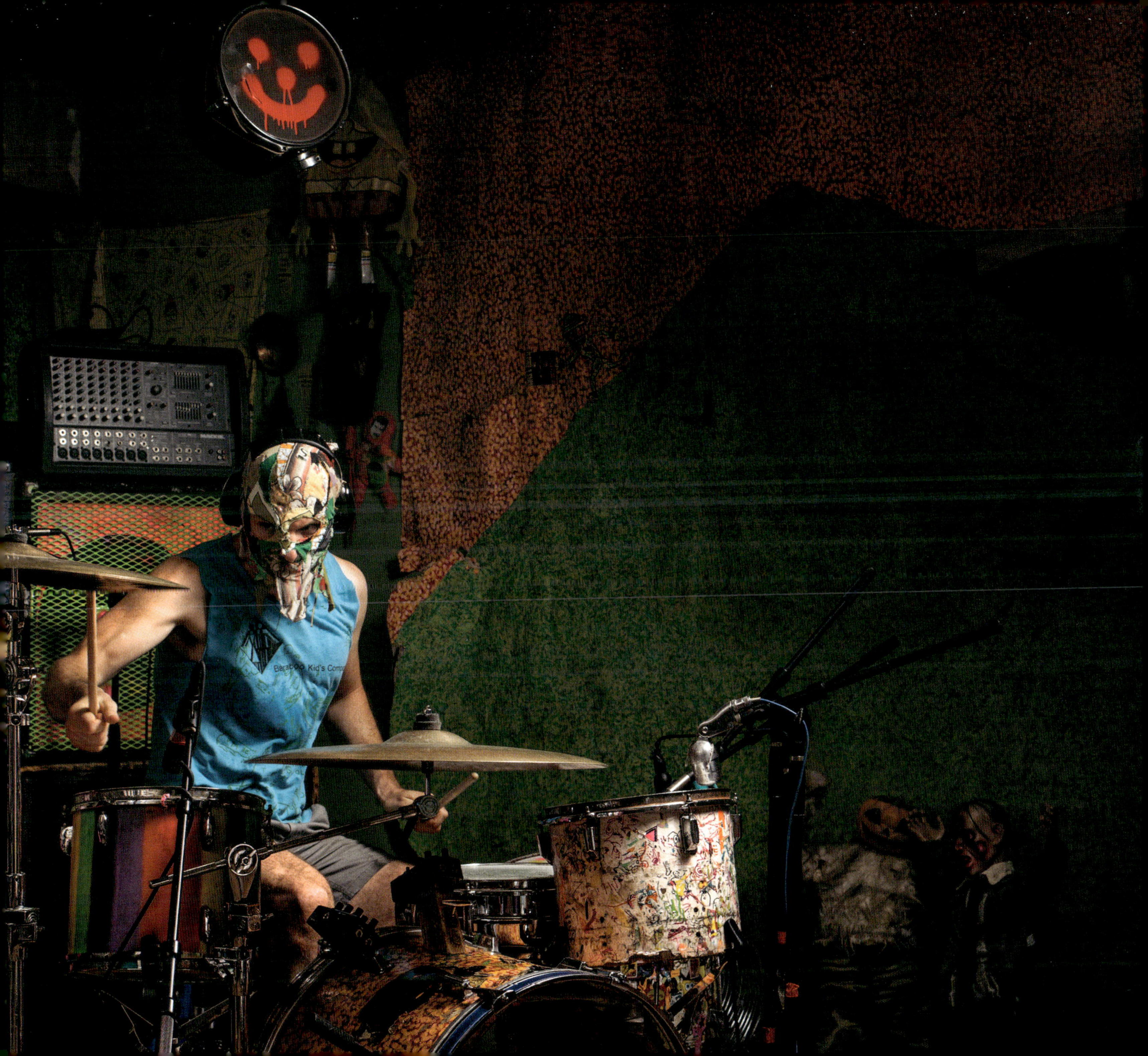
Baraboo Kid's

STEPHEN MORRIS

New Order / Joy Division. Photographed in his home studio in the UK

When I was a child I had a tiny bedroom and my dad had quite a big bedroom, so every morning I'd move my drums out of my room so I could get out of bed, and put them in Dad's and set them up. But then every night I had 'operation drums' – I had to take them all down again and put them back in my room and then I could get in bed … so, yes, I slept with them, yes … Luckily we had a detached house and the lady next door was going a bit deaf anyway, but you did get problems with people walking the dog – they would look up at the window and wonder what the hell was going on.

Back then in Manchester, there was very little to do; it was all grey. It was still in the after-effects of the war, lots of bomb sites; they knocked all these houses down, they were building Hulme [Crescents, then the largest public housing development in Europe]. That thing of looking towards the future with the big, tall buildings. They didn't know what was going to happen in later years. They were kind of sinister and a bit like they might have a spy on every floor but, compared to these Victorian buildings which were hanging on by the skin of their teeth, you felt they were great, that you'd like to live in one of them. It rained a lot and it was pretty grim.

If you wanted to hear music, apart from in your bedroom, you couldn't go to discos or anything like that: you had to go to a concert. I mean there were discos in Macclesfield but you had to be a lot older and have all the right gear to get into them so we couldn't. So the only thing was going to concerts at the Free Trade Hall and this great place called the Stoneground, and you'd go to see bands like Genesis – that was a band that I saw a lot. Phil Collins was an interesting, and probably is still an interesting, drummer. That was what you listened to. And when punk came along, you pushed all those records under your bed and pretended that you'd never liked them at all! 'Oh, no, no, no, no, I've always liked the Sex Pistols, the Ramones!' I mean, I did like the MC5 and The Stooges, but they were far across the ocean in America and you had no chance of seeing them, but then year zero happened and it was punk.

Joy Division were called Warsaw then. I had decided to become a music journalist. There was an advert in *Record Mirror* saying 'Journalist wanted', and I thought, I could do that. So I started writing reviews, which was my first experience of being disillusioned by the music business. I thought well, you can just walk in and say, 'Hi, I'm from *Record Mirror*, I'm here to review the band.' And they'd come in and thank you with caviar and stuff like that, or at least not make you pay. But that never happened, it was more, 'We're sold out, mate.' So I had to find a bloody way of getting into the gig and then writing a review, and then you got the piss taken out of you by your own magazine, but there you go.

I saw two adverts in a magazine. One was 'Drummer wanted – Warsaw' and 'Drummer wanted – The Fall'. And I thought, hmm, I could probably do both of those gigs. And then when I went back to Macclesfield I walked past a music shop and it said 'Drummer wanted for local punk band Warsaw'. So then I phoned up Ian and kind of got the job, really. Those rehearsals with Warsaw at the Abraham Moss Centre, there was this kind of thing, we had an energy. And we just started playing and everything sort of slotted together and yes it was a bit ramshackle, don't get me wrong. I thought it sounded good, they thought it sounded good, so I got the job.

It was really difficult getting a gig because, compared to today, there weren't that many venues you could play. Nobody liked punk bands. It was like us versus the establishment; we quite liked being on the outside of all that in a band. There was always the bloody Manchester mafia where you'd see bands like The Drones. They'd get gigs, and Buzzcocks and everybody else could get a gig, but you couldn't get a gig. So when you got a gig, you'd really go for it. And then we did the Stiff/Chiswick talent competition in Manchester. We knew Tony Wilson; he saw us and everyone thought we were fantastic even though it was just kind of … probably more anger that set us apart from anyone else. And then people started getting interested in us. And because we couldn't get gigs, we just rehearsed a lot, so you made a racket in various places, we just used to rehearse in pubs. One place was the community centre in Macclesfield which was just a little hall; another place was the upstairs room at The Talbot; an upstairs room at a pub in Salford. Then we settled into TJ Davidson's rehearsal studio in the old Mill, which is where all the photographs of Joy Division come from.

Working with our producer Martin Hannett on *Unknown Pleasures* was interesting and infuriating. He had to be on his own to do the mixing. Then you'd listen to it and wonder how it had got from how you imagined it, which was being very raw and live and raucous, to how it sounded on the record. It was like, we sound nothing like that! What's he done? And then if you forget it's you and it's a record, it's great; but it's a bit hard to detach yourself from it. Which is, I think, why Bernard and Hooky didn't like the sound of *Unknown Pleasures* that much. It was so different. But it was fantastic what he did.

I had to record all the drums separately; it was like he wanted the bass drum in the ballroom and the snare drum in a tin can and the hi-hat in a little cardboard box – which is dead easy to do now, but then you couldn't. It was hard to get the hang of at first. I mean, really my worst one is 'Love Will Tear Us Apart'. We'd recorded it and I'd done the drums over and over and over again. We'd stay in a flat in Baker Street and I had just got my head down and the phone goes. It's bloody Martin, he wants us to come back and do the snare drum! So I had to drive all the way back across London to do the snare drum, and every time I hear 'Love Will Tear Us Apart', all I can hear is the anger – of being dragged out of bed. On a good day I can hear what a fantastic song it is, but most of the time I can just hear: 'That bastard got me out of bed to do that!'

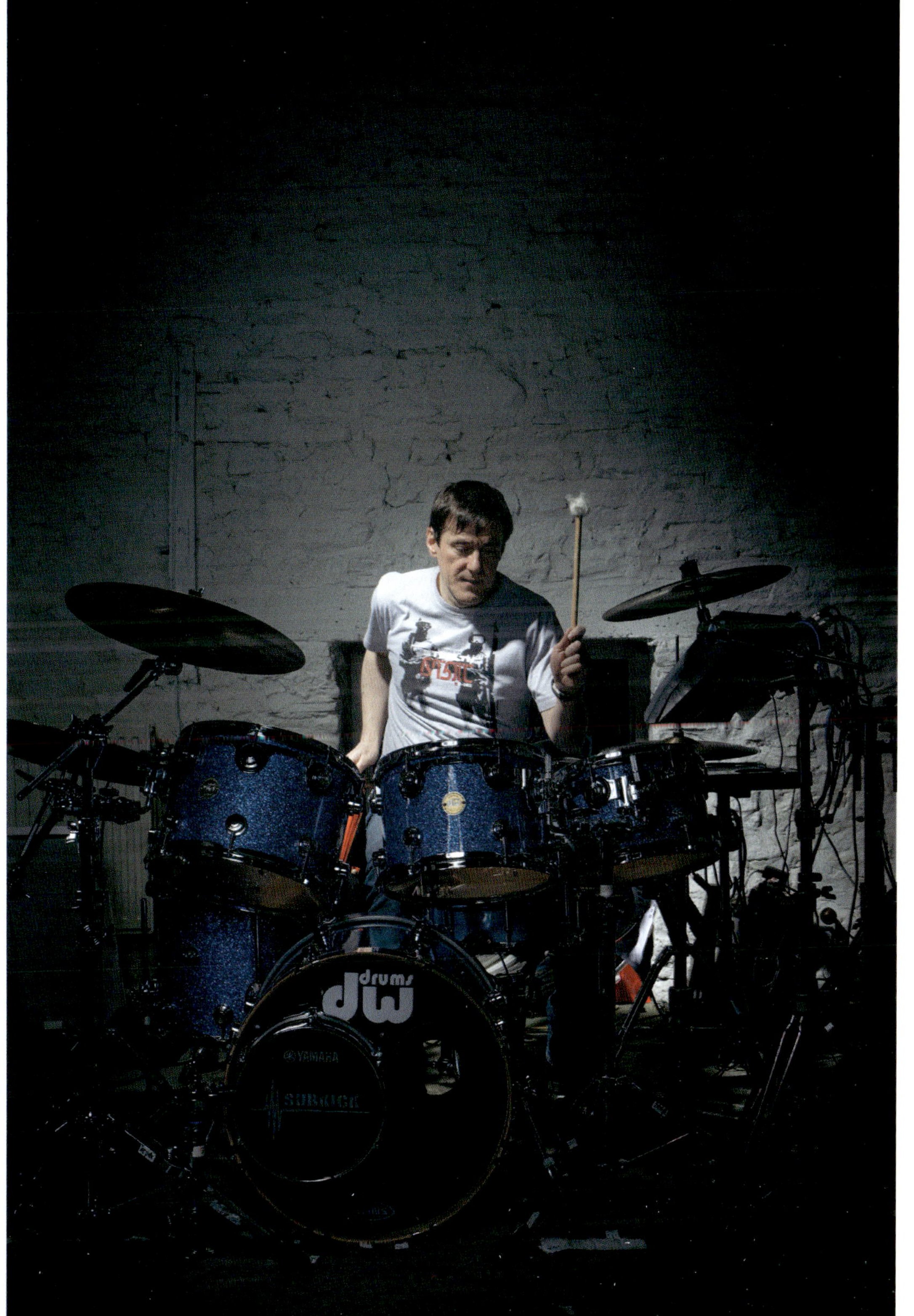
dw
drums
YAMAHA

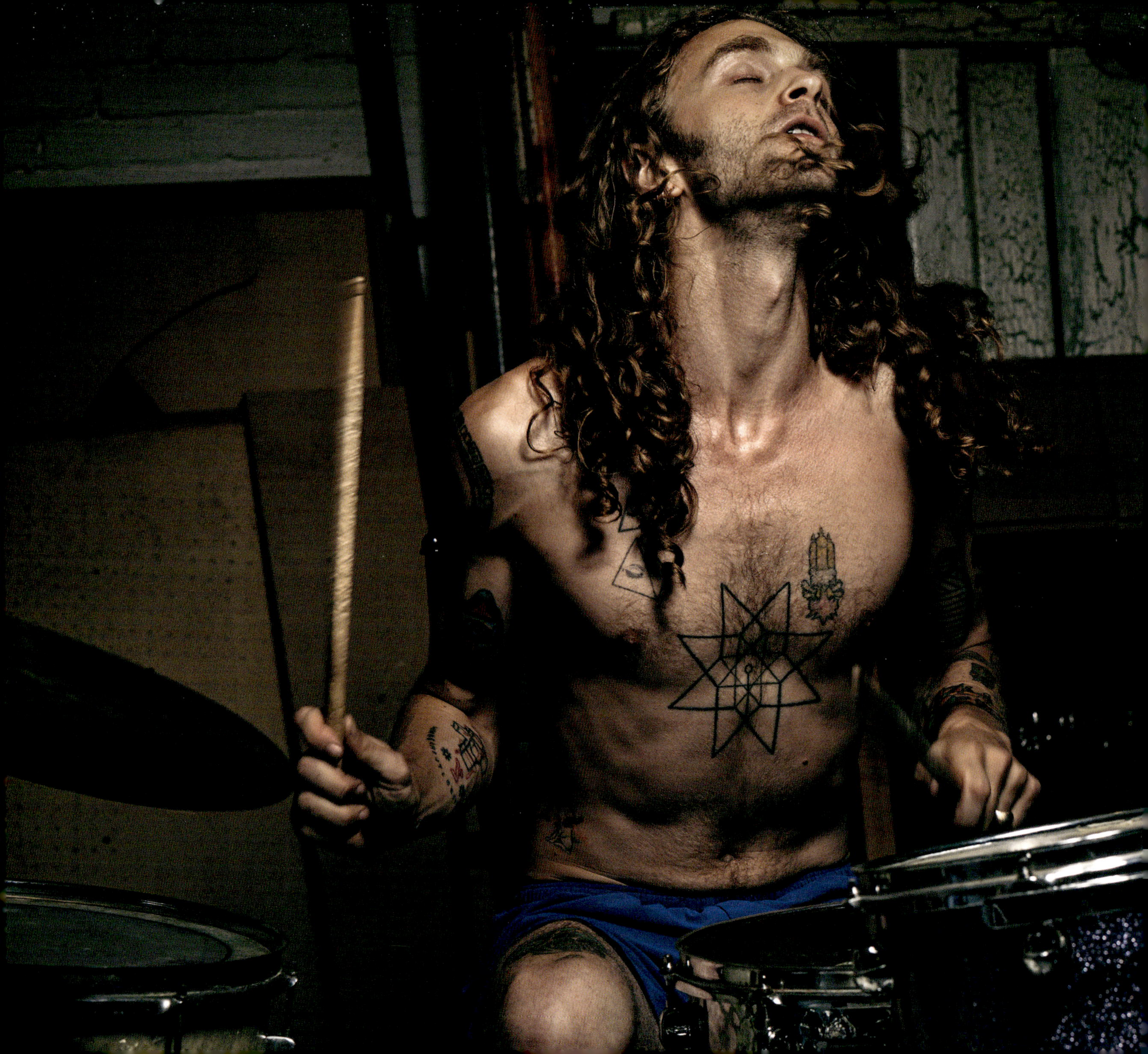

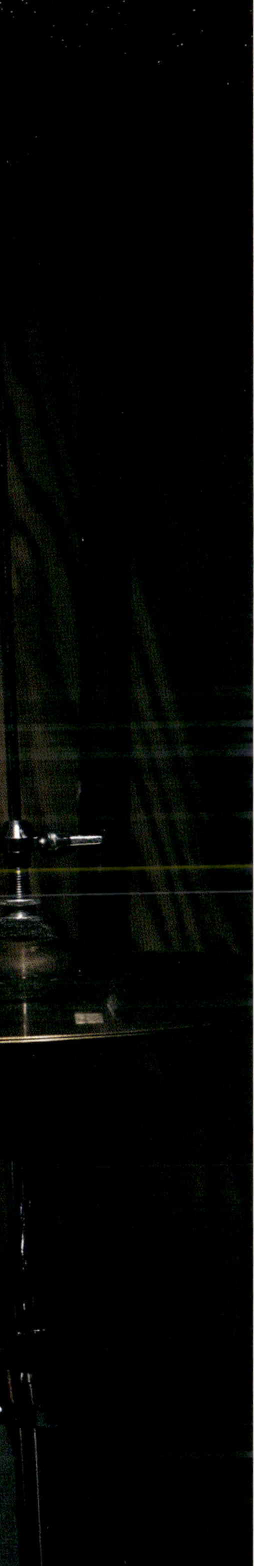

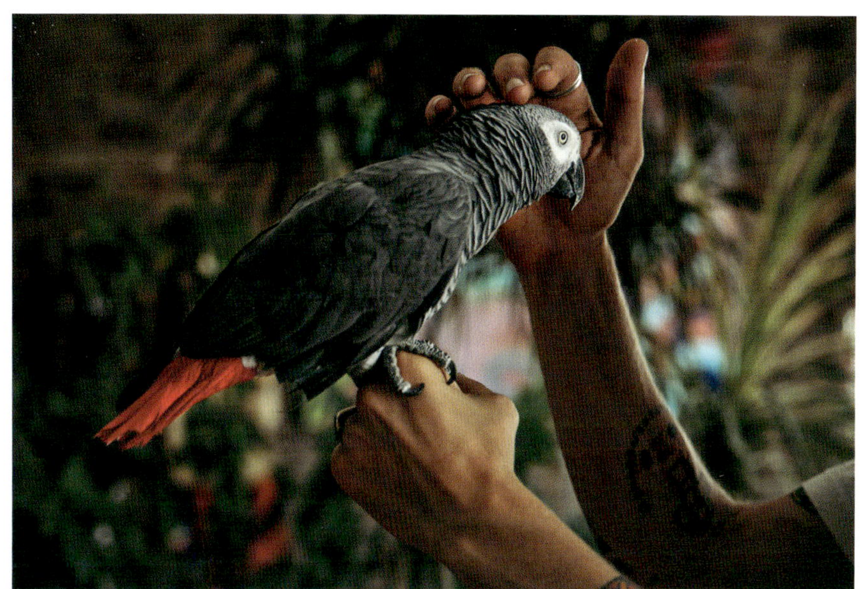

GREG FOX

Guardian Alien / Liturgy / Body Meπa / Anti-God Hand / Zs / Ben Frost. Photographed at home, New York

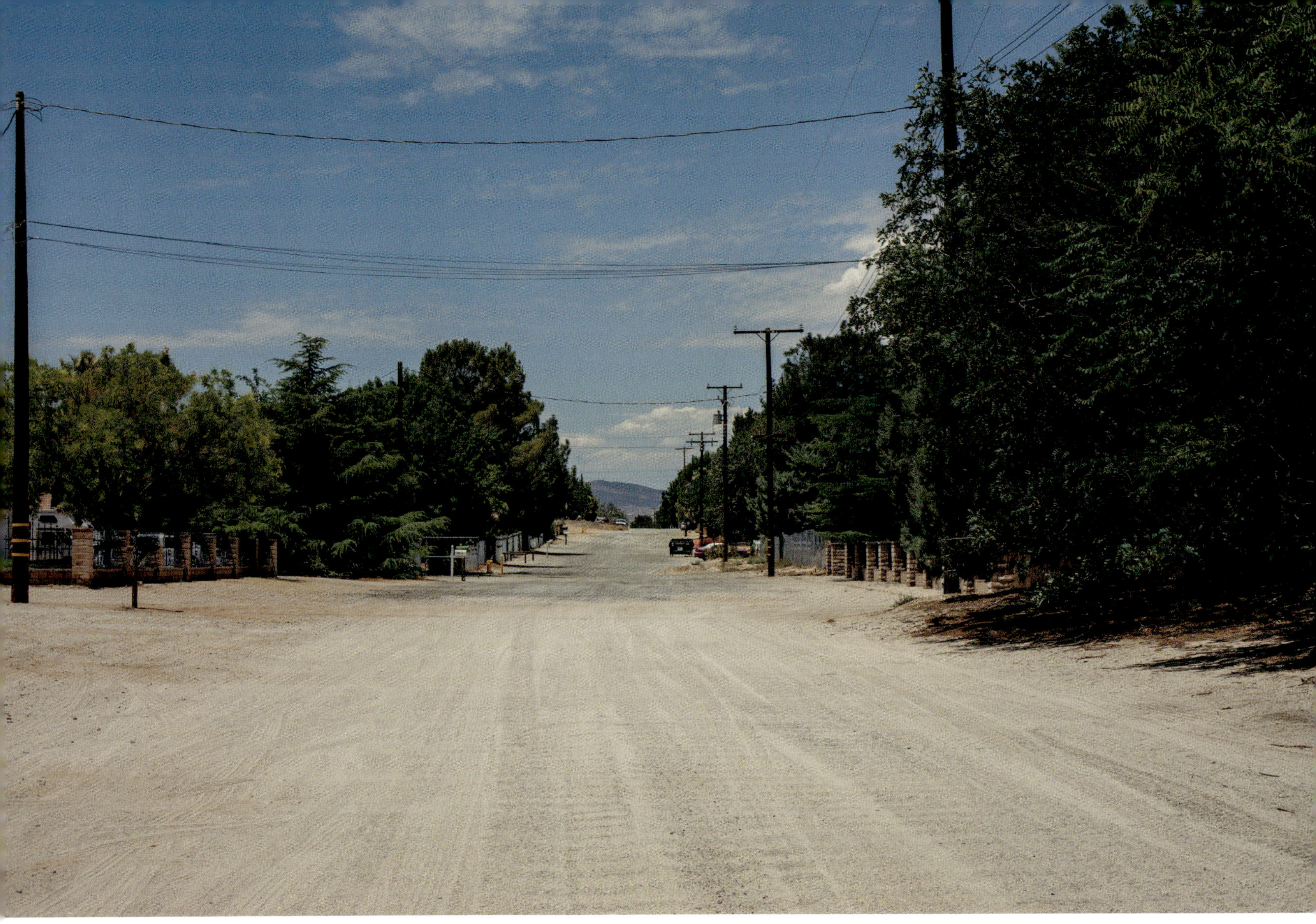

JOHN 'DRUMBO' FRENCH
Captain Beefheart & His Magic Band. Photographed at home, California

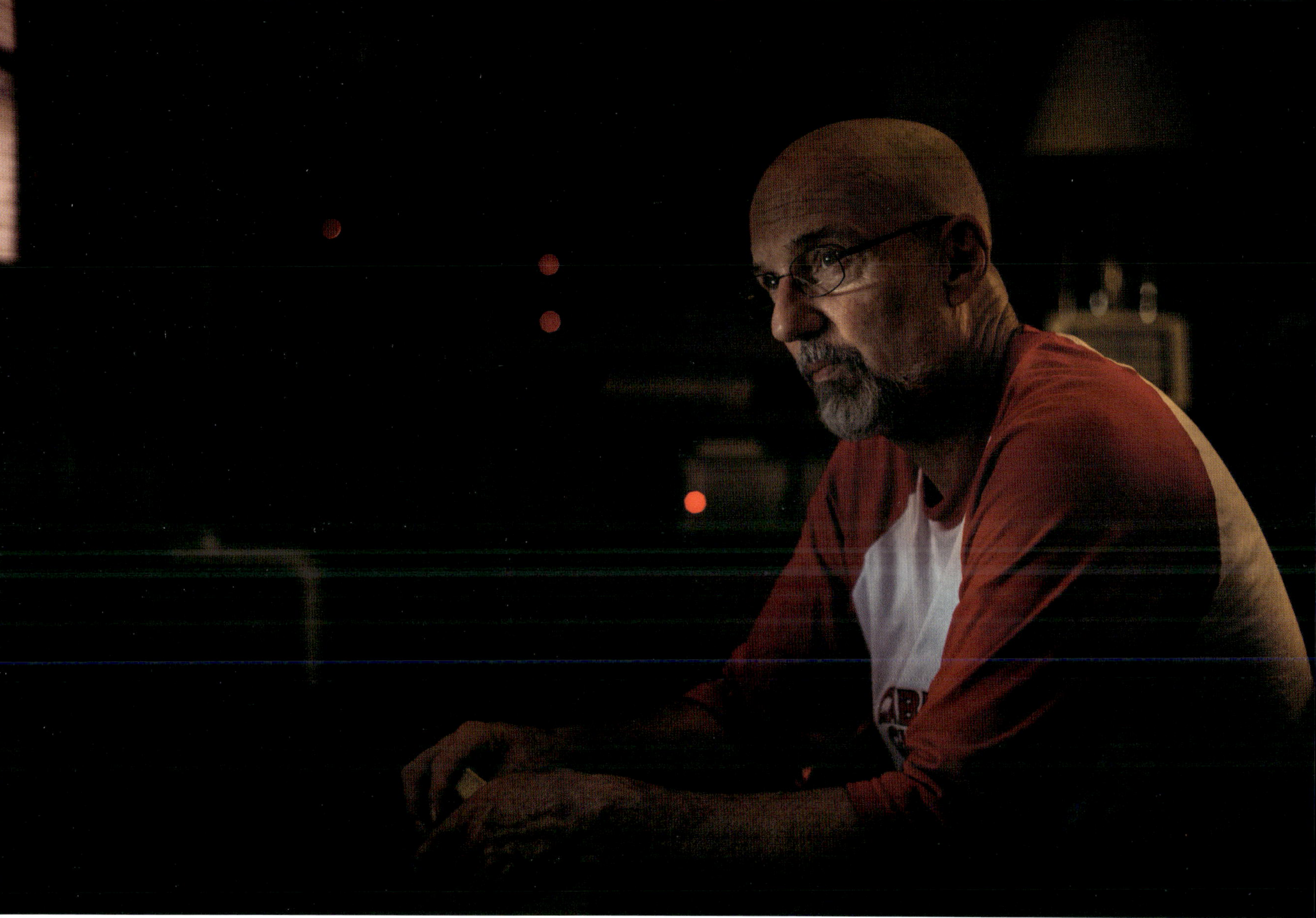

I started writing a lot of my own drum parts, sort of behind [Captain Beefheart's] back, because he wanted to have total control of the music but he really wasn't focusing on the drums at all. He would occasionally come up with some really brilliant idea on the drums, simple but brilliant, and sometimes that's the best. But in the meantime I was over there writing these more complicated, challenging things because I wanted to push myself. I didn't want to play something that anyone could sit down and play. I wanted to play stuff that would stretch me as a player. And it really did, and when I went back to playing like normal drumming I was able to put all these strange things in there and people would kind of go, 'How d'ya do that?' I never considered myself a technically good player. I consider myself a creative player and I think that's what made me stand out.

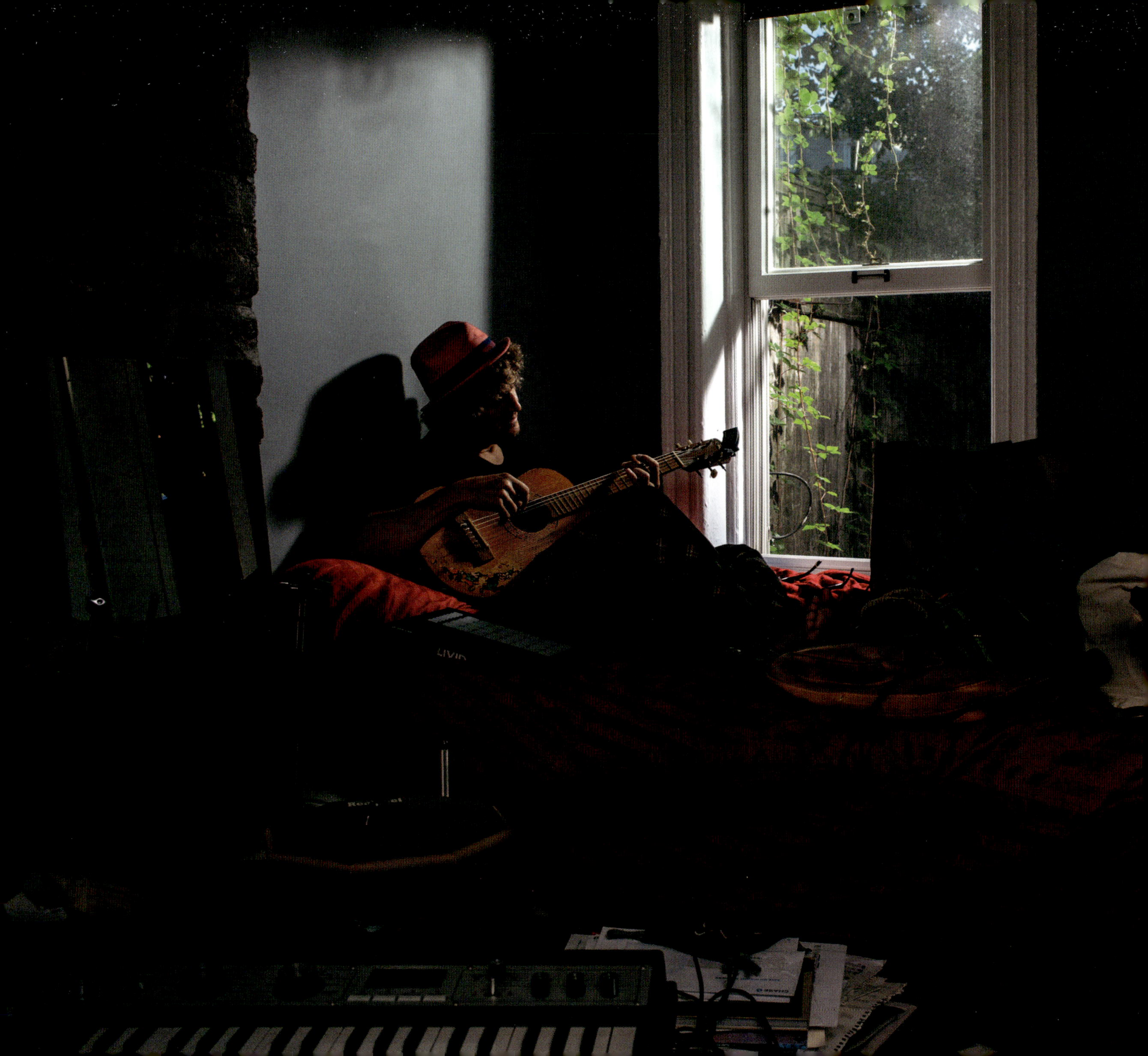

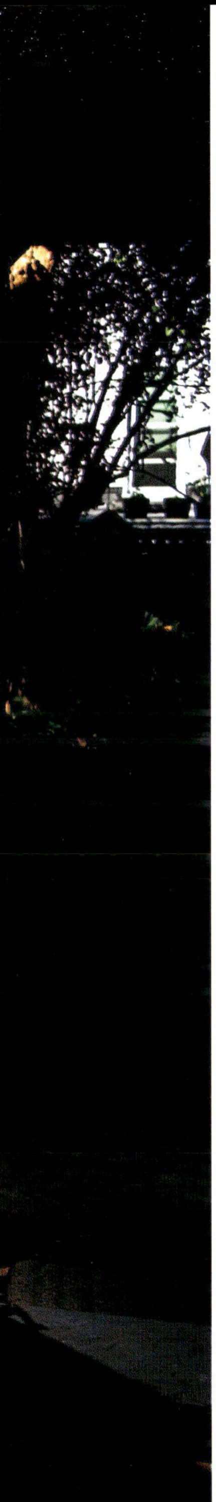

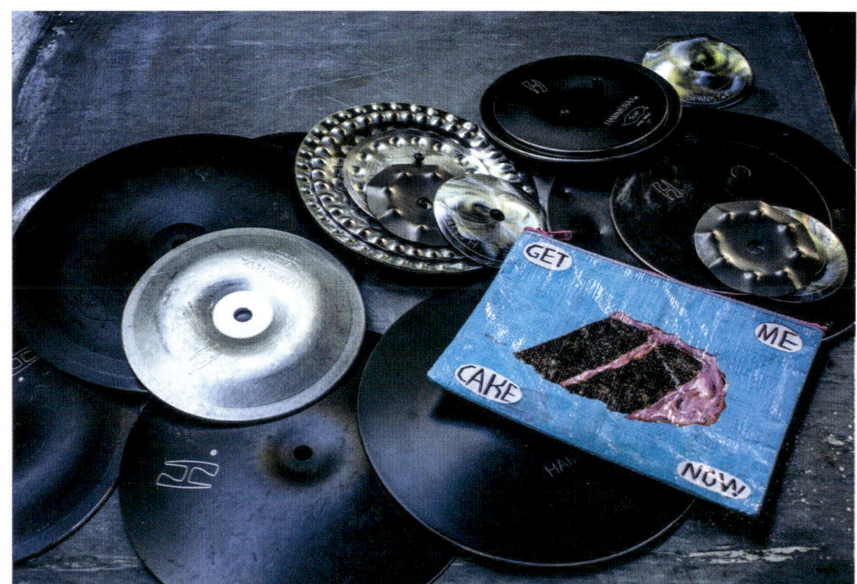

JIM BLACK

Jim Black Trio / Eyebone / AlasNoAxis / Human Feel / Tim Berne
Photographed at home, New York

In junior high there were three of us drummers playing on one drum set, taking turns. I get on the drums and I take a big drum solo, and the whole place goes berserk. I'm twelve. Granted, I was small and blond – that might have helped – but I remember listening to that cassette tape and when I start playing, the music is drowned out by screaming girls. At twelve, just starting out, from then on … it's over. I remember that real well. It's just like, yes … collective acceptance of your existence. It really changes your outlook on life.

To me it's always been like a light switch when you go to do a gig. You could be starving hungry, sad, tired, having back pain, you name it, no sleep, all that stuff. As soon as you hit the stage, it's for blood. Every gig is sacred; maybe more now than ever, because there just aren't that many opportunities to really play.

It's always nice when you're with people on the road and you're hanging out for two days with strangers and they think you're the biggest fucking freak, and then they finally see you play the gig and they have a completely different opinion of you afterwards. Because as a person you're one way and at the gig another side of you comes out. So these people are really shocked, and later they say, 'I had no idea you would play like that.'

Performing is a meditation. It's healing, it's relief, it's pleasure. The reason I think most of us do it is that it's like our medication. It's our drug. In the most positive sense; it's the balance of living in a brutal world. I know what I've seen because I've been around long enough now. That's why you strap yourself in with seat belts: 'cause you've survived this long. It's about trying to stay alive to enjoy the party a little more.

STEVE FERRONE

Tom Petty & the Heartbreakers / Eric Clapton / Average White Band / Chaka Khan / Fabiana Palladino
Photographed at home, California

I was twelve when I heard 'Take Five'. And I thought, how do you do that? And I got my hands to do it, then I started to add feet, and it wasn't that hard to learn. I have a tape of me playing when I was thirteen and I think the groove was already there.

We used to have a Saturday morning dance thing for the kids in this local ballroom, The Regent Ballroom [in Brighton], and Manfred Mann's Earth Band were playing one night for the big kids, and they came down and they did their sound check for us little kids, and every girl in the place just went crazy over it. I thought, I want some of that! I said to my friends, 'We're going to start a band.' So that was it. I started to play the drums. Nothing deeper than that. No wanting to embrace art or anything, just the girls.

We used to go up to a friend's house and we'd play 'I Saw Her Standing There'. It was the only song that we could play. The guitarist found out about this band whose drummer was sick, and he said, 'These big kids want you to go and try out for their band, you want to go and do it?' And I was all cocky, I said yeah, I'll go over there. And I go over, and there's all these eighteen-year-olds and I'm this twelve-year-old kid. I went in, I sat down and they were playing the blues and I just joined in, started playing their stuff, and then they had me come and play with them at a gig. The first gig we did was a church hall dance in Brighton, and I remember the power went out and I had to do a drum solo for the longest time until they got it back. That's probably why I've just got this aversion to playing drum solos. The poor guy came out of hospital to find I took his gig.

There are lots of guys out there who play the drums, but certain people, when they sit down and play the drums, guys like Harvey Mason, Steve Jordan or Bernard Purdie, they grab you. When you hear those guys play it's just the lilt. They don't play anything different to any other drummer, it's the same beat, the same mechanics, but just their placement of the beat ... that's I guess what they call a pocket drummer. A guy like Al Jackson, he really had this pocket that just would not quit.

I was working in France on the American bases and sitting in a canteen with all these American soldiers, and I was right next to the jukebox, and this lanky GI came over and stuck a coin into the jukebox, and I heard these drums like I'd never heard before, and it was a Ben E. King song called 'What is Soul?' I looked up who it was who was playing on there, and it was Bernard Purdie. I'd never heard that kind of syncopation played on the drums before, but I got it immediately. I got exactly what it was, and so that was a defining moment for me.

One day a guy in Paris said, 'You've got to check out this record by Charles Lloyd; it's called *Live in Russia*.' He says, 'These crazy men have gone to Russia in the middle of the Cold War to play jazz,' and it was Charles Lloyd, Ron McClure, Keith Jarrett and Jack DeJohnette, and I fell in love with Jack DeJohnette's playing, even though we were worlds apart. I played with his godson in Italy, and I was saying to him that I'd learned a lot from his godfather. We were playing one day and he had a bass solo to do, and I just did this little phrase to kick him into his solo, and he came up to me afterwards, he said, 'What was that you played at the beginning of the song? Man, it just shot me off into a different place to play my solo, it was great, what was that?' And I said, 'That's the stuff I learned from Jack.'

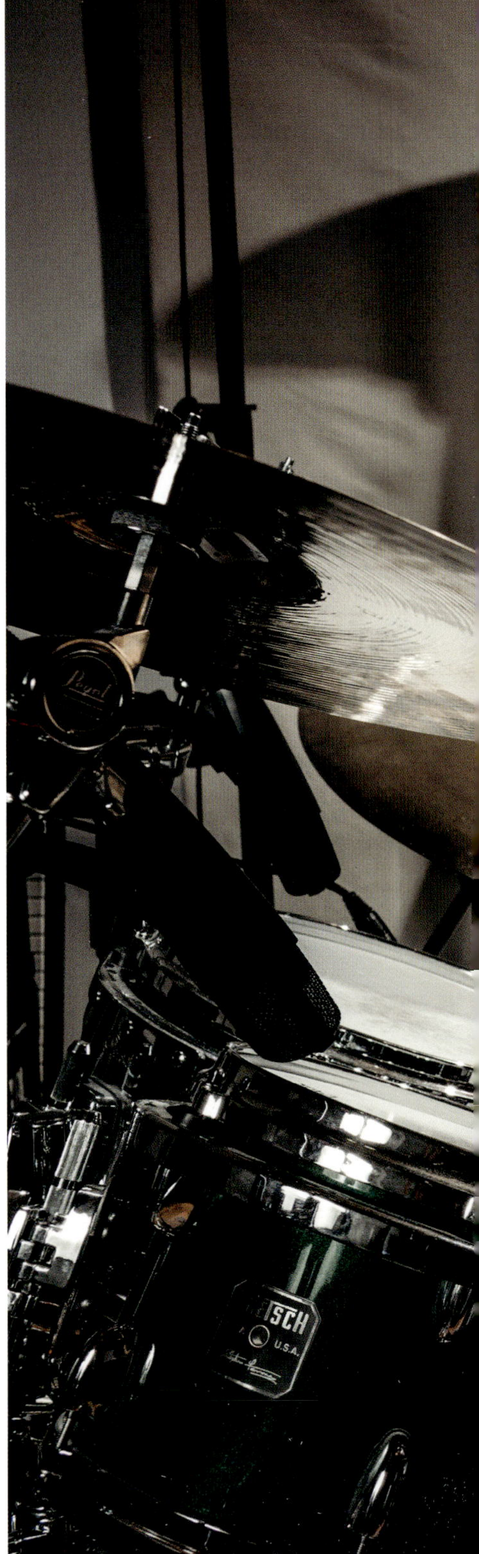

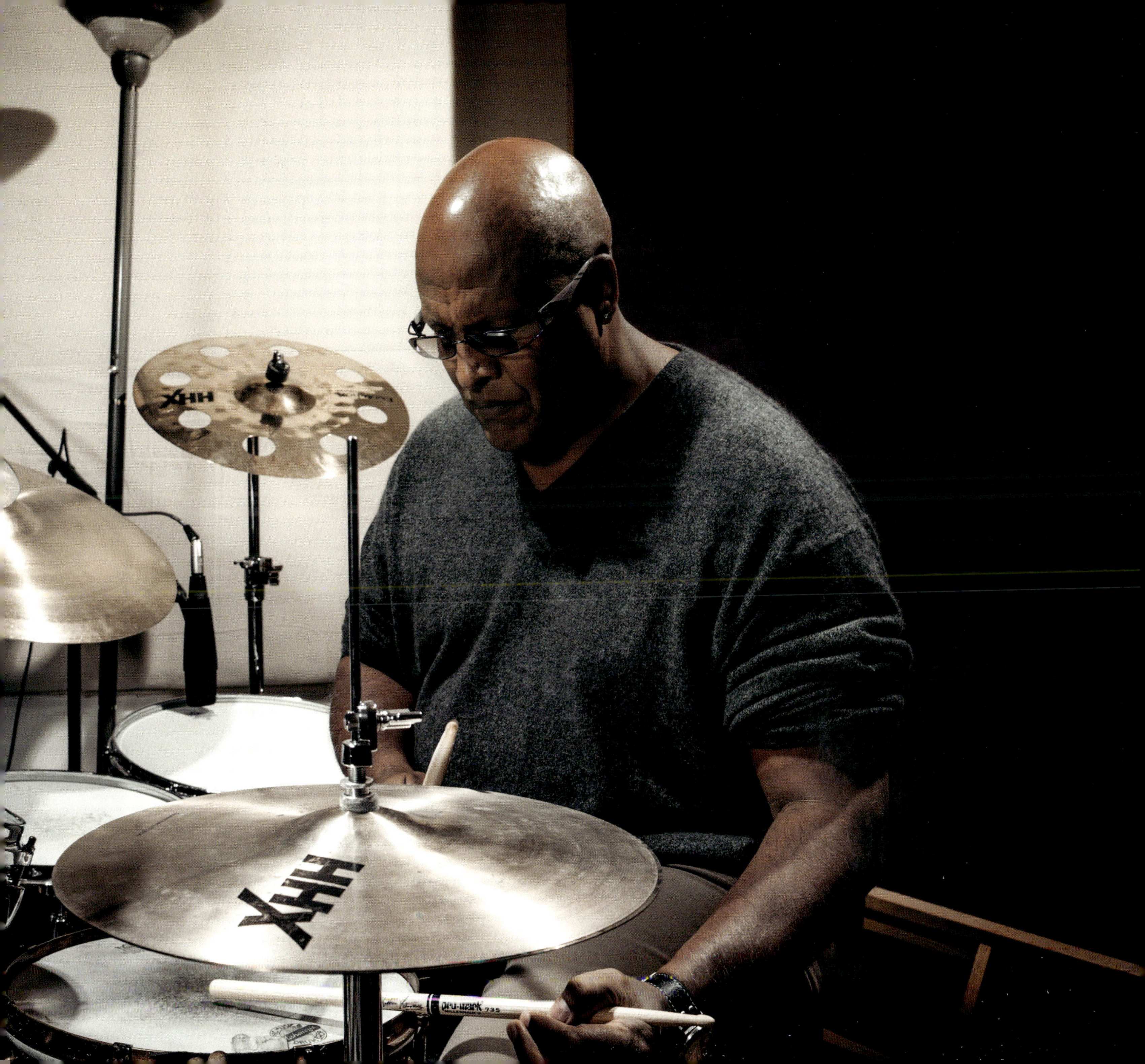
HHX
HHX
pro-mark

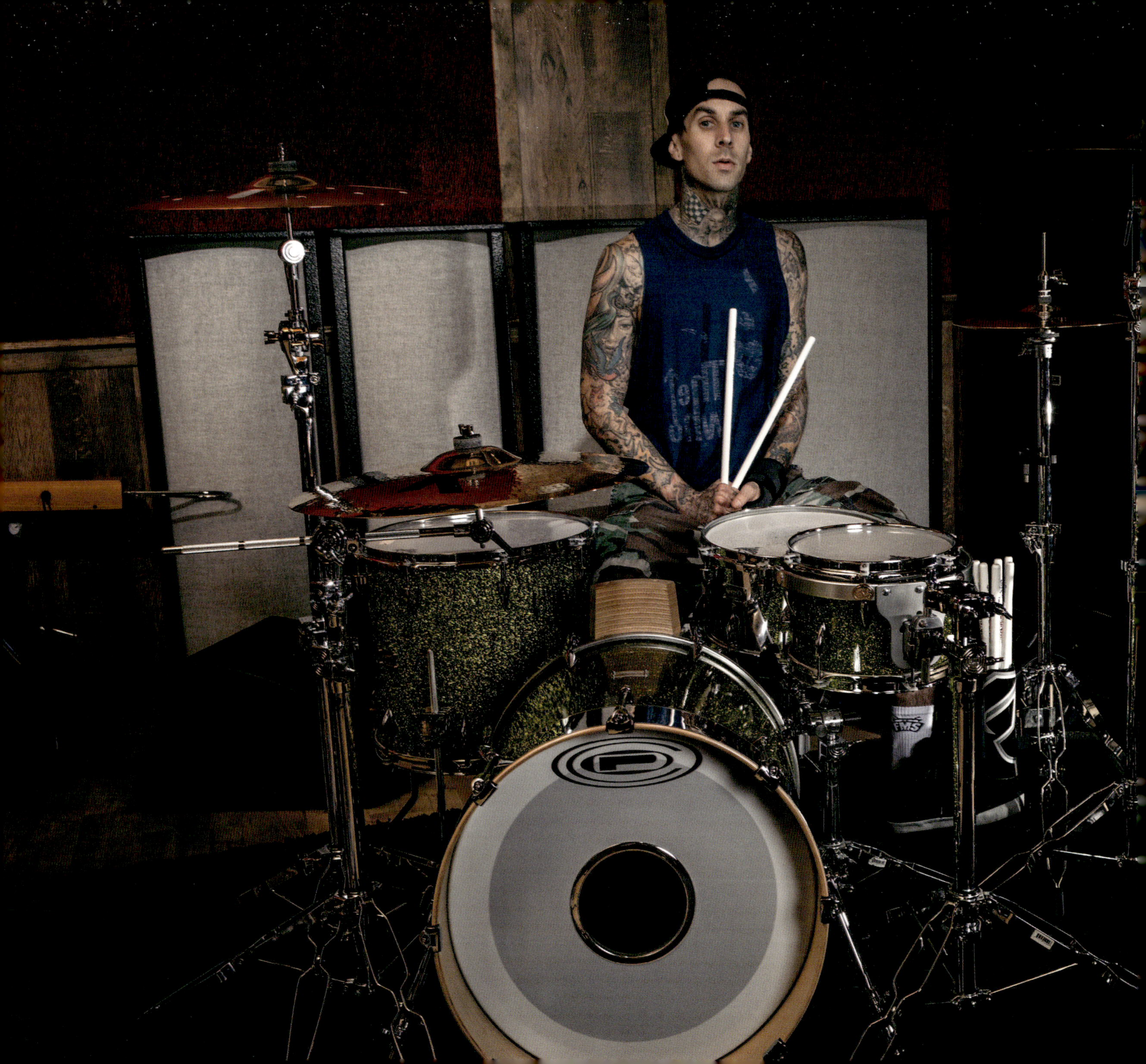

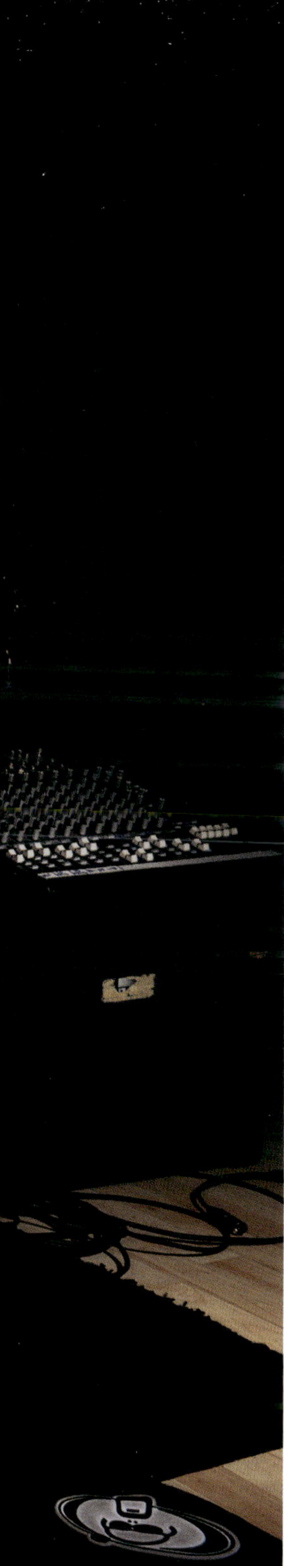

TRAVIS BARKER

Blink-182. Photographed in his studio, California

'I just love the creative process, I like a beat coming together. I like programming. I like putting on a metronome and just playing in the studio for hours without changing its tempo. Once I start playing I try to find an uncomfortable place, one that stops me, and I try to just nail that. To get comfortable with whatever makes me uncomfortable behind the kit. I've been doing that a lot lately'

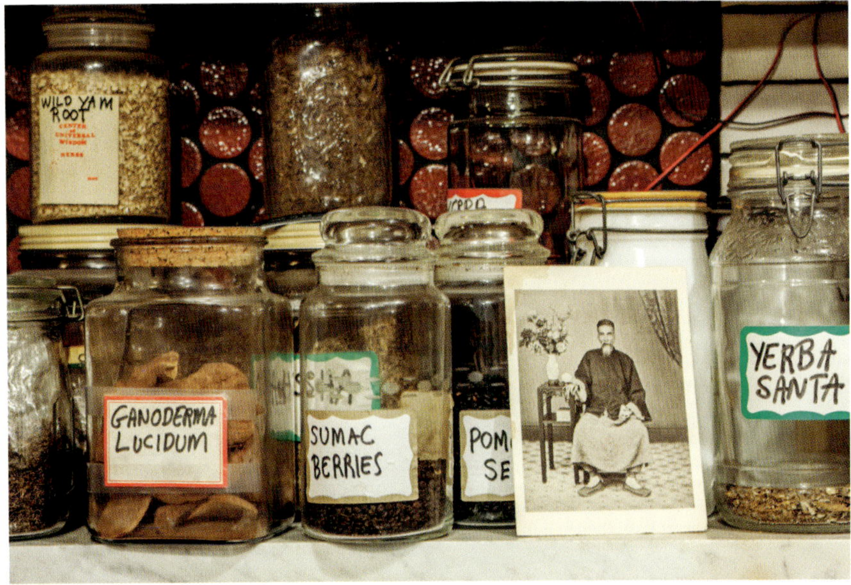

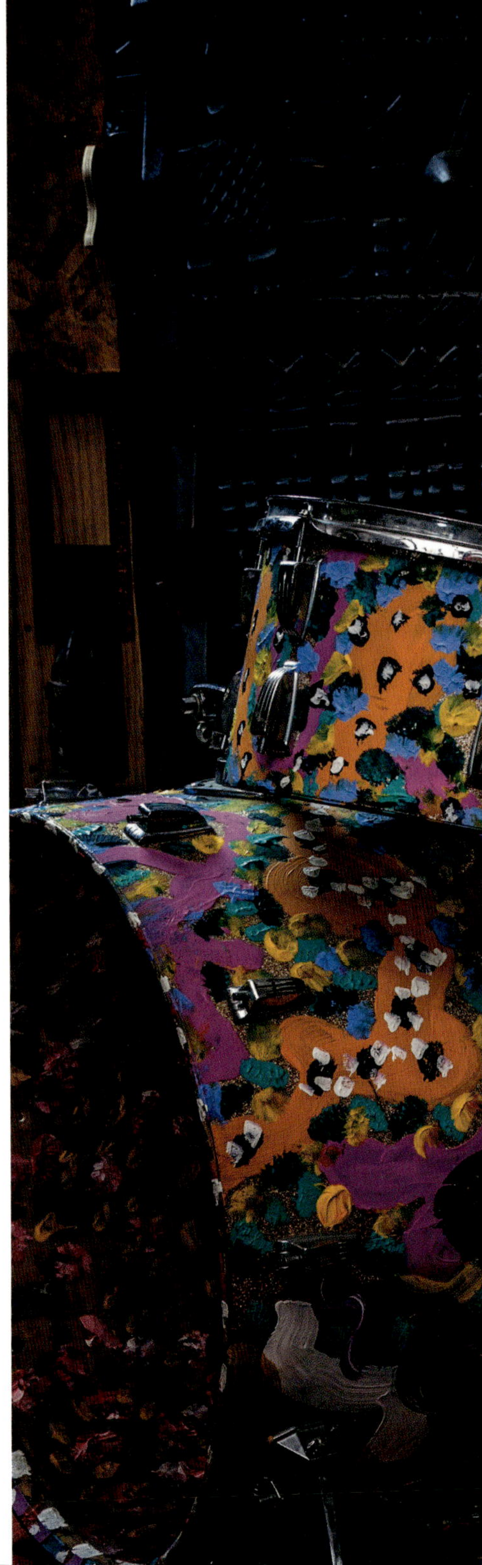

MILFORD GRAVES

Charles Gayle / Kidd Jordan / Bill Laswell / William Parker / John Zorn
Photographed in his home studio, New York

Humans love to see other humans feel good. When a human is down and they see you feeling good they start feeling good. Thing is, I've had to ask this thing myself: why do I do what I do? Why am I onstage? What's my purpose? And I ask musicians, 'What's your purpose when you go onstage?' Some people go to the drug store and say, 'Give me some medicine and make me feel good.' You go to a restaurant and say, 'Give me some food and make me feel good.' When a musician comes on, people say, 'Turn me on.' I just want to give it my all.

I like to observe who's entering the auditorium. I watch the way they walk, and I listen to the total harmonics of all the voices in the room. And when people come up and smile and want to shake my hand, they don't have to say, 'Ah, man, your drumming, your hands were moving like they do ...', they just say 'Thank you', and they smile, and I say, 'Well, I did my job.' I'm like a mediator. Somebody's given me something to give other people. One of my things – with herbs, music, anything – is to always have this contact with human beings.

If I can help human folks be better folks, even if I took drums and went out into a war zone and played and I could get killers saying that they don't want to fight no more, they want to listen to them drums, saying they don't want to think about no more fighting. So that's my thing: to get out there and turn people on and say, 'you don't have to do it that way.' Get them vibrating so they say, 'I don't want to do any of that kind of stuff anymore.' I think it works.

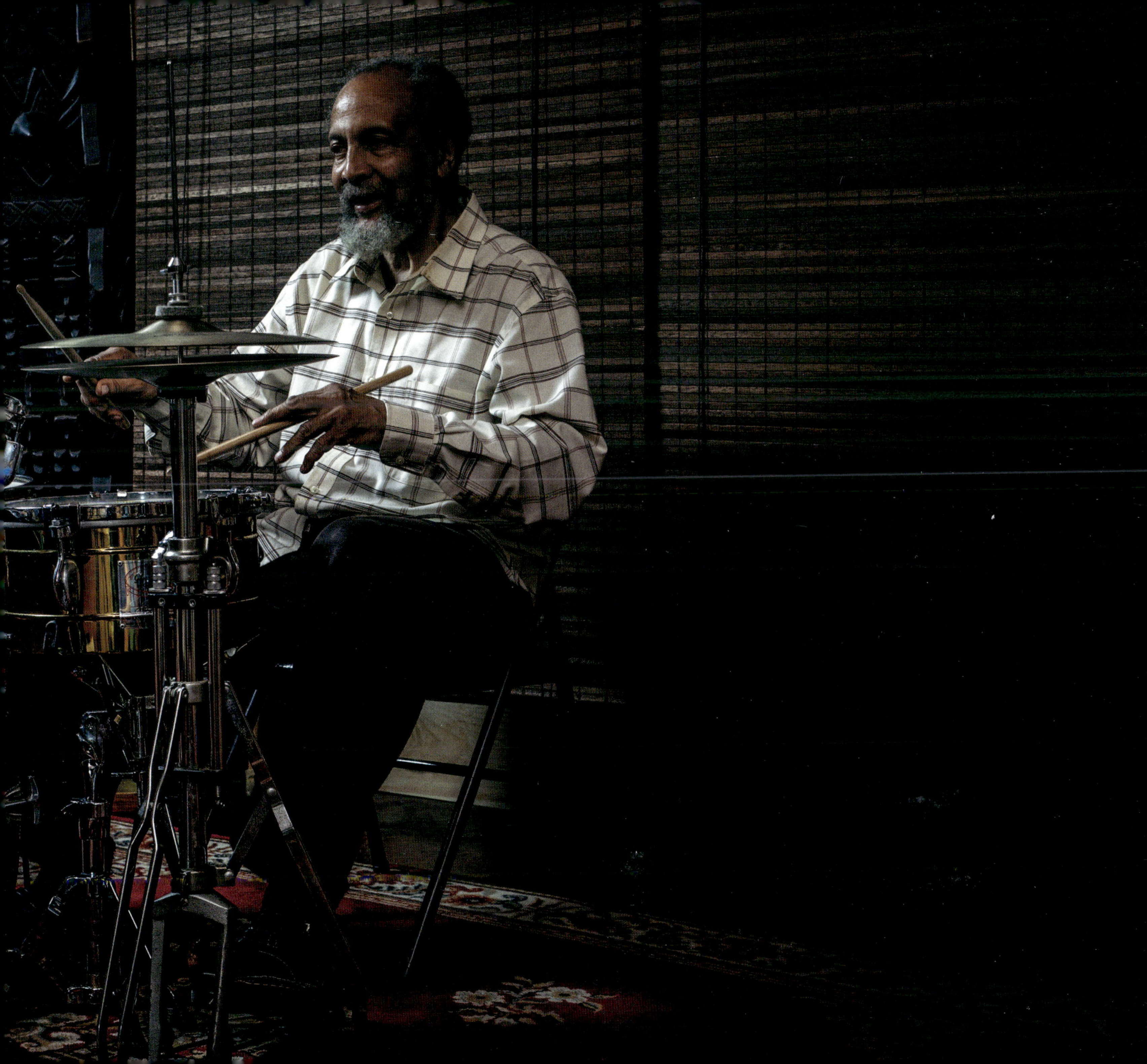

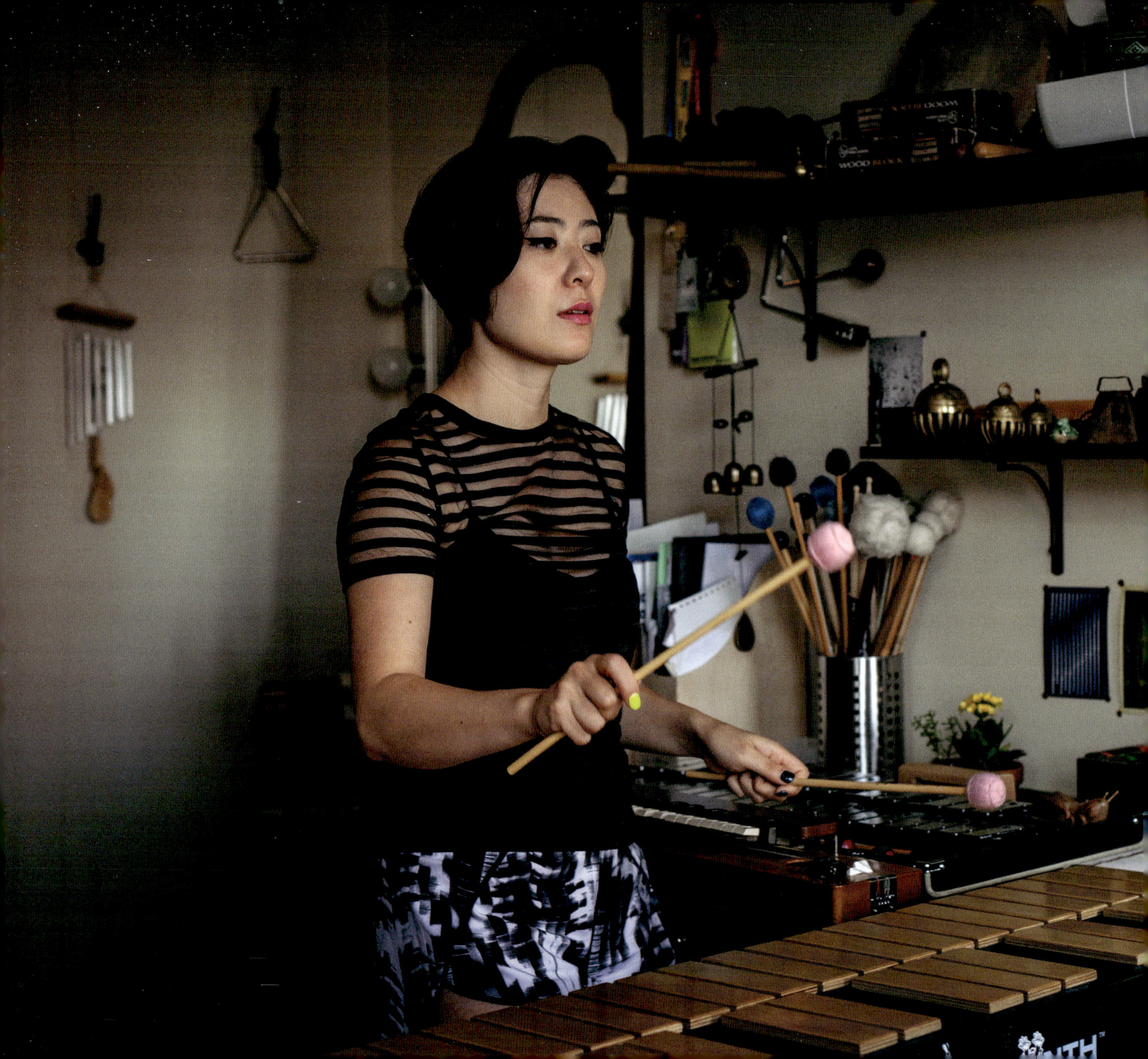
WOOD BLOCK

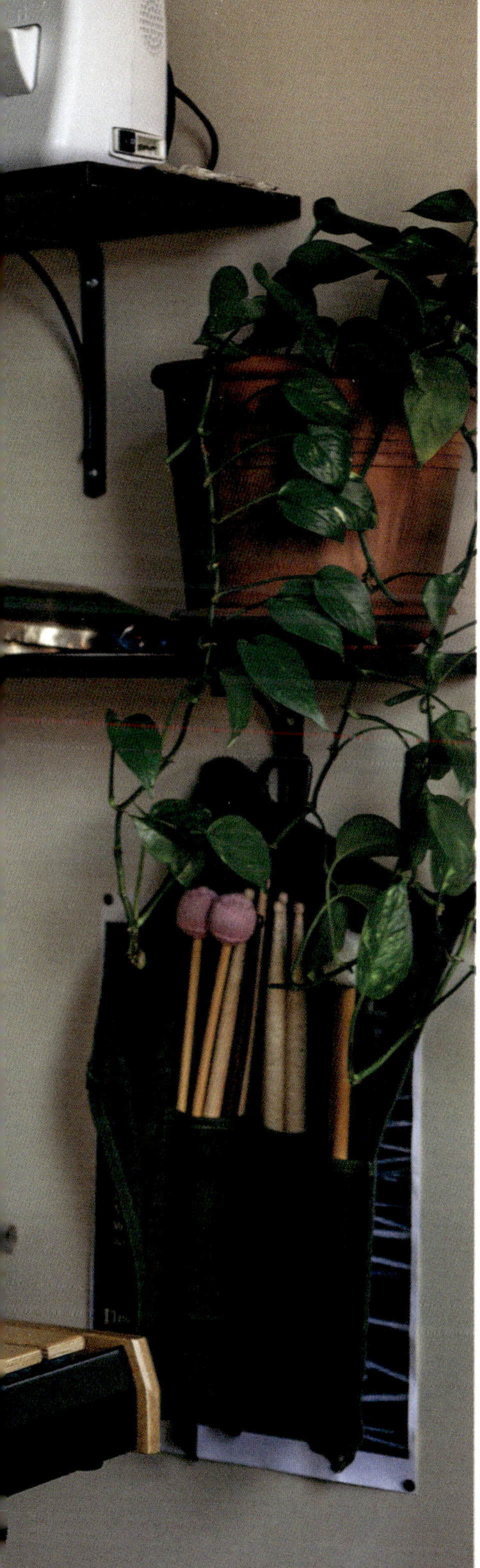

SHAYNA DUNKELMAN

Nomon / Balún / Emily Wells / Ali Sethi / Yoko Ono / Thurston Moore / John Zorn / Xiu Xiu
Photographed at home, New York

RUSSELL SIMINS

Jon Spencer Blues Explosion. Photographed in New York

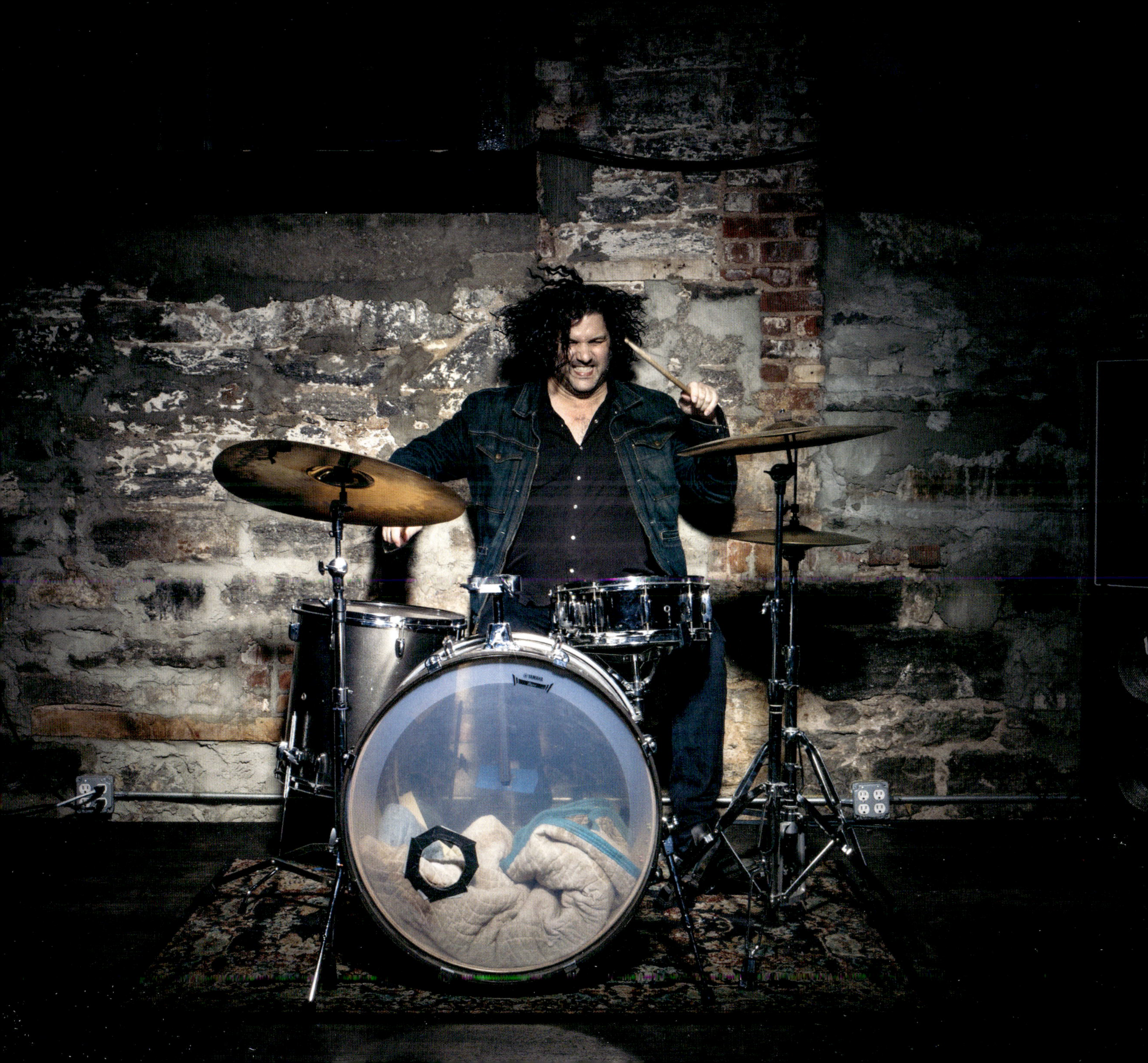

CHAD SMITH

Red Hot Chili Peppers. Photographed at home, California

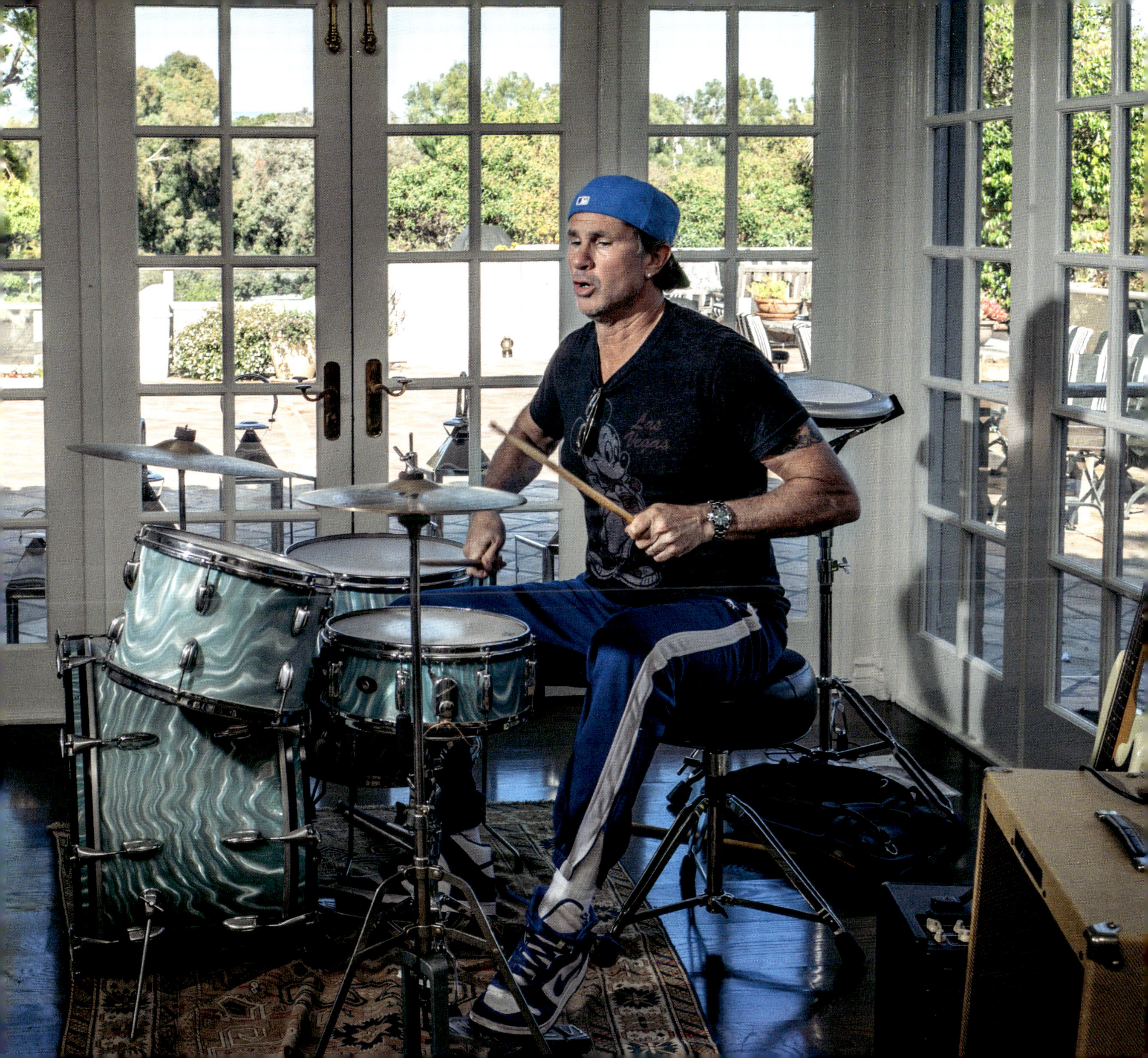
Las Vegas

RINGO STARR

The Beatles. Photographed in his home studio, California

You know the story about why I play drums? I was in hospital with TB; I was in bed for ten months. To keep us busy they brought us percussive instruments to hit. They gave me a drum and from that moment on I only wanted to be a drummer. It was so great. I came out of hospital just before I was fifteen. Then rock and roll came in. I was in a skiffle band and Lonnie Donegan was big. I loved the blues and Lightnin' Hopkins is my hero. Then country music, I always loved the motion of country. I tried to emigrate to Houston, Texas, when I was nineteen to live by Lightnin' Hopkins, but there were too many forms to fill out. Then, Elvis came in.

I have an incredible memory of the movie *Rock Around the Clock* because the first holiday I went on after I came out of hospital, my grandparents took me to the Isle of Man and the movie was on with Bill Haley and they ripped up the cinema and I thought, ah! This is great. I did love Bill Haley. I came in with him really, and rock and roll.

The Alan Freed show was a programme in England that came from Radio Luxembourg. I think it was 4 o'clock on a Sunday afternoon. My friend Roy and I, that's what we did. It didn't matter what was going on in life, we listened to that. That was the first time I heard Little Richard. When we came to America it was the biggest thrill of my life because 99 per cent of the music I loved came from America. I'd worked on the railways. I'd worked on the boats and then I ended up in a factory. I'd play at night. And it's history now, how we got a gig at Butlins for three months and I gave up being an apprentice engineer and became a musician and that's how it's been – till this day.

I think rhythm comes with the body. I think my timing comes with my heartbeat. I try to teach this to a lot of kids and some actually get the idea and some don't. It's just a foreign country to a lot of children but you can't hurt the kids' feelings, so I say, 'Maybe you should play piano or guitar' [laughs]. I think you can put a lot of time in and you can play good piano. But I don't think that happens with drums. You can put a lot of time in and probably play much more complicated than I can, but can you play with feel? Feel comes if you got it. That's how it is.

I hate the click track because I'm so aware of it, I can't loosen up and play how I like to play. The kids love the click track. A lot of producers, not just now, but over the last twenty years, love the click track. I feel it gets in the way of playing. Time for me was just something that came, I have it. You can't teach it. You can teach someone to be in time but to really just *be in time*, that's something I never had to learn. It was just there.

On *Sgt. Pepper*, I had this new kit, the maple kit. It had actual skin heads – calf heads – which I'd never had before – they were all plastic from the '60s onwards. And they're so deep; I was always looking for depth, because you see pictures of me and I have towels over the drums and cigarette packs. Something to give it more body than it had. George Harrison went to America and brought back the so-called Hal Blaine kit. So we set them all up and we had the count, 'one, two, three, four', and then it came time to do a fill and there were too many, I didn't know which one to hit. So I just said, 'Take them away.'

One of my hero drummers from the Cavern [Club, in Liverpool] was from an American band called The George Lewis Ragtime Jazzband. His drummer – in my eyes he was 110 at the time – just had a bass drum and a snare drum and a couple of cymbals. And every time he did tom-tom stuff, he'd just lean under and hit the bass drum. Made my heart sing. Less is more.

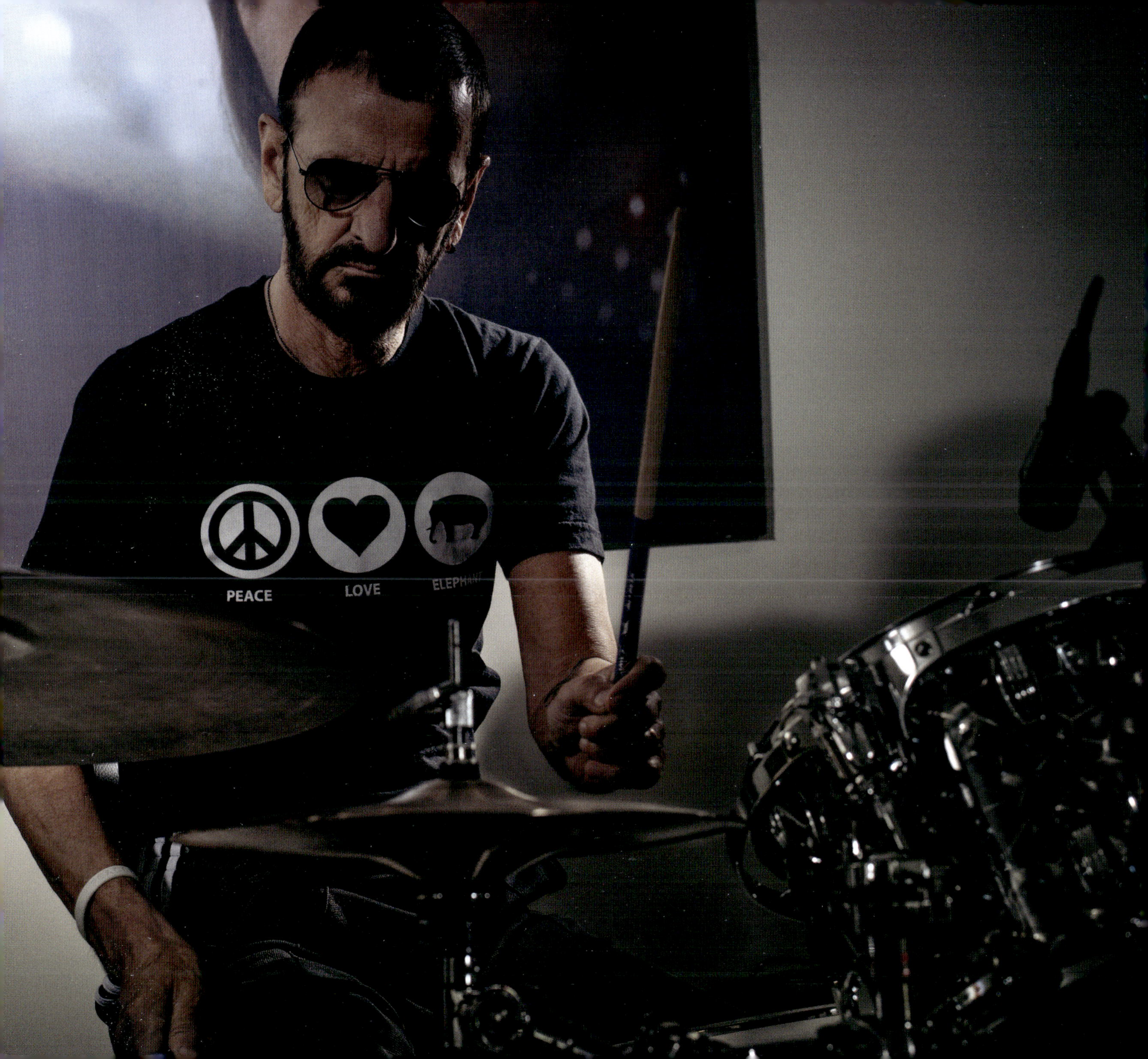
PEACE
LOVE
ELEPHANT

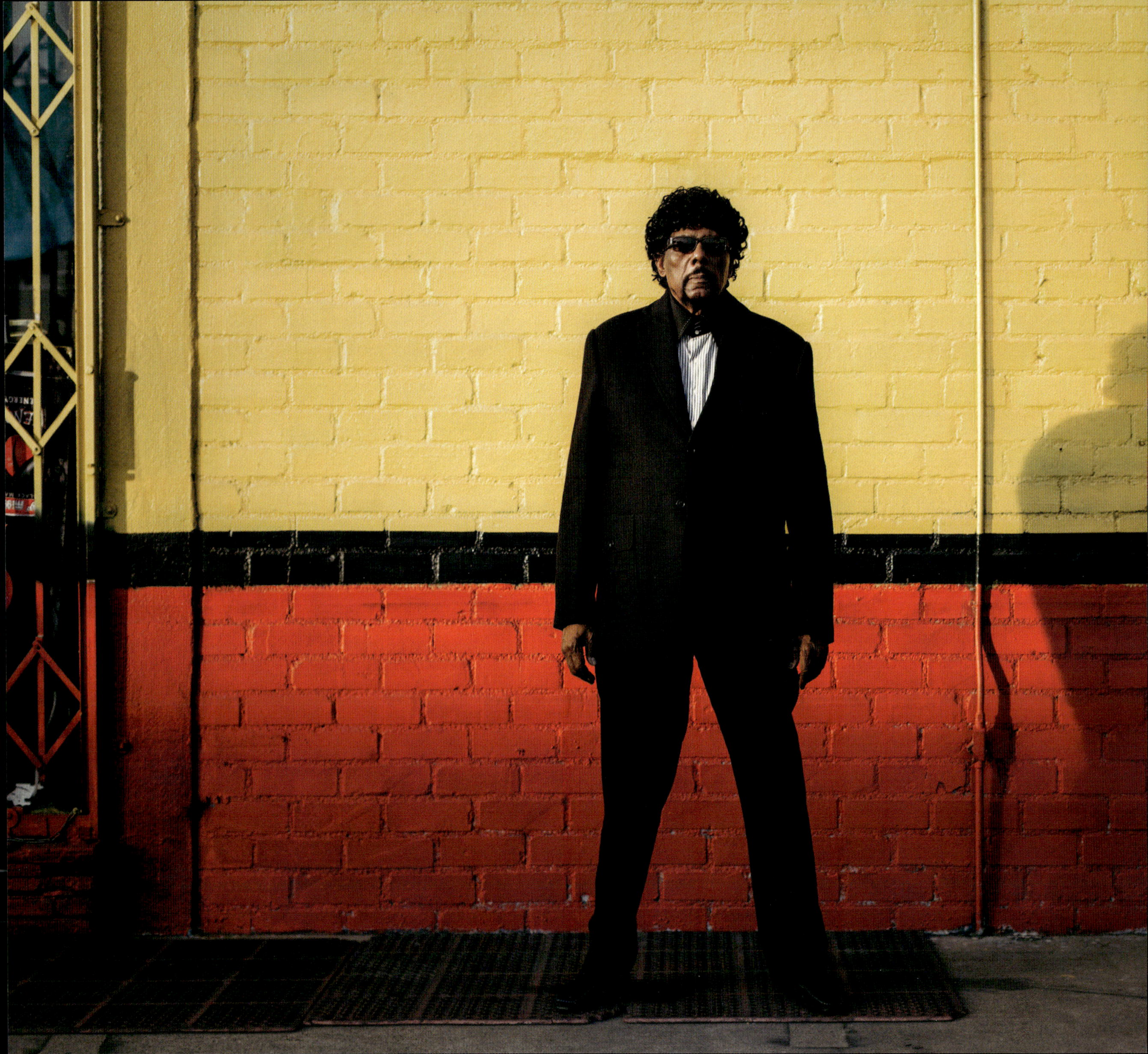

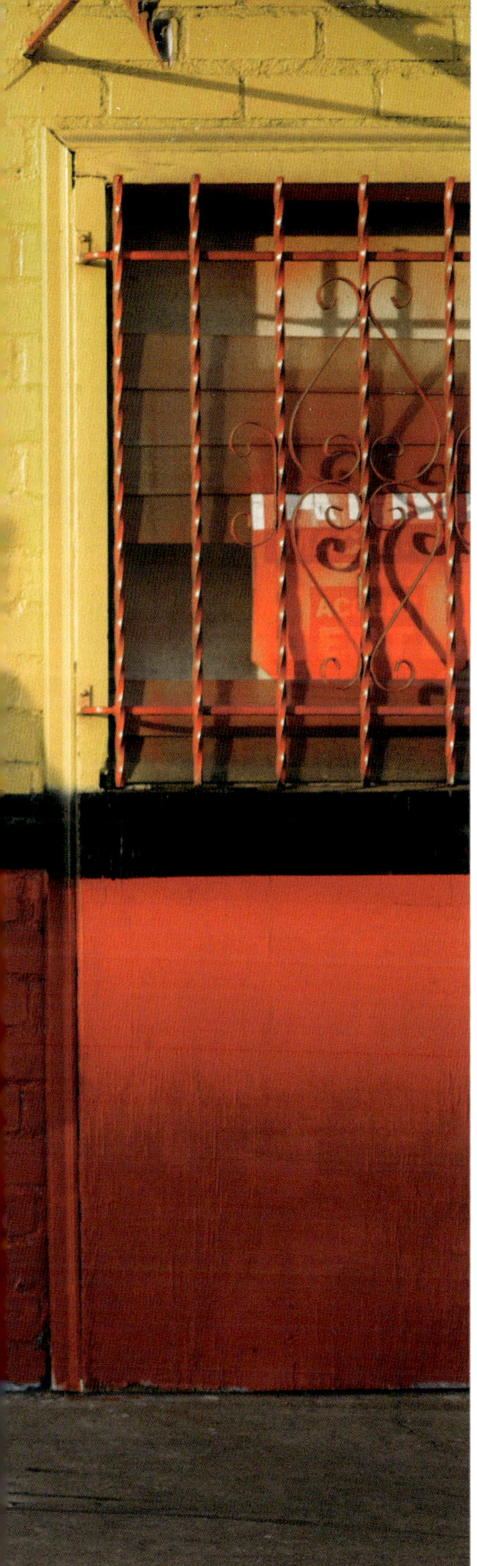

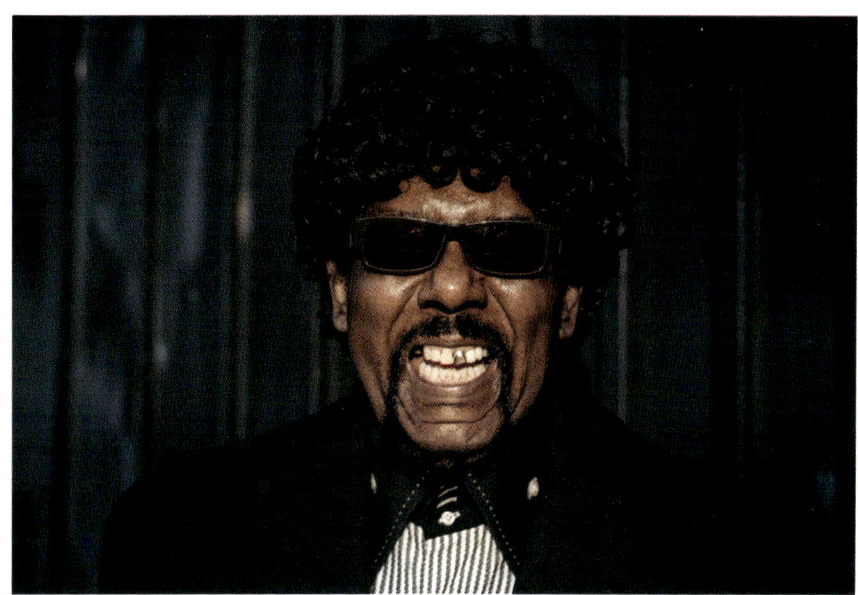

JAMES GADSON

Watts 103rd Street Rhythm Band / Bill Withers / Marvin Gaye / The Temptations / D'Angelo
Photographed in California

I got to see Art Blakey live. I didn't get to see Elvin Jones live until I moved to California. But I got to see Coltrane, Blakey, Miles Davis, Cannonball Adderley. I saw Aretha Franklin when she first started; she came here with a trio, she was playing piano and singing. They had a jazz club there so I got to see all of them. I didn't necessarily understand what it was. I used to get a headache but I thought, I got to try to stick with this to see what's really happening, until it finally registers in my mind – because I'm coming out of being a doo-wop singer into this, even though I dug certain things about it.

The longer I've been playing, the more that I find out that I don't know. And the longer that I've been playing, I guess the less technical I might play. As I get older, I play more subtle. I love to hear the complexities of other people playing a rhythm and I can hear where they at rhythmically, and it's beautiful.

Everyone moves to something. It's all music and it's beautiful. I love playing and I'll probably do this until I can't. A lot of people stop it when they get to where I'm at. The opposite sex might drive my passion; I like pretty ladies … and, like Duke Ellington said, music is a lady. People used to say – and it's true – either you got it or you don't. There's a rhythm and what comes from that is an aura. I can't say any more than that.

MATT CAMERON

Pearl Jam / Soundgarden. Photographed at the Pearl Jam studio, Washington

My first gig was a talent show when I was fifteen years old. I was in a Kiss cover band and during my drum solo I fell off my drum riser, which was two school desks kind of put side by side. Everyone was watching me and I fell off the stage. Luckily, that didn't discourage me.

As a musician you really try to prepare for that moment of performing. But once you get up there, you realize you sort of have to improvise as well and you have to feed off the audience. Sometimes the audience can sort of determine where the performance is going, depending if it's a good audience or a bad audience. And it's always good to have those experiences where the audience doesn't give a shit and you've just got to barrel through.

I remember some of the early Soundgarden tours, we would play at places in Florida or Alabama in the Deep South where people just didn't really know our music and didn't really care and didn't want us there, but it's a good challenge to try to win some new fans. Yeah, we followed the lead of Black Flag, a lot of those SST [Records] bands. They definitely did blaze a trail in the States to be able to tour nationally without any kind of label support. They had a circuit that the rest of us followed. We played one place in Texas that actually had chicken wire in front of the stage to stop the crowd throwing bottles. Luckily they didn't throw any bottles at us, but it was like a sport down there.

There are better opportunities now to be an independent player. We used to have to write letters and send out cassettes and collect business cards and write down numbers on a Rolodex and things like that. Now, everything is more at your fingertips. It seems like it's easier to get your music on a compilation record or get in touch with a small label but I guess the flipside is that there is so much more music now that it might be hard to wade through. I think it's great though that the playing field is more level. There are a lot of groups that are able to just do their thing and develop on their own and put out records through iTunes or Facebook and all those things. I think it's a pretty exciting time.

The human element is what makes music interesting. There is so much computer these days in music and you can sort of tell. I can tell when it's not four guys in a room banging it out. The beauty about making records back in the day was you wanted to get a full statement going on a record. From start to finish you wanted that to be cohesive and you wanted it all to relate. Now, record companies are always looking for a single, not necessarily complete albums anymore.

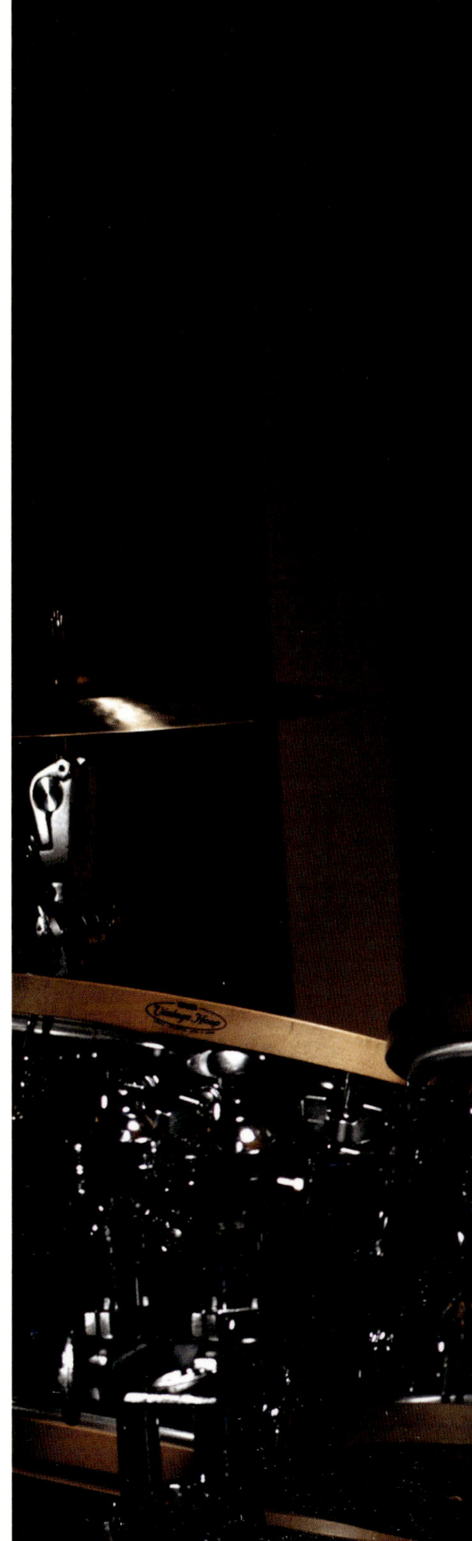

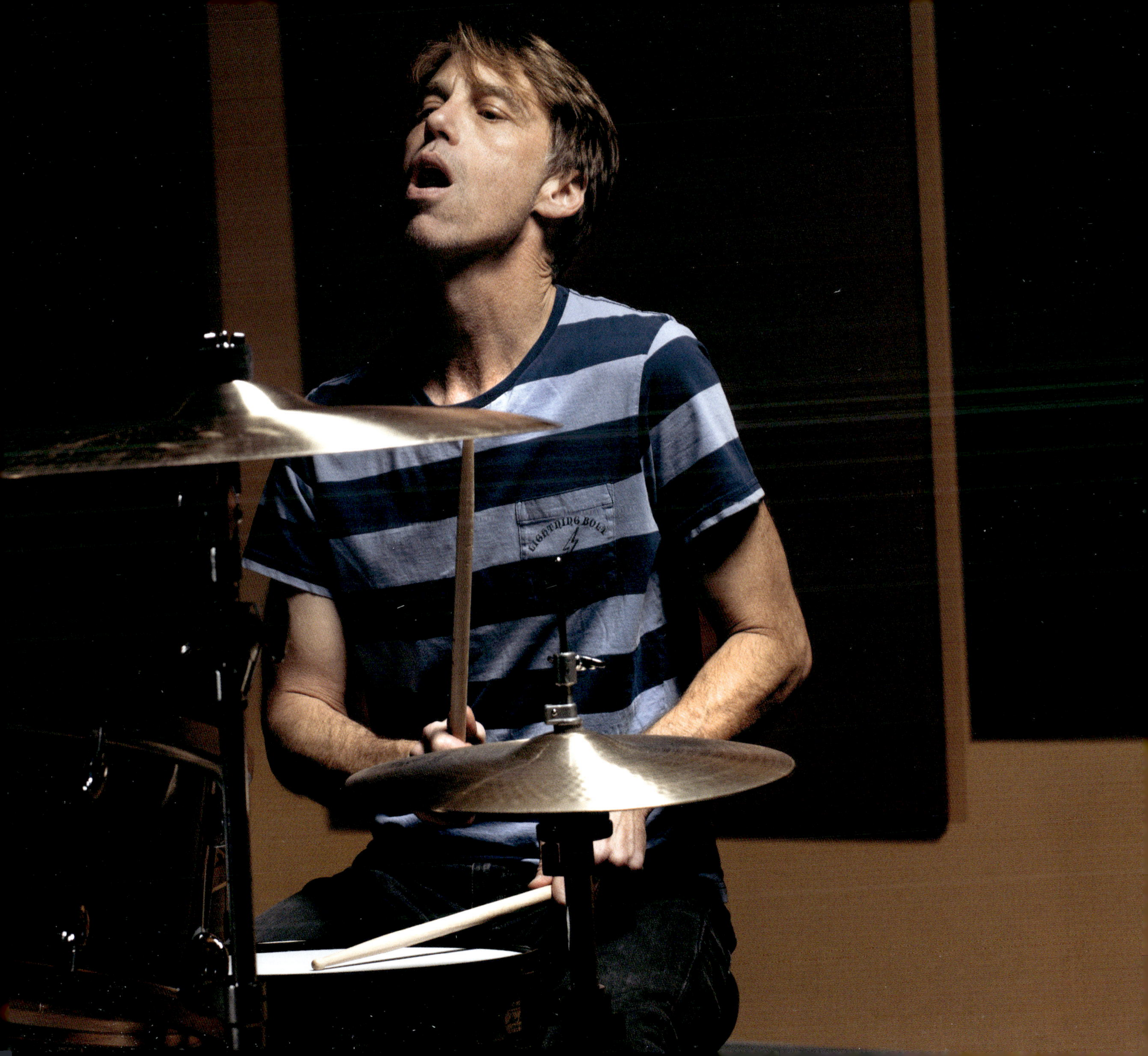
LIGHTNING BOLT

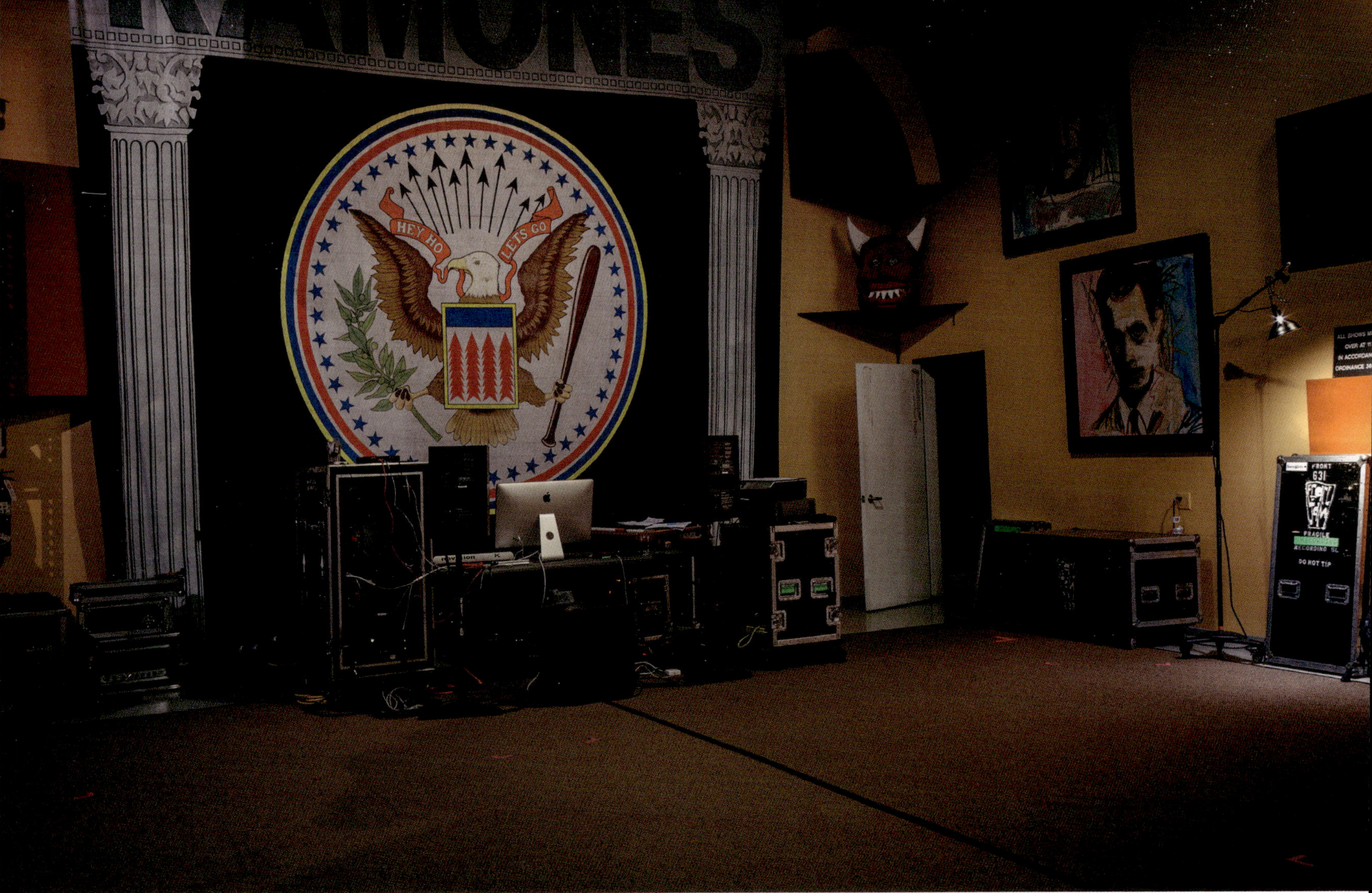
HEY HO
LETS GO
FRONT
FRAGILE
DO NOT TIP

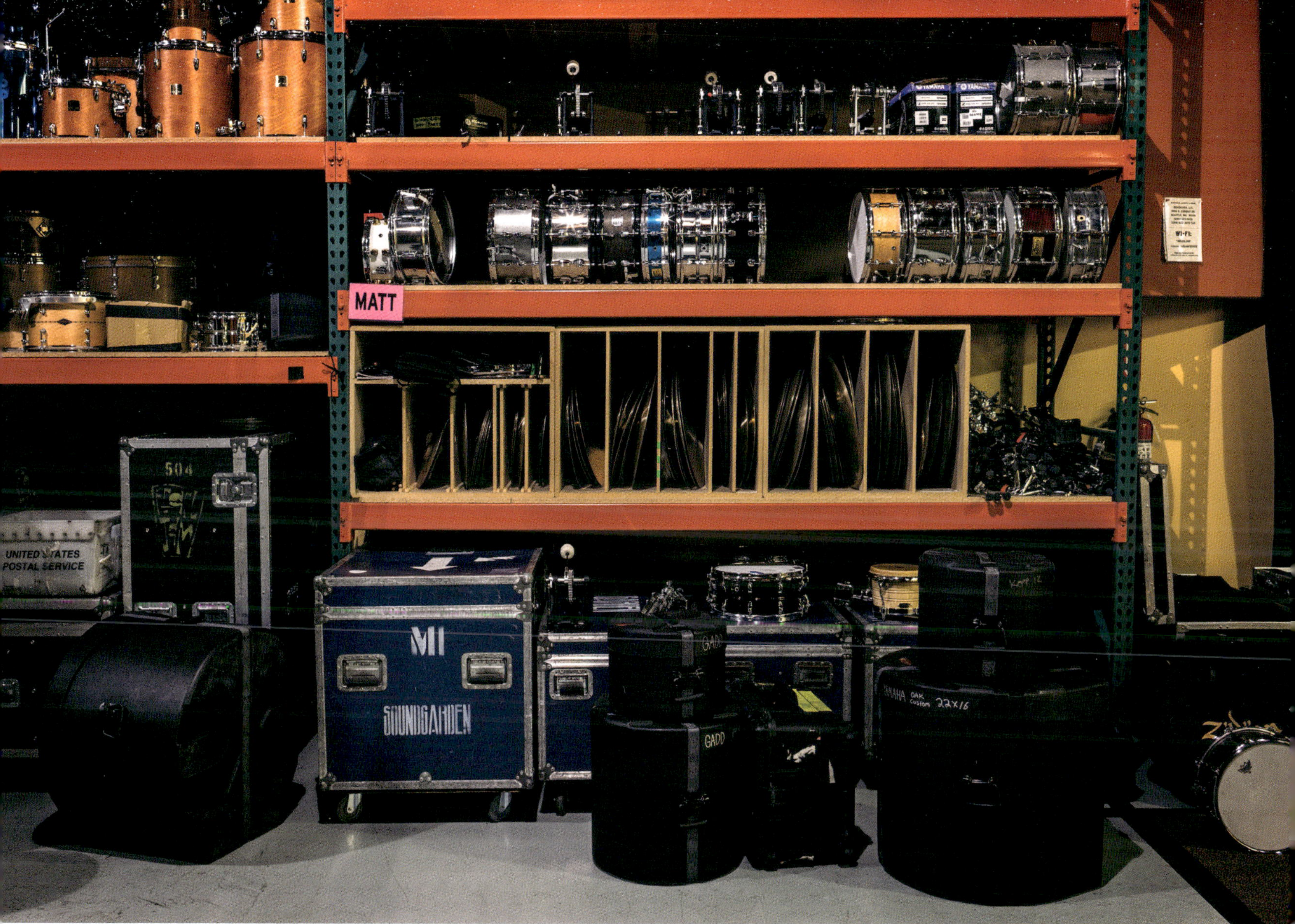
MATT
504
UNITED STATES
POSTAL SERVICE
M1
SOUNDGARDEN
GADD
GADD
YAMAHA OAK Custom 22x16

ROGER HAWKINS

Muscle Shoals Rhythm Section (Aretha Franklin / Percy Sledge / The Staple Singers / Wilson Pickett / Paul Simon). Photographed at home, Alabama

My dad tried to show me how to play the guitar. It hurt my fingers and I didn't like it. I took piano lessons. On my first recital at the school, onstage, I froze up in the middle of my little song, and the music teacher had to come from backstage to put my fingers on the piano where they should be and start me up again. I finished the song and that was the last time I ever played piano.

I was either twelve or thirteen when my father bought me a set of drums. It had a bass drum, a snare drum and a 12-inch cymbal. That was just a dream come true for me. This fellow, I can't remember his name, was a piano player and we got together. We had heard that there was a talent show over in Florence, Alabama, so we went. Of course we lost; it was just piano and drums. When we finished, a band came out onstage. One fellow, he was kind of like an Elvis type, had his hair combed back and had this white sports coat on, and the other two guys, one was a guitar player playing a Fender, and then there was this keyboardist. I was amazed by them. I thought, those guys need a drummer. And so when they got finished playing, the keyboard player was standing up leaning against the wall smoking a cigarette and I said, 'Excuse me, my name is Roger Hawkins, do you guys need a drummer?' It was Spooner Oldham. He says, 'Well I don't know, I'll talk to the guys and I'll get back to you on Monday,' and so he calls on Monday and says, 'I talked to the guys and they said yeah they'd like to have a drummer.' I said, great! So my dad took me to Spooner's house and we, you might want to call it jamming but … but it wasn't exactly. I mean it was every man for himself, really. So we played some of the old songs, and I just loved it. I really didn't know what I was doing but I loved it. That was the first band that I was in.

From there it went to nightclubs. They weren't really nightclubs, they were beer joints, just old funky places, and my dad would take me; he watched me play till I could go to bars by myself. Sometimes it would last two weeks, sometimes it would last six months. Two of the guys here in town wanted to move to Atlanta to hit the big time, so we moved to Atlanta and got us a job in a club, and when I was about seventeen I heard that the fellows at FAME Studios were moving to Nashville. That's what I wanted to do, because even before FAME there was a small studio in Florence and Rick Hall was involved in it – if Rick Hall were to walk into the woods naked he would come back out with a hit record. It was upstairs, and right across the street was a pool room, and so I would sit in the pool room and eat hamburgers just waiting for anyone I could talk to to come down.

I tried to learn as much as I could, and then later on when I heard that they were moving to Nashville, I thought, man, I'll quit this club stuff and I'll learn how to play in the studio if they'll let me. So I moved back and I did whatever I had to – deliver hamburgers or whatever I needed to do – just to be around the studio. And of course I had already met Spooner. Years later he was at FAME Studios, he and Dan Penn, and I'm hanging out as a young guy, and they said to me, 'When we get finished writing this song, we'd like for you to play on the demo a bit.' And I said, great! Of course there was no money in it, but I would get to play on their demos, and that's how I got started.

At eighteen I was married and had a small child, and of course that brings responsibility, but I had been drumming all this time. My family and my wife's family would say, 'You know, it's about time you settled down, got a real job.' I did do a few little jobs. Around this time I also did some body shop work in a car place, but all this didn't feel good to me out in the hot sun. I'd played on this Dan Penn demo that Rick put out as a single, and so I'm underneath this old car with my wrench in my hand and I'm taking this bumper off the front of this car and I'm down under it, and there's clods of dirt falling in my face, and then I hear this song on this old radio they had there, and it was Dan Penn singing and it was me. It was me. I loved it. The song was '(Take Me) Just as I Am'. I ran in and I said, 'Hey, that's me playing drums on this thing over here, on the radio.' The guy says, 'Get back out there and finish that car, boy, Mr So-and-so's going to be over here on Thursday, expects to have it ready.' So that was it, back to work.

Around that time I applied for a job driving a laundry truck that paid $75 a week. That was a lot of money to me. I applied on a Thursday and went and talked to the fellow, and then over that weekend I decided, if I don't get this job driving this laundry truck, I'm going to play drums and that's all I'm going to do. I don't care if I make three cents or $3 million; I do not care. So I called the man on Monday and he said, 'I'm sorry, but one of my buddies' son needed that job. I'm sorry but since he was a friend and …'. I said, 'I understand, thank you.' That's when the door slammed on the world. It was just me and the drums after that.

The first hit I played on ever was a big hit, 'When a Man Loves a Woman' by Percy Sledge, and it got people's attention, and as a result of that they would start bringing their artists to Muscle Shoals. They'd bring them to FAME and we got to record with Wilson Pickett and a whole lot of artists. [The Staple Singers'] 'I'll Take You There'; that was something that came out of me that day that I really wasn't expecting and I actually loved what I'd done.

I can only imagine what artists thought when they came here. When we used to go to Europe in the '70s, after doing a whole month's tour we'd fly back into New York and then it would be Atlanta and then it would be to Huntsville, Alabama, and then from Huntsville to Muscle Shoals. The airports get smaller as you get closer to home and so by the time you got to Muscle Shoals it really did look something like a chicken coop. It really did.

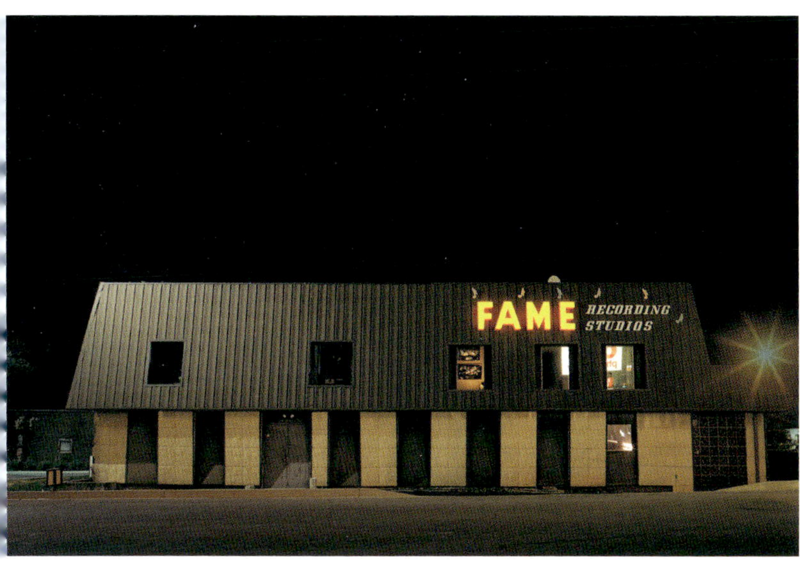
FAME
RECORDING
STUDIOS

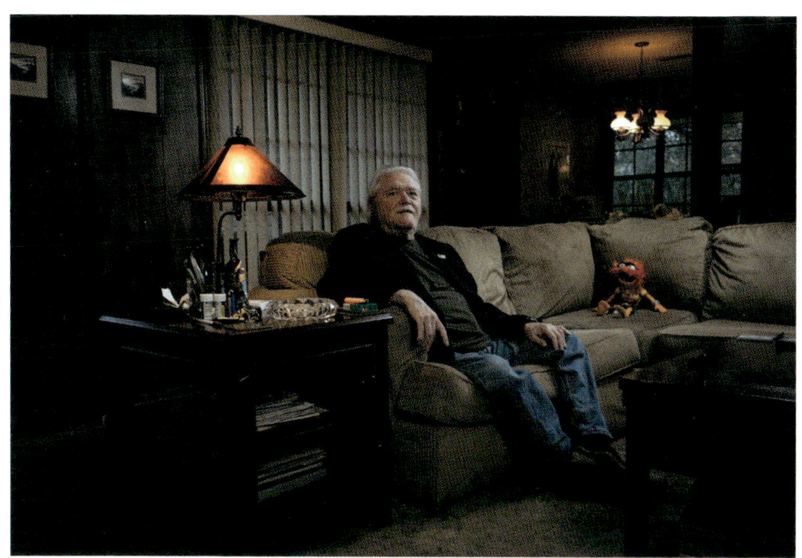

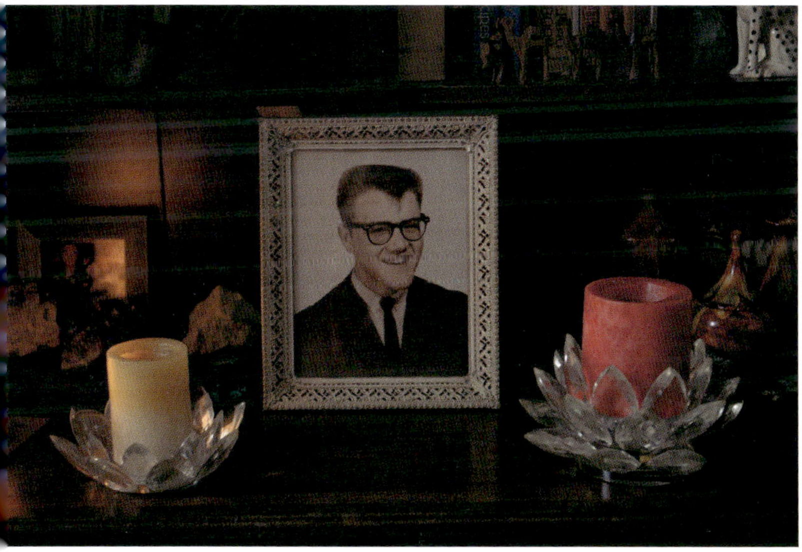

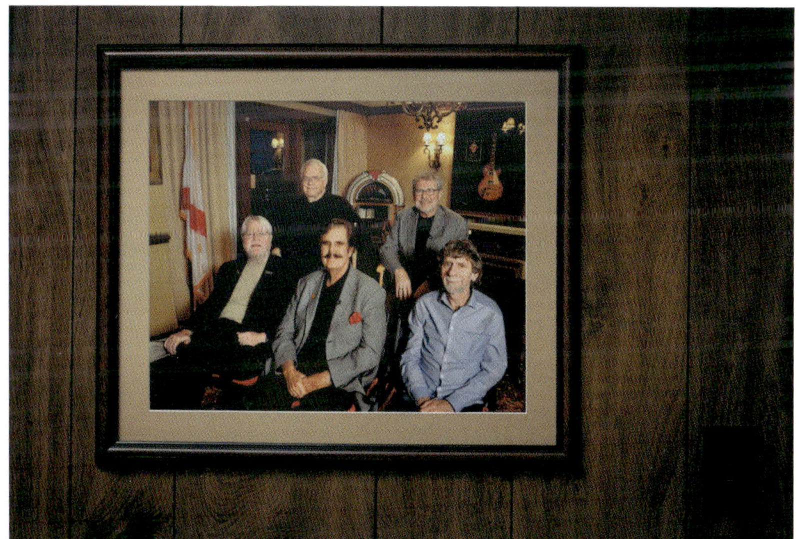

"IF RICK HALL WERE TO WALK INTO THE WOODS NAKED HE WOULD COME BACK OUT WITH A HIT RECORD"

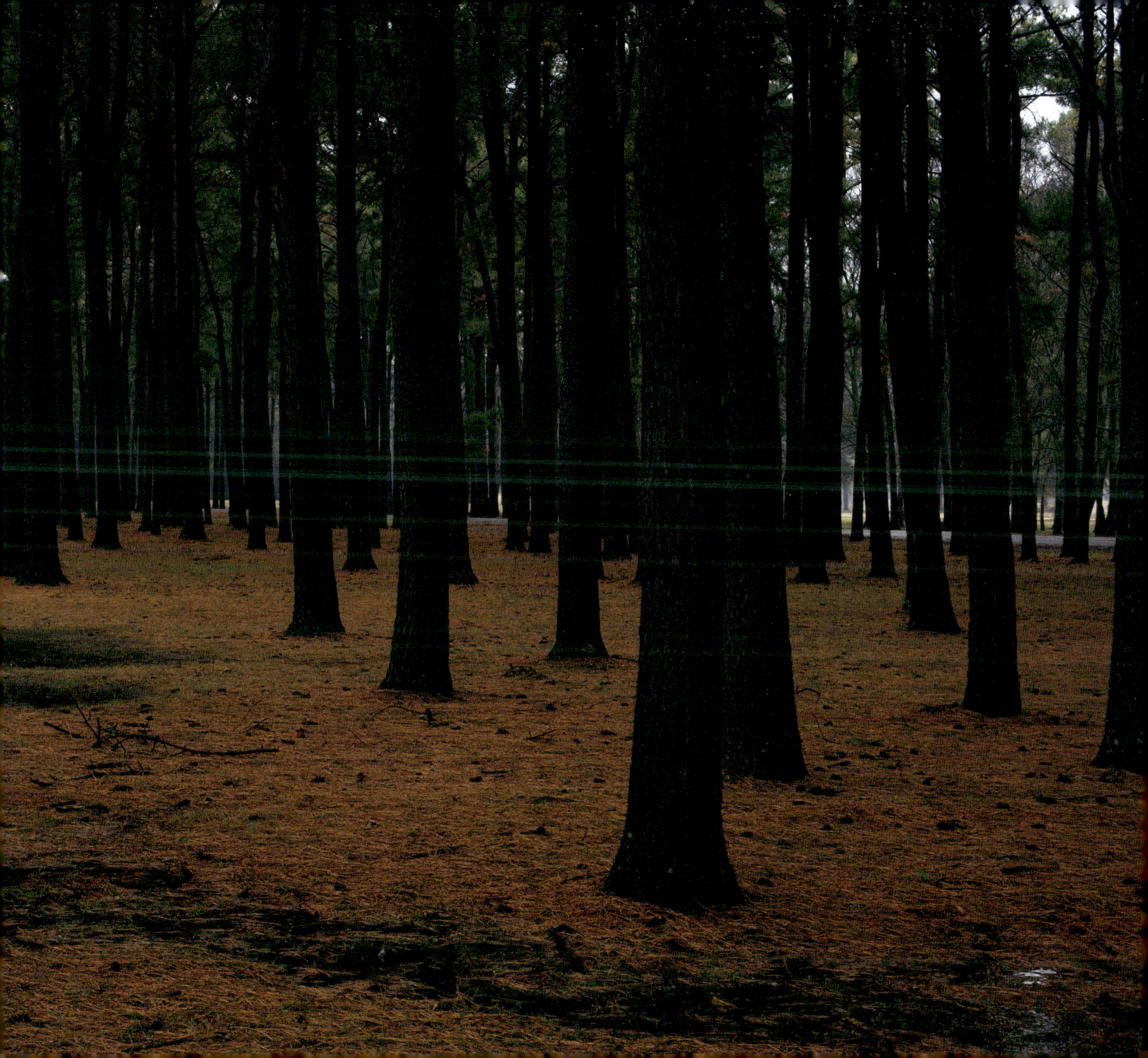

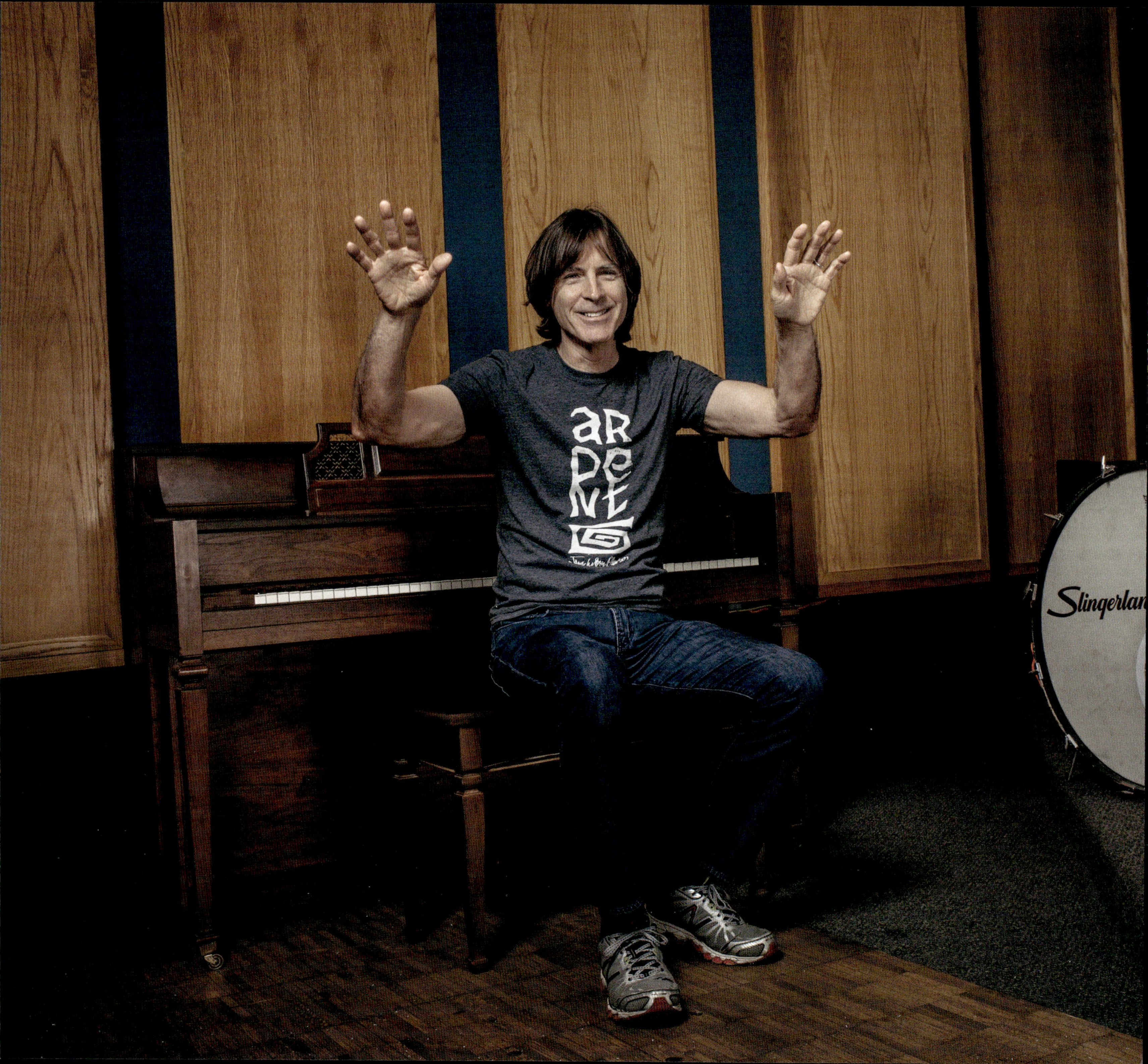
Slingerlan

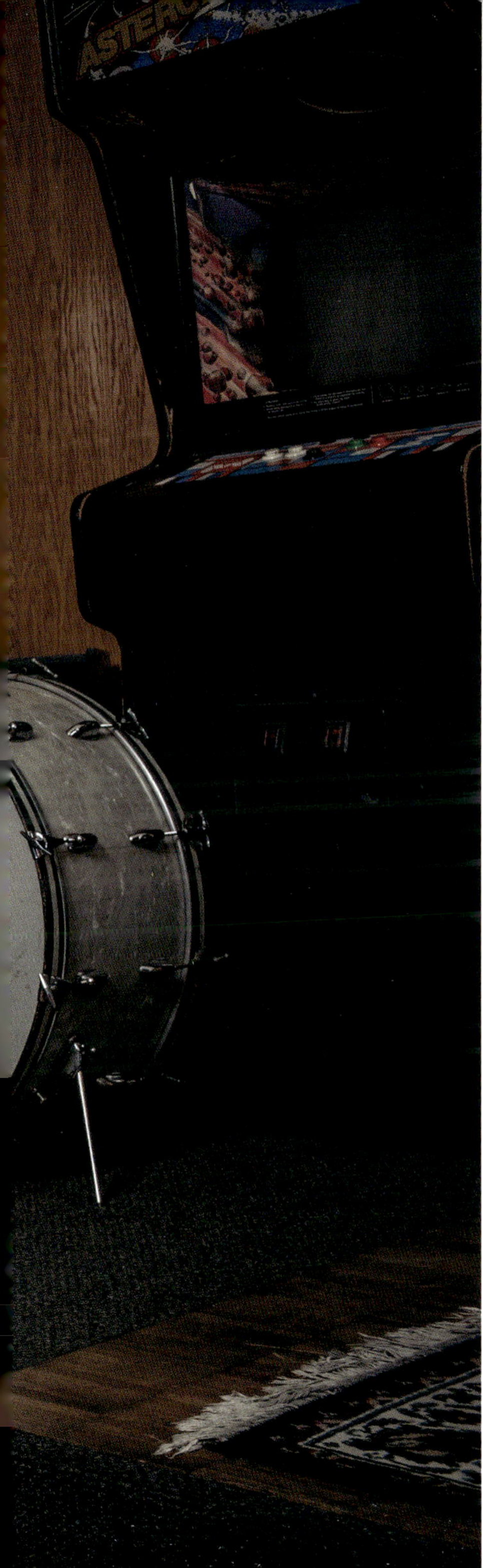

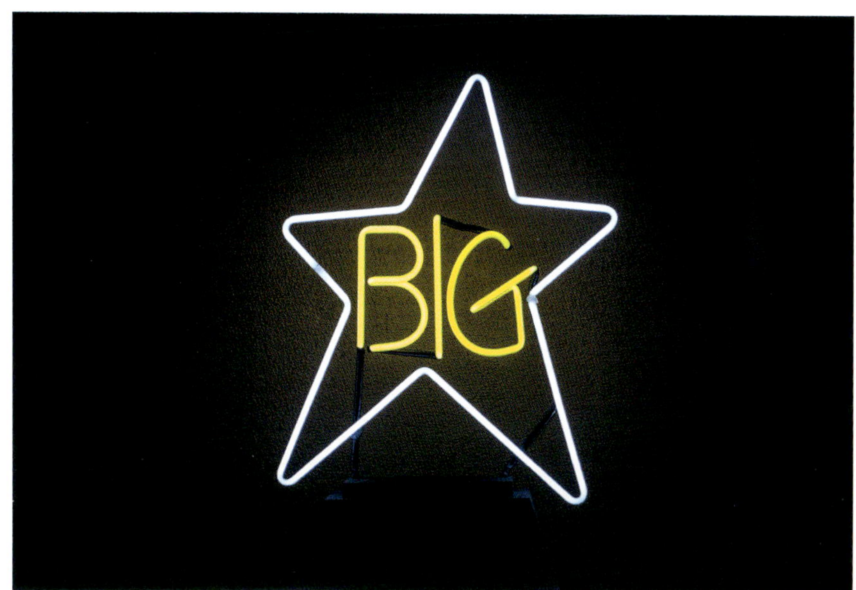

JODY STEPHENS

Big Star. Photographed at Ardent Studios, Tennessee

My brother and I wound up in a band with three lead singers, and we would do Three Dog Night [songs] and whatever required lots of singing. I was still in high school, and my brother and the lead singer in this band were going to the University of Memphis, and that year the director at the university got the rights to do *Hair*. We auditioned and we were hired as a band – that was pretty cool. My eyes were opened. From that I was introduced to Andy Hummel. After one of the *Hair* performances, he came up and asked if we wanted to come over and jam, and I said, sure. The people that wound up there were Chris Bell, Steve Ray and Terry Manning. That was the beginnings of Big Star [before Alex Chilton joined the band].

Ardent Studios is where I now work, and where all the Big Star records were recorded. John Fry, the owner and founding father, gave us all keys to the studio, and we could go in and just make the best of some of the most incredible creative tools available at the time, and that was amazing; we could spend an evening working stuff out. At the end of the night we could listen back to what we'd done. You could walk away with a whole tape in hand and have a record of being creative. There's nothing like the interaction of people, all in the same room together, playing off each other and the immediacy of all that.

I just love great songs because they feed some sort of hunger in me that's just innate. The greatest drummers are the ones that played on the greatest songs, like Ringo and Jim Keltner, Al Jackson, Charlie Watts, Keith Moon and John Bonham. It's that perfect match of player and song. It's kind of mind-blowing that those songs just come out of thin air; they really do just pop out of people's minds.

GEORGE HURLEY

Minutemen. Photographed in California

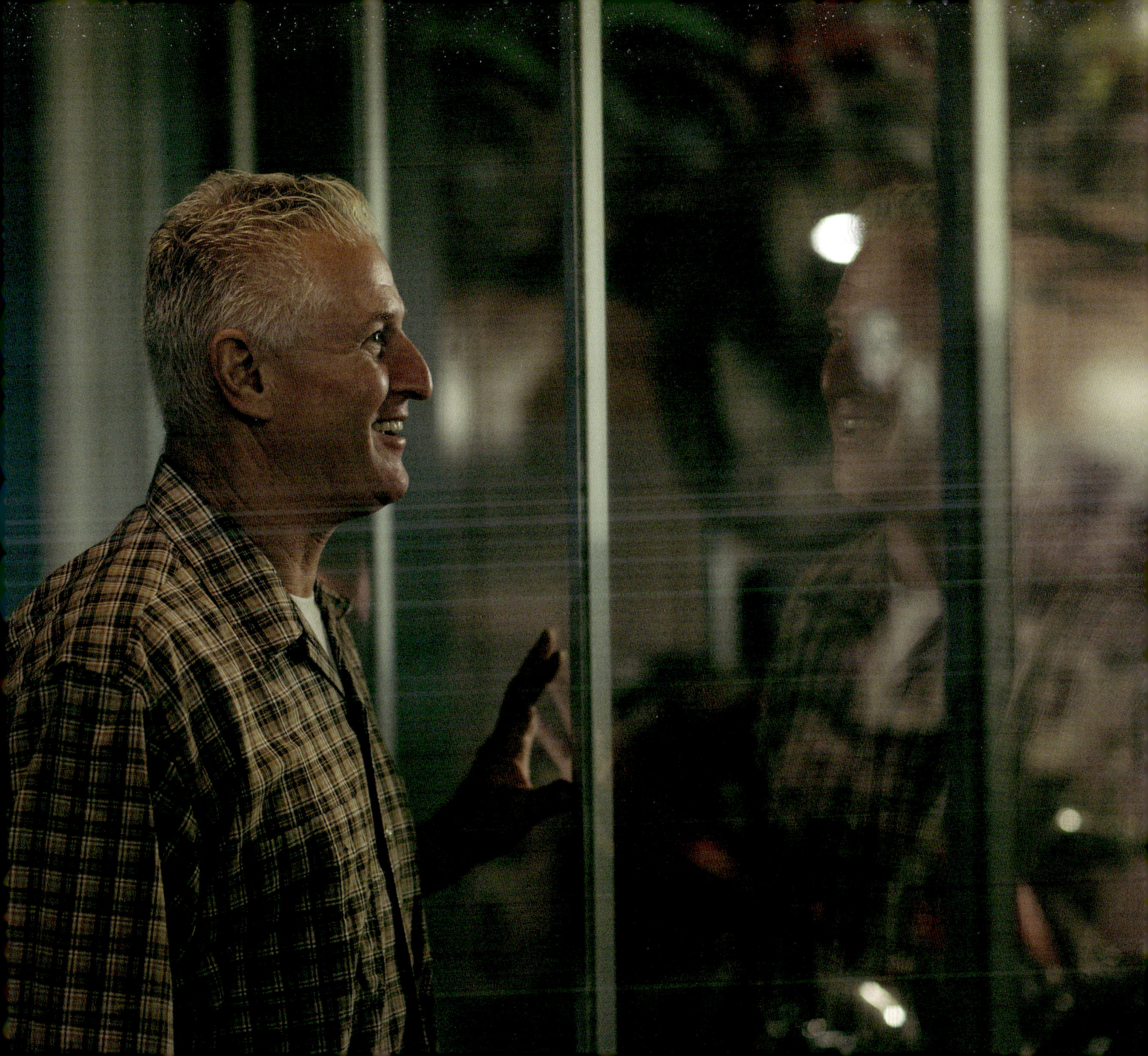

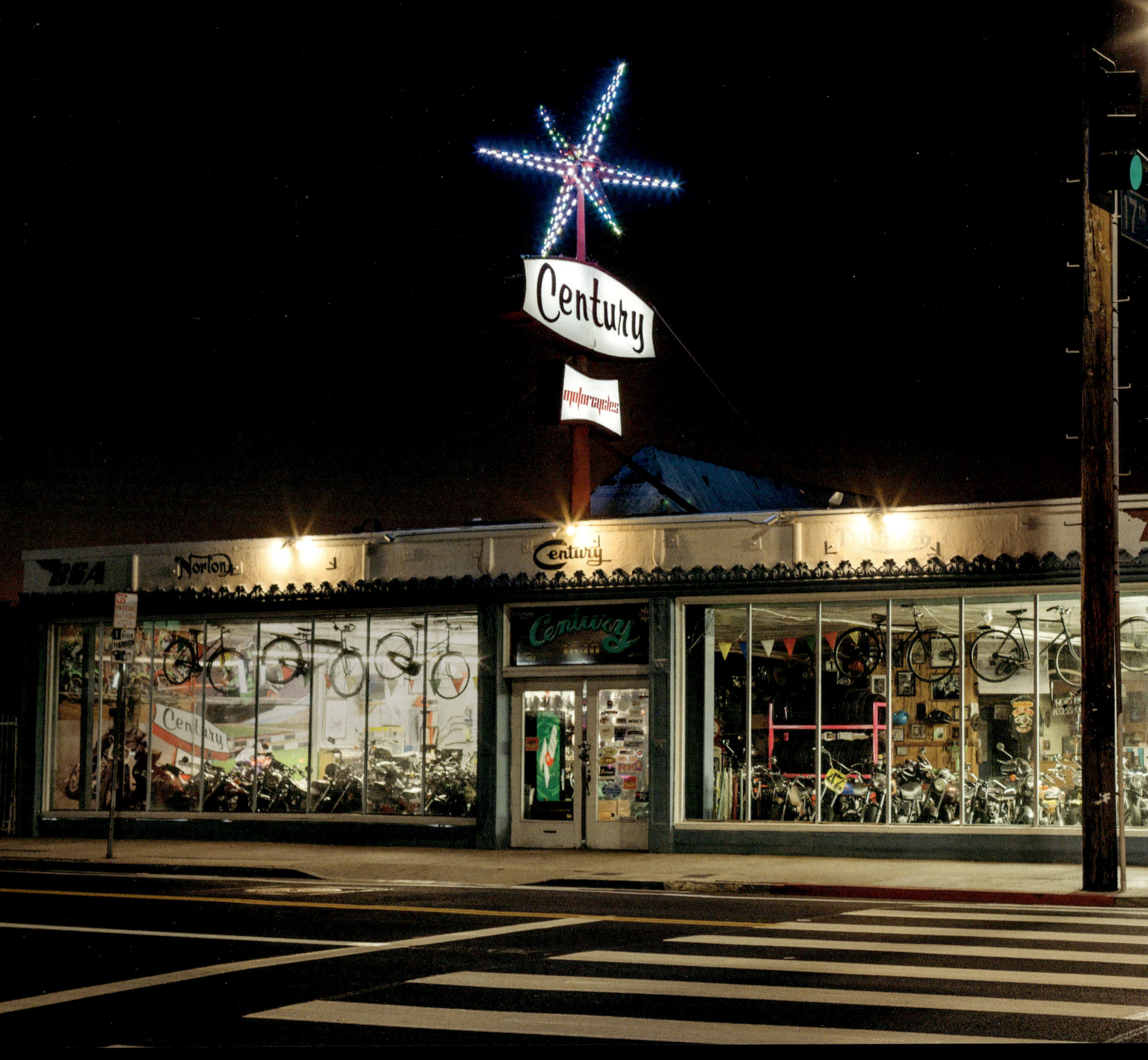
Century
motorcycles
BSA
Norton
Century
Century
Century
17th

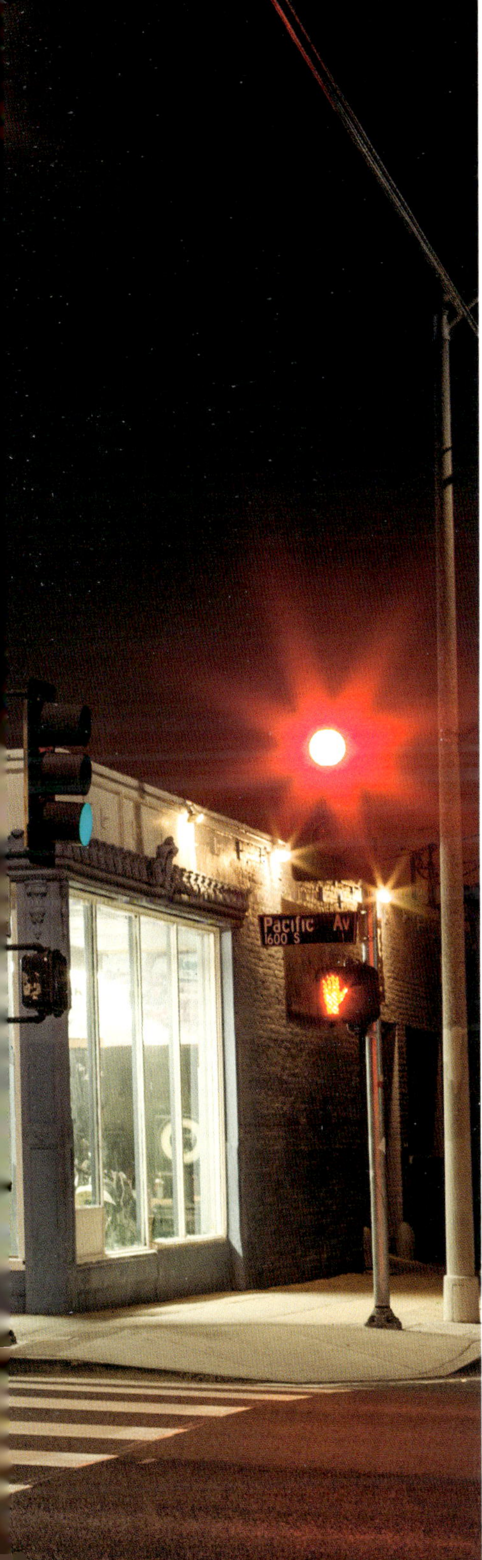

Motorcycles have always been fascinating to me. It's the closest thing to flying, I guess. On the very first album Minutemen put out, if you look on the back, you'll see me with a big old scab on the side of my face and my eye because I wrecked my motorcycle two days before the photo shoot. I was pretty sore. I've always been around motorcycles and I've always been fascinated with this shop [Century Motorcycles] in my town here. It's got a lot of beautiful bikes. A lot of English bikes – Vincents, Triumphs and Nortons. And I used to go there when I was a kid. I was dreaming about motorcycles and Evel Knievel.

When I was growing up my cousin Darlene was the most famous girl in the whole neighbourhood. She had these big, big boobs and there were always guys over there in hot rods and stuff. She had a stack of 45s, all the '60s bands, and she was pretty hip on music. That is how I really picked up on a lot of this type of music – The Animals, The Beatles, you name it.

I didn't start playing drums until I was nineteen. I'd wanted to play all my life but I didn't get a kit until I was nineteen. Guess how I got it: I traded a motorcycle for it. After I got that set my neighbours hated me. When that drum set came home and they could hear me playing up through the alley; it never stopped. I played every day after that for ten hours a day. I would go into the night and I wouldn't even get up to turn the light on. I'd just listen to my stereo, play my drums and when I was done for the evening I would take them all apart, lock them into this case and make sure that nobody could steal them. I was so obsessed with them it was ridiculous. I couldn't sleep at night; I'd hear a little twitch outside, I'd think someone was taking my drums.

Within two years I got together with a bunch of guys around town and we'd have our little jam-outs. Then Mike Watt was asking me for the longest time, 'Hey, can we do some songs together?' I had been in a couple little bands or projects before that. I just really wanted to get out there but I was a little bit shy too. Then we got this band Reactionaries going. It was a four-piece band and that was the prelude to Minutemen. That band broke up after I think maybe six months. So then we got rid of the singer and we decided to do it as a three-piece: me, Mike and D. Boon. And we just started writing songs and when we had enough to do a gig we begged Brendan Mullen, who ran The Masque, the local punk rock club up in LA, and finally he let us in. We started doing gigs there and so the Minutemen were born.

The whole idea then was that anybody could be in a punk rock band. You didn't have to be pretty, you didn't have to be good. You could just grab your stick and do your thing. We could be our own band, play our own music – we didn't care how we sounded. We wanted it to look like anybody could do it. We screamed and yelled and made a bunch of noise. Something came of it. We got a little bit of sound out of it that was unique. I never thought it would go as far as it did. We had our own gigs going plus we were seeing a lot of other new bands coming out. There weren't a whole lot of punk rockers in LA at the time. And then punk really exploded.

So now we were going to take this punk rock show on the road. That was like a Lewis and Clark expedition. There is a lot of space in between California and the Midwest; towns are hundreds of miles apart. We recruited a couple guys as roadies. Some of them, as soon as we crossed the California border they couldn't take it, they had to go back. They were gung ho in the beginning but they couldn't do it. You're going down through the South, Texas, Alabama, and you're hoping you got a gig the next day. We were hungry. We didn't have money to do this; we were really just running on faith. We'd get a gig, meet a few people. As strange as the music was and as new as it was to these people that were actually showing up at the bars, these little bars in Nowheresville, they liked it. They would bring us home and we would appreciate their hospitality. We would go in and raid the refrigerator and eat because we were starving. We had to learn how to do that because, otherwise, we probably would have perished on the road. If the car broke down we managed some way to rig something together to keep it moving. We blazed a trail all the way through to the East Coast and back home within a couple months. We made it alive. We did it. We kind of blazed a little trail there. A lot of people behind us used those clubs, that trail. So it really paid off for a lot of people too. It was a real expedition.

JACK WHITE

The Dead Weather. Photographed at Third Man Records, Tennessee

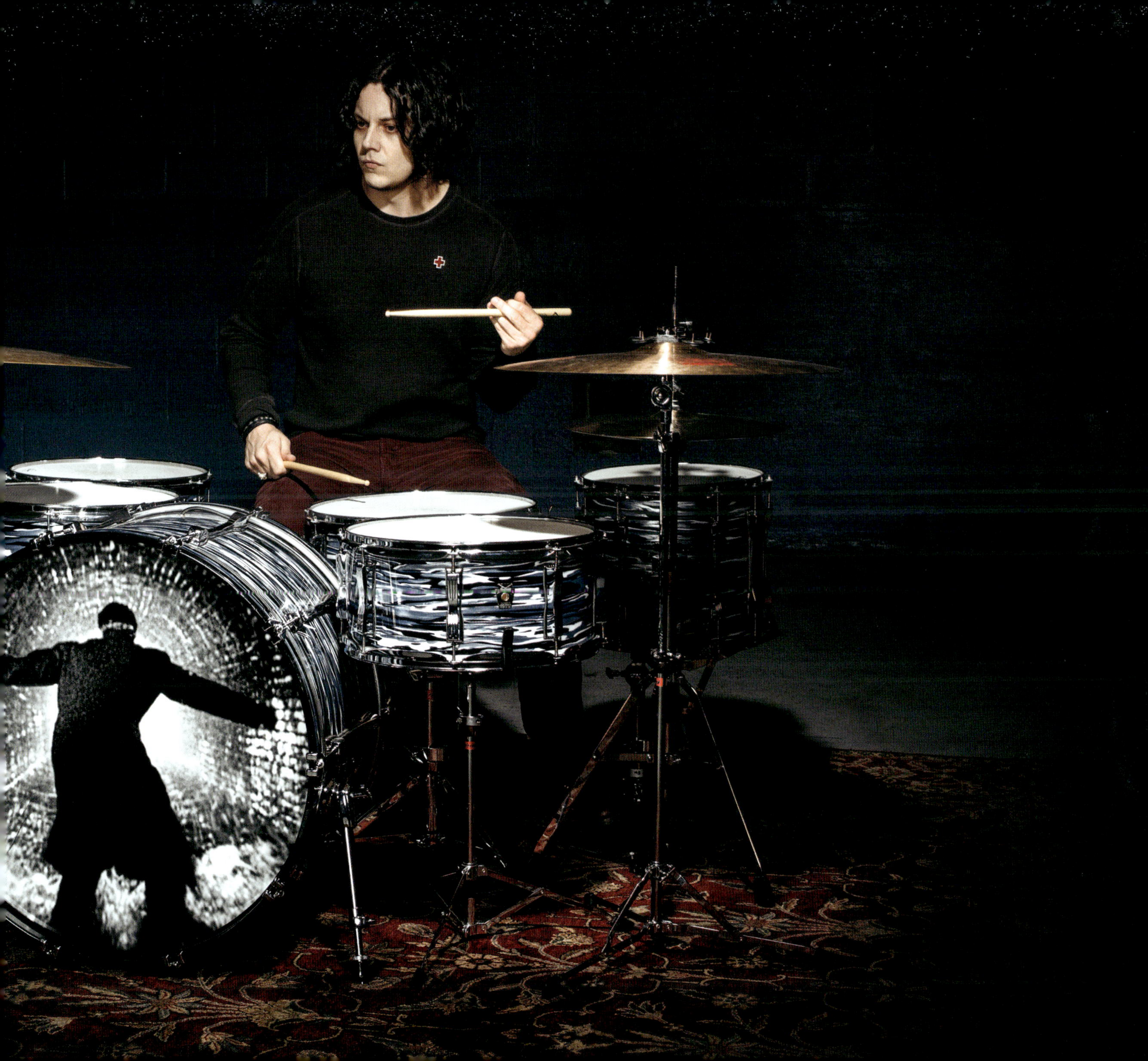

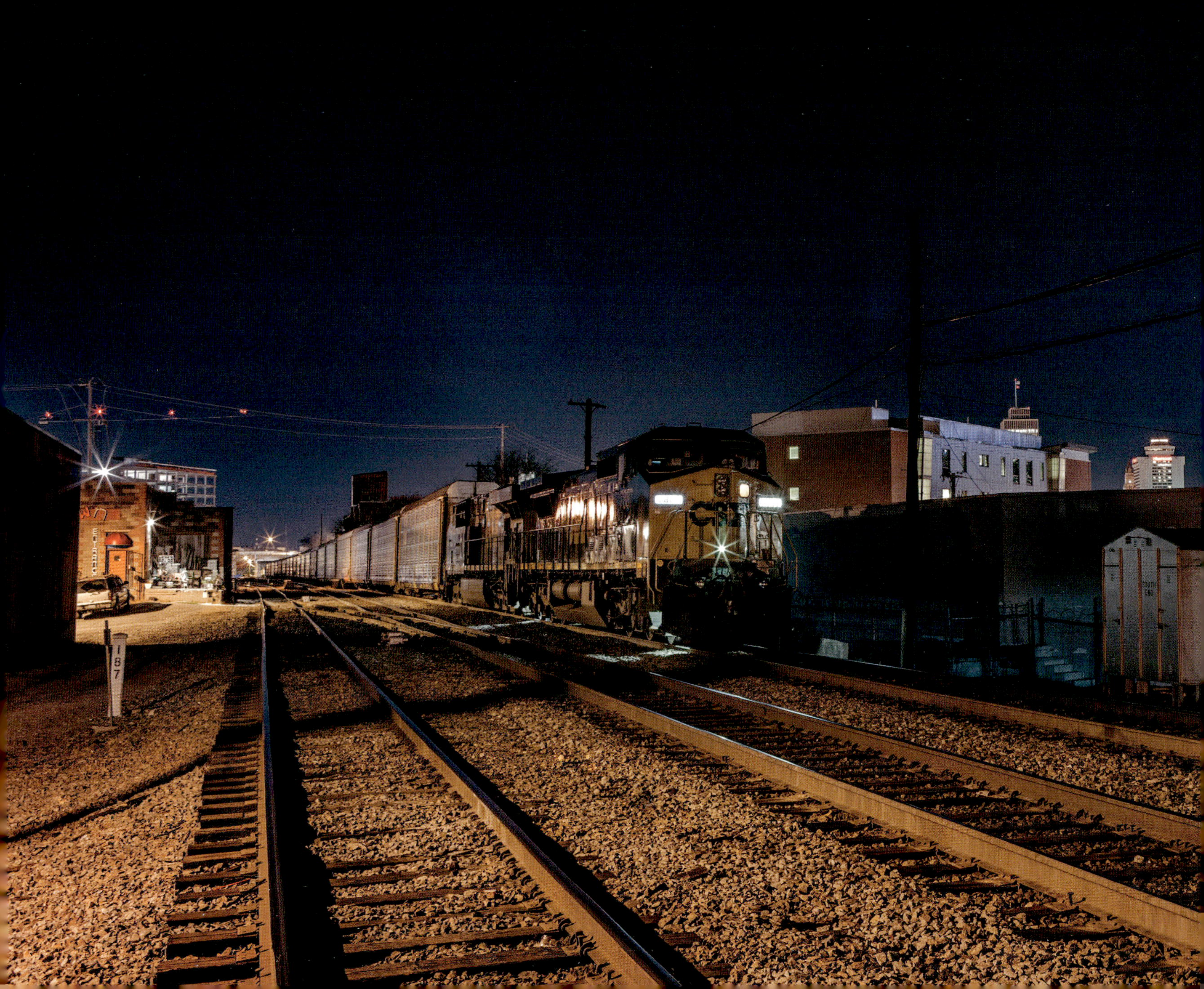
187

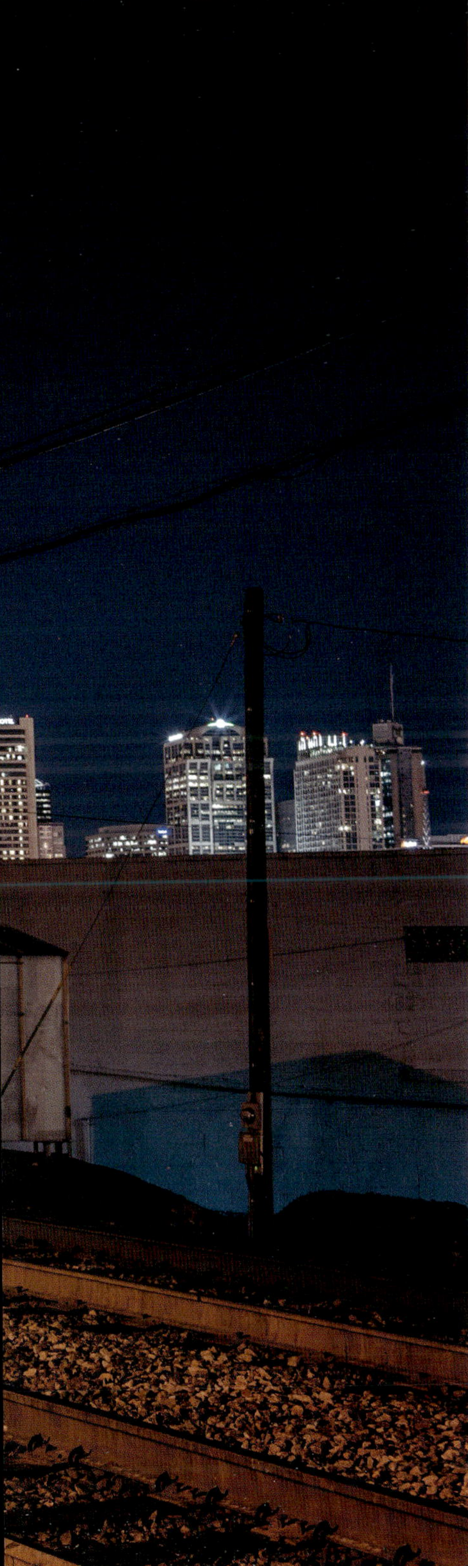

Somebody told me early on, when you go onstage you have to act like you own the joint; and I always say that to younger performers when I'm working with them. And when we put on live shows here, they say, 'Easy for you to say, Jack, you do own the place!' If you see a performer onstage and there's any sign of nervousness or second-guessing or insecurity, as a viewer you lose respect for that person. Even if the music's no good or your performing's not that good, if you act as if you own the place, it sort of sells it.

Take a drum beat like John Bonham's: he means every hit he's putting down. It can almost sound calculated when you listen to a Led Zeppelin song, like math, because it's so perfect. Every single beat he's putting down is on purpose. There are no side things going on, and that's pretty hard to do, to make it succinct like that and still come across. He's just magical at that. I have to say, John Bonham is the law. Some drummers get up there and they just sort of play and they're doing things that they think sound good, or they try to show off and be impressive to people, but that gets old after a while. It does the song a disservice and it does the team you're a part of a disservice.

As the drummer you set up the structure; they're going to build a building around you. You're like the girders inside the building and you have to leave the spaces for doors and windows, and for all the materials to be put on top of you, so you can't cover up what they're doing. You have to be the structure that they're based on, but you have to emphasize what it is they lie on top of you and help them, to give them the best foundation.

I think the most underrated drummer is Meg White, because I think people confuse playing lots of drum fills as being good at something, and that's just so not the case. I mean, in the last thirty years there've been so many drummers that just have a million drums in front of them and play a million beats per second. It doesn't mean anything. That's an important thing to remember when you're buying a kit like that. It's like a guitar player who plays insanely fast guitar solos: it doesn't make it better, it makes it worse. And the people who can play simply, like the two-, three-note things that the blues musicians were playing, those are so much more heavy and soulful, more powerful. It's the same thing with Meg's drumming; it's so childlike and simple that it captures people's attention and they move to it, they're inspired by it.

There are certain things humans are attracted to, we don't even know it. Like the beat being on the one. Funk music is a sexy kind of music; not in a Barry White kind of way, but in a way that really sells it to you. It's all about the one. The importance is on the one, like a zap – that really appeals to me. It's like someone dropped a bomb on me, the gap there. That feels sexy to me – not necessarily the sound of the drums or anything like that, but because of everything being on the one.

I called somebody today on the phone and in the background a train was going by and it reminded me of when we first got this building. Someone said, 'Oh, it's too bad the train goes by.' I was like, 'What are you talking about? That's the best part!' I really do love it, and it was nice to hear that on the phone in the background. It's something you almost think shouldn't exist anymore. It's such a timeless thing. It could be 1840 right now when you hear that sound.

JACK DEJOHNETTE

Miles Davis / John Coltrane / Keith Jarrett / Bruce Hornsby / Paul Simon
Photographed at home, New York

Everything is connected but it takes time for us, the human species, to make those connections. I don't think of music in categories; all music is world music. I look at all the so-called genres and incorporate them all into my music: electronic, reggae, folk, rhythm and blues, classical. My career is full of cross-pollination. I do a lot of playing with younger musicians. There is an exchange of youthful energy and imagination and wisdom between younger musicians and older musicians.

My first memories of music are of listening to my uncle's records when I was a small kid. His name was Roy Wood and he loved jazz. I used to listen to his records and play the Victrola and drop the needles in. I'd listen to Count Basie and Duke Ellington, Slim Gaillard and Louis Jordan – I was fascinated by it. I was fascinated by all kinds of music. So I started taking classical piano lessons when I was four. But I used to listen to all kinds of music on the radio: country, classical, gospel, the blues – it was all great to me.

How I started drumming was a drummer left his drums in the basement at my grandmother's house. My uncle became a jazz DJ so I had access to a lot of jazz records and I taught myself how to play the drums. I just went down there and started playing [along to] the records. I did a lot of jam sessions in Chicago. I used to go to play piano and to watch the drummers there and I got good enough where I could play just as well on drums as piano (actually, I play better drums than I play piano). Due to my experience as a pianist and an accompanist, playing standard tunes and having my own groups, I felt it made me a better listener.

Great drummers inspire the artist to go beyond what they normally would do. In my case, it's an improvisational situation. If it's a drummer who is playing the Top 40, you need a great drummer who plays the time down and plays the arrangements and makes it sound like it's the first time he's played it every time. Elvin Jones, Philly Joe Jones, Max Roach, Art Blakey: these are great drummers because they understood the whole ensemble and they knew how to get the best out of the musicians. That's the drummer's job: to make it feel good, to inspire the musicians and also be inspired.

Music changes with the times and jazz changes with the times. When I was growing up, everything was on records, then it moved to CDs, then it moved to digital, so the economy was different then. Record companies were supportive and stayed with an artist and developed an artist, not just waiting for an instant hit; they would bill an artist. But now that's all changed. But what drove musicians, and what still drives musicians, was to be the best they could be, to try to play with the best musicians possible, to play for audiences all over the world and make a good living from it. And it is also their art – it feeds their creative juices. People used to go and hear somebody or hear a record, or buy a record; now people go to YouTube. People used to come to concerts not with their iPhones and their recorders – people used to come with their ears and their hearts.

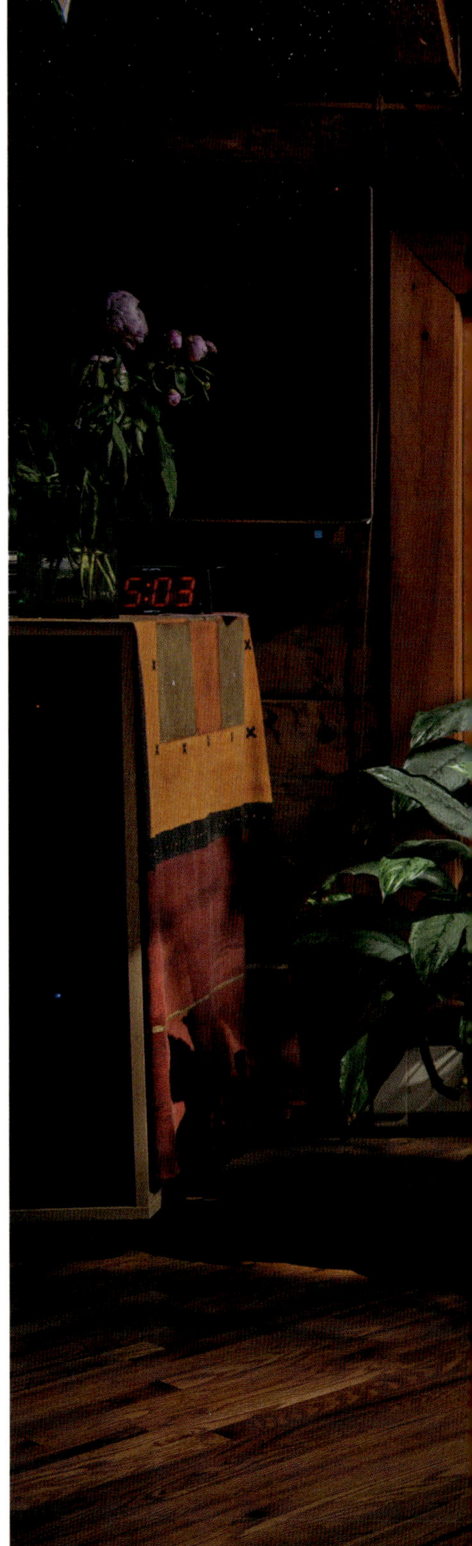

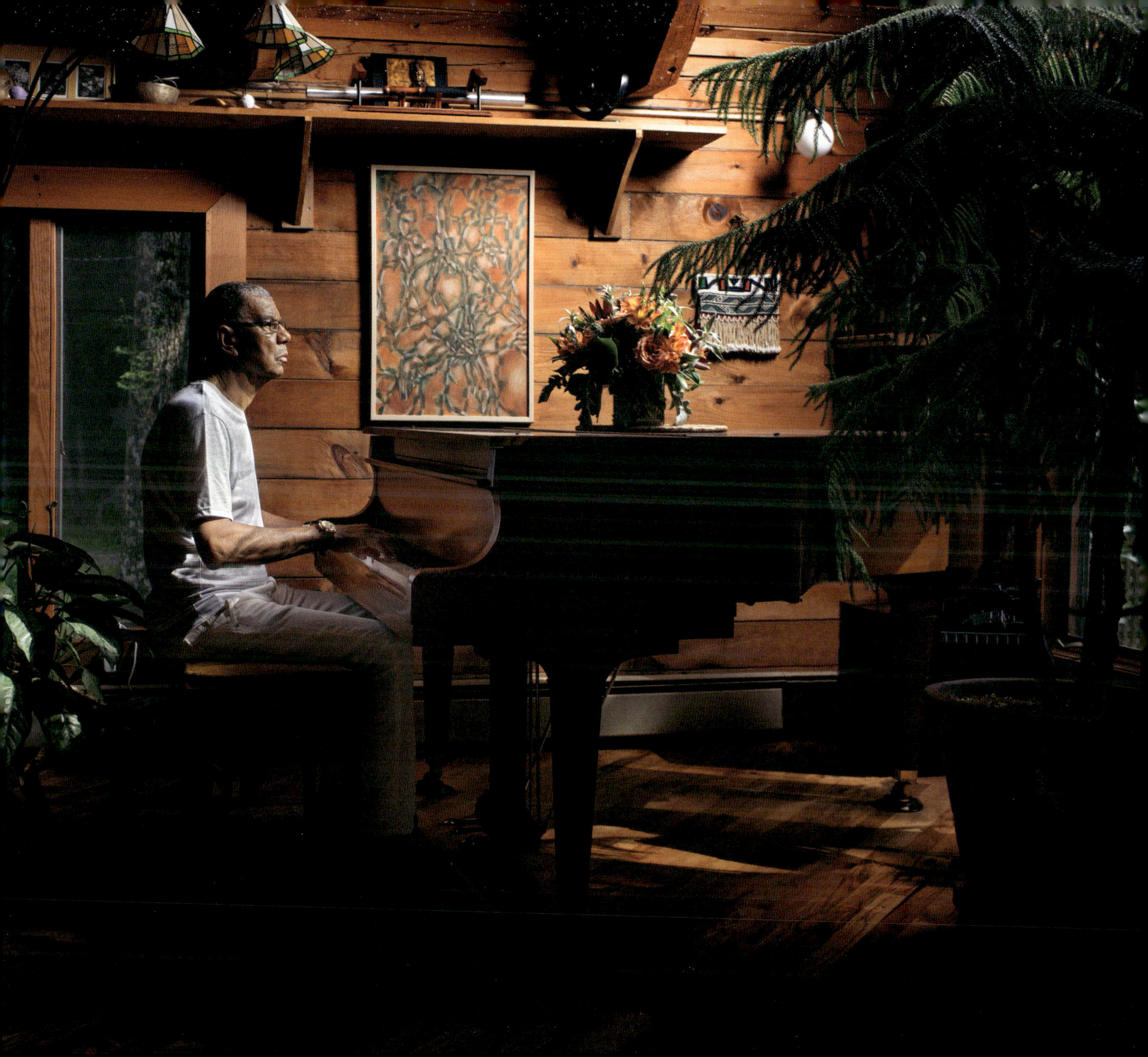

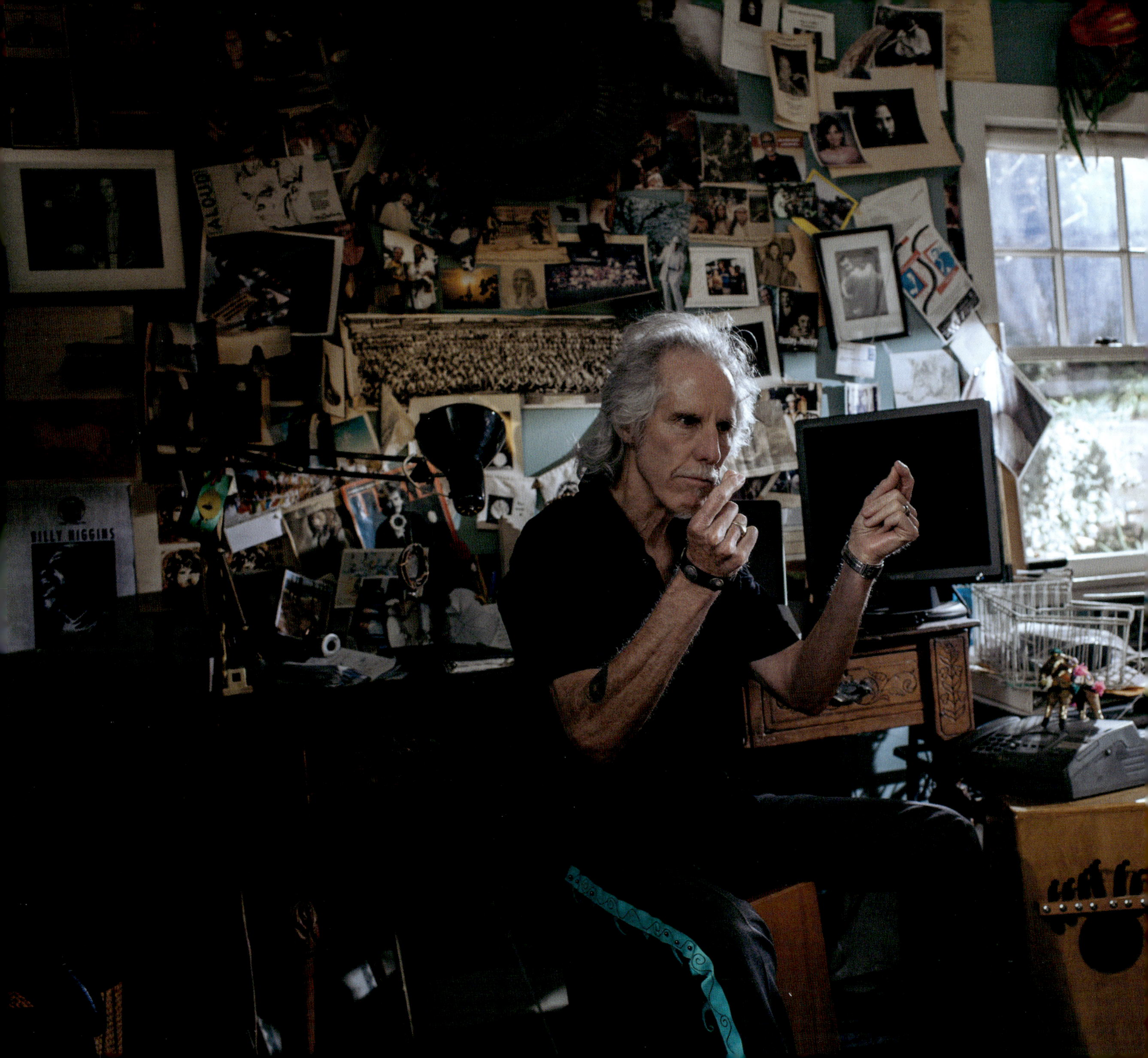
ALOUD
BILLY HIGGINS

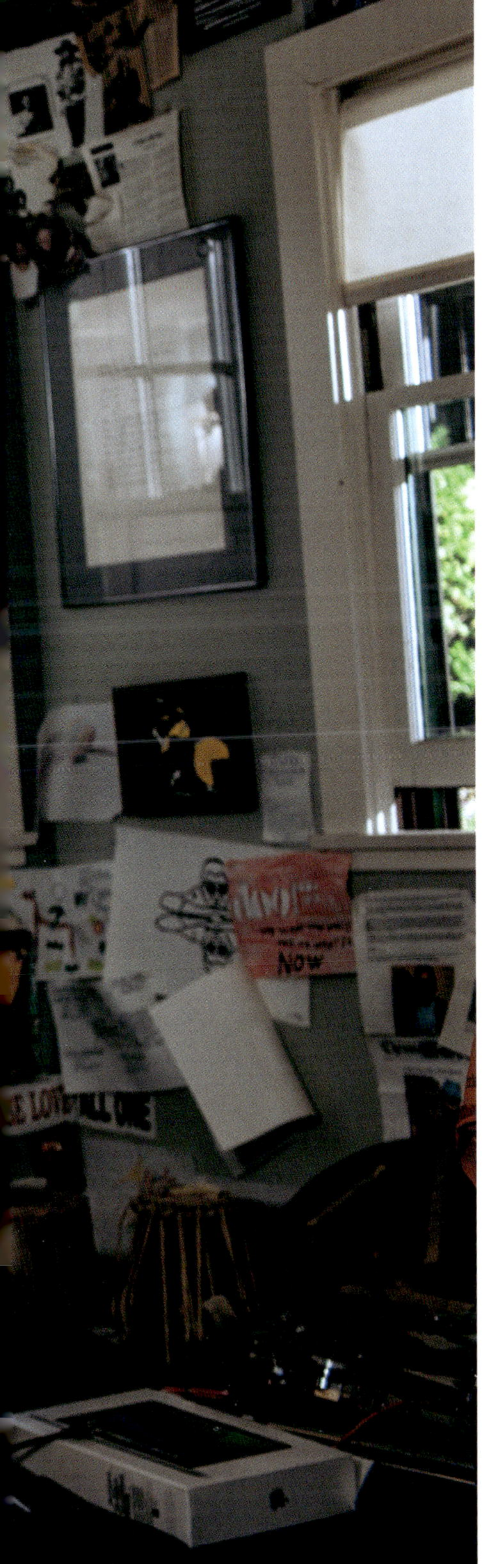

“IT’S ALL ABOUT TOUCH, IT’S NOT ABOUT POUNDING”

JOHN DENSMORE

The Doors. Photographed at home, California

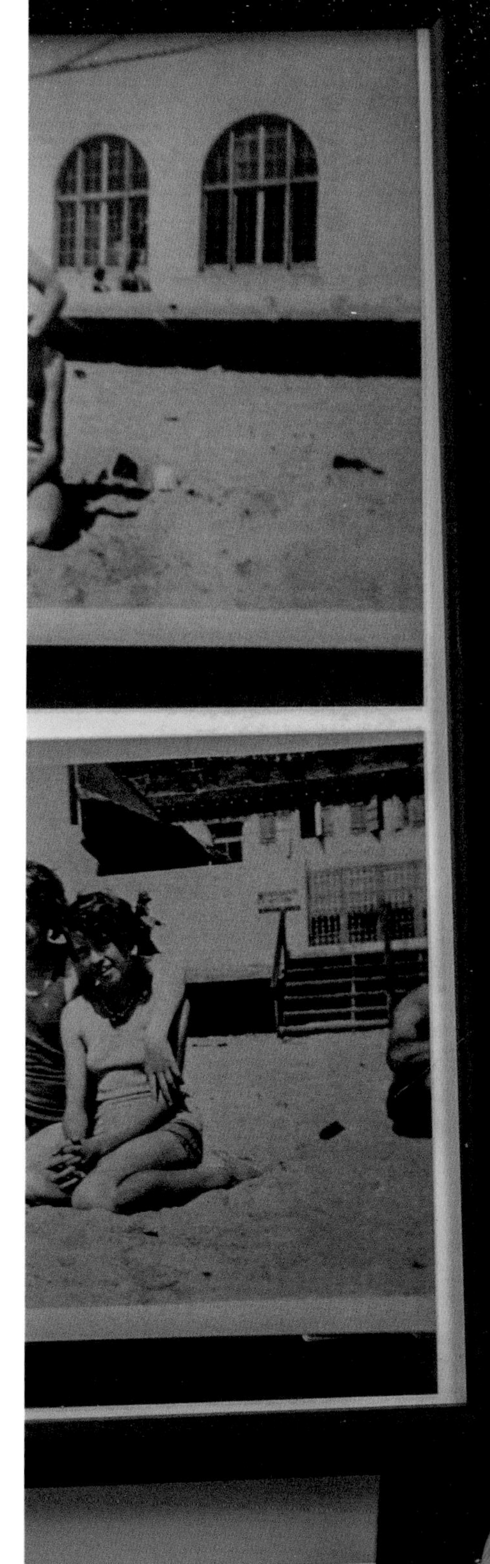

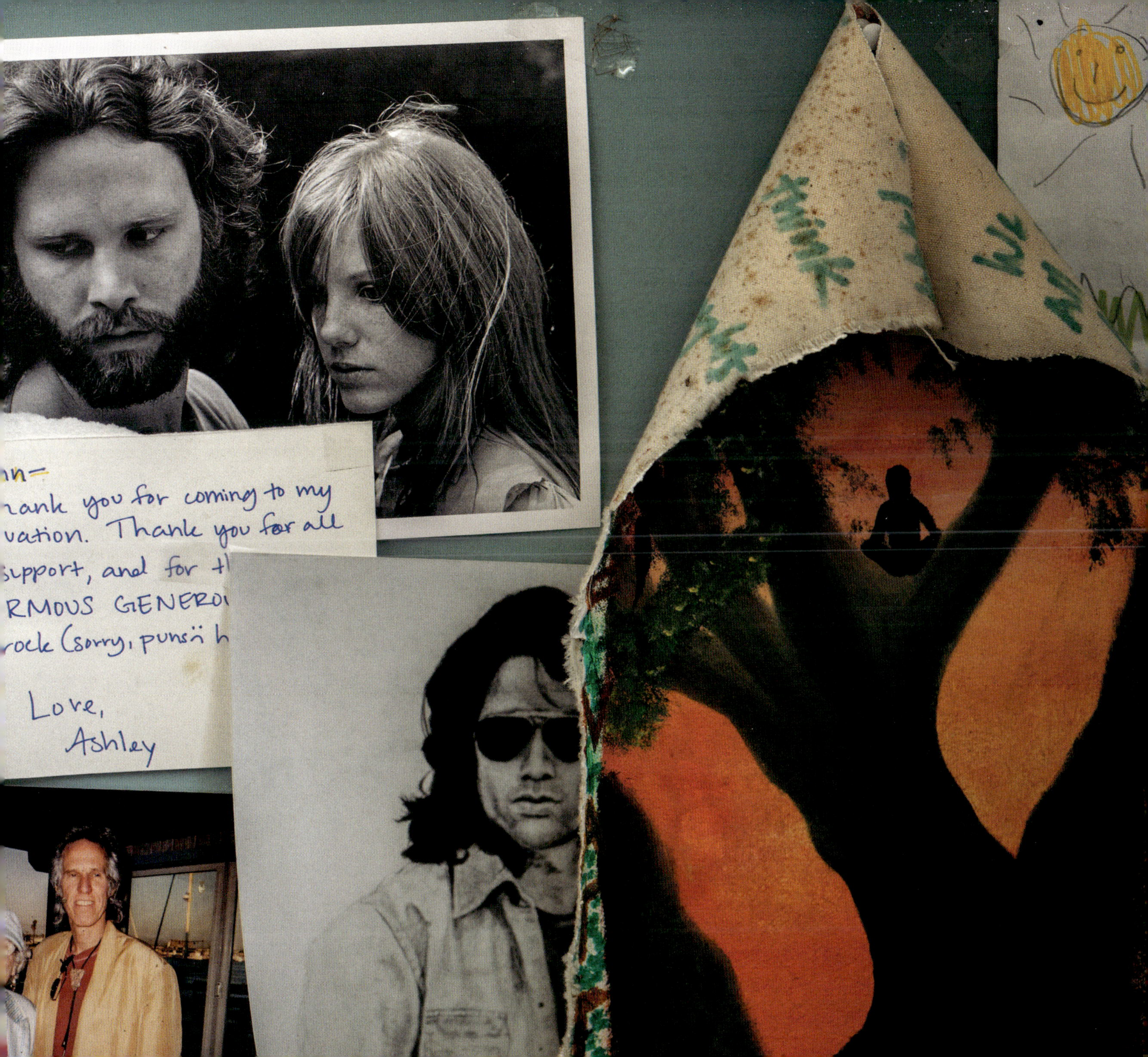
hank you for coming to my
vation. Thank you for all
upport, and for th
RMOUS GENERO
rock (sorry, puns h
Love,
Ashley

"I TAUGHT MYSELF BY LISTENING. I TRY TO INVENT MY OWN WAY OF PLAYING. IT'S STILL A PUZZLE TO SOME PEOPLE, THE WAY I PLAY MY DRUMS"

TONY ALLEN

Fela Kuti & Africa '70 / The Good, the Bad & the Queen / Rocket Juice & the Moon. Photographed in France

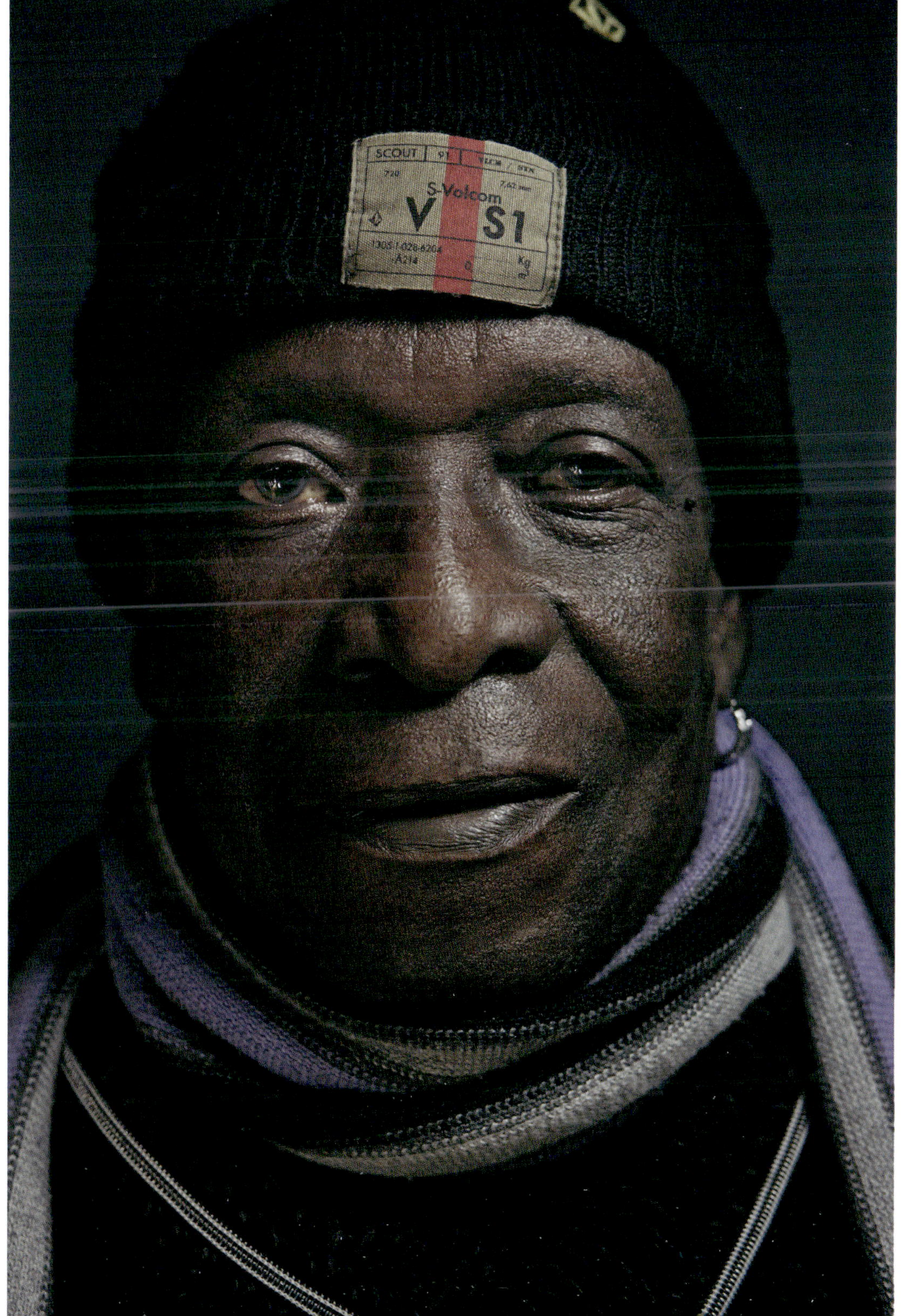
SCOUT
S-Volcom
V S1

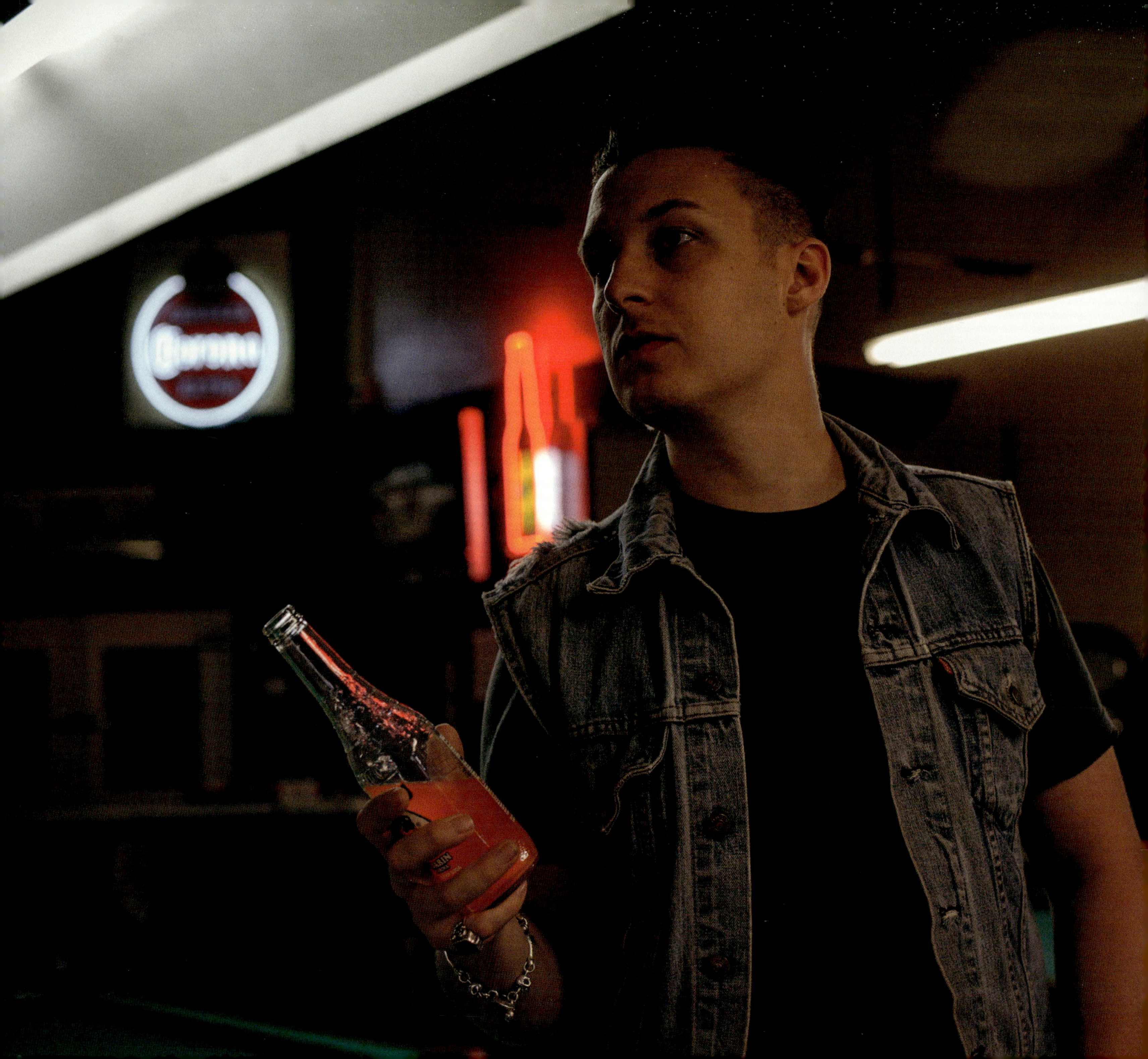

MATT HELDERS

Arctic Monkeys / Iggy Pop. Photographed in California

Before I played drums I was a DJ with vinyl, in my bedroom. I was about thirteen or fourteen. That got me listening to dance music, hip hop and stuff like that. We were about fifteen or sixteen when bands like The Strokes were coming out. The rest of the band and I used to hang around and go to school together, so we kind of all made the musical transition at the same time, from just listening to Dr Dre and stuff like that to guitar music that we considered to be quite decent. At that time there was the rap metal thing – like Limp Bizkit and stuff – and that was a bit dangerous; we weren't really into that. So when guitar music came along it seemed more genuine and traditional and it got our attention.

I've always been interested in making music in one form or another. There was the DJing stuff, that side of things, which I still have a big interest in. Even though I was listening to hip hop, there were bands like Oasis and Pulp as well. And English hip hop: Roots Manuva's *Run Come Save Me* was the album for us at that age. It still is one of my favourite albums. Hearing people with a familiar accent made you think, oh, maybe we could do this – make music.

BRYAN DEVENDORF

The National / LNZNDRF / Pfarmers. Photographed in the UK

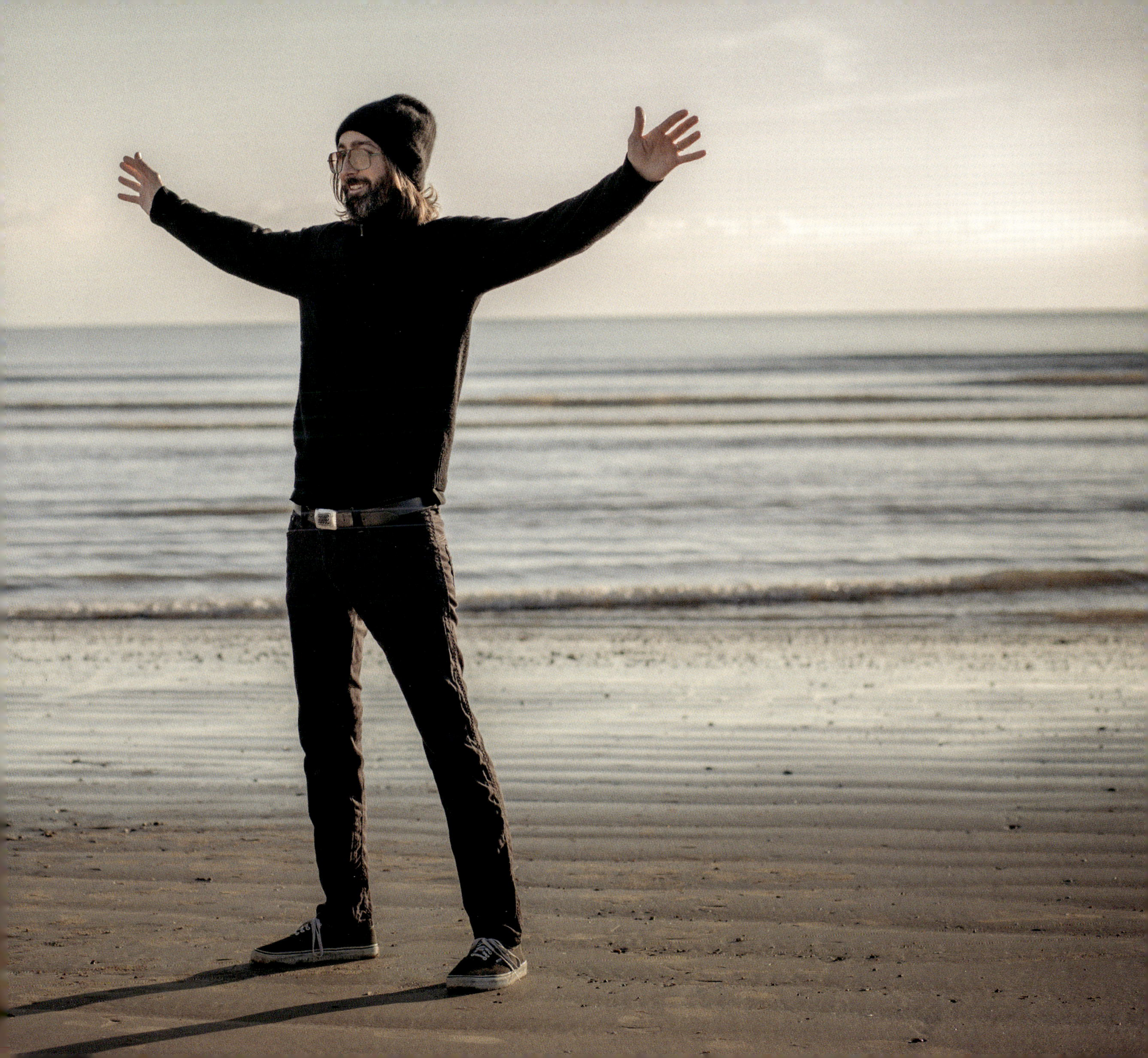

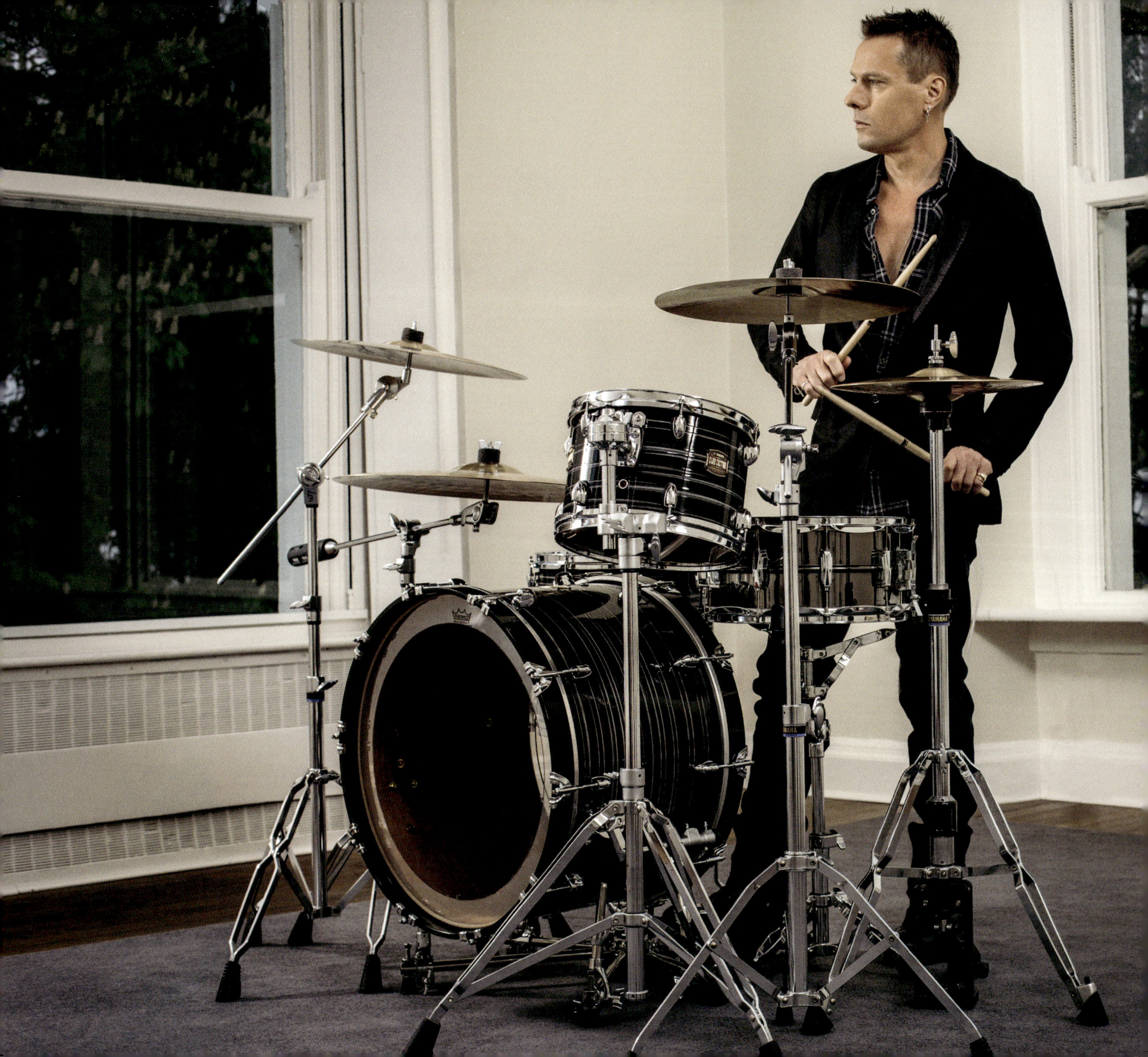

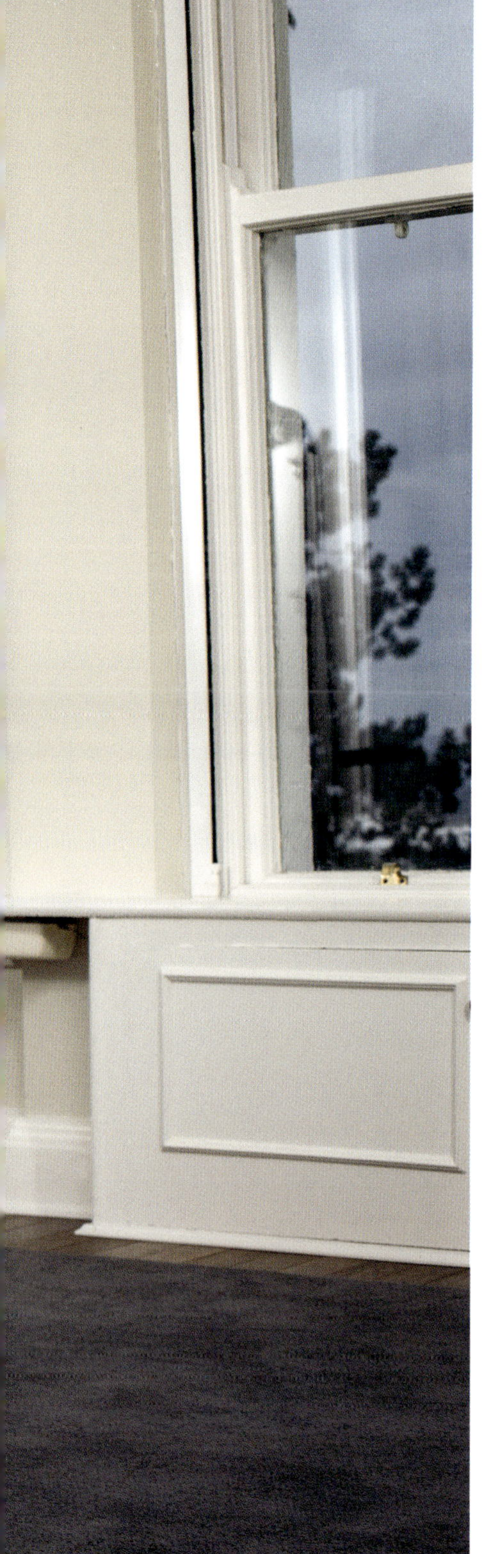

LARRY MULLEN JR

U2. Photographed in Ireland

I formed the band in Dublin in 1975 around the time of the punk explosion – a time when it seemed that anything was possible. Being able to play your instrument proficiently was the least important part of that movement; attitude, though, was essential. This was really great news for us as we were not accomplished musically but we did have a singer with an attitude. Early on, most bands try to learn how to play other people's songs: we were no exception. At school we rehearsed every Wednesday afternoon in Mr McKenzie's music room. After months of unsuccessful attempts to cover the most basic tunes it was agreed that we would have a stab at writing our own songs. The first song written was aptly named 'Wednesday Afternoon'. Surprisingly, it nearly sounded like music. Writing that song was the kick-start we needed. From that point on, learning how to play and write our own songs, both together and individually, became the main focus for the band. We argued endlessly over musical indiscretions – we still do. I believe history will show that our musical handicaps have turned out to be our strength. My bandmates are my greatest musical influences.

As a kid in the early '70s I was a huge glam rock fan. In 1973, Cozy Powell released one of my favourite 7-inch singles, 'Dance with the Devil'. It reached number three in the UK charts. It's a rare and beautiful thing for a drummer to have a chart hit. It would confirm what I already thought I knew: I wanted to be a rock drummer. If glam, pop and rock along with 'Dance with the Devil' were my drum wake-up call, then *Hunky Dory*, *Ziggy Stardust* and *Aladdin Sane* would become the most important musical benchmarks for me at that time. Released in 1971, 1972 and 1973 respectively, these albums were for me the perfect trilogy with a particular musical through-line. Classic songs and melodies, with one of the all-time great rock drummers, Woody Woodmansey, playing on all three: I had found my teenage musical nirvana. Even though I had no clue what Bowie was singing about.

The date 23rd September 1997 is etched on my mind. The day before the show we flew from Milan to Sarajevo. I sat in the cockpit during the flight. Everything was fine as we flew through Italian airspace. As we entered UN airspace things changed dramatically; air traffic control ordered us to leave the area immediately. We later discovered there had been a perceived threat from anti-aircraft fire. We eventually landed to the unbelievable sight of hundreds of Stabilization Force (SFOR) peacekeepers – including Irish soldiers – waving and cheering our successful landing. Our audience was diverse, made up of music fans from all over the region. Some had come by train – the first time trains had run to the city since the beginning of the conflict. The SFOR was well represented at the show, taking up one whole side of the stadium. During the opening songs, Bono started having problems with his throat. He eventually had to stop singing. That's when the real magic began. Bono conducted the audience as they sang every song for the rest of the set. The show was a powerful and humbling experience. I was conscious throughout that Koševo Stadium, where we played, had been used as a morgue during the war and newly dug children's graves surrounded us. I was invited to walk through the streets of Sarajevo with some local residents who had lived through the siege. They were anxious to tell their stories and show me the massacre sites marked with the 'Sarajevo Rose', where red resin was used to fill in the mortar shell scars as a memorial to those who were killed. I was profoundly moved by my time in Sarajevo. I never want to forget.

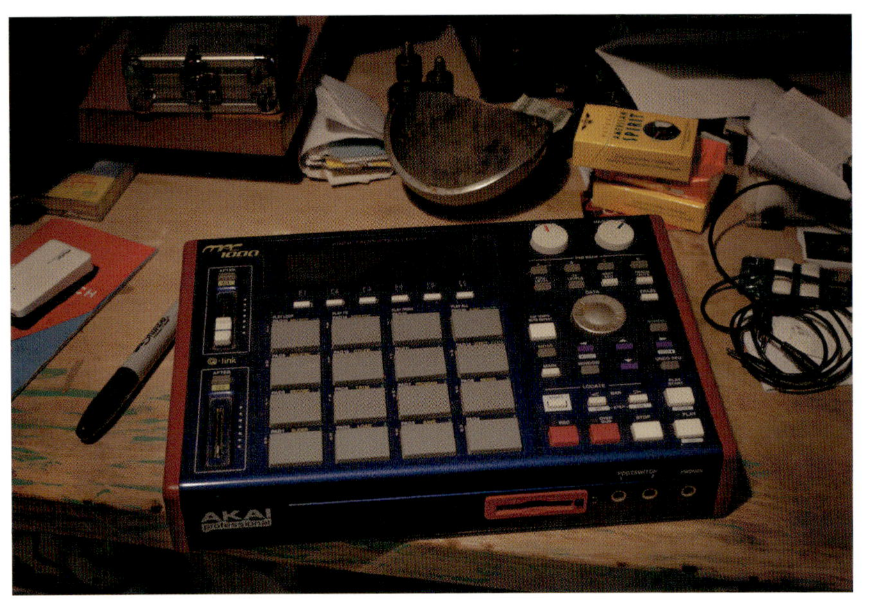

RYAN SAWYER

Cass McCombs / Charles Gayle / Mike Wexler / Susan Alcorn / Thurston Moore / Gang Gang Dance / Matana Roberts. Photographed at home, New York

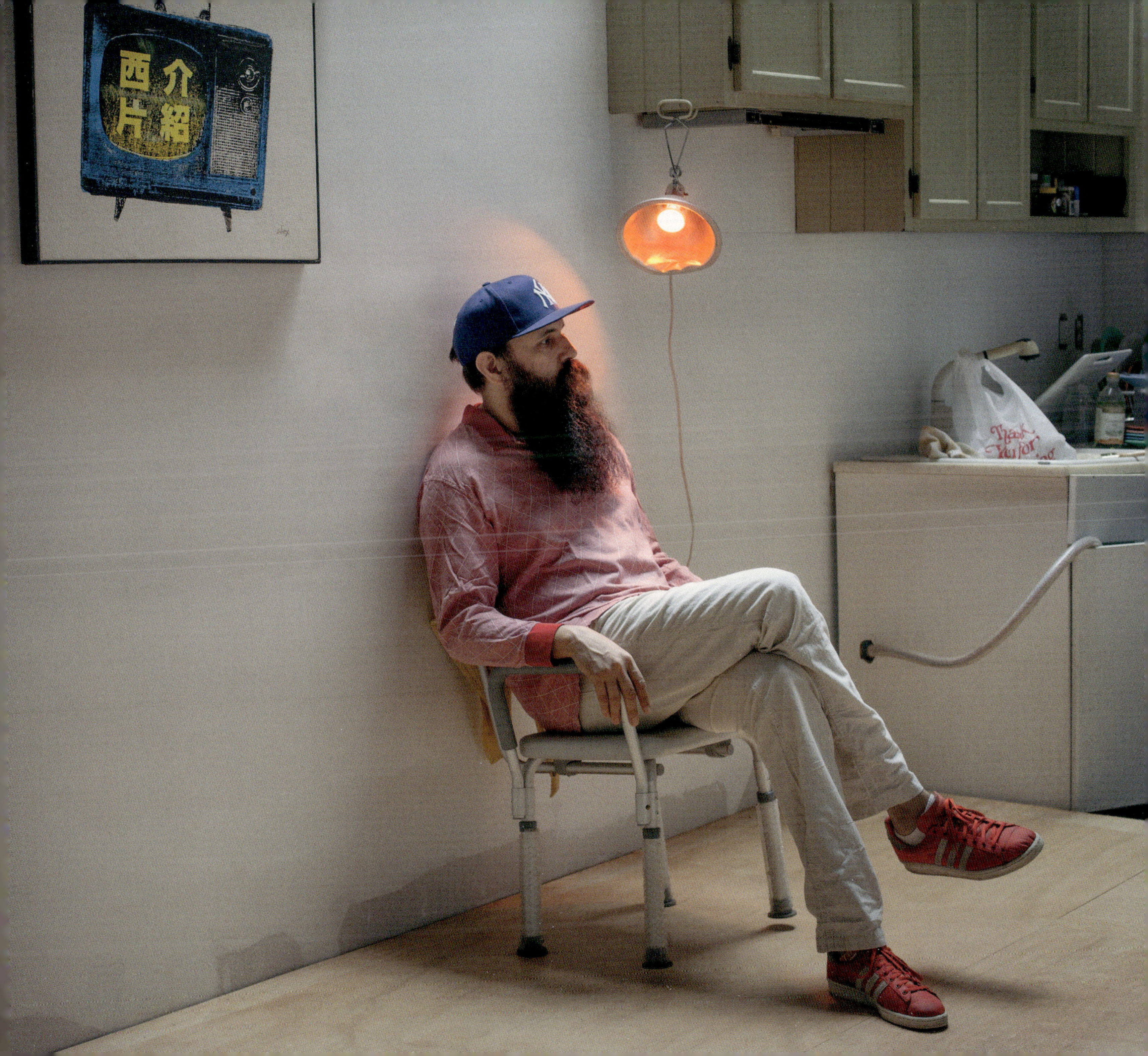
介紹西片

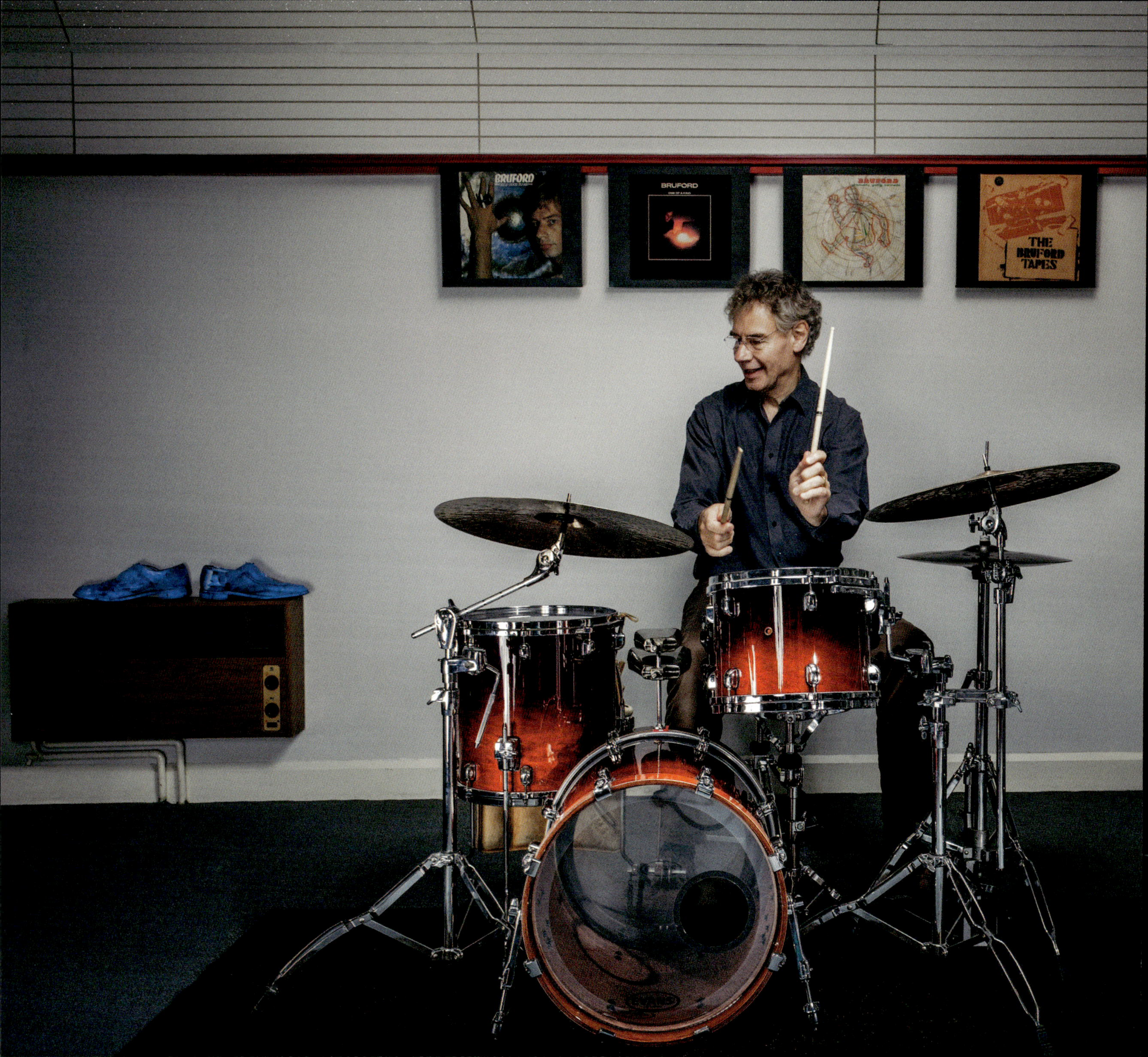
BRUFORD
BRUFORD
BRUFORD
THE BRUFORD TAPES

BILL BRUFORD

Yes / King Crimson / U.K. / Bruford / Bill Bruford's Earthworks / Pete Roth Trio
Photographed at home in the UK

My sister gave me a pair of brushes of her boyfriend's when I was about twelve, with instructions to swish them around on the back of a thick card album sleeve. It sounded just like the real thing. A pair of sticks followed, and then a red sparkle drum kit when I was about thirteen. The first time I played in public was with a bar band in a Swiss hotel on vacation, aged fourteen. Everyone loved it. And that was the beginning of the end.

I was influenced by almost anyone who crossed my record player. Miles Davis for economy and style; David Bowie because he was always moving and would never quite let his audience catch up. Among the drummers, I was transfixed by jazz. The BBC was televising jazz regularly on Saturday night prime-time TV, so those programmes were my first encounters with Art Blakey, Sonny Stitt, Lee Morgan, Freddie Hubbard. It was a mystery: how come they didn't play any wrong notes?

I used to practise upstairs in the loft and in my bedroom. Parental support was through gritted teeth, which gritted even more with the arrival of an anonymous note through the mailbox asking me to cease and desist. My parents had never really met a professional musician, so they didn't know what that was, or what it meant. Like all parents, they were nervous about something they didn't know anything about. They kept saying, 'But what will you do when you're 25?' Then when I got to 25, they'd shift to, 'But what will you do when you're 30?' and so on. If they were still alive, they'd still be asking me how I earned a living. I'm not sure myself, come to think of it.

GREG SAUNIER

Deerhoof. Photographed at home, New York

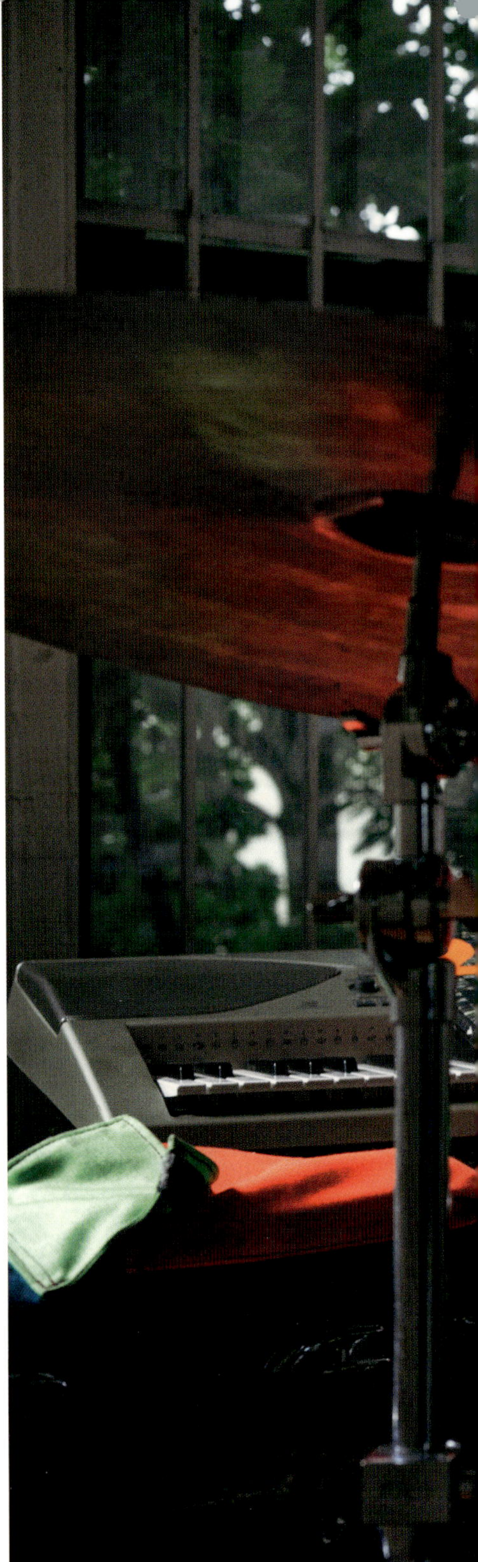

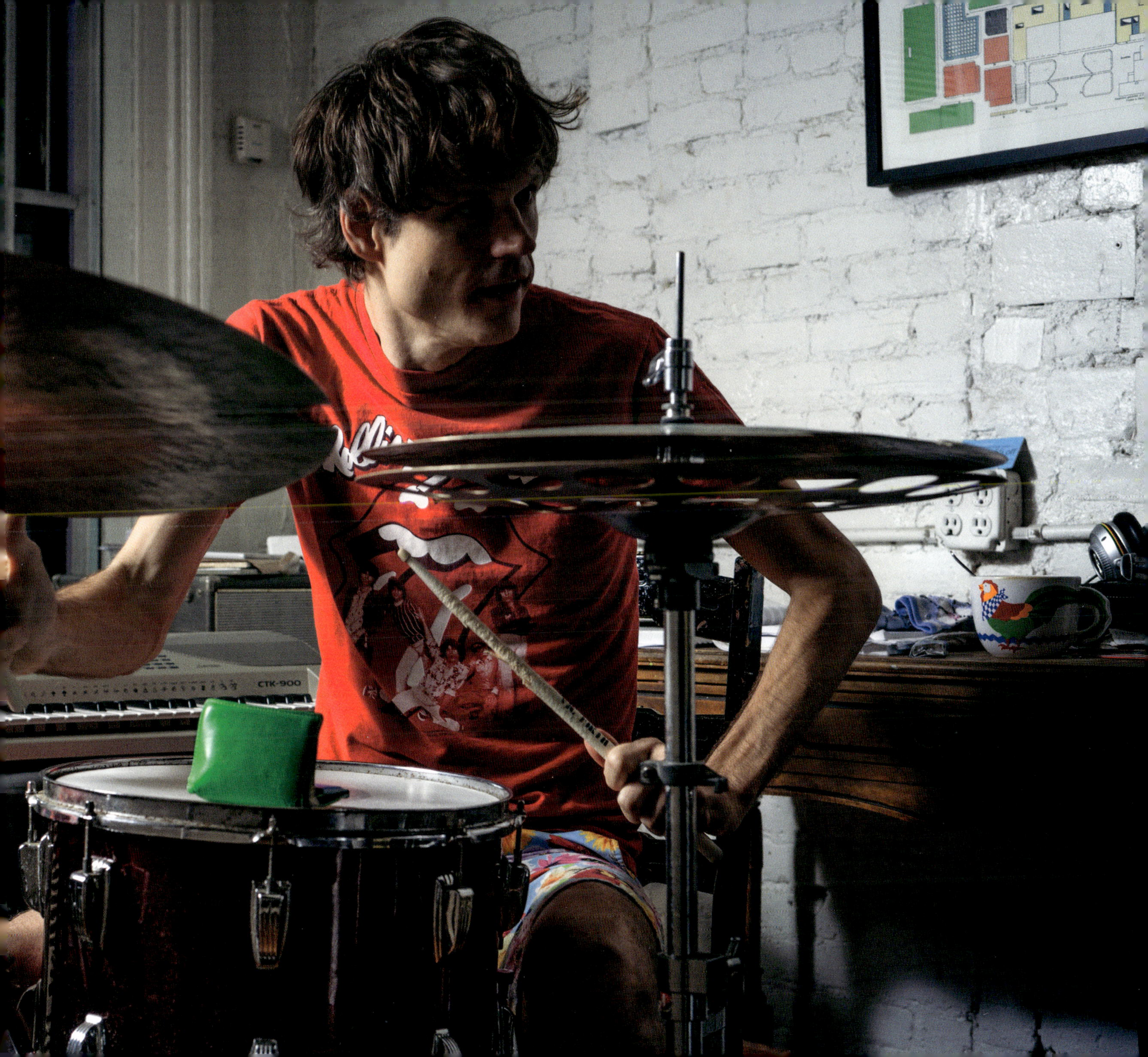
CTK-900

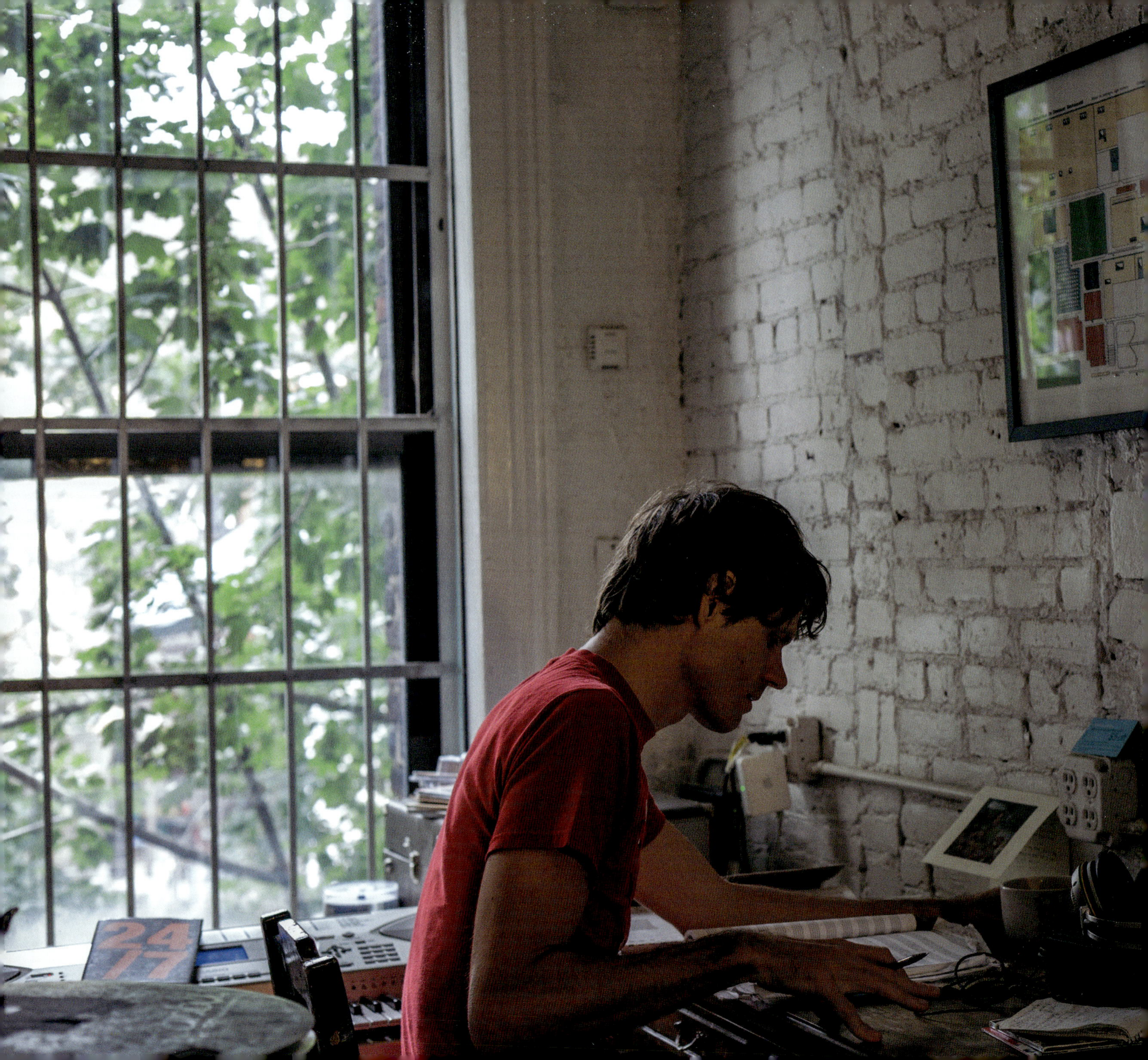
24
17

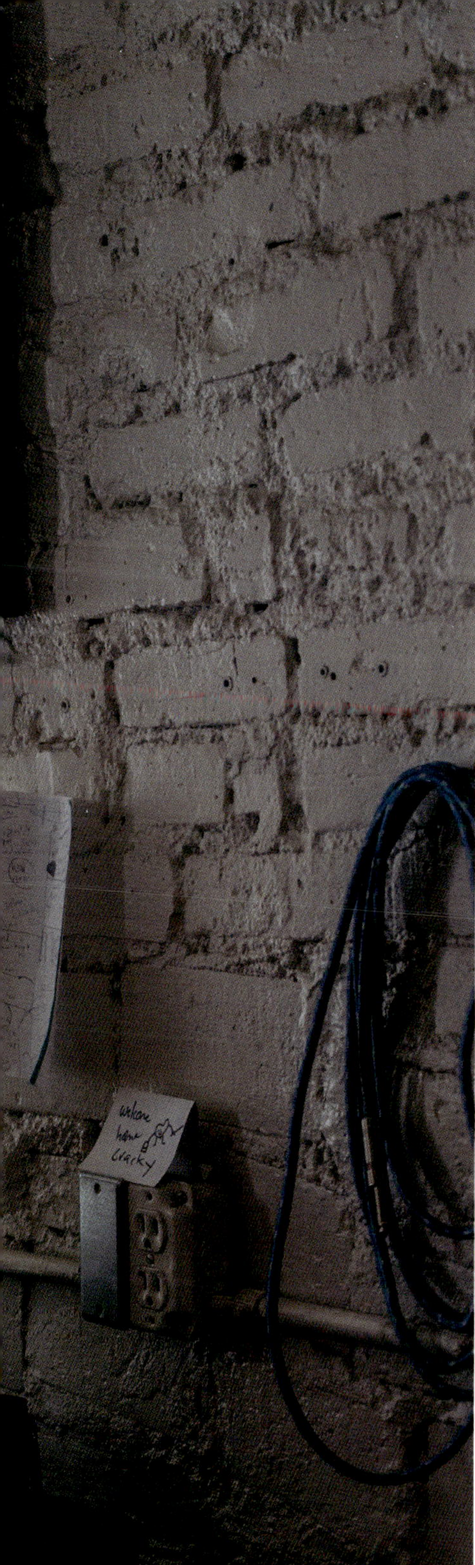

I was horrified one time reading an article where they'd done a study on how much people hear music in their head. For the experiment they would just call people at random points during the week and ask, 'Is any music in your head?' They found normal people maybe had music in their head 20 per cent of the time, something like that. For musicians it's up to 50 per cent of the time. I was like, where's the insane asylum? I've got music in my head 100 per cent of the time. I can't get rid of it.

Something that particularly delights and inspires me about other drummers or musicians is when they're not afraid to fuck up. They're willing to do so; in fact, they dare themselves to, they goad themselves and the people they're playing with and say, 'I'm about to screw you up. Try this!' It's fun to tease each other when you're playing. It's fun to tease yourself and to set yourself up to fall by attempting some really insane fill. There's no way you can crash and burn by the end of it in front of everybody, really loudly, or it's going to be obvious. That creation of tension is something I respond to a lot with drummers, rather than the drummers who make it safe for everybody – which I do think is a nice thing. A common goal of drummers is to make everyone else relax.

Steve Jordan is a really cool example because he's someone who obviously does a great many sessions and must be professional; he mustn't cause other people to screw up. He needs to be reliable, but he wouldn't be Steve Jordan if he didn't have a certain desire to tickle the people he's playing with and prod them a little bit, to inspire them to come up with things that they wouldn't have come up with if he hadn't been there. All those Keith Richards records: on paper it's like a day-one-drum-lesson rock beat, the beat he's playing, but he plays it with this certain flair. We're talking about microscopic things between each hi-hat hit, just a certain ever-so-microscopic unevenness between things; not every note hit is exactly the same volume and that gives it something that feels like it's pushing you. Even as he's got his sunglasses on and he looks perfectly relaxed and he's Mr Cool. At the same time you know that underlying it, he's trying to make you do something – the other musicians, the listeners – trying to make you dance. He's trying to make you not be able to sit perfectly still and feel calm. It has to do with a willingness to take a risk and to potentially cause everything to fall apart and screw up. Even someone as reliable and professional as Steve Jordan has a bit of that devil inside him that wants to take a boring, mundane room or situation and give it some spark, give it some life and wake everybody up and make them smile. I think that's maybe what it is for me.

I've had many nine-to-five jobs, like most people have, where you're in a cubicle doing data entry. There's not a lot of room there either to express yourself or express your existence as an animal or a human on this earth or to imagine things or to be creative in any way. I respect musicians who understand the privilege that music is: it's the chance to go nuts and to really reach for things that day-to-day life often prevents you from being able to do.

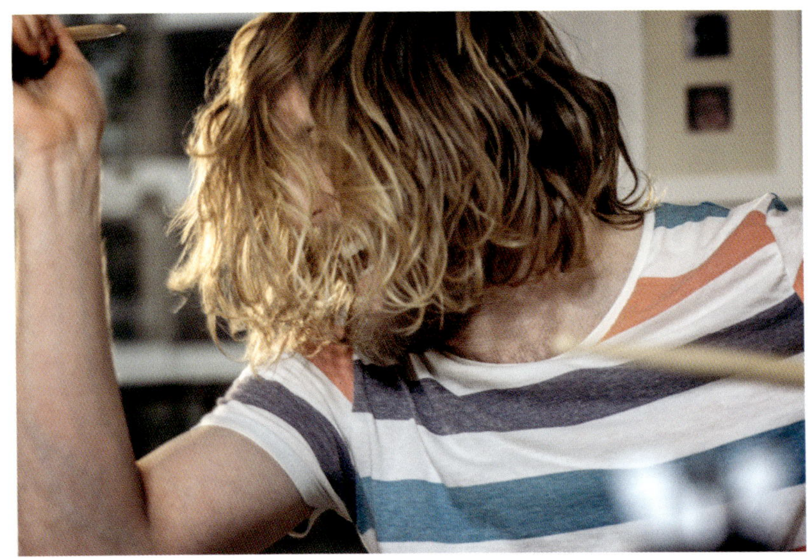
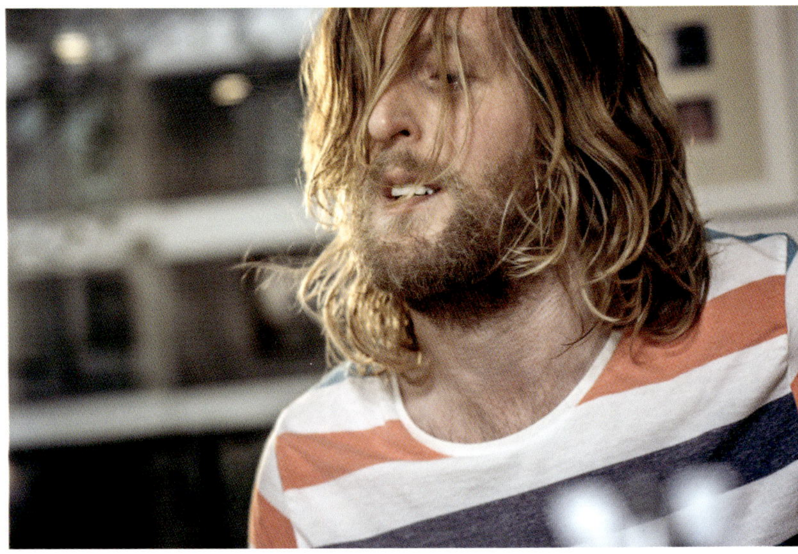
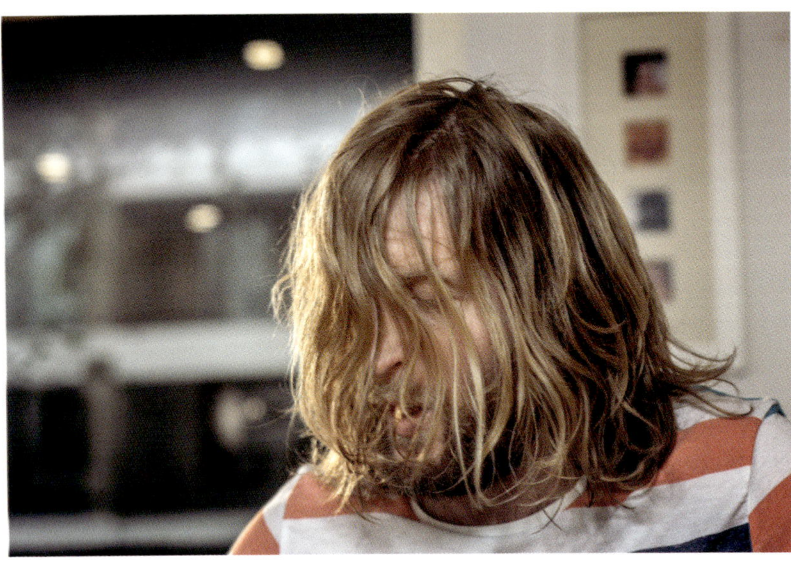
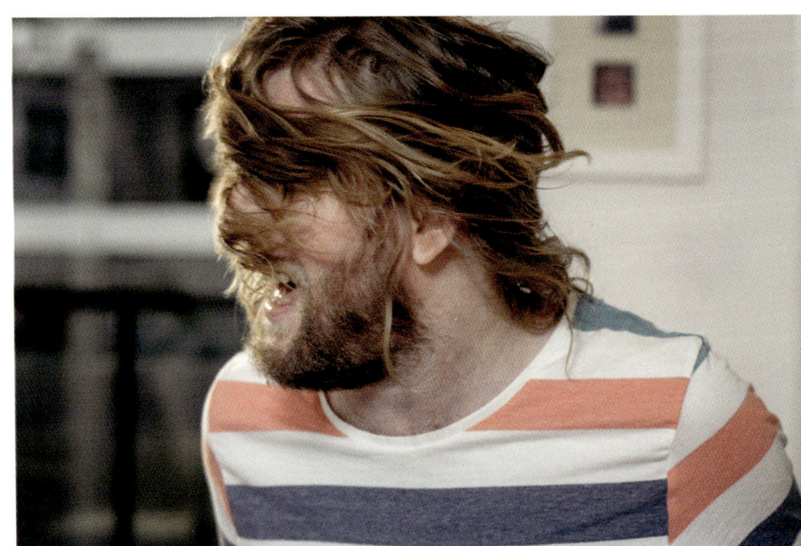

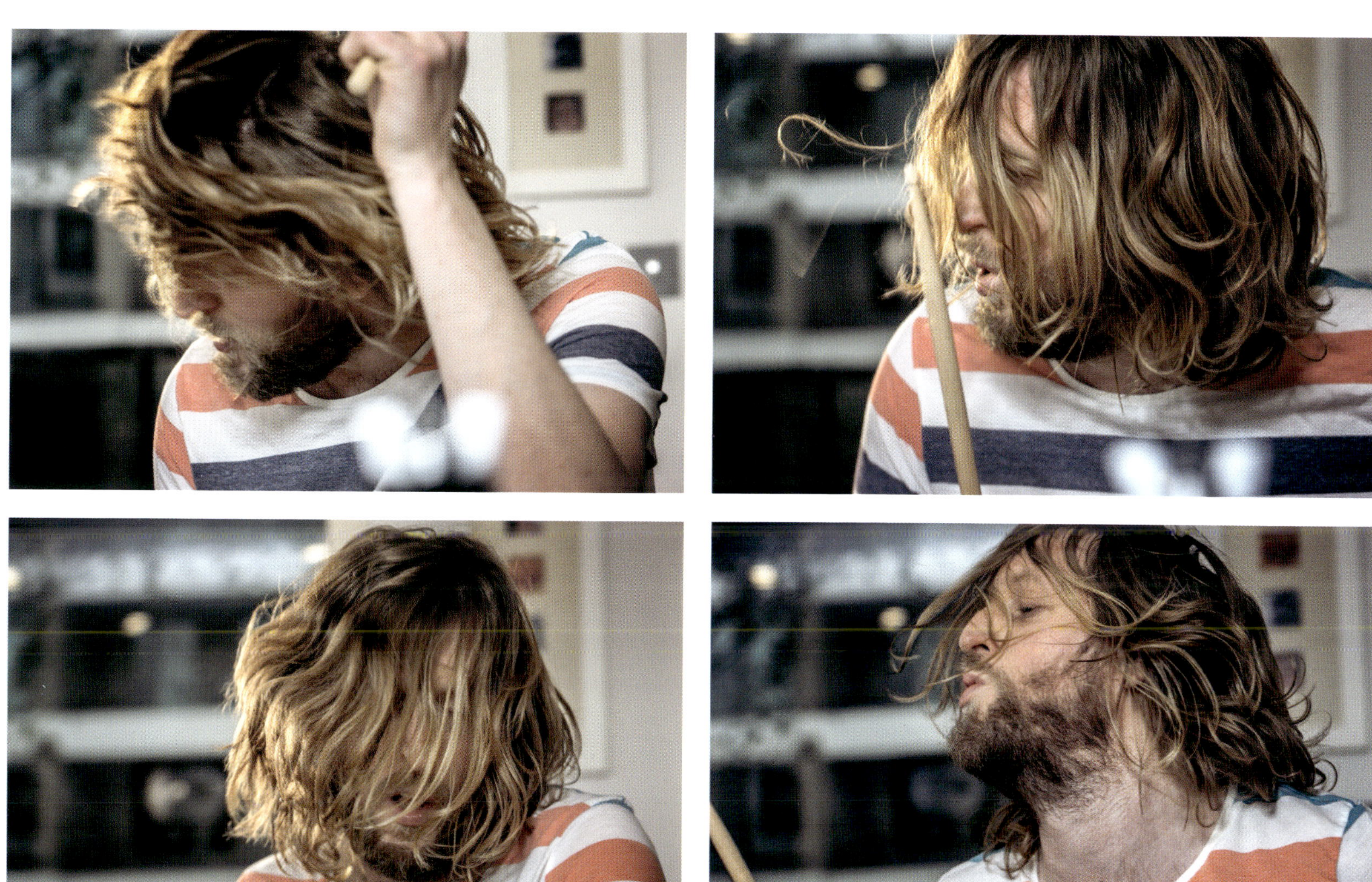

ANDY BURROWS

Razorlight / We Are Scientists / Tom Odell / Mark Ronson. Photographed at home in the UK

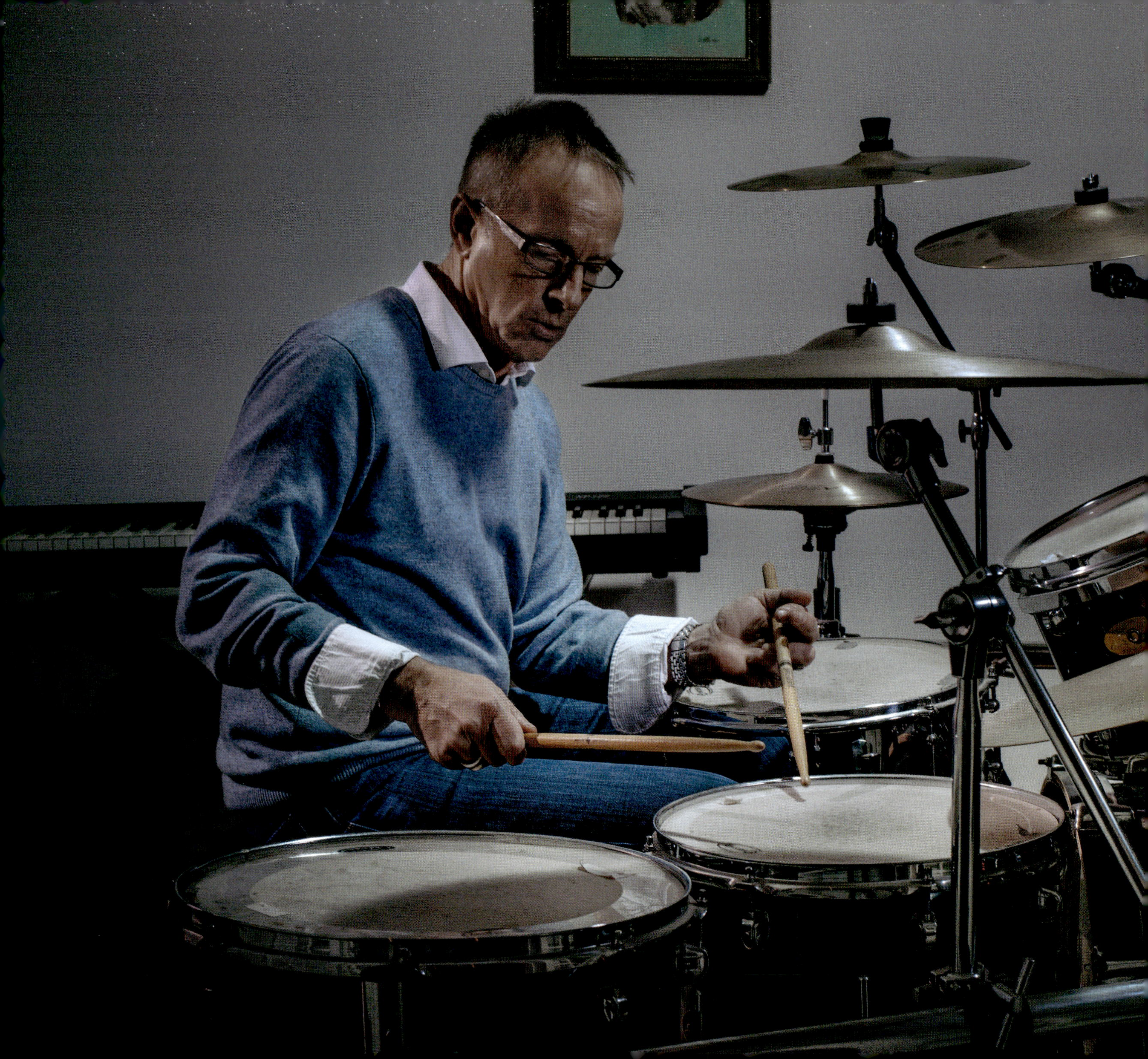

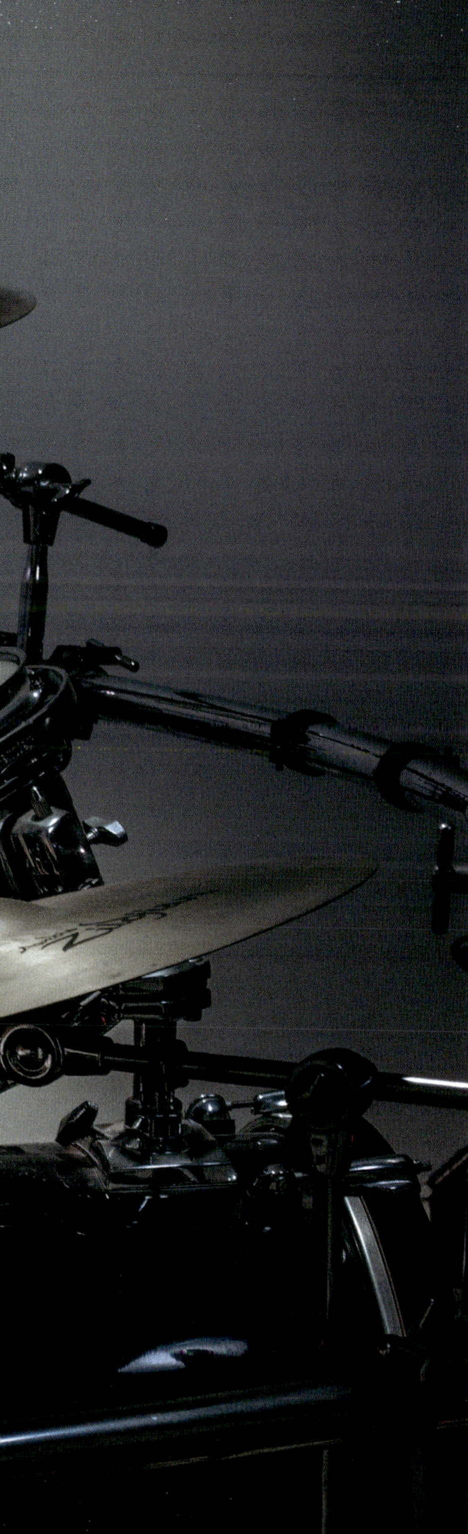

TOPPER HEADON

The Clash. Photographed at home in the UK

When we were on the road we'd play four or five shows without a break. You don't get tired, because you're young and you're doing something you love. But in the end I think we were exhausted. I was just up seeing Mick and Paul a few months ago and we were saying how we didn't realize at the time how much it was the chemistry of the four of us that was special in The Clash. You don't realize that, and you're arguing and bickering because you're also kids, and you're spoiled and you've got all these outside influences. We were saying it's been really strange because what we're known for today happened thirty years ago, and it still seems to get bigger all the time, to new generations. We got the Ivor Novello Award for Outstanding Contribution and we've never been able to follow it. Mick has tried with Big Audio Dynamite and with Carbon/Silicon, but you can't follow The Clash. Last time I saw Joe, before he died, he was playing at the Shepherd's Bush Empire, and I went backstage to see him and he was really disheartened because when he was announcing a new song there was polite applause, but as soon as he did anything by The Clash the place went mad ... he could never follow it. Mick and I could never follow it. We all kind of tried in various different ways, but we didn't realize that the four of us were greater than the individual parts.

When I got into The Clash it was a punk band, but because I could bring all the funk stuff in, and Mick was a brilliant songwriter and he'd go off and write, it just ... it didn't become a punk band, did it. We had the punk ideals, but by the time we did *London Calling* it wasn't punk rock music anymore.

I really want to get across what a genius Mick was to put that band together. Mick had got me in for London SS; he knew me already. I left and joined a soul band. But when he got Paul on board, and then him and Paul went out and got Joe, Mick remembered me and we met up in the Rainbow [Theatre, Finsbury Park]. I can remember him saying, 'I want you to come and audition.' And, remembering what it used to be like, I said, 'Oh, yeah, all right, I'll be down tomorrow.' I didn't turn up. And then he phoned me up again, and I still didn't turn up, so he really hassled me. When I went down there I thought they looked fantastic. They had this feel. They were very threatening and tight, incredibly powerful, but musicianship-wise it wasn't really my cup of tea. But I joined the band and something happened, I was the final bit of the jigsaw.

Not that I'm not taking any responsibility for it. But until I joined The Clash, I wasn't a great drummer. I was okay. I was a good drummer, but I wasn't powerful. When I joined The Clash I had to relearn my whole style, playing as loud and as hard as I could. It changed me from being an okay drummer into a great drummer. It was just the chemistry. I had to relearn all that and do it really loud and powerful to drive the band. It's like Joe said, and it is true: a band is only as good as its drummer. Often, with The Clash, offstage I found myself a bit superfluous, because it was about the image and about the whole thing – the politics, which Joe was in charge of, and the look, where Paul was the best-looking one. We all tried to look as good as him. But onstage, that's when I came into my own, because I had to hold it together. They'd all go, 'Where the fuck are we?', and I'd show them.

I loved it; it was a completely mad set-up. We didn't have a proper manager – we had a manager who was a used car salesman – we had roadies ... my drum roadie had never drum roadied before. The tour manager, Johnny Green, had never toured. It was chaos the whole time but it was great fun. What people often don't realize is that the first time we went to the States we sold out the New York Palladium. Most bands did CBGB, or little clubs or whatever. So that was our first gig there, sold out at the New York Palladium.

STEVE GADD

James Taylor / Eric Clapton / Paul Simon / Chick Corea. Photographed at home, Arizona

One afternoon when we were working in Rochester, Chick Corea played a new set of drums I'd just got. How he approached playing answered a lot of questions I couldn't answer about drummers I loved whom I had heard but hadn't seen. It made sense of what Tony Williams was doing, Jack DeJohnette, Elvin Jones – and you know, studying them, listening, slowing the record down so I could figure out what they were doing.

When we went to play the music that night in the club, everything sort of went to another level. I've never experienced anything like that, that much of a transition. When I saw Chick, how free and how without rules he sat behind the drums and approached it, it just opened up a whole different vocabulary for me. When we played, the music evolved overnight.

What inspires me is wanting to share with other people how good music makes me feel. It's nice if you can communicate that to someone. If it's really exciting and intense on the bandstand, it's great when you can look out and the people are feeling the same thing. Everybody is having a good time and it doesn't make any difference where they're from or what they look like. If the feeling gets you, then you're all sharing the same thing. In clubs it's one thing. In big arenas that back-and-forth thing still happens, it's just on a different level. But it's always special when you can feel that energy and love coming back.

In the 1970s New York was unbelievable. The energy, the city was great. You could still afford to be there. You could have your own apartment; you didn't have to have five guys as roommates. There was a lot of work, a lot of advertising, jingles, a lot of record dates. Broadway was always going on – that's always been a thing – but there were clubs too, a lot of clubs where you could play.

The club that meant a lot to me in the '70s was Mikell's. That was on 97th and Columbus. We played there with Stuff, a band of guys who were studio musicians. We had a little group and we went and played the club at night just because we liked playing together. You'd start at ten in the morning and do recording all day up till ten at night, and then go play at Mikell's. It was like a party. It was non-stop. Back in the '70s no one thought that drugs were ever going to be a problem – we all found out different later on. I was getting called to do work with people who were my idols; if it was a choice to try and stay awake or go to sleep, I'd want to stay up and play music. And part of my life was falling apart. I started using so I could work and then at some point I was working to use, and I didn't even know what had changed. It was a subtle change.

Music was the only thing I could get lost in and still feel like I was able to give something good to somebody because, in a lot of other areas in my life, I wasn't able to keep it together. I held on to music for dear life because that's the only thing that made me feel that I was still connected.

I have a close bond with guys I met in those years who are still alive, even if I don't talk to them for years at a time. When we connect it's like the last time I saw them was yesterday. They were good times, the whole conglomeration of different, great music that I was involved with. I didn't think it was ever going to end. It was just like everything I touched in that period just went, just got out there. It was great. It was definitely being in the zone I think, because – and you don't realize it until it's passed – there was a lot of good stuff that came out of that period.

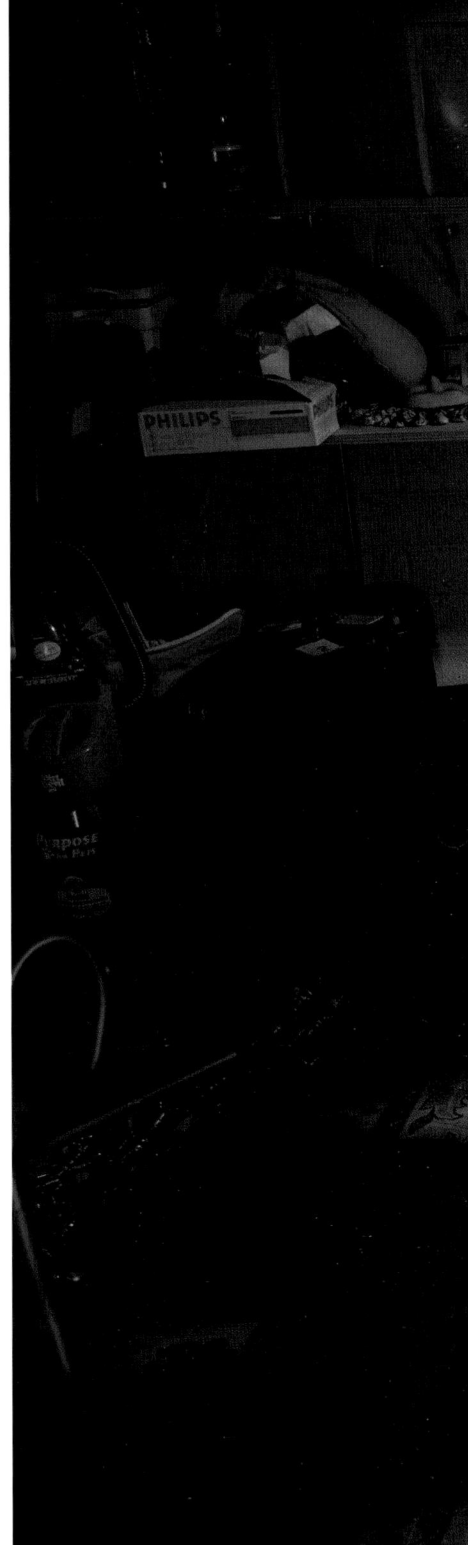

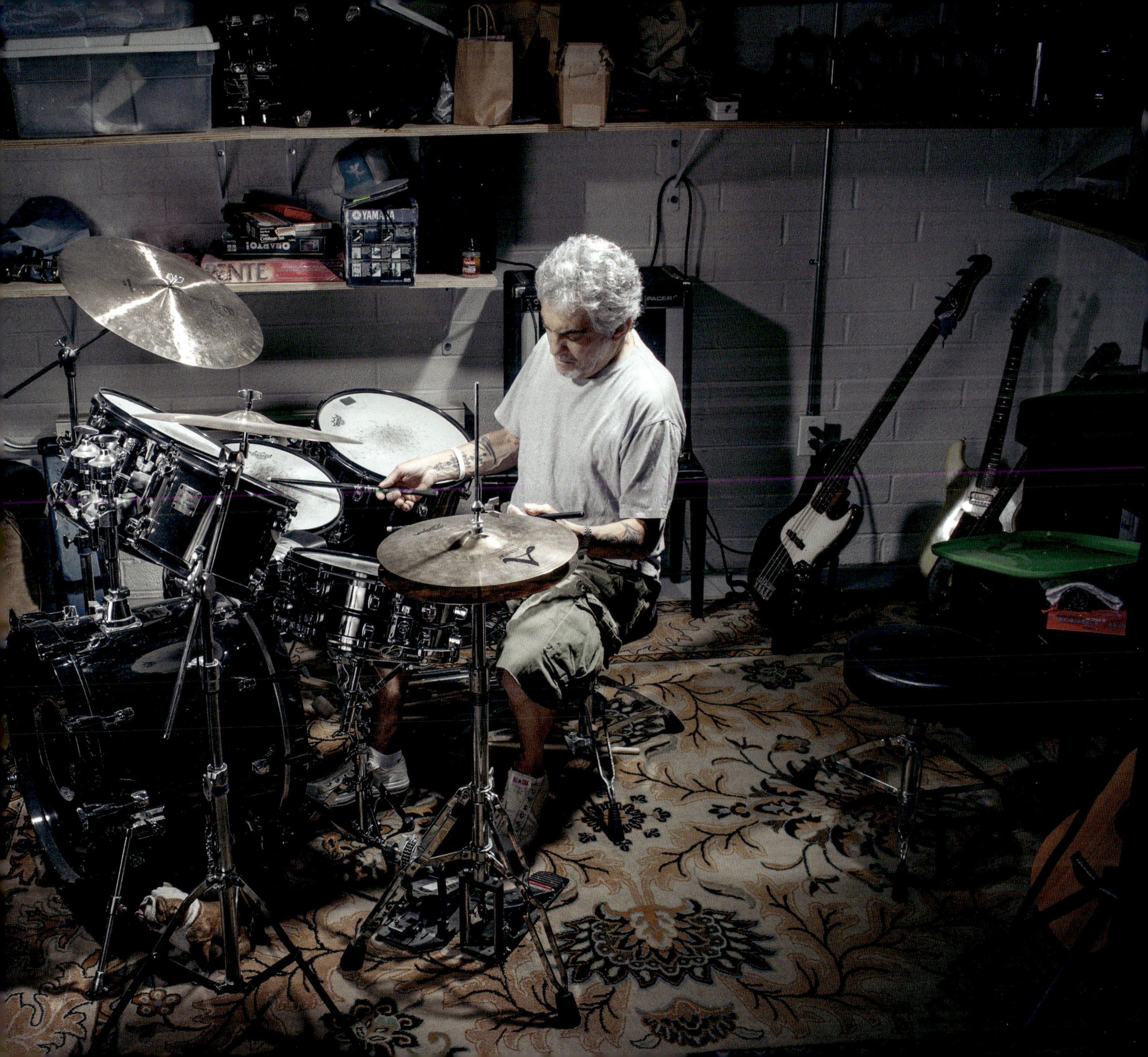
YAMAHA
PACER

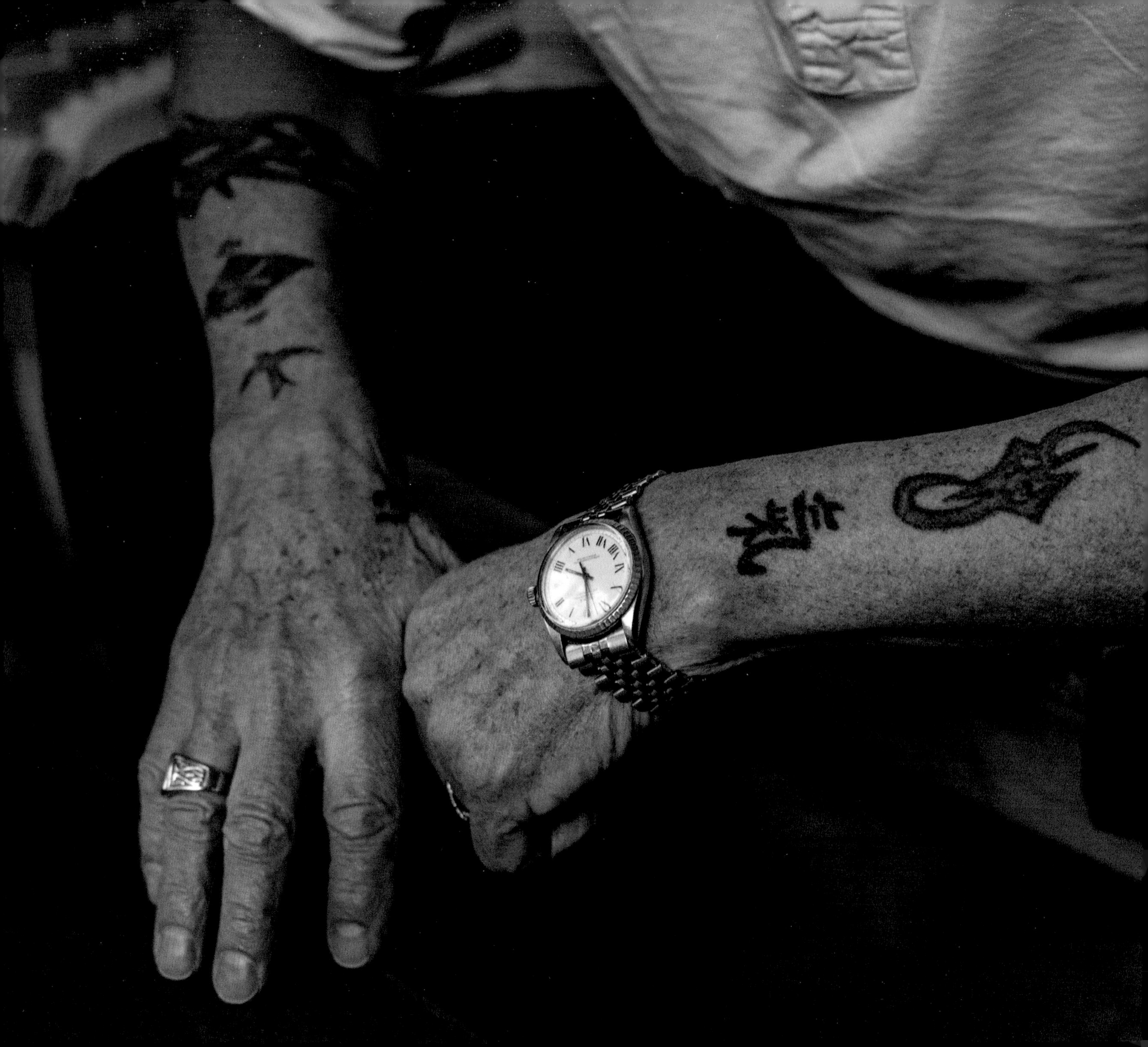

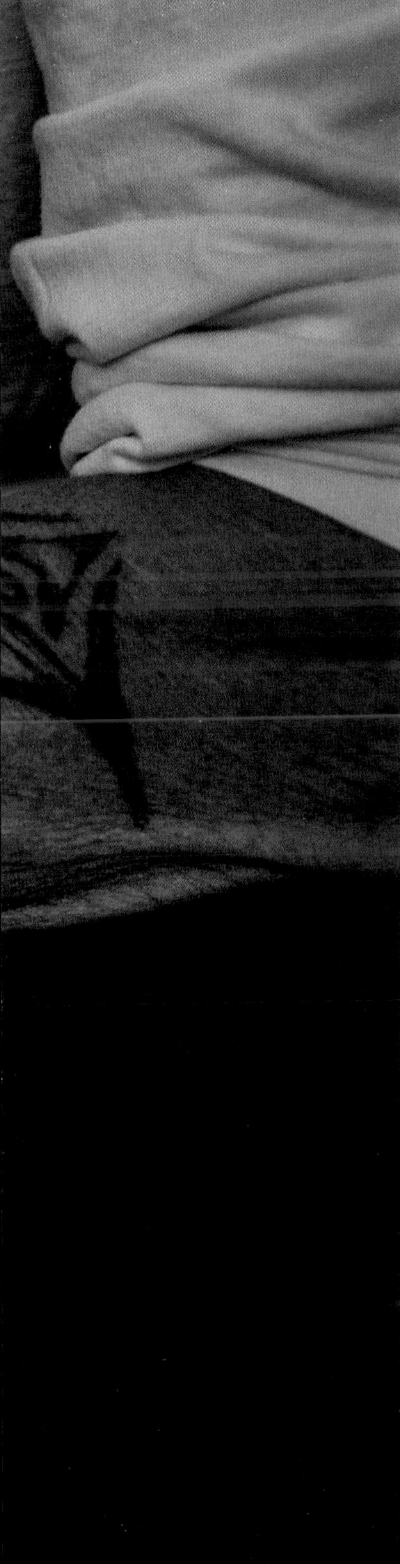

“I HELD ONTO MUSIC FOR DEAR LIFE BECAUSE THAT’S THE ONLY THING THAT MADE ME FEEL THAT I WAS STILL CONNECTED”

JOHN STANIER

Battles / Helmet / Tomahawk / The Mark of Cain. Photographed at the Battles studio, New York

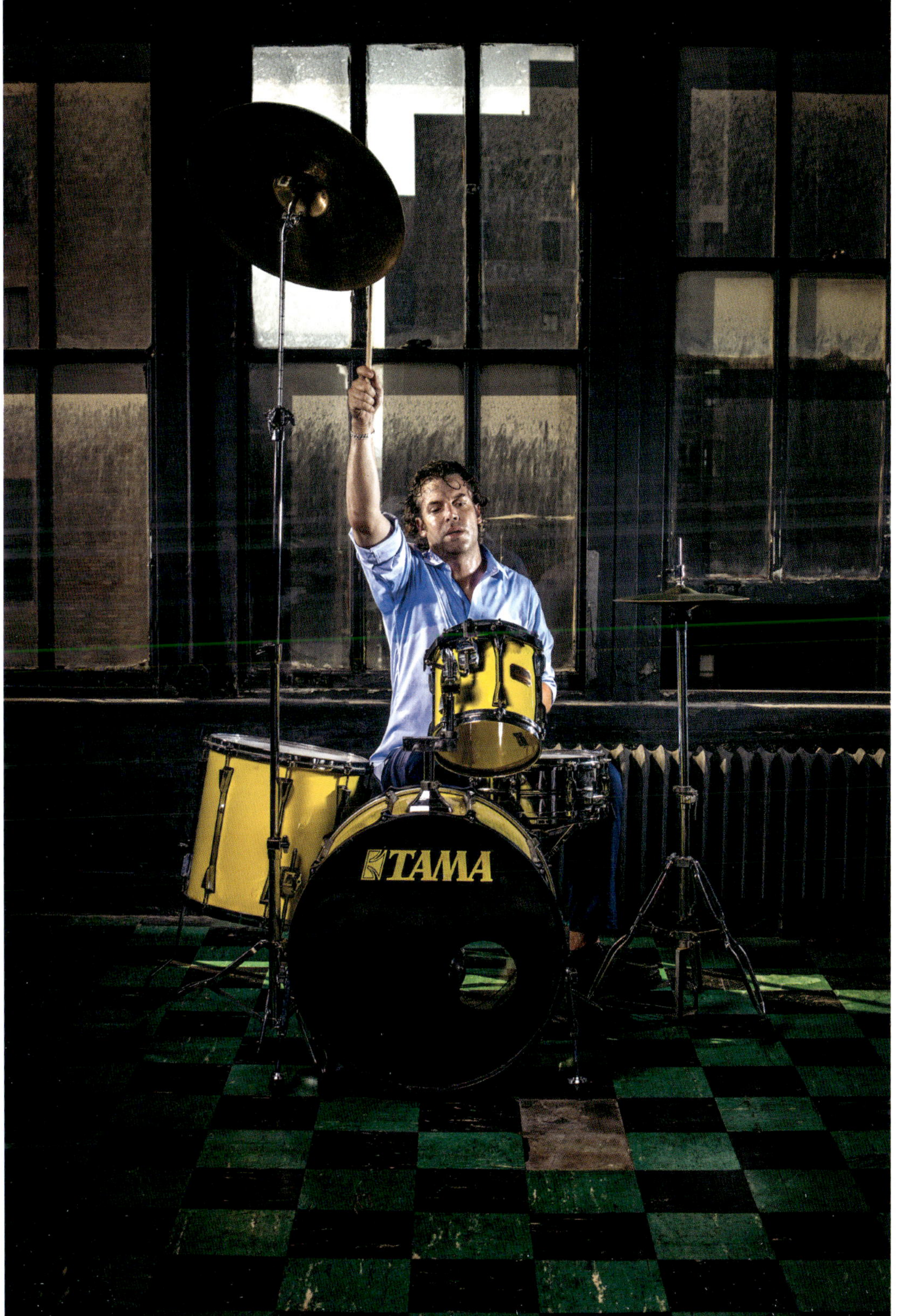
TAMA

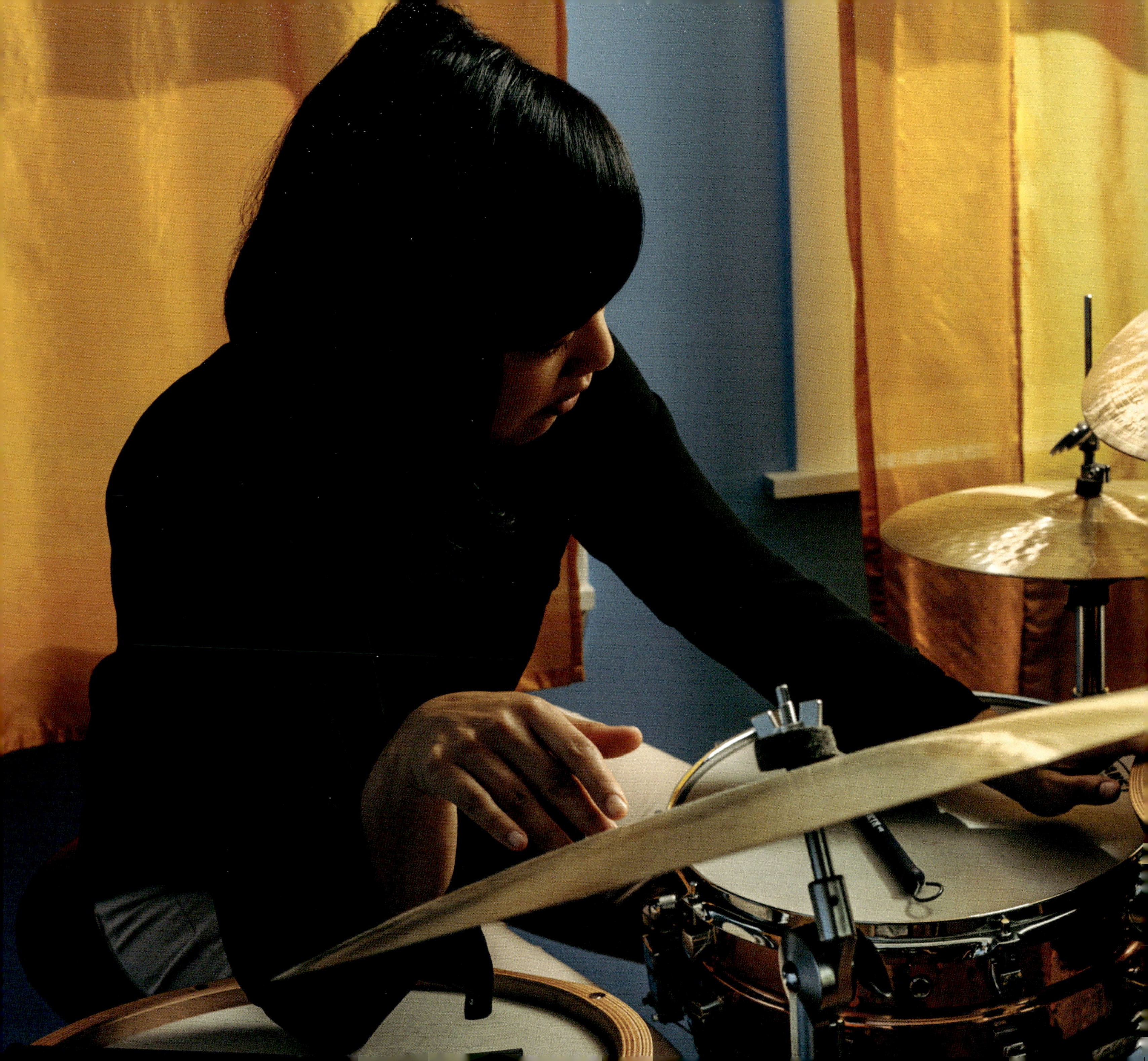

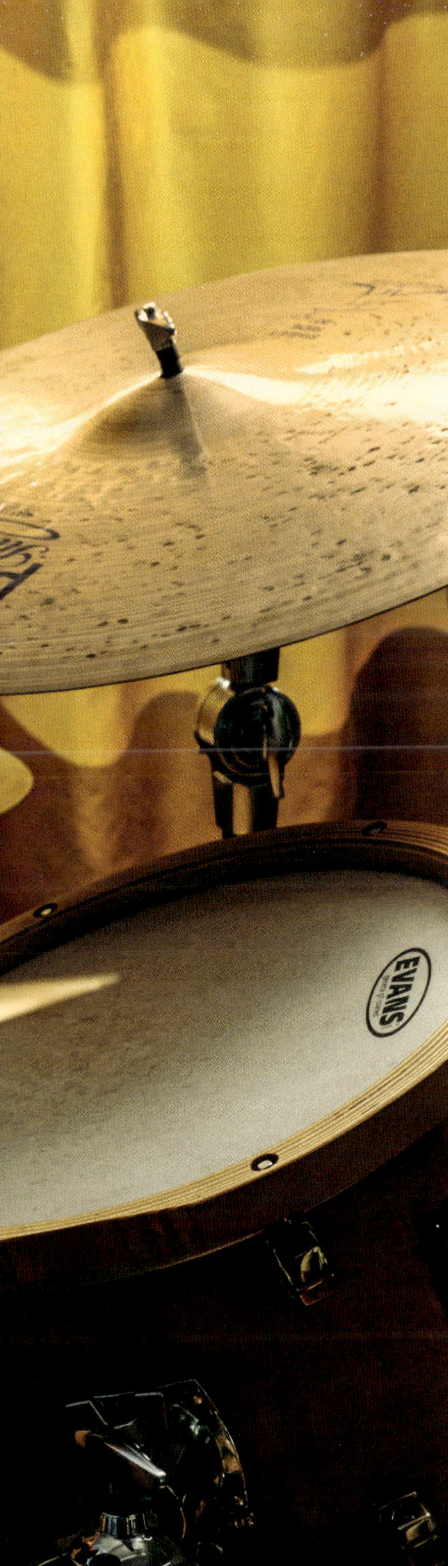

SUSIE IBARRA

Susie Ibarra Trio / Mephista / Electric Kulintang / Dave Douglas / Pauline Oliveros / Wadada Leo Smith
Photographed at home, New York

I've been very lucky to study with great teachers. I studied with Vernel Fournier. And I remember sitting at the back of the [Village] Vanguard with Andrew Cyrille and him telling me, 'If you study with me you'll study jazz and if you study with Milford Graves you'll study the drums.' And I said thank you; I had heard some recordings of Milford's, so I reached out to him. I was already playing professionally when I came to him and we sort of got connected in that way – he was teaching, I was studying drums. I also sat in on some of his herbology and martial arts classes and he started to play out live more at the time. I'm connected to the people I studied closely with and then, through me, my students are connected to that lineage; it's unspoken and powerful to be connected that way through music. I stepped into that lineage by studying one-on-one with certain master teachers, and then you pass it on.

I have a lot of friends who are traditional artists, although I'm not a traditional artist. I think there's a connection where you understand that there are certain things that come through certain groups, but I just tend to express it a little more abstractly. It all comes from a lot of traditions, if you unravel it and break it down. You can learn to play a large vocabulary but, at some point, you just have to put it to the side and create something, and have a personal voice. But there's also a mix of what influences you and whoever you're performing with and what you're playing in the moment. What's the purpose of the performance? Who are the people in the audience and what's the intention? I guess, aesthetically, I have always been a contemporary artist so I don't know how not to be, but for me it's all connected. How do you create new extended techniques? They might come from mistakes, which might be the most amazing moments, or it might just happen on that evening in that performance, or when you're playing or practising: something just moves differently. Feeling is very important. Really, my body is an instrument and then I sit down at the drums, and the drums may carry that out, but first it is in the body for me.

Time within music is flexible, yet there's a pocket. There is a pocket but there's a flexibility in how you feel that. It's always there no matter what kind of style you're playing. Rhythm is one of the most complex things to get, it's so innate. Rhythm and the drum – the rhythm voice – it's so old. But at the same time it's also one of the most complicated, hardest things to learn when you really go deep into it. Time wraps and envelops everything, even if it's subliminal or subtle.

I'm big into space. I'm very conscious not to overplay in an ensemble. It goes back to the idea of: what's needed to really make this music sound great in this moment and how do I contribute to that? Drums and the percussion family have such a big role of creating drama. I think to be able to listen you have to have space in the music; to be able to communicate, to be able to play music well together.

EARL YOUNG

The Trammps. Photographed at home, Pennsylvania

The difference between the Motown sound and the Philadelphia sound was that Motown musicians, they played in-house – I mean they played with just Motown. And Philadelphia's musicians, we played for anybody that came who wanted a drummer. So we played for The Spinners, Johnny Mathis. When B.B. King came into the studio he would sit right in front of me with his guitar and he would play; he'd say, 'Earl, put it right here.' He played and we jammed and the album came out good. So it was an honour for me to be able to play with B.B. King and Johnny Mathis and Wilson Pickett. Wilson Pickett's another soul singer who came into the studio and he likes to stomp; he's like, 'I want to feel that groove right here.'

Memphis sound is laid-back funk. Motown was great for their tambourines in the songs. The Philly sound, well, our sound was mostly like, I usually like a lot of skip beats, and that's the difference. Now the Motown sound was more of a four/four back, like 'Dancing in the Street'. Now Philadelphia, when I played 'The Love I Lost' and 'Bad Luck', that was more of what they call … we'd put a little tuxedo on it. That's basically the three different sounds.

The '70s was the bomb because every little club had a disco ball. Everybody put a disco ball in their room and said, okay, open disco night, bring The Trammps in. We worked everywhere. Some paid good, some didn't. But we worked every night. You had the platform shoes and you had the big lapel collar outfits with the bell-bottom pants and you were cool. And the thing about it, everybody came to the show was dressed. All the ladies were looking lovely, and I mean nobody went out if they didn't look good. People talk about 'disco sucks', but everybody in the club was dressed, no fights, everybody came to dance, just like *Saturday Night Fever*. People came to dance, they came to date, they wanted to have fun, they didn't get all sloppy drunk. So I loved that era. That was really a great time in my life that I enjoyed.

With The Trammps, everything we cut was about having fun, like 'Zing! Went the Strings of My Heart', 'I Love You' and 'That's Where the Happy People Go'. And 'Disco Inferno' was from *The Towering Inferno*, the movie with the party on the roof. Well that's where the song came from, 'burn baby burn', people getting loose getting down on the roof. That was when the real hit came. I was working in the club in Brooklyn, a home club called 2001 Odyssey. That's where they filmed *Saturday Night Fever* with John Travolta. Since we were working there all the time, they took our song, 'Disco Inferno' – they needed one more song to put in the movie. And I'm glad they did that because the album sold 25 million copies. The album went all over the world, so that meant it took us all over the world along with it.

We used to do a lot of dancing, so I used to do a lot of splits. We used to do a little thing where you jump off and run and split. I was working in Madrid, and I went and did a running split and the stage had splinters … the splinter, it was all in my butt, and they took me to the hospital there. I never forgot that and I stopped doing that move.

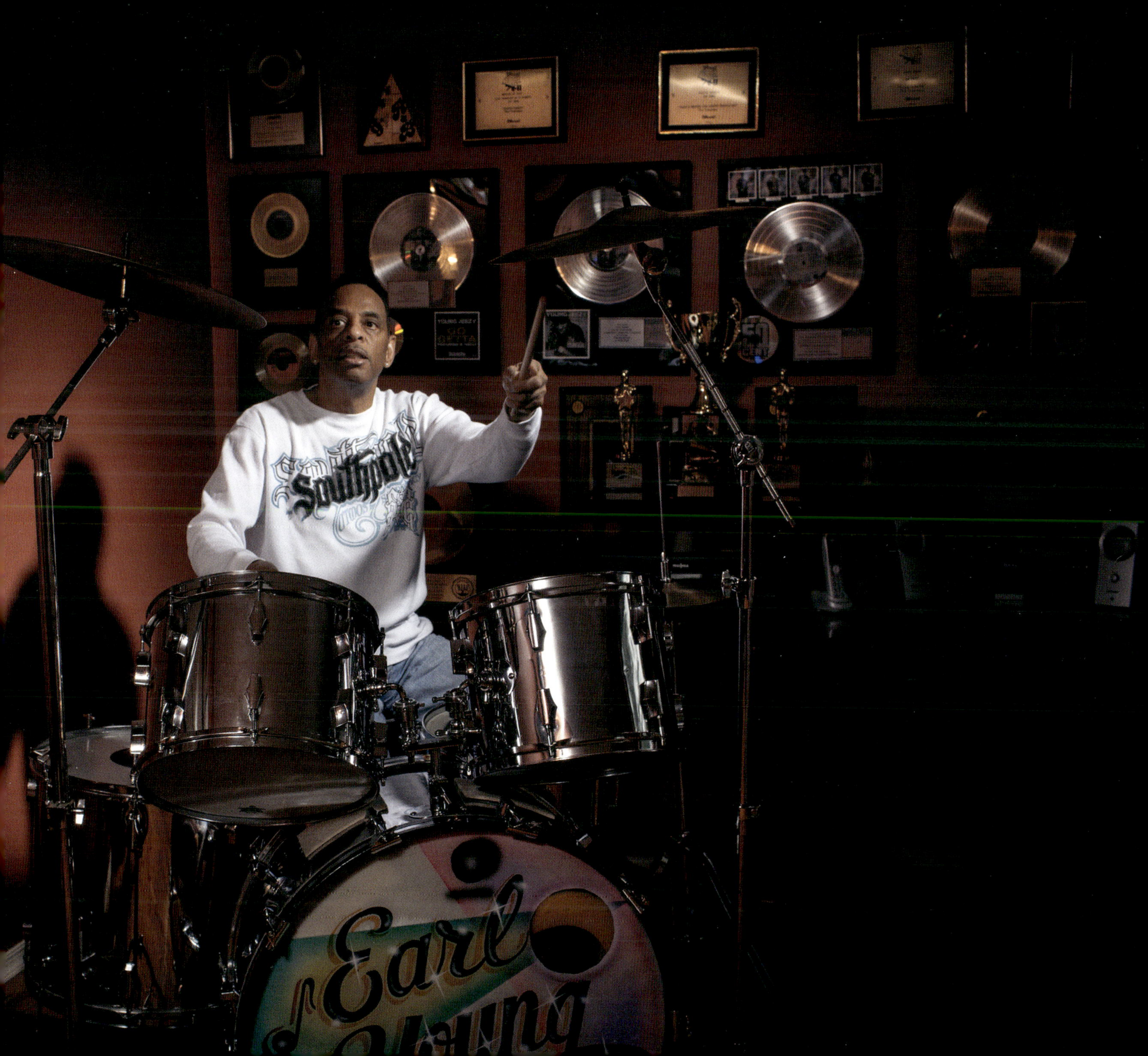
Southpole
Earl

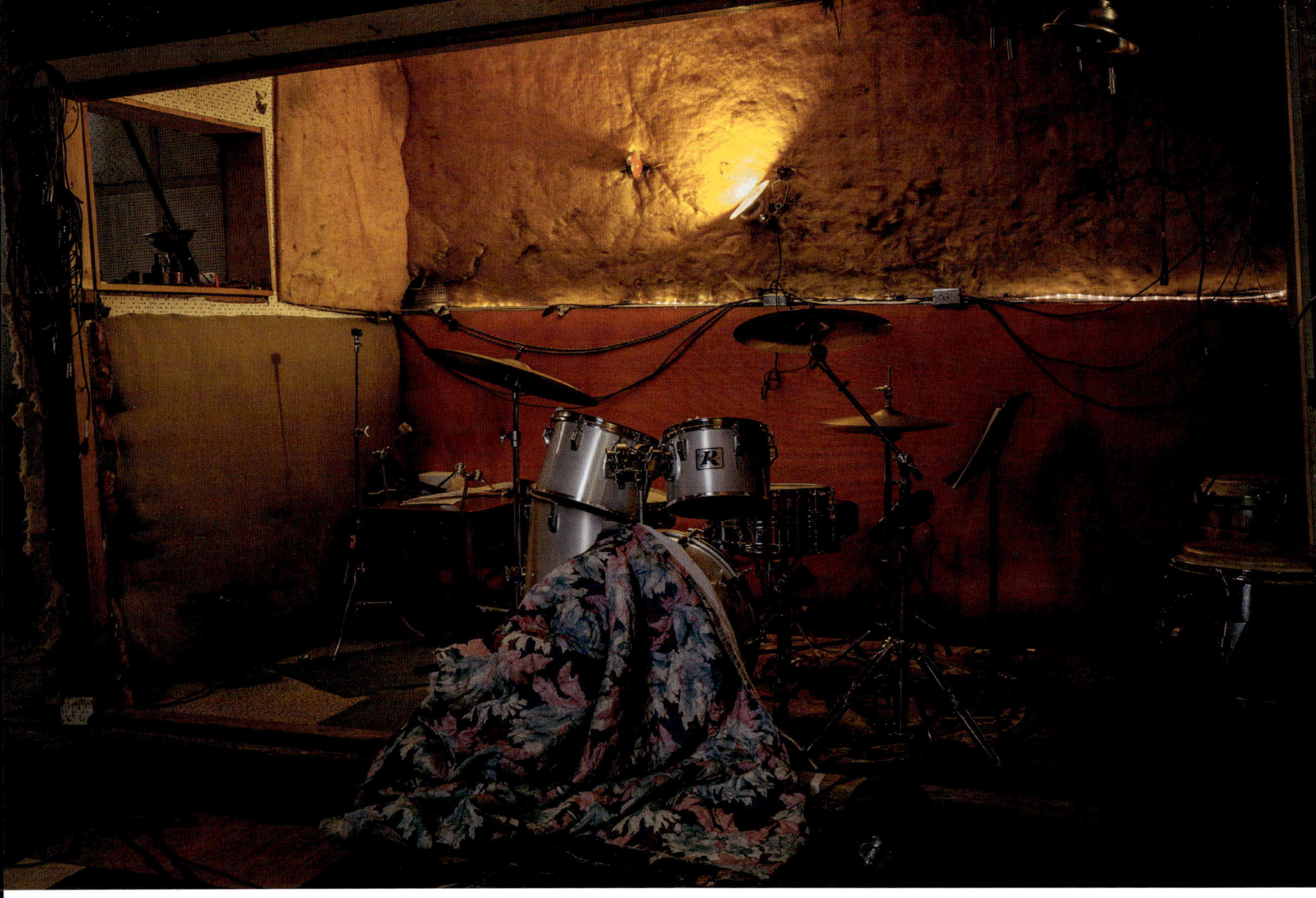

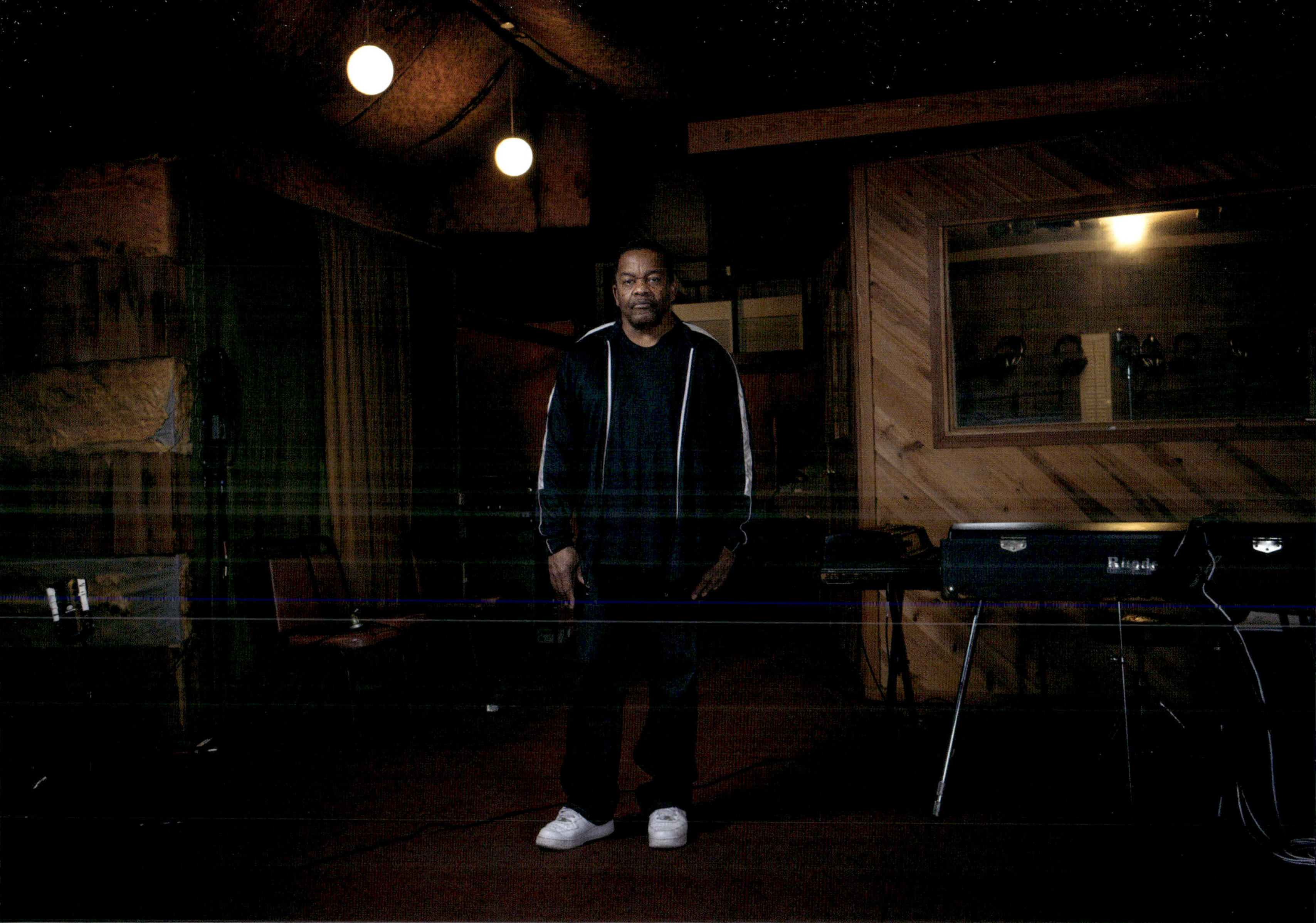

STEVE POTTS

Booker T. & the MG's / Gregg Allman Band / Paul Rodgers / Al Green / Neil Young

Photographed at Royal Studios, Tennessee

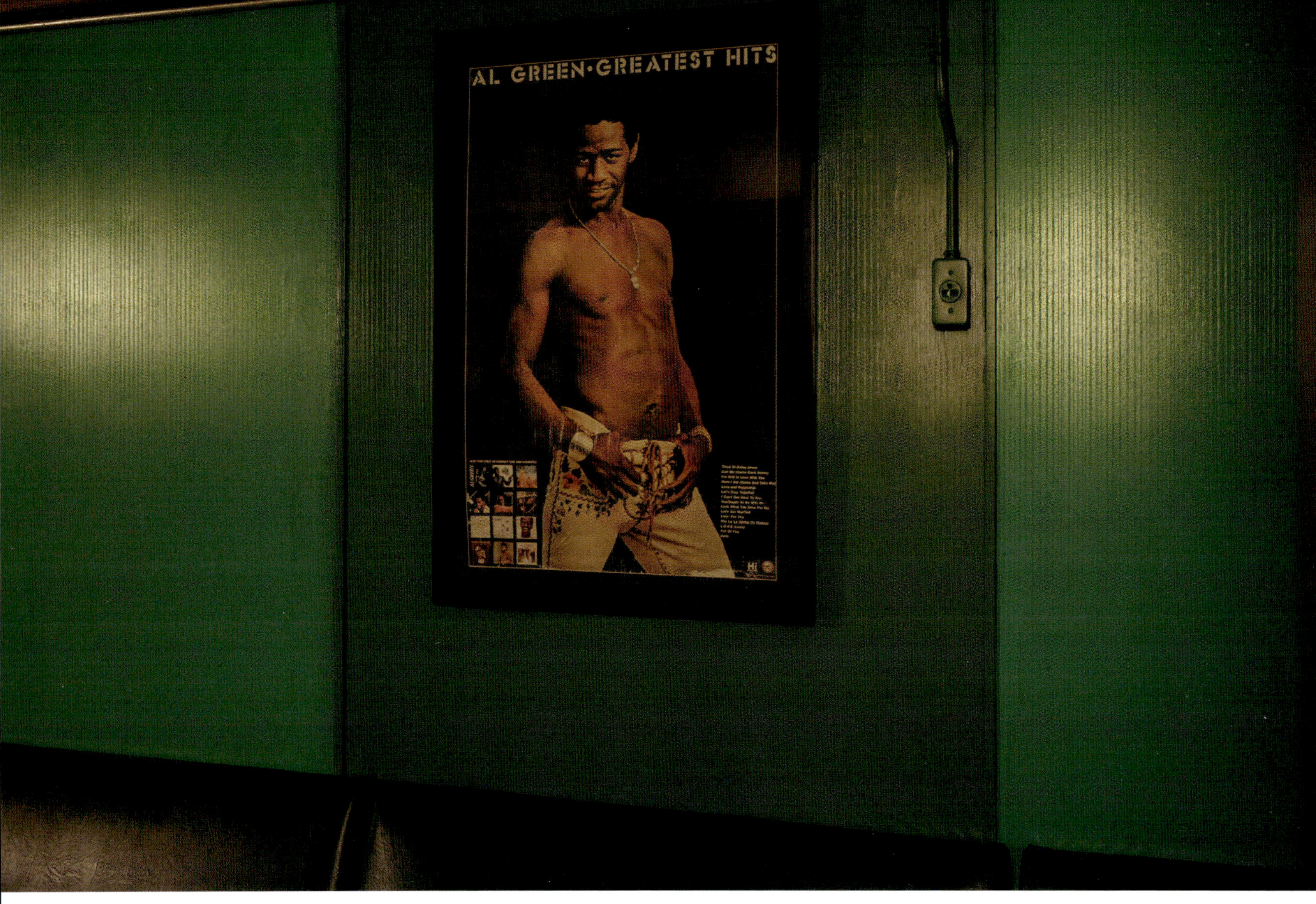
AL GREEN·GREATEST HITS

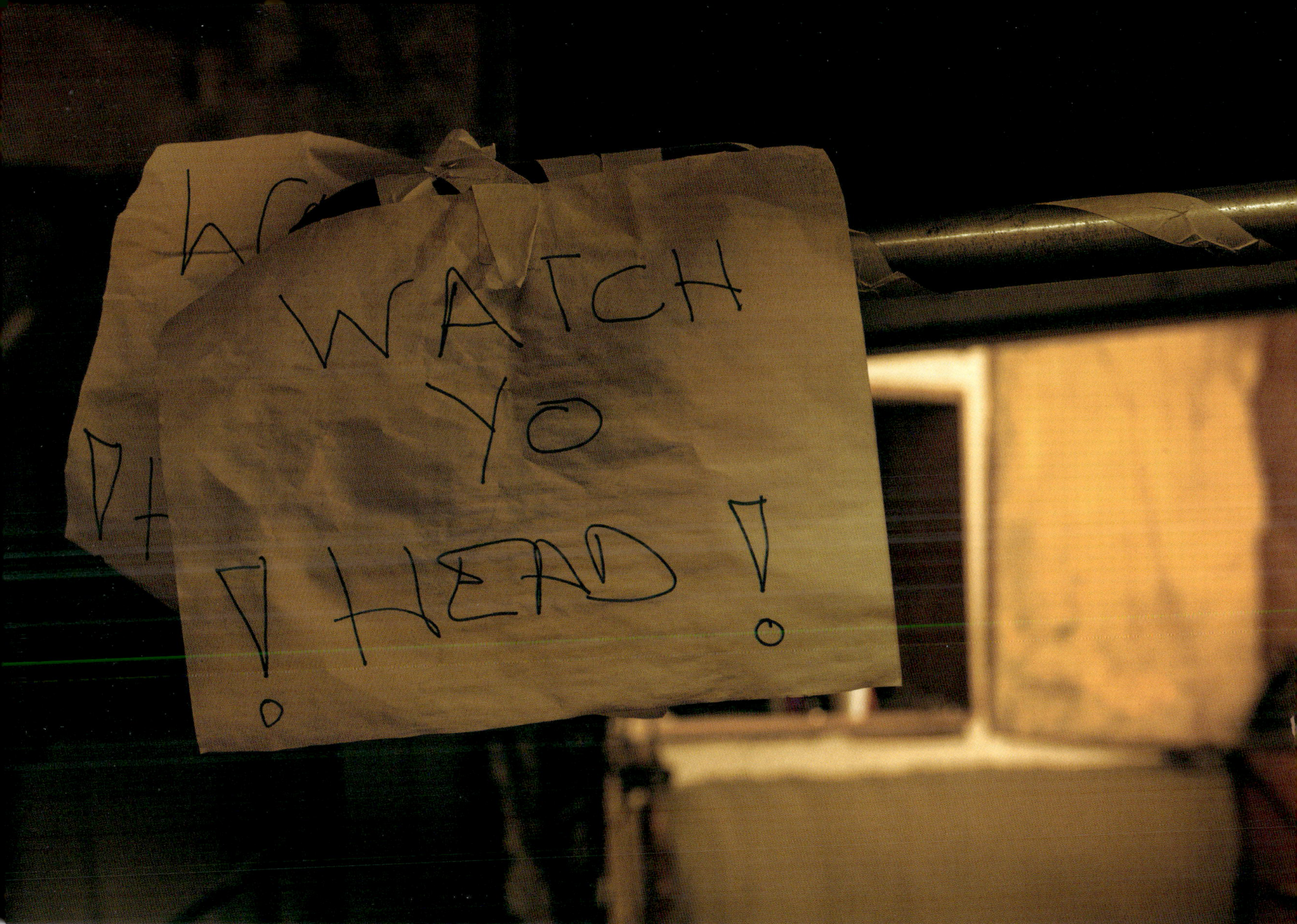
WATCH
YO
HEAD !!

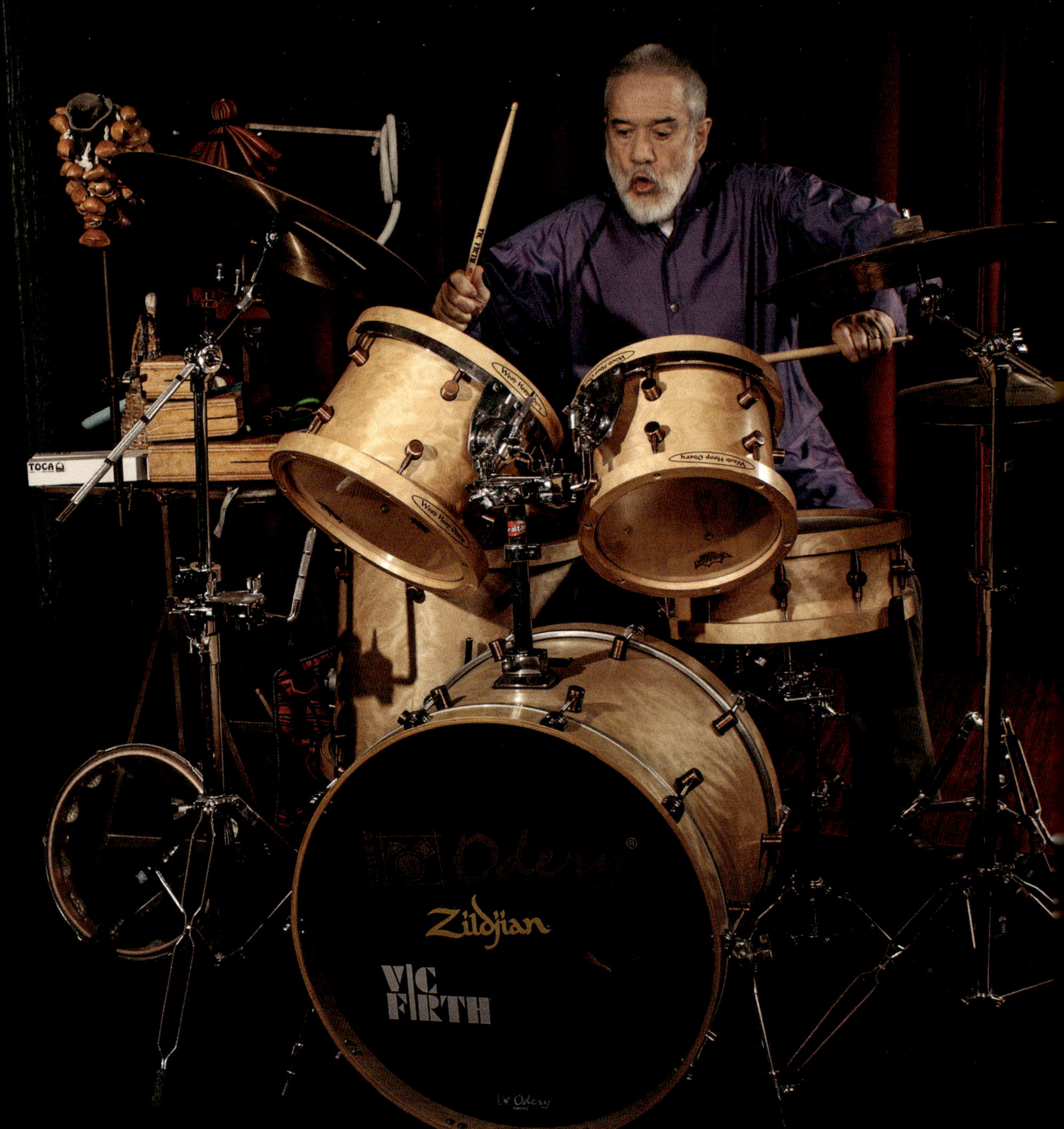
TOCA
Zildjian
VIC FIRTH

AIRTO MOREIRA

Miles Davis / Chick Corea / Weather Report / Cannonball Adderley / Paul Simon
Photographed in his home studio, California

My biggest highlight is when I played with Miles at the Isle of Wight. There were almost 700,000 people there. It was – oh, boy! Jimi played. I think Janis Joplin played. I know that the only band that was considered a jazz band there was us. The audience loved it. To play for such a big audience was beautiful.

We flew in a chartered plane from New York to London with all the musicians and reporters. I don't know how many hours we drove until we got to the shore to take the ferry. Then we got to the island and we couldn't move because there were too many people all over the roads. They had to call a helicopter to pick us up. Then we flew over everybody and we landed backstage, maybe 100 or 200 feet from the stage. Everybody was very loose and going everywhere, kids and everything. This was in '69 I think, it was right after Woodstock. We played for an hour and ten or fifteen minutes maybe. That was it. Then we finished. They got everything and put it back in the helicopter and we flew back to London and then back to the States.

When I listen to certain things that I did a long time ago, I can feel, see and hear the difference, the changes that I went through. Right now I don't play so aggressive anymore. I don't have to be real fast. It's like I'm playing much more comfortably today than I used to play a long time ago. I'd sweat a lot because I couldn't control the energy the way I can control it today. Today when I play, the energy is still very good, but it's a different kind of energy. It's not always uptight, pushing all the time.

Some music really makes people feel good. That's the positive energy that the music has that comes from the musicians. It's healing. That's a spiritual energy from the good spirits. I always love to put that energy out. Sometimes people cry, they say, 'Oh, wow!' There [were times] onstage when I saw the Amazon rainforest or I thought I was flying in space. It's like each one of us, we have a different way to translate that energy, to receive that energy. But it's amazing what you can do with God's energy.

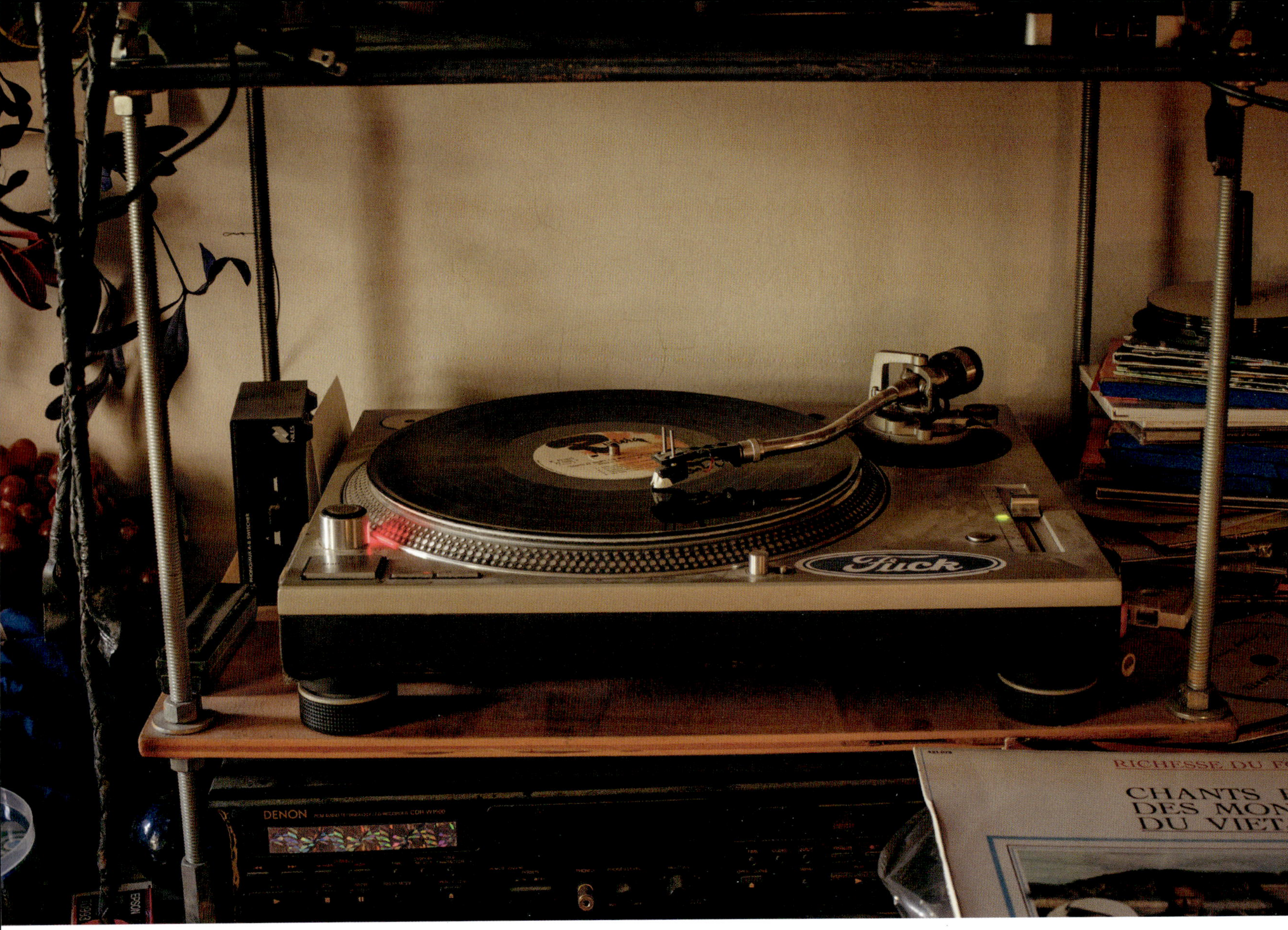
DENON

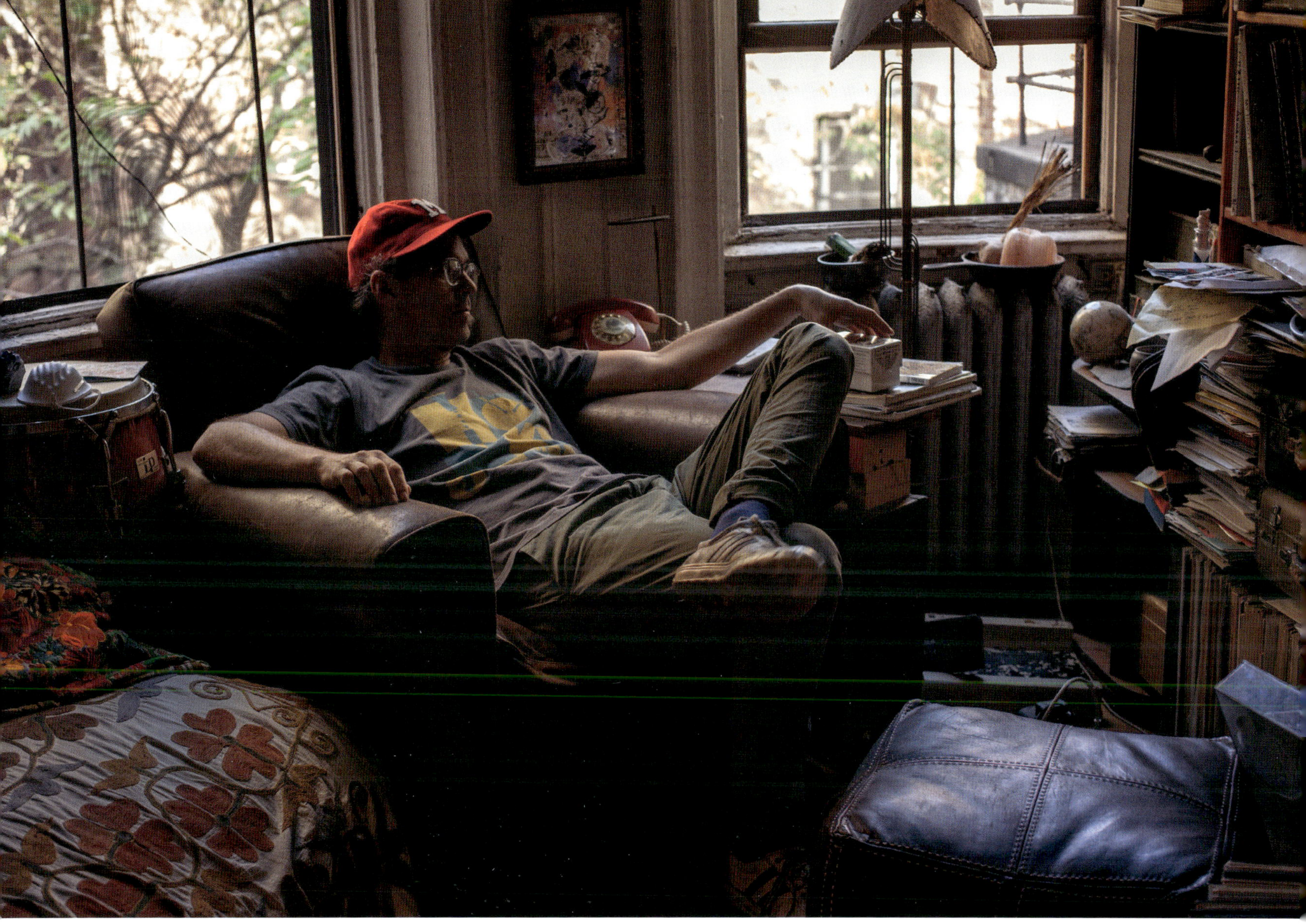

KENNY WOLLESEN

John Zorn / Bill Frisell / Sex Mob / New Klezmer Trio. Photographed at home, New York

TERRY BOZZIO

Frank Zappa / Jeff Beck / Missing Persons / U.K. Photographed at Drum Channel Studios, California

I was very lucky and got the gig with Frank Zappa, who had, you know, a musical scope that incorporated fusion to comedy music to classical music, to jazz to rock – you name it – in his own style. But at the end of that three-year period with Frank, I felt like I was out of the Marine Corps for Musicians. I was a real strong player but hadn't really developed my own style, at least not consciously.

With U.K. and with Missing Persons, that's where I started to develop something more linear and melodic, and started using my stacked sounds and bells and things that are my little trademarks. So it took me until I was thirty years old before that occurred to me. I always tell the story about 'The Black Page' on vinyl. Frank took one little lick out of a ten-minute-long drum solo and it was a lick I ripped off from Tony Williams, and he used that for the introduction. There I was, immortalized on vinyl ripping off Tony Williams. That's when you start to go, wow, where's my own style, where's Terry? That's my experience. First, learn the basics; second, learn from others and then third, try and develop your own style.

If it wasn't for Frank … I mean, those kinds of gigs don't exist [any more] where somebody not only makes you famous and well known but also gives you credibility – because he's such a well-respected genius in many, many areas. I am kind of a shy, conservative person and he pulled a lot of that stuff out of me where I just went nuts because he gave me the opportunity to go nuts. I was spitting and standing up and wearing a studded leather jock strap and doing all that heavy-metal-rock-and-roll posturing that was sort of the fad at that point.

I learned so much about music – and very difficult music, challenging music. I learned how to project to an audience, survive on the road, play a variety of styles and experience all the cultures, from travelling to Japan and Australia and all over Europe and behind the Iron Curtain. We went to Yugoslavia back in the early or mid-'70s, before the Wall came down. Plus, getting to play with [George] Duke and Napoleon [Brock] and all the wonderful musicians I played with in that band. And Frank wrote 'The Black Page' for me. I mean, just so many things that gave me this cred, a cred you can get if you play with Miles or with Weather Report or with some big band. But those kinds of gigs don't exist any more.

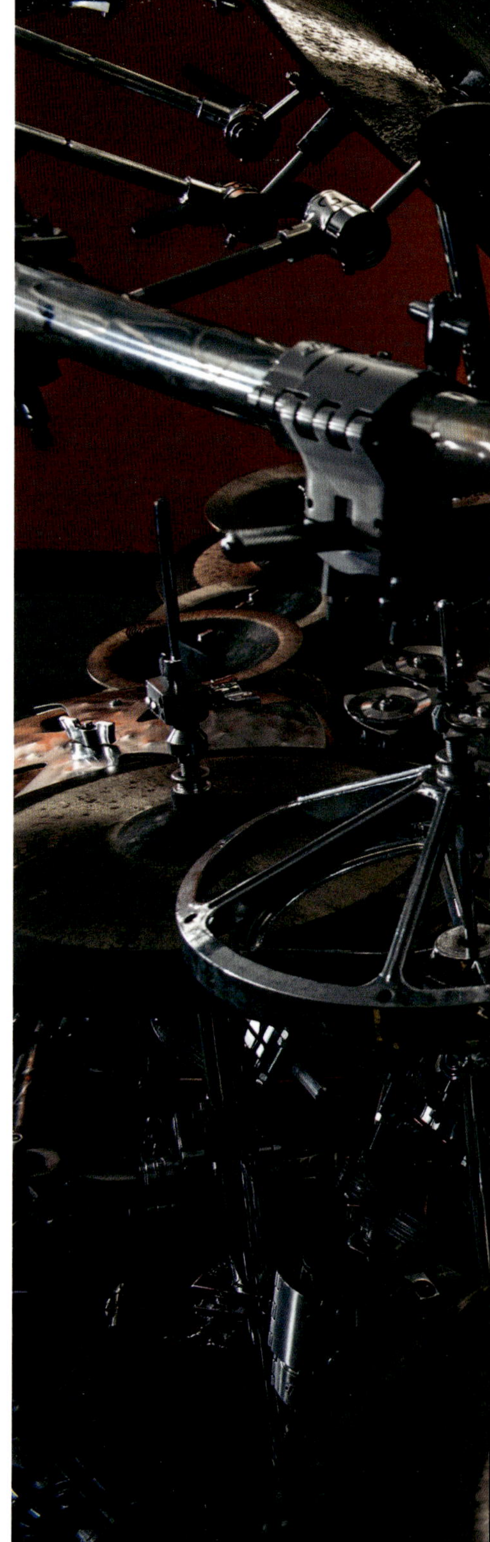

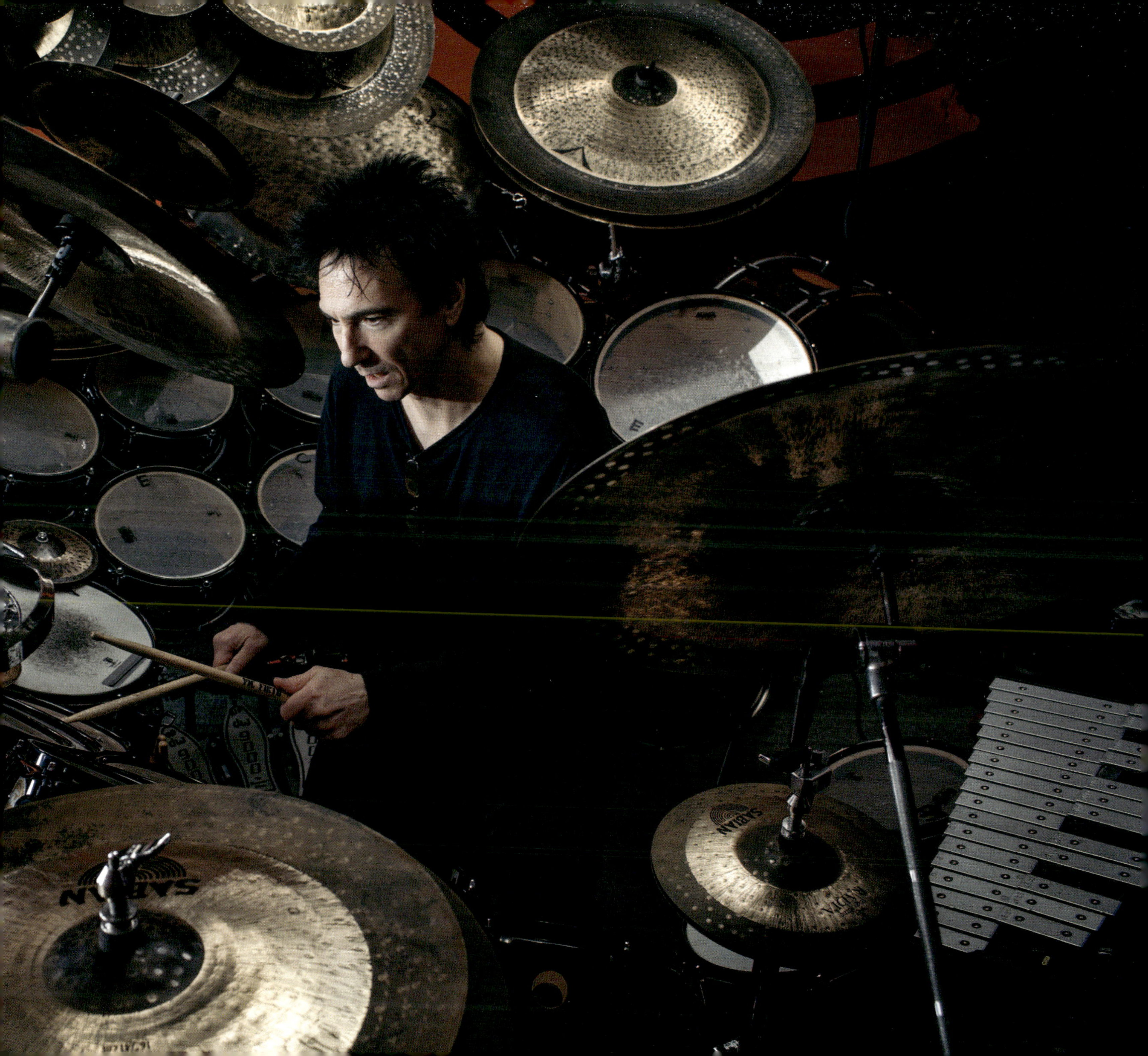
SABIAN

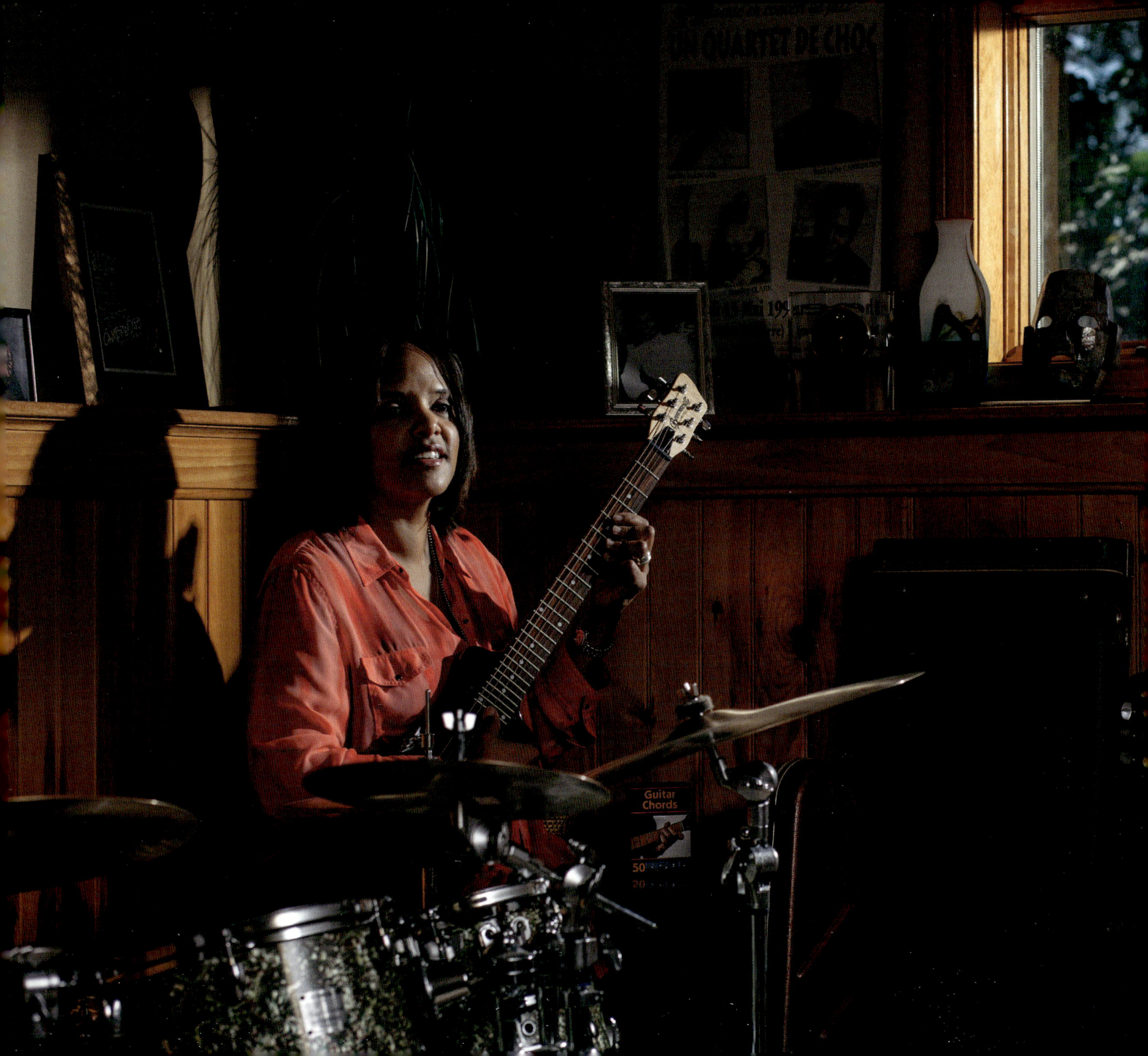
UN QUARTET DE CHOC
Guitar Chords

TERRI LYNE CARRINGTON

Herbie Hancock / Wayne Shorter / David Sanborn. Photographed at home, Massachusetts

Over the years inspiration has been mysterious to me – I'm not always sure where it comes from. Listening to Jimi Hendrix's *Band of Gypsys*, recorded live at the Fillmore East, was the first time I heard rock with a funkiness to it and it made me see that all music has a dance. I felt transported – and heard the blues in it as well, which is the foundation of jazz too. It made me see a connection. John Coltrane's *Ballads* was so beautiful to me. To hear this powerful band play so pretty was one of the first times I realized how attracted I am to melodies. Before complex things or high-energy things, I am satisfied with a nice melodic piece. Joni Mitchell's *Don Juan's Reckless Daughter* – I love anything Joni, she is my favourite lyricist. She is a poet and her mind intrigues me, and the way she puts the melody to lyric. She is so free and so sophisticated musically as well. The song 'Paprika Plains' on this album sounds like ascension to me.

Recently, I was playing with Wayne Shorter and I was trying to fit into his quartet, but it was not really working. Then I stopped trying so hard and just played, and he said after the show that it came together when I was myself and not trying to be anyone else. I was so happy to learn such a powerful lesson – to be reminded of something so powerful – at this stage in my career. Once, while playing with Herbie Hancock I had an out-of-body experience, and after the show he said, 'Now you are doing it – playing life, not music.' That was for sure a highlight for me.

DENNIS CHAMBERS

Parliament / Funkadelic / Santana / Stanley Clarke and George Duke / John Scofield / John McLaughlin
Photographed in Nevada

My mom was a background singer for Motown. That's how I got started in this crazy business. She left Motown when I was two to put a band together in Baltimore. The band used to rehearse at my mom's apartment or my grandmother's house. The only thing that would keep me still was when they would come around to practise and I would sit there and watch the drummer play. Strangely enough, I still remember the colour of the drums, which was a champagne sparkle kit.

I have friends who would testify that – especially in the summertime – no matter what time of day, you could hear me practising. Crazy enough, it worked out. Nobody called the cops. I think the reason was that my practising time was when people were at work. My later teenage years, man – I don't even know how or why my neighbours let me play like that. I would play like I was in a stadium. Sometimes when I would start up with the music, because I had this gigantic stereo as well, I would play along to the records. Or, if not, I would just be listening to the stereo. I remember my neighbour, Miss Francine, she would say that when I would start playing her pots and pans would bounce around … but they never called the cops.

I spent eight years with Funkadelic. With them it was eighteen, nineteen band members on the bandstand. When we would play, sometimes the bass player, Rodney 'Skeet' Curtis, would change some things and then all of a sudden we would go right there. Instead of just letting him go and stick out like a sore thumb, we would just add to him and see where it went. And a lot of times we went down … like a whole other alley, and then what came out of it sometimes was new music.

The '70s was a great time in music, everybody was experimenting. When I sit there and talk to someone like Jack Bruce or Ginger Baker … Jack was a jazz bassist; Ginger Baker wanted to be a jazz drummer. He *was* a jazz drummer, actually, but yet they put a band together, Cream. It was a rock band. And I think it was either Jack or Ginger, I can't remember who said it: 'We were a jazz band but we just forgot to tell Eric.'

Music has changed of course. It's funny. Not that many people are contributing to a new way, a new sound of playing the drums or playing music. I was watching a Quincy Jones video and he said it best: normally with the rappers, in this day and age, in this era of time, people are doing more sampling – they are sampling things that have already been done. That's fine and dandy, but what happens in twenty years if you don't create something new – where would music go? And that's what I feel about drums. There's nothing new about playing the drums, the only thing new is what you say on the instrument. How you feel. But if you copy somebody else's way of playing the drum, where will that go in twenty years?

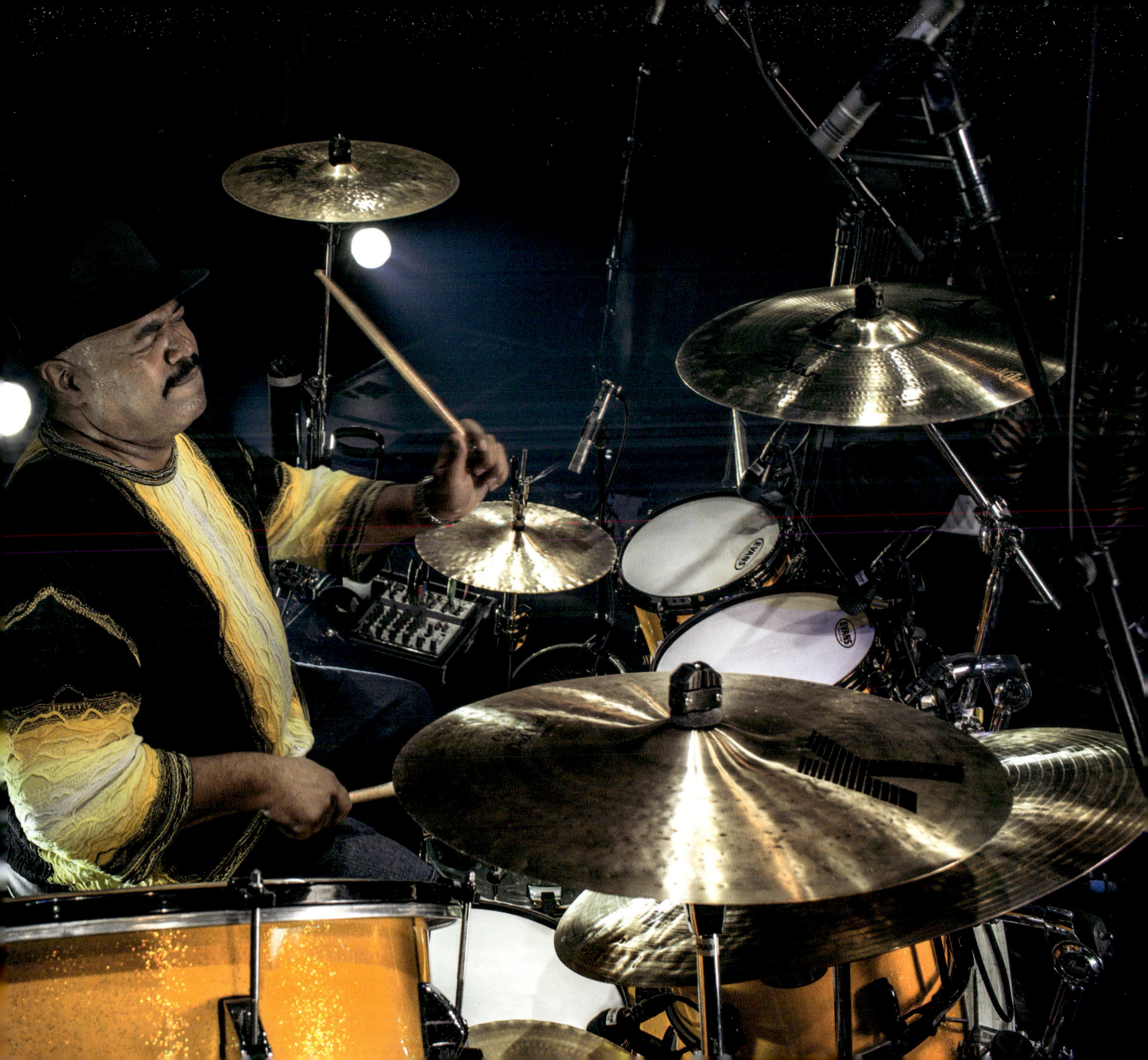
EVANS
EVANS

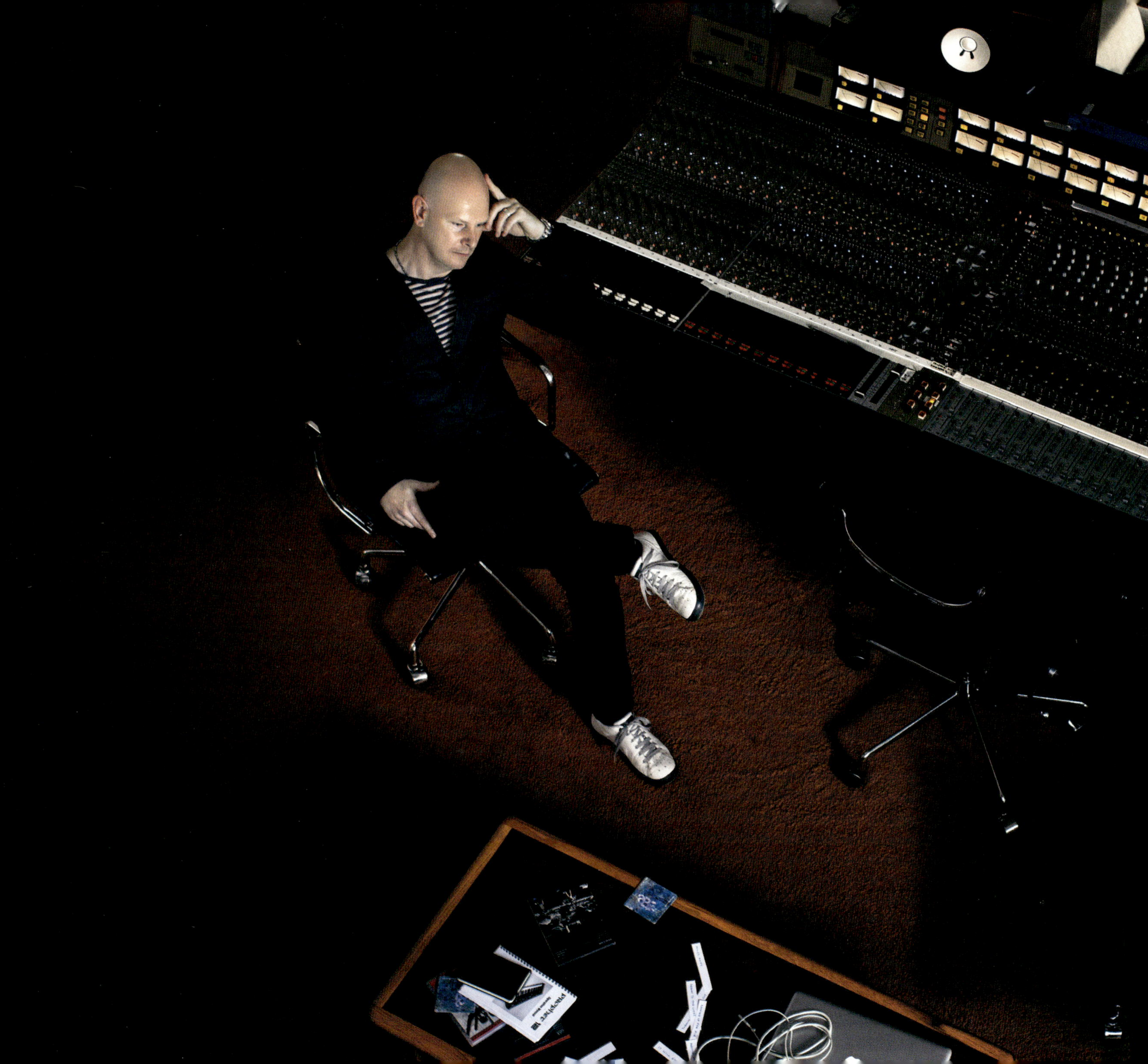

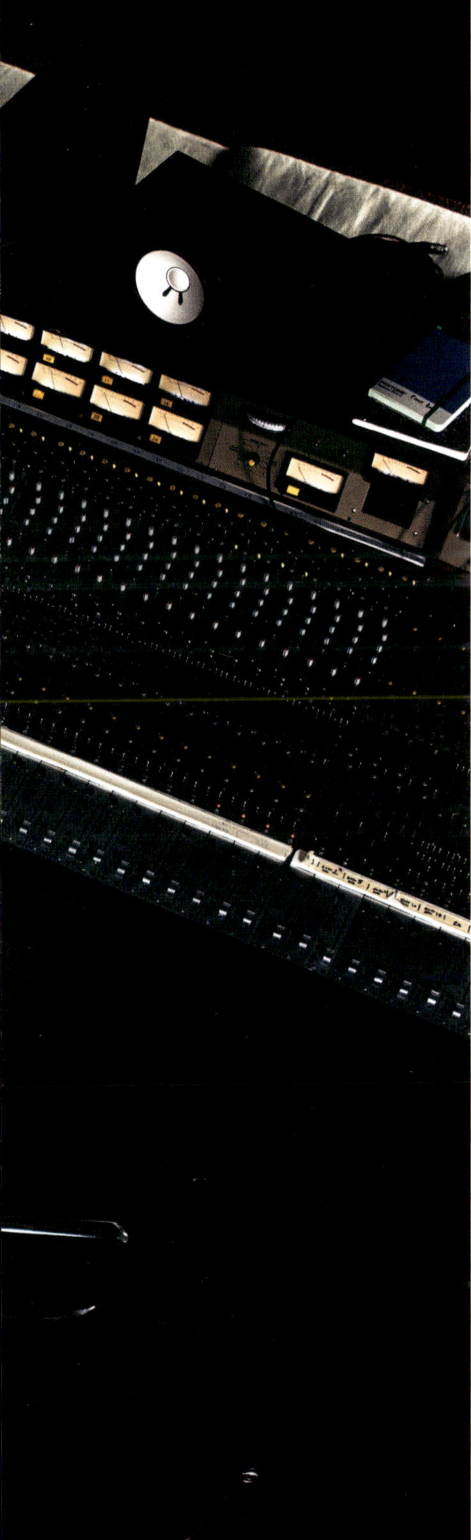

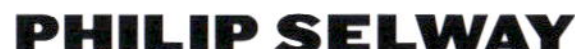

PHILIP SELWAY

Radiohead. Photographed at the Radiohead studio in the UK

I am led by the nose, really – pretty much self-taught in a lot of ways. There have been certain periods where I've gone to places like Drumtech up in London. I reached a point in my playing when we were about two albums in where I realized that there were aspects of my technique which were letting me down, so I wanted to go and work on those things, and it made a difference. But actually in terms of how I play I have been very lucky in being able to plough my own furrow and that it's been learned in relation to what's been going on in Radiohead as well. I think it shows in how we play because we all have got very distinctive voices, each of us, but we've been playing together so long that it holds together. It does mesh together. On one side you have an insecurity because you think, I've not been trained, and I've not got all these chops that all these great session musicians have got. But on the other, it's a more direct route to finding your own musical voice. You end up backfilling in some ways; you're just trying to pick up some of those techniques and that broader knowledge you feel you need to do the job.

Particularly with a band, it's just having that understanding and having something click musically between you. That doesn't come from hours on end sitting down and practising your paradiddles, although that is a very worthwhile thing to do. That's not to demean sitting down with that stuff, because I mean it's brilliant, it really does unlock a lot of musicality itself as well.

I always go on about this performance self-help thing that you need to silence that 'silent critic' in you. And that's been a very strong voice at points. Because of the nature of being in a band, you kind of bluff your way through it – an awful lot of it, anyway – it's not as if you've done years of training. Although you do in a way, because you play, you rehearse and everything as a band, even though there's not a certificate at the end of it to say you have done all that. Then again, there might be a contract at the end of it.

The more experience you get the more you prove to yourself over the years, and the more you can recognize what's good and musical and what you bring to whatever musical set-up you're playing in. And that's not an egotistical thing: that's just a sense of actually starting to feel a bit more accomplished in your chosen craft, I think. Once you have that sense of your own musicality, it's amazing how little you have to throw at it for it to come out. In fact, it's the classic 'less is more' approach. If you are trying to throw in stuff you think is going to make you seem more accomplished as a player or using the stuff to impress people, that's not going to connect … it just feels fake.

Having grown up playing in a band with five people and a lot of instruments in there, you learn to leave a lot of space. We all have to, for each other, because you have five people playing relatively simple parts, but in the way they are all interwoven you have naturally got something quite complex going on there already. I'm sure some people could be very rude about my sense of time in music – it's flexible, it's not a metronomic thing for me, although that does have its place and it can be great to play to a click or sequence at points. But again, coming back to the whole thing of a band of five people, you kind of find your mid-point between you, or your interpretation of the pulse, and that's what gives it its particular character. I have my ebb and flow but actually that's a very natural process, a natural feeling. And music is all about feelings, after all. It's kind of about how those feelings play themselves out; just getting caught up in the flow of the music, and it's playing you rather than you playing it.

BRIAN CHASE

Yeah Yeah Yeahs / John Zorn / Drums and Drones / Alan Licht / Toby Driver / Mary Halvorson
Photographed in his studio, New York

Jazz has been a big part of the new music tradition in New York City. It's been great to be exposed to that world, how it's very much alive today and how the boundaries of jazz have kind of morphed to embrace rock and noise and concepts from the classical music world. So it's music without borders or boundaries, which does kind of relate to the Brooklyn music scene today in terms of eclecticism.

Awareness of time and the breakdown of the day doesn't really exist in performance. The level of functioning while playing feels very different to the level of functioning in the outside world. A lot of it has to do with awareness, because when I'm playing music I'm connecting to a different part of myself, and that part of myself is very much focused on playing the music and expression and connecting to the performance on a deeper level. So if I'm doing that while thinking about all the chores I have to do and appointments I have to keep and all the other burdens that are typically on my mind, then that's not doing a service to the music.

I often think about this idea of getting to the edge and jumping off. A lot of the technical aspects of the music are designed to get us right to the edge of being conscious of keeping time – and those are important, but I feel they still only get us up to the edge. For us to really get into it, we're going to have to have faith and jump off. And so to make up for that extra little distance, that's where we have to let go. So we use the technique to get us to that point where we can let go and really get into it.

When I practise I spend so much time on technique, the way in which I play and not just what I play. Remaining conscious of my posture, my hand position and the way the stick functions as an extension of my body then become primary concerns. In this I value looseness, ease and grace. Then there are the moments when I am overwhelmed by the passion of the music, and at these times my restraint for the sake of an ideal in form often becomes compromised and my body becomes a metaphor for what I am feeling as my experience. The muscles in my face can become tense with the excitement, my neck can lurch forwards with eagerness and my grip can tighten from the intensity. Not that this necessarily helps the music – and sometimes it can detract from the concentration, from the focus – but it can be fun to watch. There is a joy in the openness of playing and for me that is what there is to communicate.

There are a lot of perspectives that come into my position at the back of the stage. One thing that comes to mind is being inside it compared to being outside it. My example would be us playing on *David Letterman*. When I am on the inside, what I'm doing is playing on *David Letterman* and I have a function: I have to get up there and play drums, play the song and play it well. The idea of being on the outside is being aware that I'm on the *David Letterman* show and if I started thinking about that idea, I would probably freak out. I'll be aware of it because I'll talk to friends or family and they'll say, 'You're on the *David Letterman* show!' And I'll be like, 'I know!' So the more I can stay on the inside of it while at the same time respecting the situation for what it is, that really helps me stay sane.

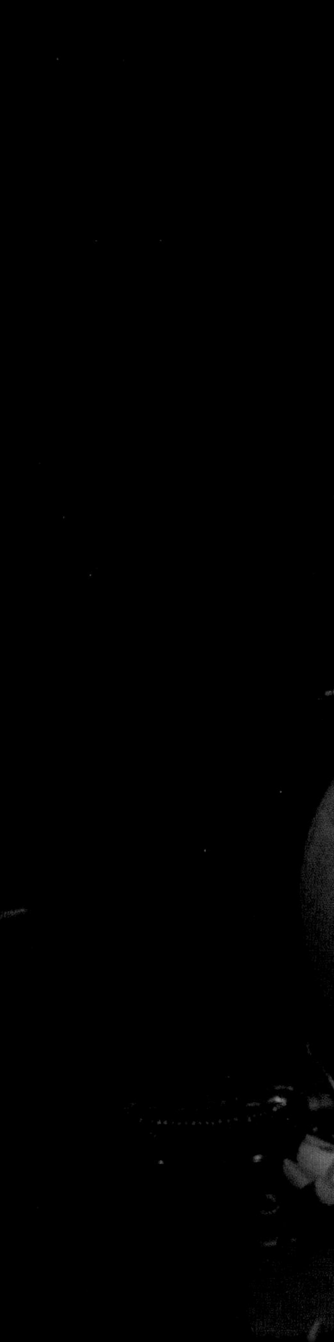

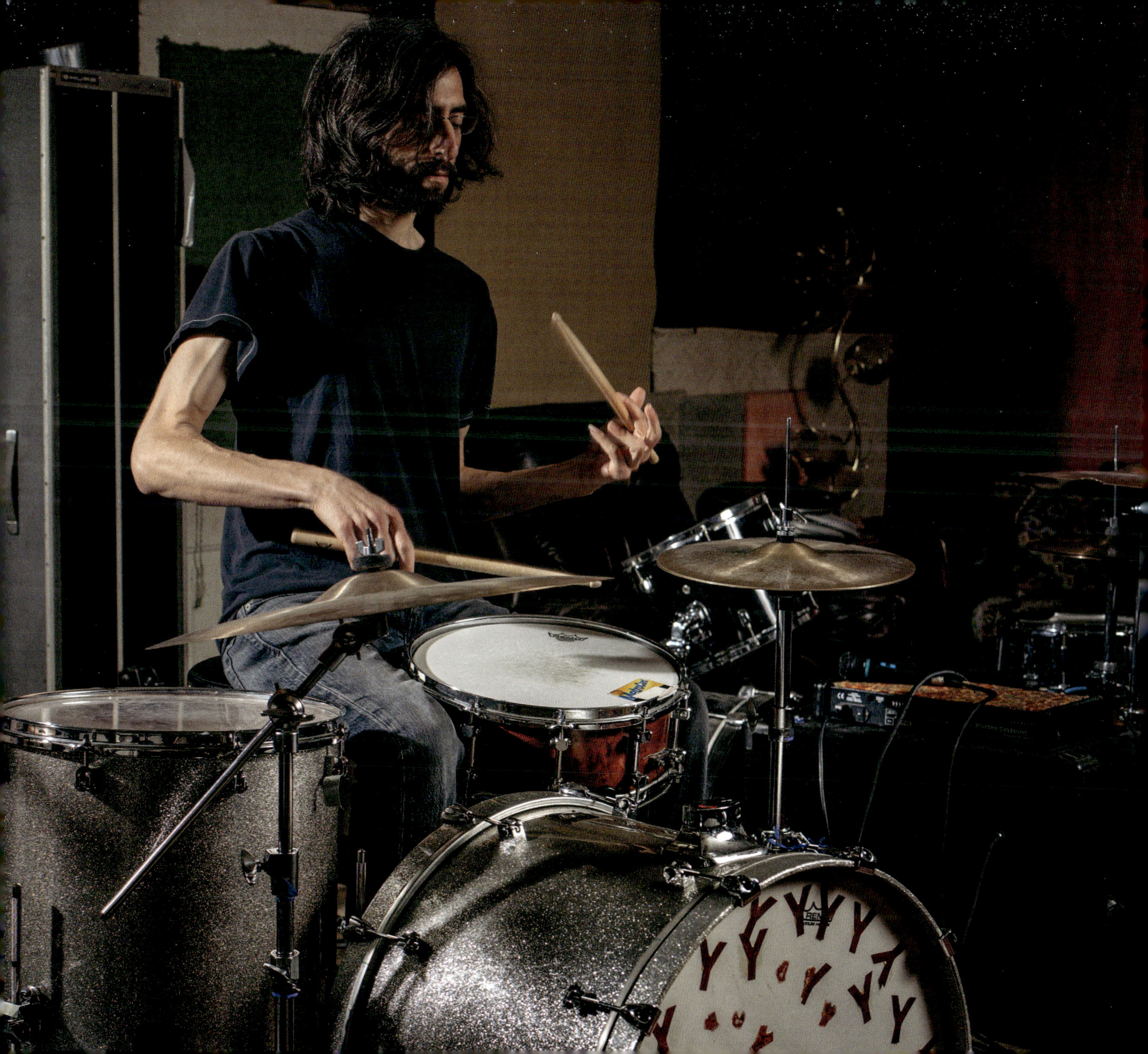

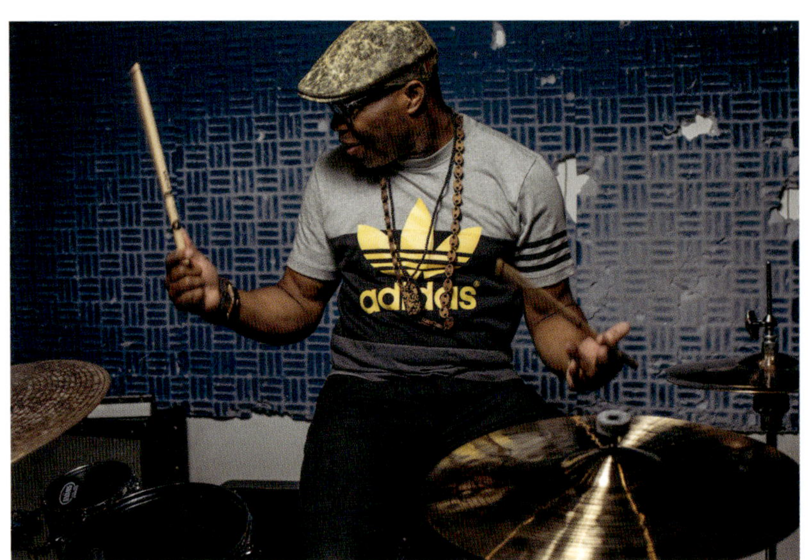

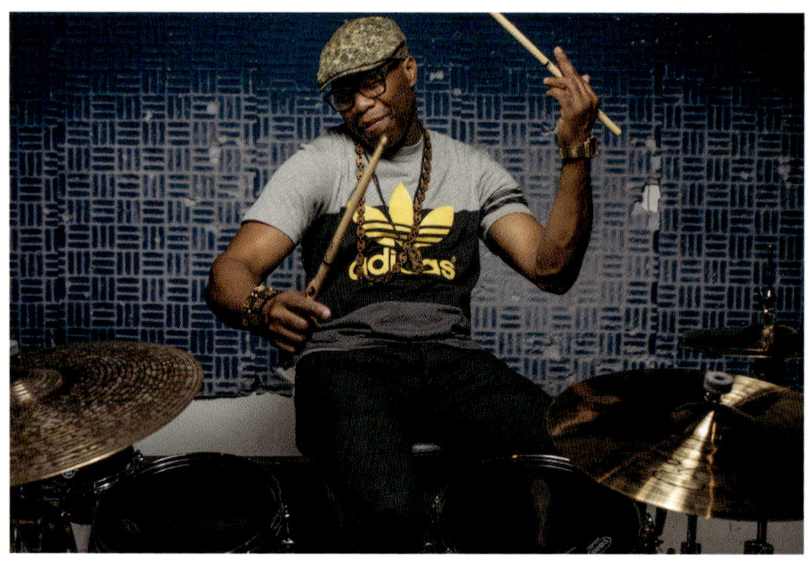

DARU JONES

Jack White / Nas / Pete Rock / The Ruff Pack / Slum Village. Photographed in New York

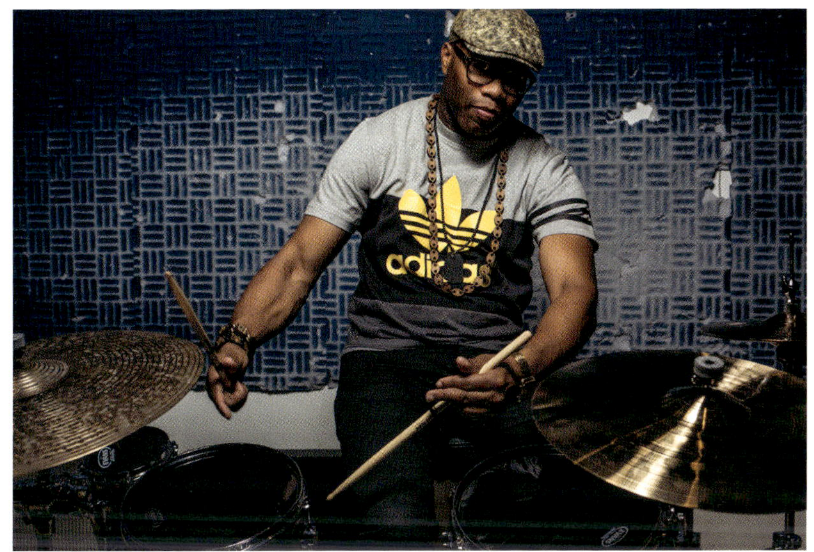

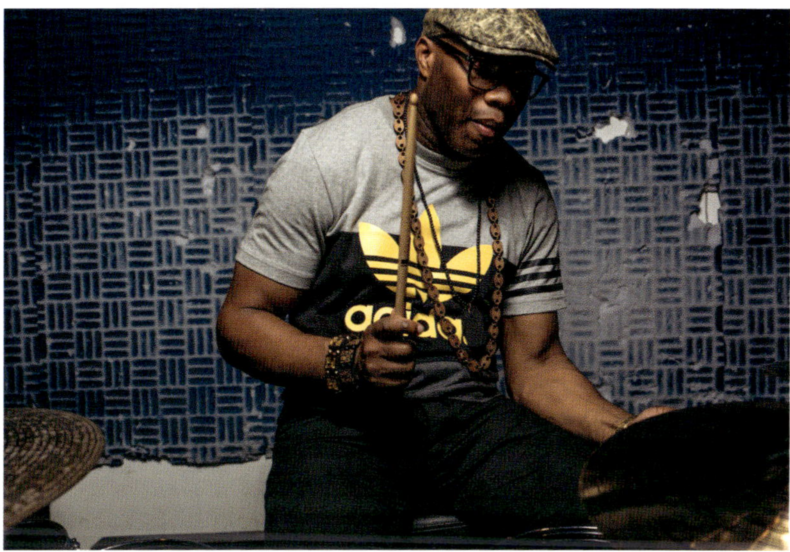

Playing in church when I was a kid was all about being a team player and playing for the spirit to come in. It wasn't like how it is nowadays in the church – now, it's all about chops and who can play the fastest. At that time it was about playing in the pocket. So I'm in church trying to play all this Vinnie Colaiuta, odd metre stuff – that got me in trouble. They'd tell me, 'This don't work for the Gospel.' Nowadays it does, but then, if you were not keeping on time they would nudge you off and the next guy would get on to replace you. After that happened to me a couple of times I learned how to have better time, so that was a big deal.

My parents, they're both organ players and pianists. They are musical directors as well, directing the choir. The type of church I went to, we had service every night of the week except Saturdays. There are things I learned from that experience, like learning how to play from my heart and soul. I'm not reading from a chart. I'm playing and I'm just intuitive to whatever the vibe is around me. Even when I walk or talk, my interactions just kind of flow like music, like improvisation, if that makes any sense. I kind of live like that. It's a vibe thing – I'm really big on that – it's about the spirit and checking out what the vibe of the situation is. That's what early jazz was: improv, and call and response.

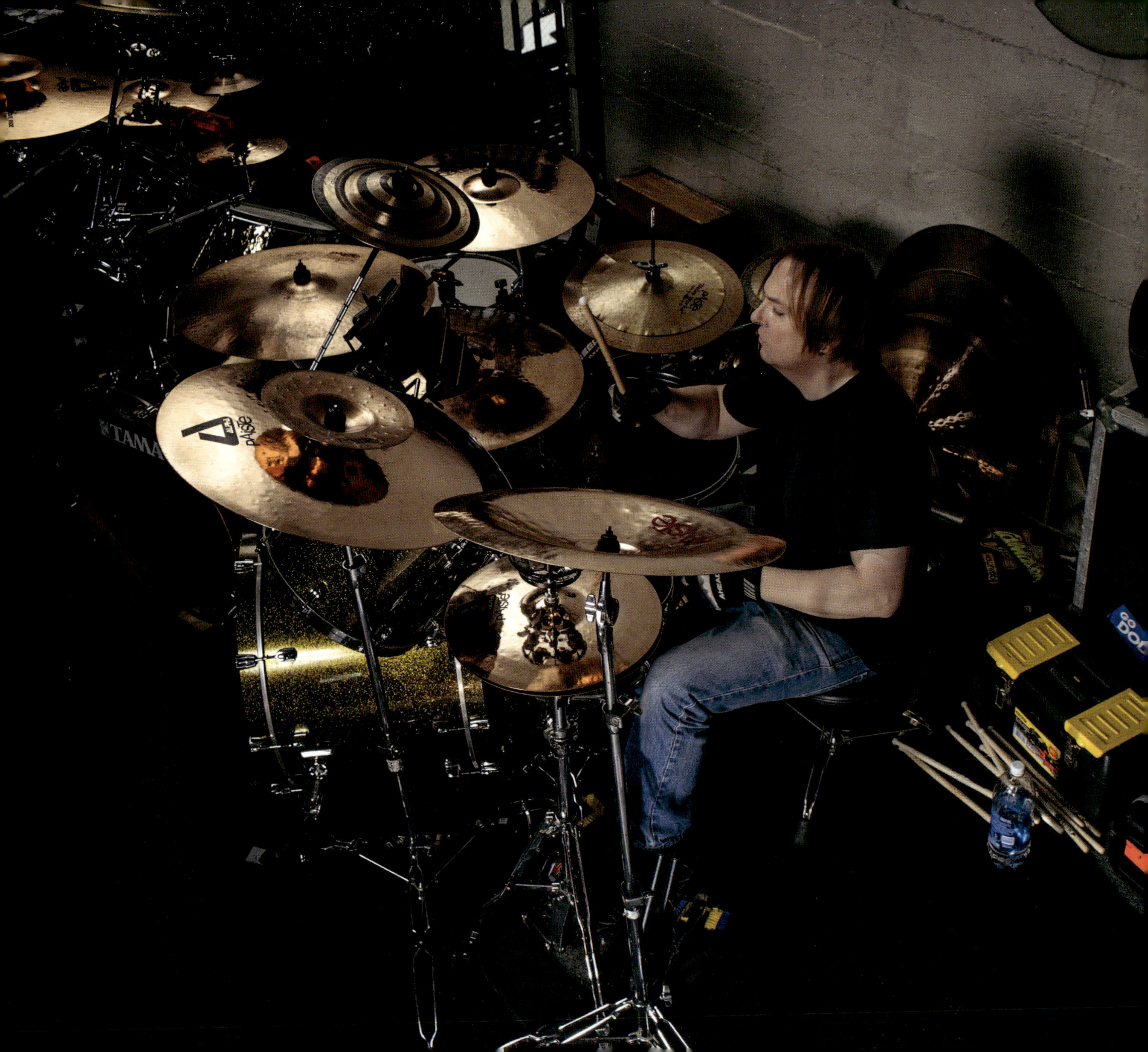
TAMA
paiste

DALE CROVER

Melvins. Photographed at the Melvins studio, California

When I joined the band they were into so many different types of music, all under the same category, punk rock. I thought, wow this is really amazing, you can pretty much do whatever you want and it's accepted. But it wasn't really, it's just like anything else. Everybody wanted to mosh, so if you played anything slow it was like, 'What the hell is this shit? You guys suck.' We took a lot of flack for that and for looking kind of weird. We did opening slots for bigger bands like Nine Inch Nails. We played a show in Dallas where people were going crazy before the show had even started. They tolerated us for about half our set and then they started ripping up the floor. It was at a hockey arena and they had this covering on the ice. We were getting pelted with all kinds of stuff: the floor, recorders, coins. It's weird because it's not like they'd just go, 'That music is no good, I don't care.' It really made them angry, which is great.

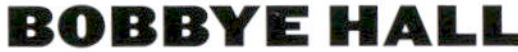

Bob Dylan / Marvin Gaye / Stevie Wonder / Stevie Nicks / Carole King / Bruce Springsteen

Photographed in the desert and at her home, California

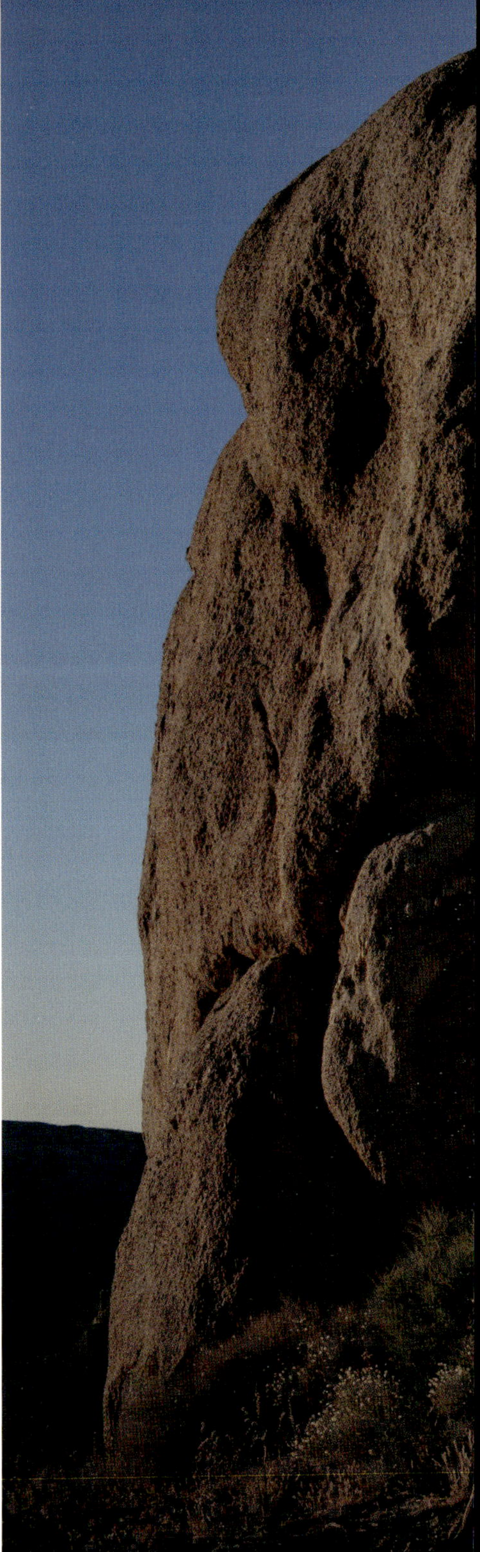

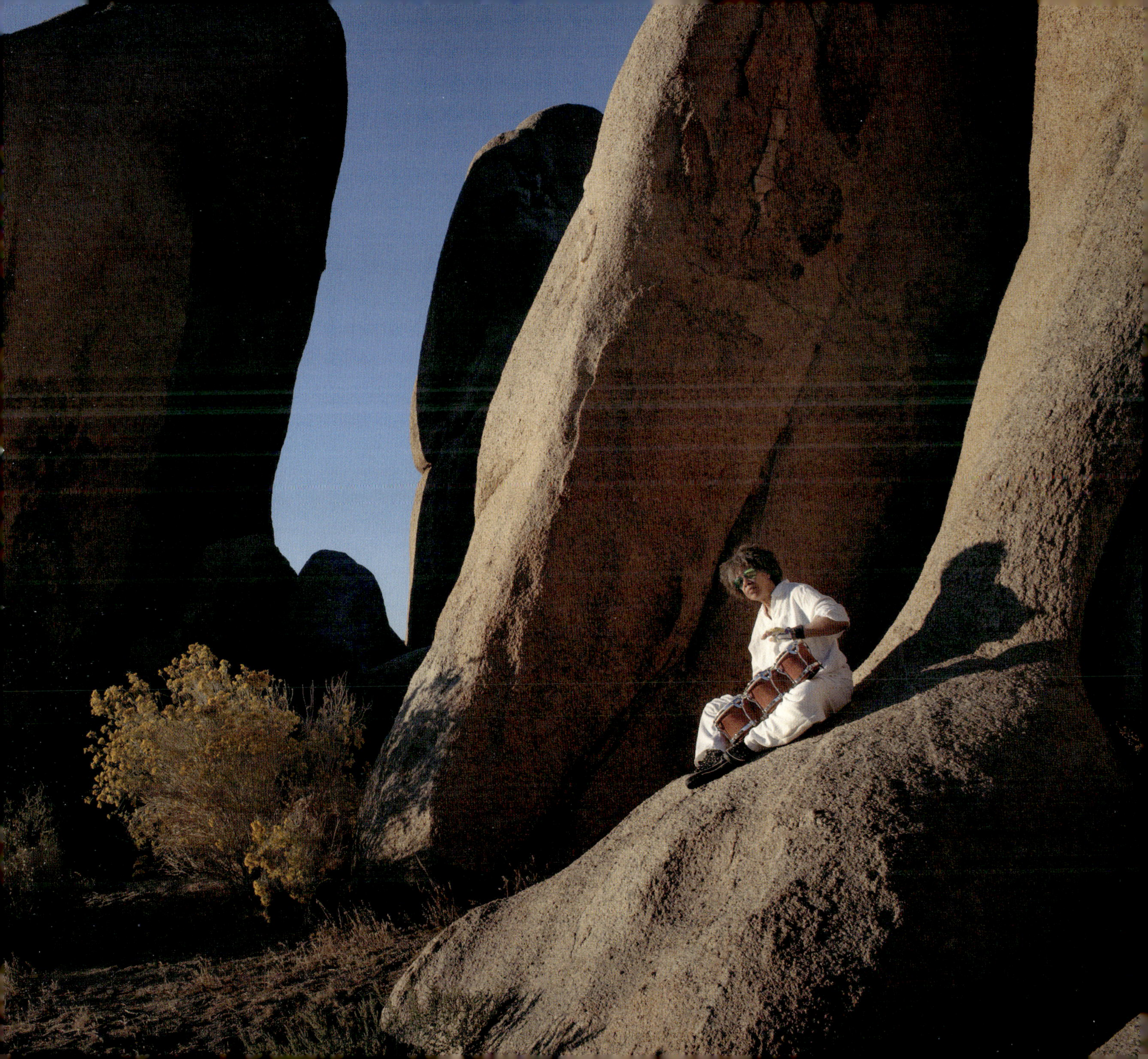

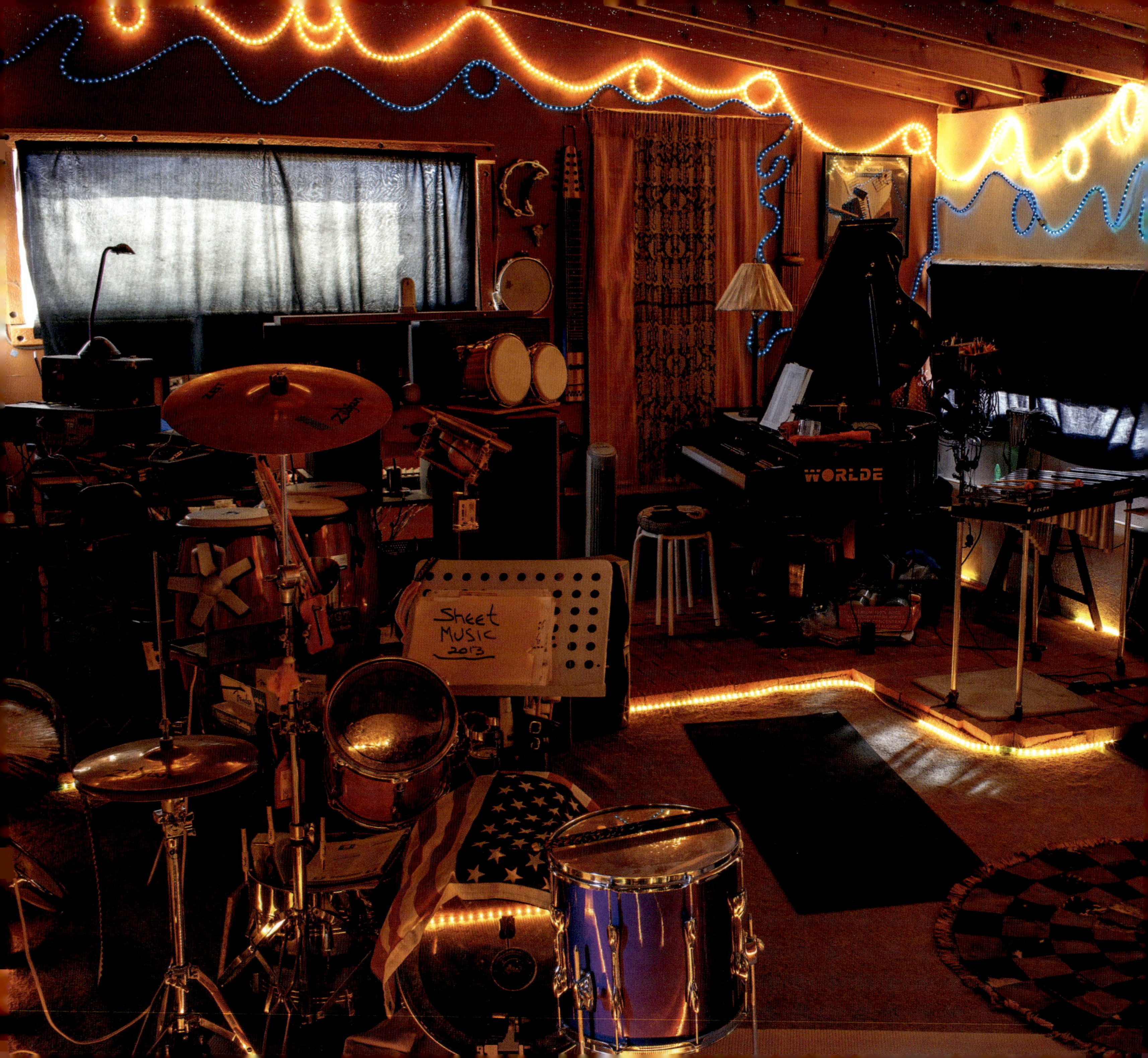
WORLDE
Sheet
MUSIC
2013

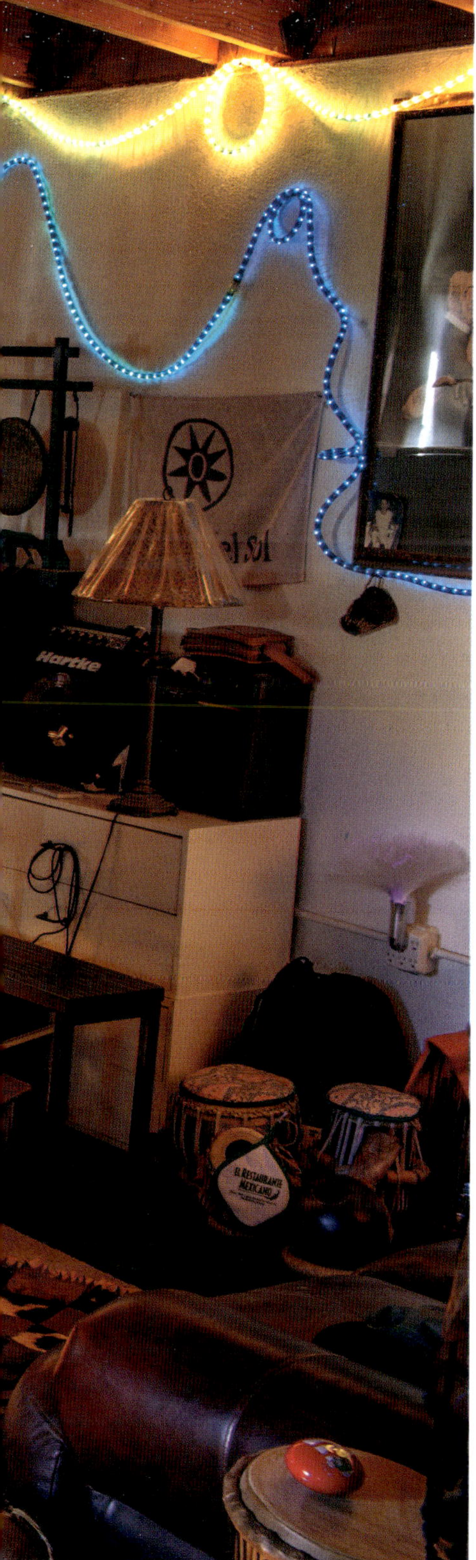

My mother would play a lot of blues. I would be lulled to sleep by listening to the blues. I just knew that instead of using words I wanted to play. And being an only child, I had a chance to do that. It was right around that time when my parents needed to work things out and, for me, beating on things – pots and pans – was a way of not involving myself with what adults were doing. I began to work out my own feelings, and passions grew from a very young age.

During the summer my mother would let me go play in the studio, and I would play at Motown. Berry [Gordy] would have me play with Stevie. Stevie Wonder. I'm ten or eleven and I'm running around the studio, and he would play drums and his harmonica and I would play the bongos, he would play the bongos. He would play the drums, I'd play the drums. We would just have the empty studio for ourselves. But I never travelled with Motown, I was too young. So I just made the sessions. I was staying with my parents. They would send a car for me to take me to the studio. We got no credit, but that was the norm back then. He saw this vision of the Motown sound before it was the Motown sound.

Berry was very rich and very powerful and very imaginative and always in the future. When I think about it, he was a great inspiration for me. He let me play in the studio. Now, I'm a liner note legend.

I was so new to California. I came out to Hollywood in 1970, on 15th January. I had a thirty day ticket. Either I make it or I'm gone. And I'm still here. I was a baby in Hollywood. I stayed at a place called the Hollywood Studio Club when I first came out here. I was the only chocolate thing in there. It was a residence for women in the industry in Hollywood. I had a friend, she was clairvoyant. I'd come home and she'd ask, 'How was your session?' and I'd say, 'Well, I was working for this group, they call 'em The Doors, I think.' And she'd go, 'Oh my god, you're kidding me, Bobbye, you're working for who?' She would tell me about these people and that's how I knew who I was working for.

When you play there is a place that you go, when you are in your passion. It's not something that you do, it does it to you. You are the receiver and it doesn't have the fingers and the thumbs to do it, so it comes into you and you are doing it. And when you do it, it's like you're not here anymore. Can I get back there? No, because those are special doors that I went through at that moment. It's almost like abduction: you came back and you looked at your watch and it was a different time. You can't really explain it.

HOWARD GRIMES

Hi Rhythm Section (Al Green / Ann Peebles / Otis Clay / O. V. Wright / Syl Johnson)
Photographed at home, Tennessee

Willie Mitchell hired me, he liked me. He set a time and I took off running, because that's all I knew. He stopped and said, 'Hold it. What the hell you doing?' He said, 'Look, we're going to all get there at the same time, slow down.' I started getting energized, I started feeling him, his tone. The talk, he was so laid back. He had something I had never learned, that calm. And humble, too. He set the time and he said, 'A one, a two, a one, two, three, four'. I started, and I didn't realize at the time but I felt so comfortable, I could handle his music. He never told me what to play, he never told me how to play – he set the time. And by him setting the time, I didn't know [but] he was teaching me time.

Later on as I started recording, I learned how to count through him. And he said, 'Well, now I think you got time to learn.' He says, 'So where you hear it at?' I would start even down a little level under him and he always agreed with where I heard it. I had got so to his level, I came under his level with my feel. He was so laid back and I felt it should be laid back even further. He never did say, 'We're too slow, you're dragging' – he always accepted. So I got more comfortable, more relaxed, and he just allowed it, he never said nothing. So many producers and writers were saying, 'Willie Mitchell gonna lock you in like a time machine.' That's probably why I could do all the things like cutting the records.

When we cut the Al Green record – it was such a big record, 'Funny How Time Slips Away' – we were playing the song and it wasn't quite where Willie wanted it. He said, 'Howard, I want you to play the hi-hat, get up on the beat.' I knew what he was saying but I actually didn't know how to project it. And then he told me, 'I want you to make love to the drums.' I thought he was crazy: I can't make love to the drums. And then he said, 'Think about your wife. When you're making love to your wife, think when she's soft, she's ….' My mind kind of went into what he was saying. But I thought he was crazy. But hey, what happened? I got real light. I got so light, and when it happened he said, 'That's it, what's what I want.' It was like something supernatural took over my body. I got so light, the feel came and everybody fell down with me on that pattern. And when we cut the track, he said, 'That's one of the greatest tracks. It's going to be difficult for a drummer to try to play that feel.' And that's how I found out the way he thinks. He used mostly sex as a reference on how to get me to play, and I love women, but I didn't know that was the part that goes with the way you cut records.

Nobody never knew Blacks and whites were recording together. We were the only ones that could be accepted, but they didn't want nobody to know that there were whites and Blacks [together]. We couldn't even walk out the door at the same time. I came up at a time that was very prejudiced and racist. It used to disturb me. The first time I found out, I asked Floyd Newman one day, 'Why we all can't leave and come out of the studio together?' He said we weren't integrated. I kind of felt a little down about it, I didn't quite understand why. I was trying to figure out why we could play in the studio together but couldn't be seen.

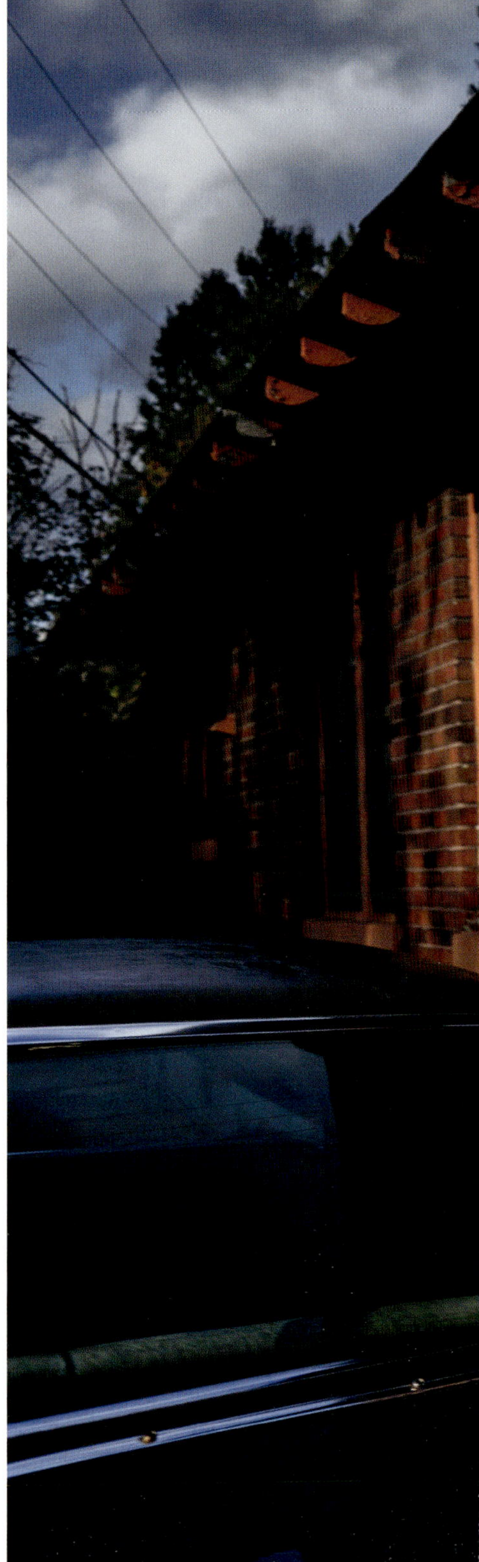

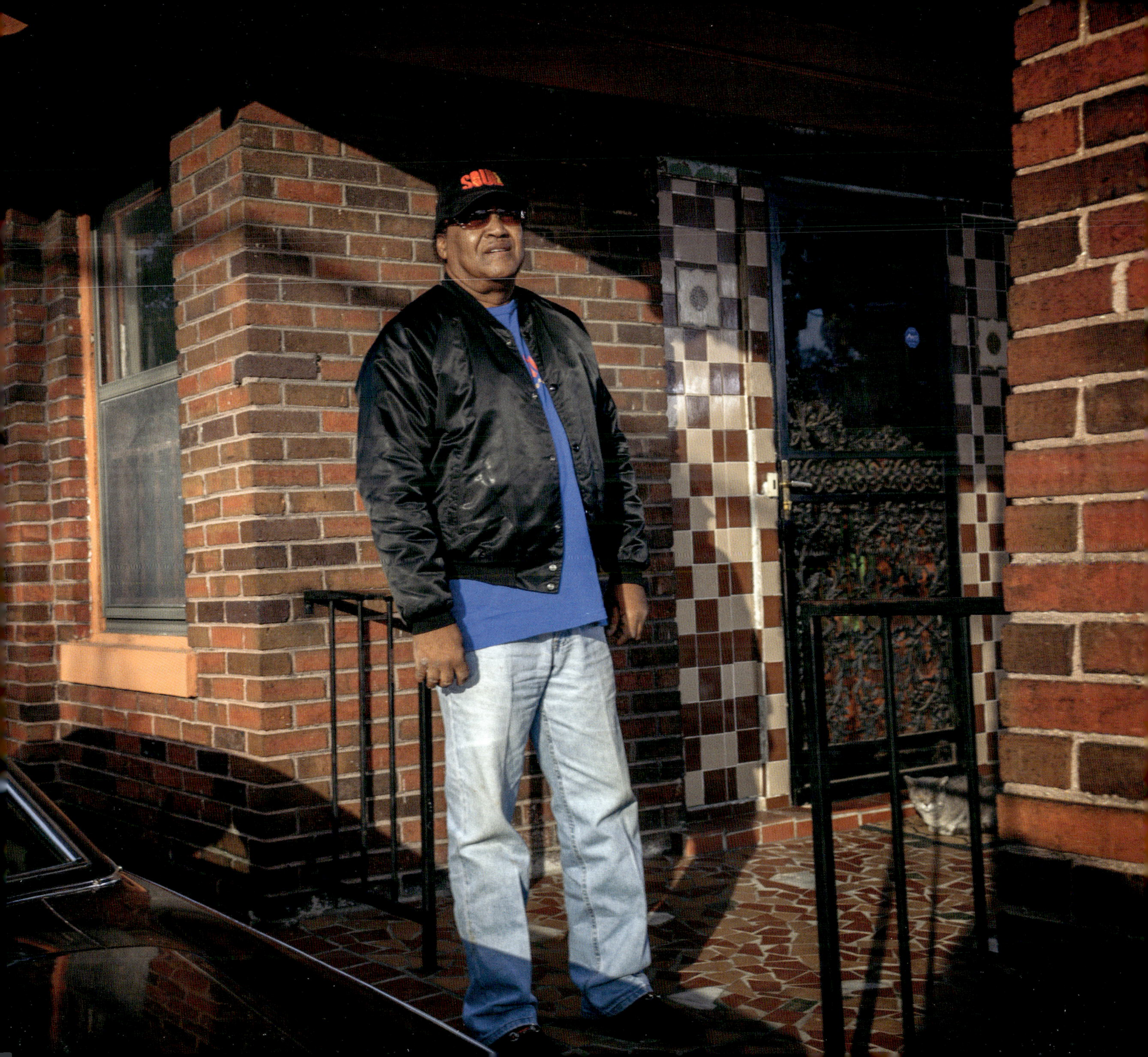

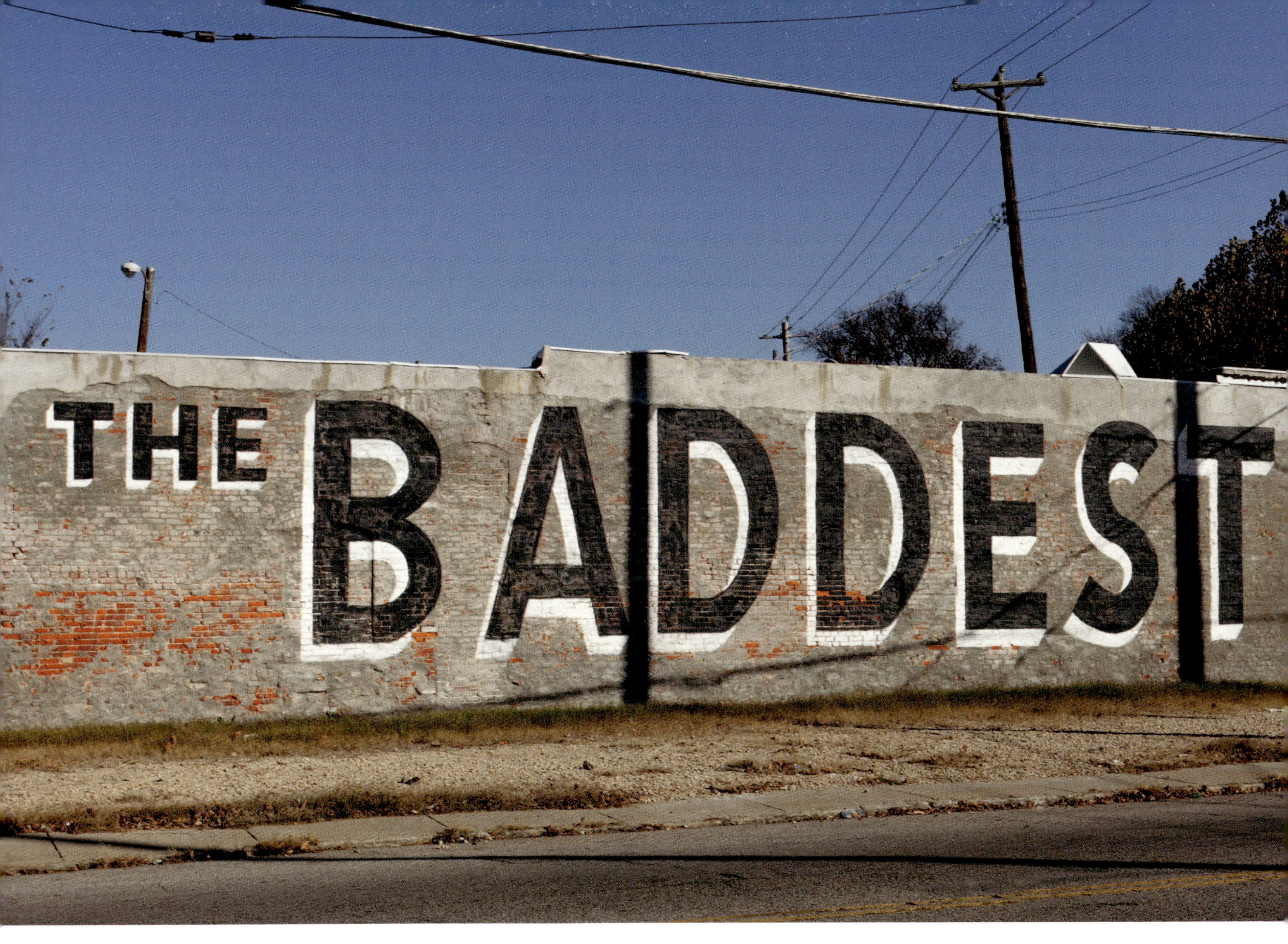
THE BADDEST

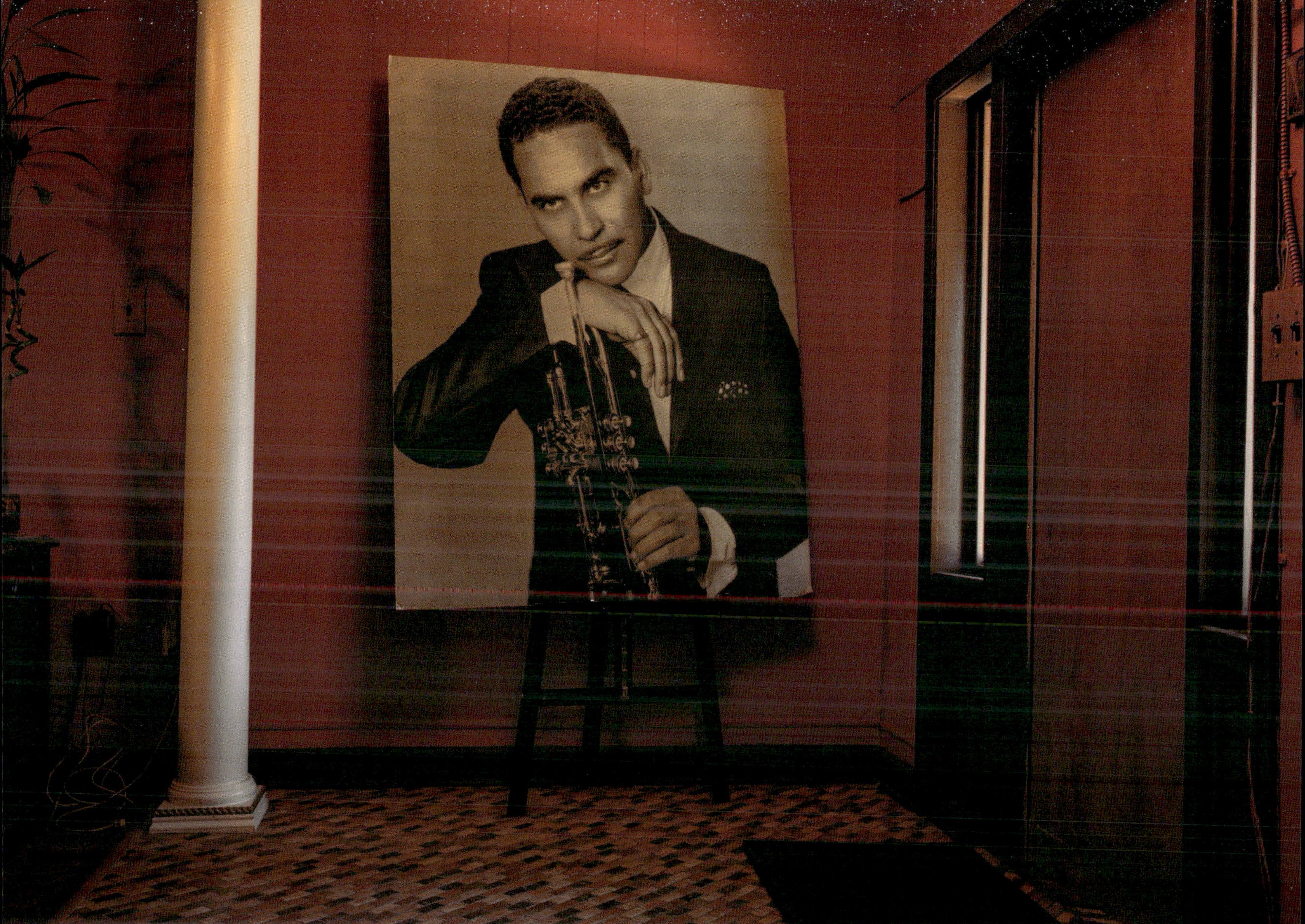

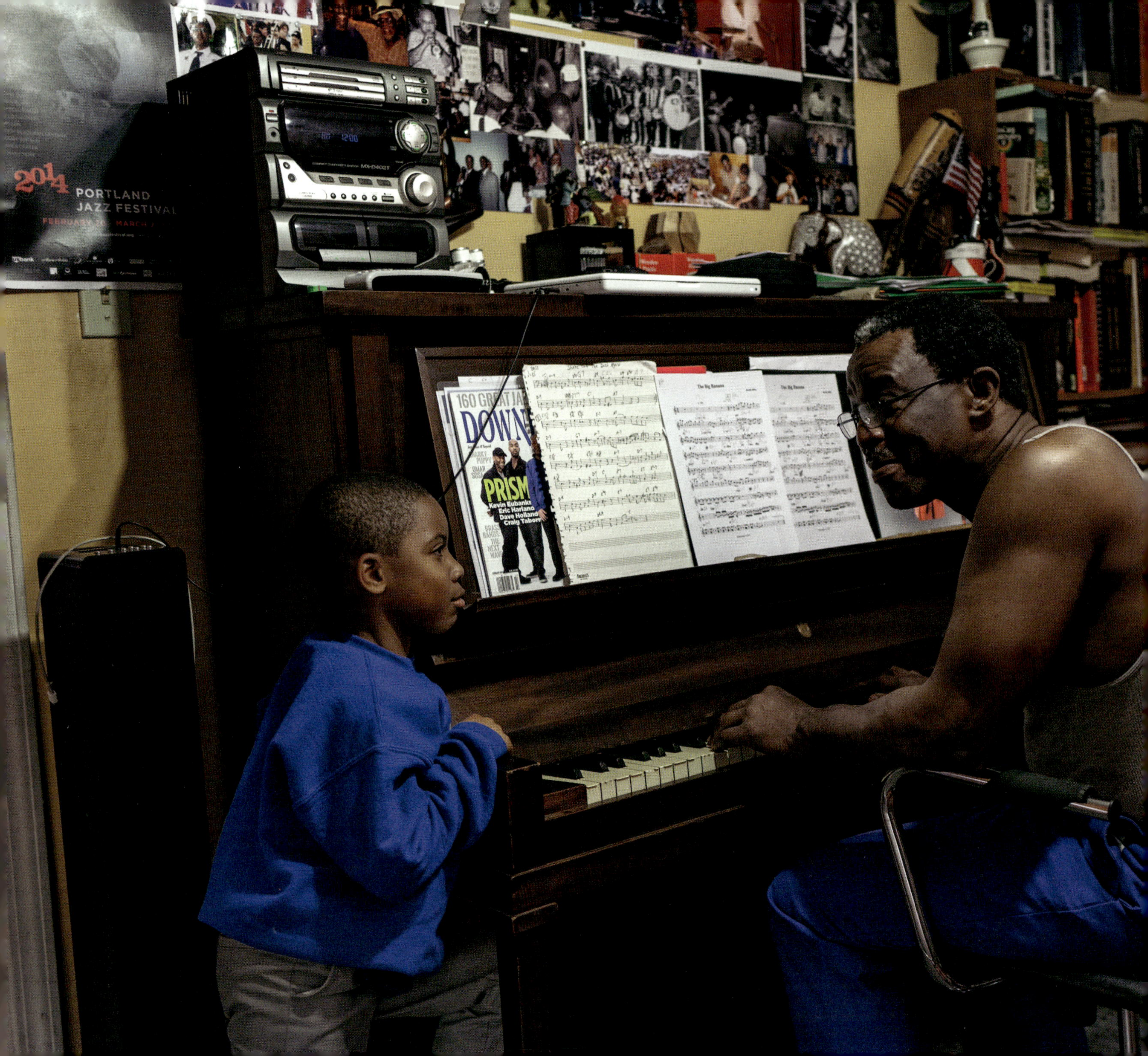
2014
PORTLAND
JAZZ FESTIVAL
PRISM
Kevin Eubanks
Eric Harland
Dave Holland
Craig Taborn

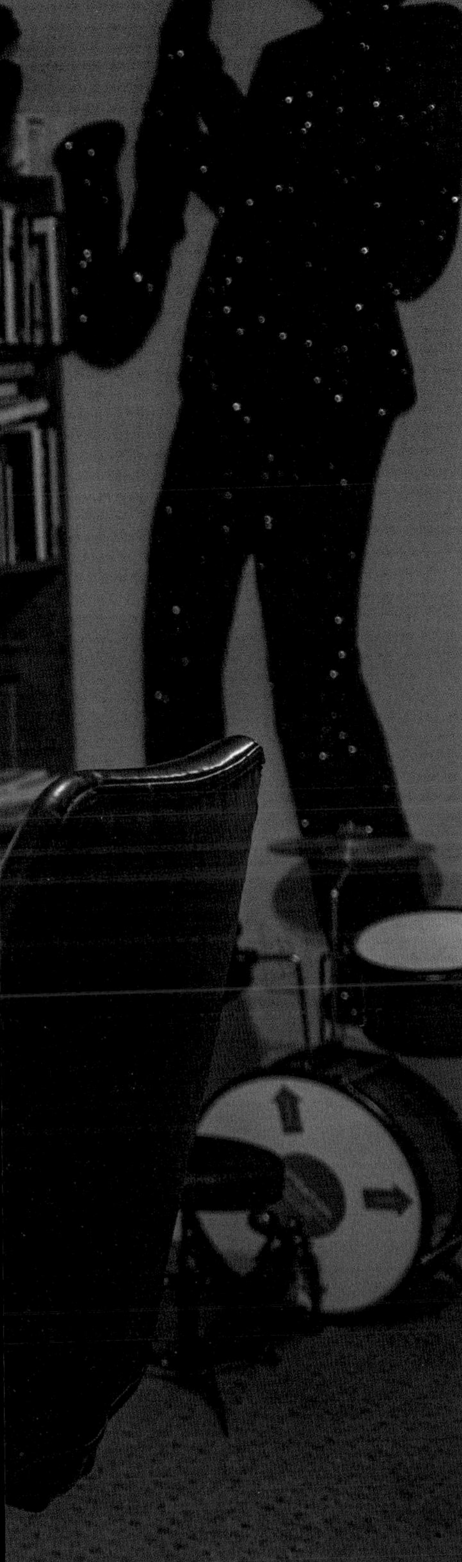

HERLIN RILEY

Wynton Marsalis / Ahmad Jamal / Dr John / Dianne Reeves / Cassandra Wilson / Jazz at Lincoln Center Orchestra. Photographed at home, Louisiana

My mother's father, he played the drums in the church. He was one of the first people to introduce the drums to the church service, like in 1930 or something. When I was a boy, I went to church with him all the time. I couldn't wait till he got up from the drum set so I could have a chance to sit down and play. And even though that music was done in a church – it was for praise and worship – when I got to play, I was playing in front of people. It was very helpful in my development because there was a certain spirit in playing music in the churches in the South. I learned to play the tambourine, I learned the power of repetitive rhythms and how it evokes a certain kind of spirit inside of you. When I got behind the drums I didn't want to just play the regular church beat, I wanted to play some James Brown rhythms, some 'Cold Sweat' or something. My grandfather would just look at me and say, 'Nah, it's not the place for that. Keep it straight.' That taught me that there's a time and place to be experimental, to play odd metres and other weird things. There's also a time where you should just play straight and play the time, because that's the foundation of the music.

My grandfather, in 1913 he played with Louis Armstrong. When I was a boy growing up, he would actually sit at the breakfast table with me and he would have two butter knives in his hands and he would actually beat out rhythms on the table for me and challenge me to do those things. It was cool because I didn't realize the historical significance of him doing that. He was born in 1902 so he had a connection to music from the 1800s. So when he was teaching me, this was in the early '60s, so that was seventy years of history that was coming through him that he directly laid on me.

It was wonderful to have my grandfather, first of all, but then when I got old enough to go to Preservation Hall and check out some of those other guys who were my grandfather's age, those older drummers from that era, I got to hear their perspective on the same style of music. So that was very rich for me. I got to understand and be part of the brass band tradition of New Orleans. When you listen to most New Orleans drummers you will hear a significant flux of the bass drum, because here in New Orleans we've learned to play the drum set from the bottom up as opposed to from the top down. When you hear the brass bands coming up the street, the first thing you can hear is the bass drum and you can hear it from blocks and blocks away. People start turning off lights and locking up their houses to get outside to the procession, to the parade.

Drummers … well, anybody who's young and who's trying to develop something, they're trying to get information, and in order to get information you have to be humble enough to receive it. A lot of times drummers, once they get a certain amount of information, then they feel like they've arrived. But you know, you never arrive in music – I've been doing this for forty years and I'm still learning different aspects of playing. There are some students I've had before who play the drums a different way than I do, like they have this whole hip hop way of playing. So when I have a student and he's good at that style, I'll ask him, 'Hey man, show me how to do that.' Because music is bigger than the individual. You have to learn in order to be really, really great.

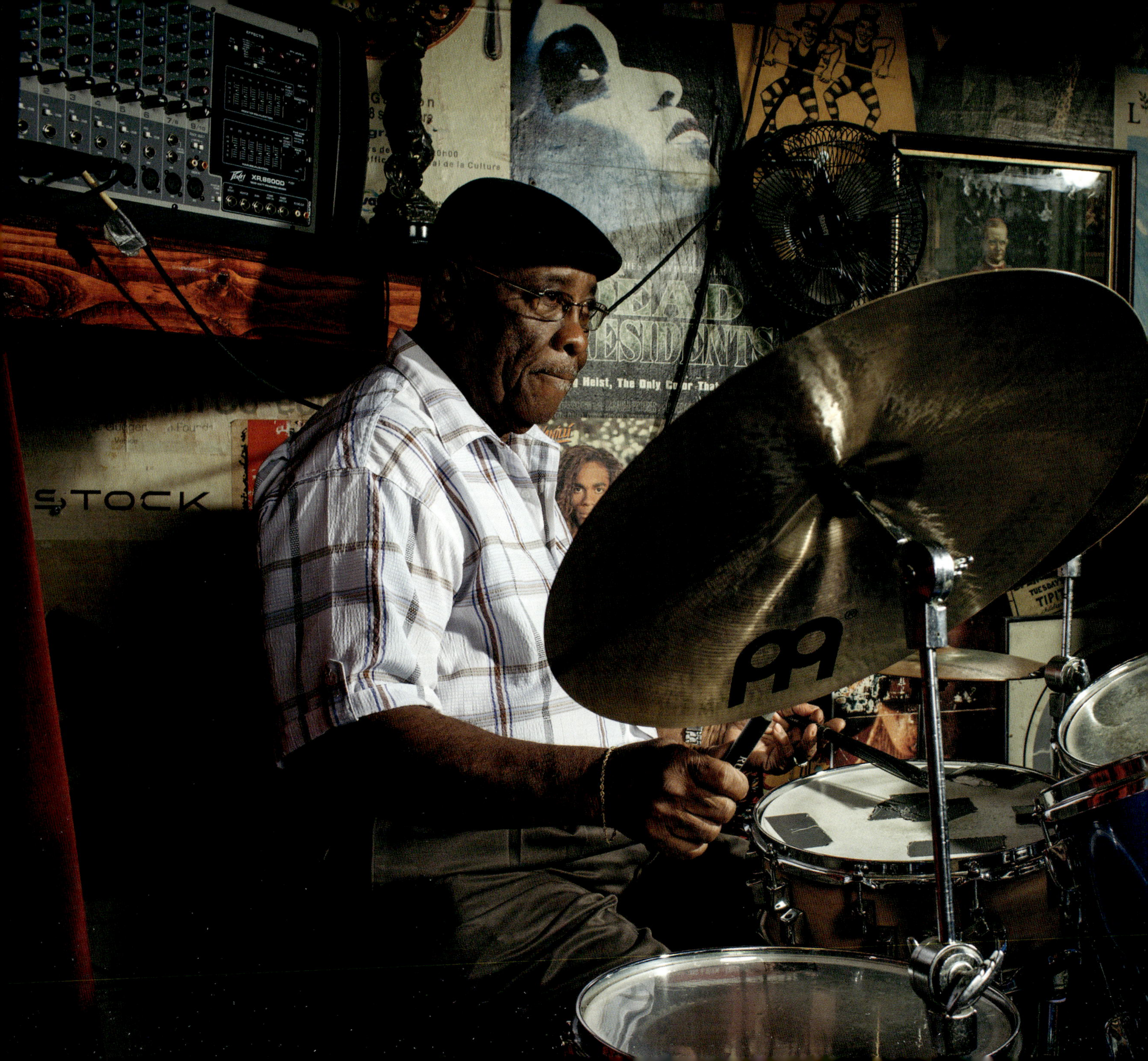
XR8600D
Heist, The Only Color That
STOCK

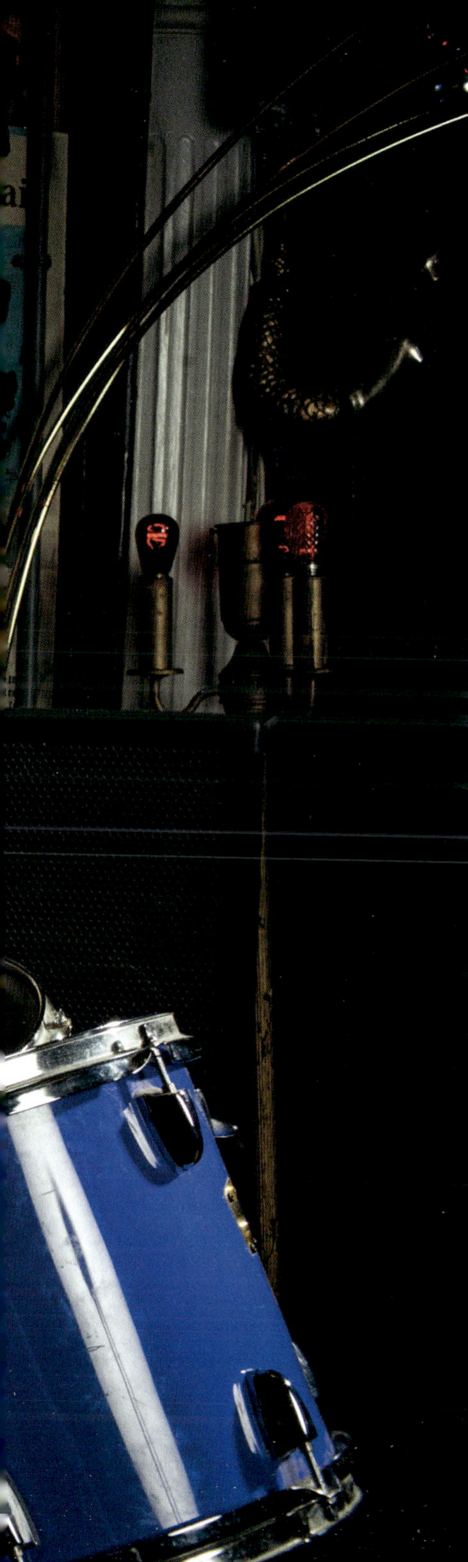

JOHN 'JAB'O' STARKS

Bobby 'Blue' Bland / James Brown / B.B. King. Photographed in Florida

I'll say this much: with James, Bobby Bland or even with B.B. King, you wore a suit. You wore suits when you played. We played in New York with James; we had to wear a tux. With James, you were one of the best-dressed groups on the road. All of his uniforms for the band were tailor-made. But the only thing that bothered me was those platform shoes. And let me tell you, I told everybody I met, 'I cannot play in these things, I can't walk in these. These things'll break my ankles if I try to walk in these.' They made you about 8 feet tall. So when I'd get onstage, I'd pull them off. I had shoes there that I could slide my feet into to play with. You walked onstage in them and, if they took pictures, you stood there with them, but so far as play in them, no man, no siree bob, I couldn't play in them.

When I joined James's group, there were five drummers onstage and I just asked the question, 'You have five drummers, why am I here?' And he said, 'You'll see.' No one certain drummer was doing everything, and he told me, 'I just want you to watch the show for this week.' So I went and sat on the side of the stage and watched what they were doing against what he was doing, how they were playing with him. He sat me in and said, 'You've heard this now after this week, I want to hear you play this tune, but I want you to play it ...', and he said he wanted me to play it the way that I heard it, and it started that way. I really never had a basic audition with James.

See, I had already been performing with Bobby Bland, so that was a blues gig, and he was rather popular because of all the tunes that he did. I recorded all of his stuff from '59 up to '65, [so] I was accustomed to seeing crowds, but after I went with James, that was a whole different job. I mean, I had never seen that many people at one time for one artist like that. It was mega. That's when I started hating the theatres. I used to love to play the theatres: you do your show and get off. But James did five, six shows a day. From ten o'clock, eleven o'clock in the morning, people in the theatres. I saw a triple line at the Apollo almost three blocks long waiting to hear us. You'd play a show, they would open the side door and let the people out, then close the door. And as soon as they closed it they'd open the front door, and fill it up again. It was just truly amazing, and you'd sit there and watch it.

I've never been a flagger, as they call it, on drums, but I've never been that show drummer. I sit there and play, and I'm lazy, I don't like to have to reach up here or over there for cymbals or whatever. I sit with everything right there where I can get to it. So after he started weeding drummers out, it got down to just Clyde [Stubblefield] and myself, so each one of us had to learn to play everything that James did. I don't play like Clyde; Clyde doesn't play like me, so therefore you get two different takes, you get the same groove but there's a difference in the groove. That's when I started getting the overseas travelling too. I'd never gone overseas until I joined his group.

Clyde knew me from playing with Bobby Bland. We became like, are still ... we're brothers. We don't have to communicate. We know how to play off each other, and when we were with James, with regards to where he was, if he would point back at one of us to take it up, we could take it right where it was. He played little tricks with you, too. If he'd catch you not watching him, then he'd point to you and if you didn't do it, then he wanted to fine you – I don't know how much because I never paid fines. There have been quite a few gigs that we played where we really went off – like the crowd was there but you shut that out and you're into your groove. I never will forget a gig at the Olympia theatre in Paris. We got into a tune, we really got into it. I mean we couldn't hardly stop the groove. James just went off stage and we just kept pumping. I don't know what it was, you can't explain it. And we could not stop, and we just played and played, and the longer we played, the harder the groove got, and when he came out at the end, that's one of the few times I know we had him – we wore him down. After the gig was over with, when everything was through, you could still feel that pulse. It was amazing. That groove, it was still there.

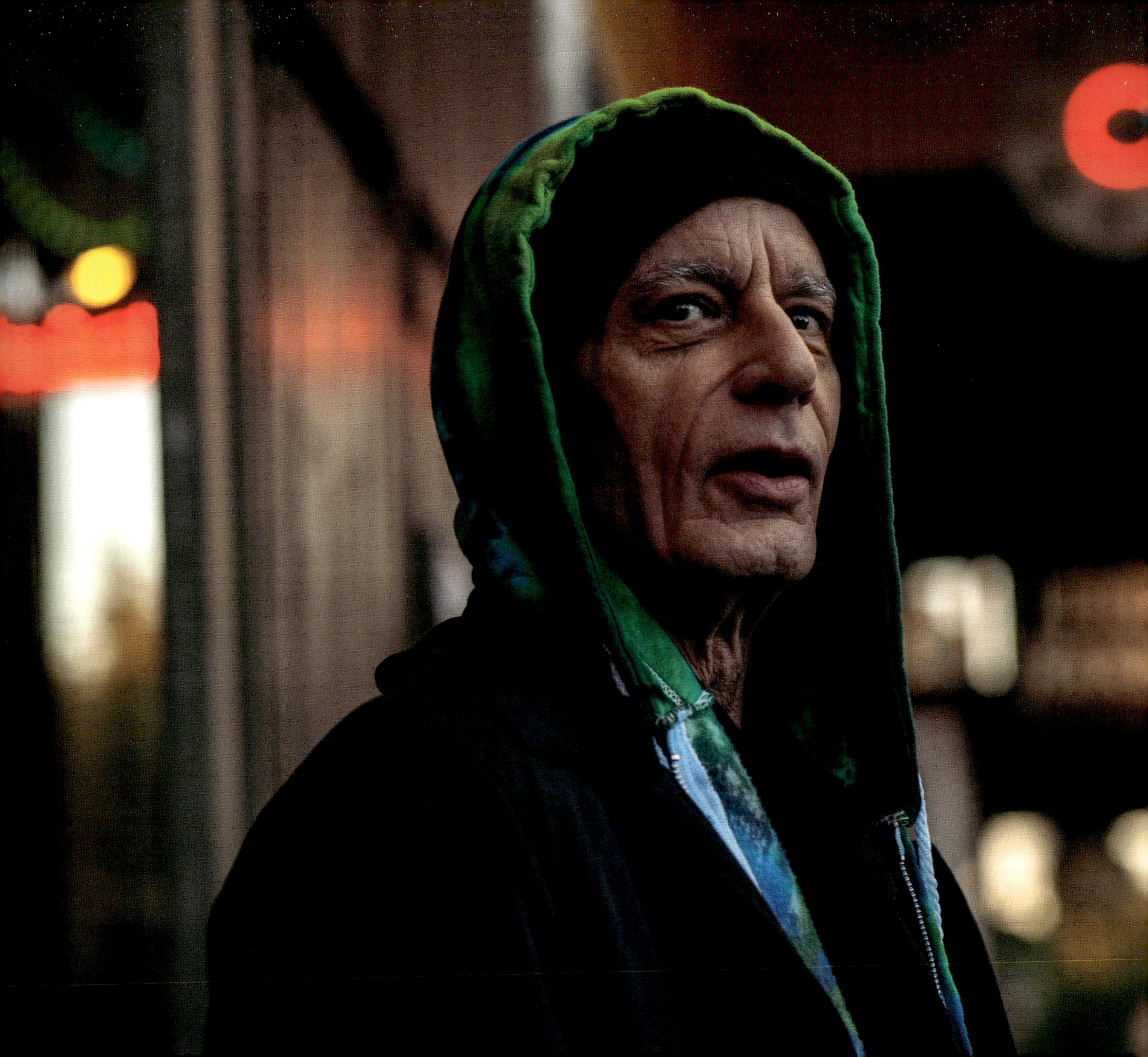

JOHNNY VIDACOVICH

Astral Project / Nolatet / The Trio. Photographed in Louisiana

“I LIKE PLAYING THAT’S RIDICULOUSLY HEAVY. SOMEONE WHO STAYS BEHIND AND MAKES EVERYTHING SO PIMP – LIKE JOHN BONHAM”

JULIE EDWARDS

Deap Vally. Photographed at the Deap Vally rehearsal space, California

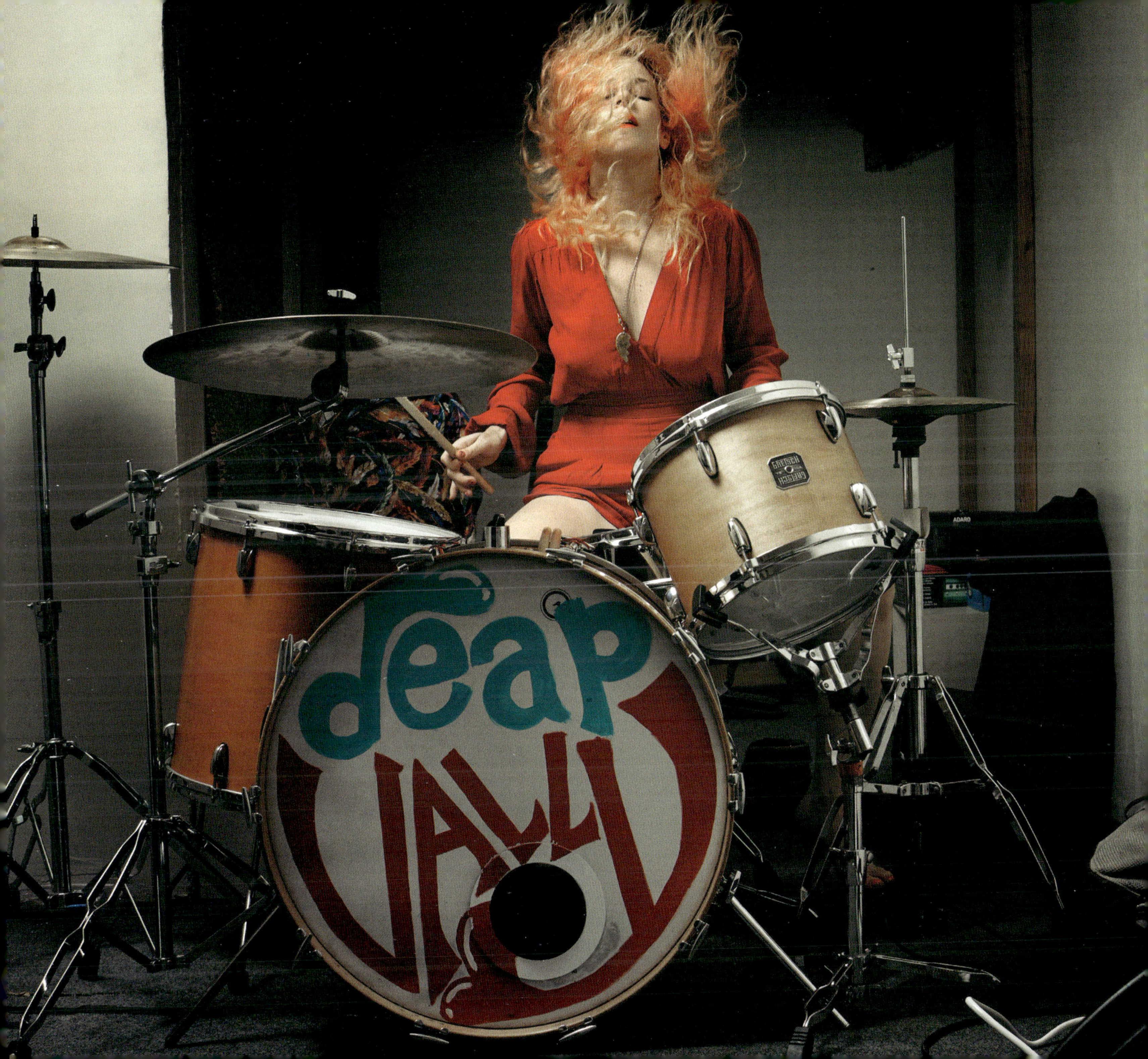
deap
VALLY

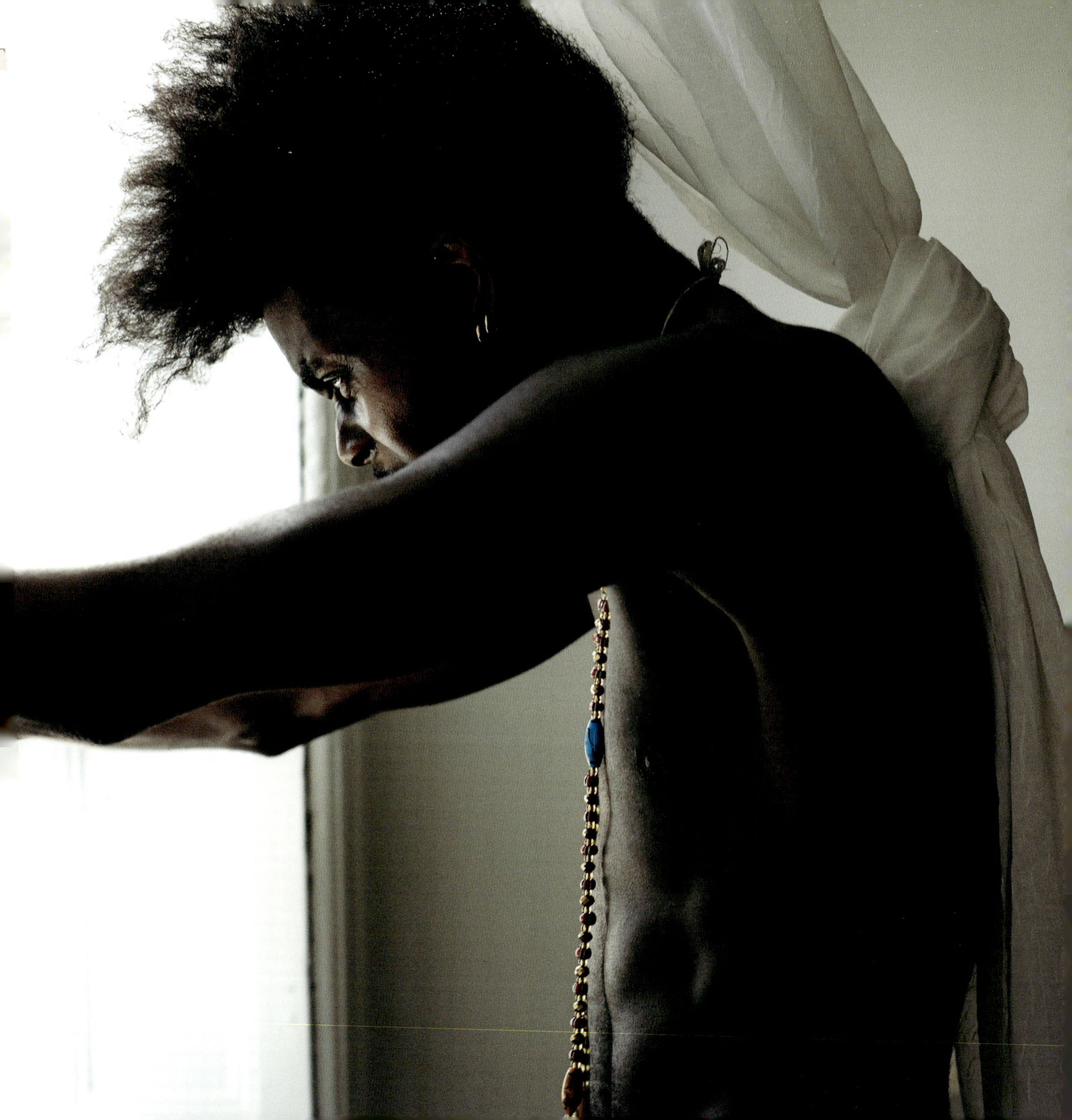

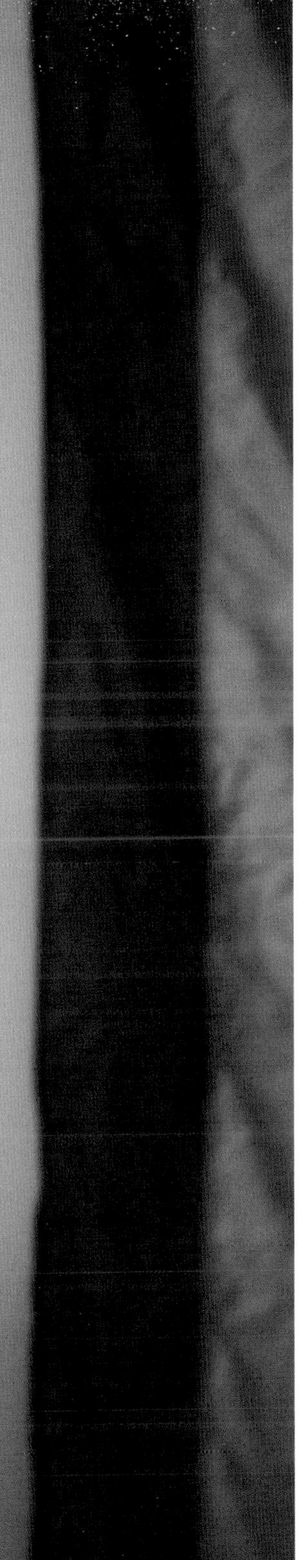

PAULI 'THE PSM'

Gorillaz / Damon Albarn / Harry Styles. Photographed at home, New York

The drum machine's got a spirit in the same way that a human drummer has. The traditional thing to say would be like, you know, a human drummer has energy and it's alive and will bring its personality and its touch and its flavour. No, the drum machine is exactly the same: it's an instrument, and you're programming the drum machine in the same way that you programme your body to play the drum kit. When I play a drum machine, I really go to town on the fact that it's an instrument that needs to be pushed to its limits in the same way a clarinet or a drum kit or whatever should be played. I think drum machines are amazing. Look at Jam and Lewis – those guys made patterns that drummers cannot play. Look at what Skrillex is doing now with dance music. You can't keep up with that stuff. Questlove, he replicates drum machines. Look at what J Dilla did with the drum machine. That is more than what any drummer can do. Except Quest or Chris Dave.

The first time I met Tony Allen I was onstage at the Africa Express Christmas party. And Damon [Albarn] is playing synth, like how he plays synth on his African vibe, and then Flea's playing bass and we're going nuts. I thought I was doing alright, but I can feel this presence of this guy coming from behind me. He's kind of just watching me. I was like, who's this old Black dude? This old fool, get out of here, I'm playing drums. At the end of the song, he taps me on the shoulder and he goes to take the sticks from me. I'm looking and then I realized it was Tony Allen. He says to me, 'Today you're not great, but one day, you will be a man.' I was like, what the heck? Okay … So he went on drums and everyone was like, 'Ahhh! Tony Allen!' But I was like, ah shit, that's Tony Allen, he just rubbished my whole life.

I watched him play that whole set and it was amazing, it was just like he was floating. I wondered how he was doing it – he kept the whole band together but it was like he wasn't even touching the drums. He's so light. He's a great drummer. He doesn't play the notes, he hears the notes, he feels the notes, he goes to play it but he just tricks you into thinking it's happening. It's not even there. He's a magician. The guy is beyond drums. There was a song at the end that he didn't really want to play and he said, 'Yeah, you can play now.' I played this song and I played my heart out. But playing my heart out is not the same as a great drummer who just floats. At the end of it he says to me, 'I'm playing a gig next week at the Jazz Café. You need to come.' I was like, okay, cool.

I tried to learn everything about Afrobeat in that week. I go to the Jazz Café and Tony says, 'I need you to play four songs today.' He plays the whole set and then he goes on the microphone – it's an evening with Tony Allen – he goes, 'Okay, thank you. I'm now going to bring out from London: Pauli.' And I was like, shit. I kind of thought he wanted me to play but I wasn't kidding myself thinking Tony wants me to play. So I'm playing these songs and at the end he comes up to me and says, 'Last week you were not a man but today you've done me proud. Well done.' And I was like, Ahhh! Tony Allen, sick! He is drums. When you see him, you just think: You are drums.

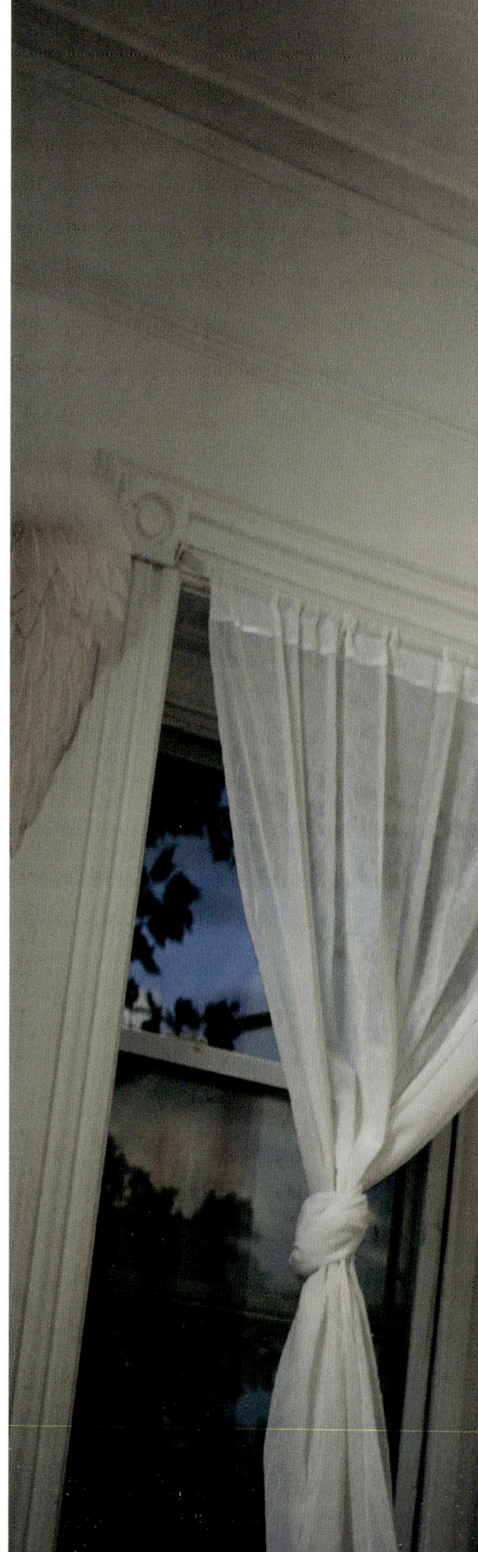

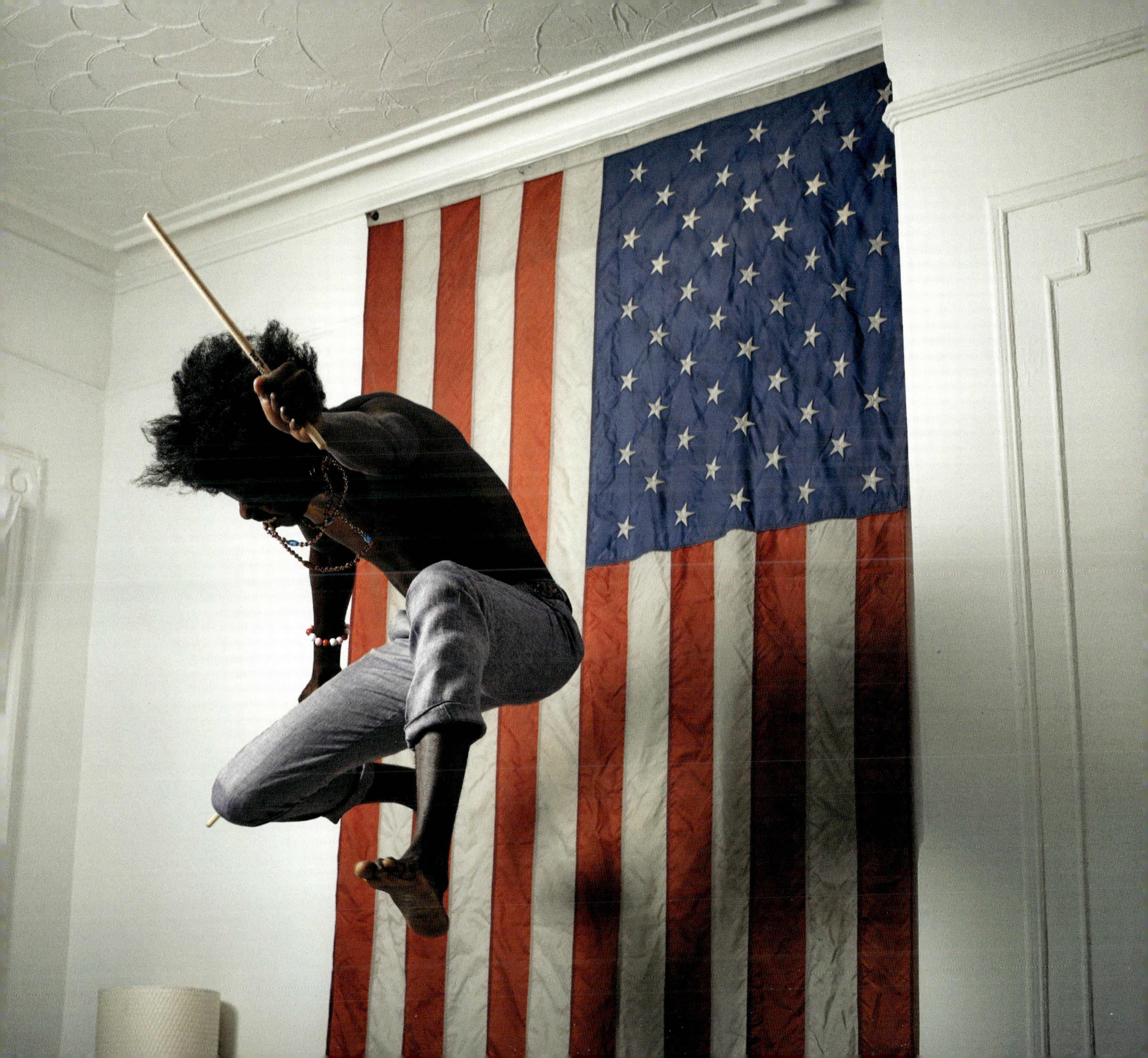

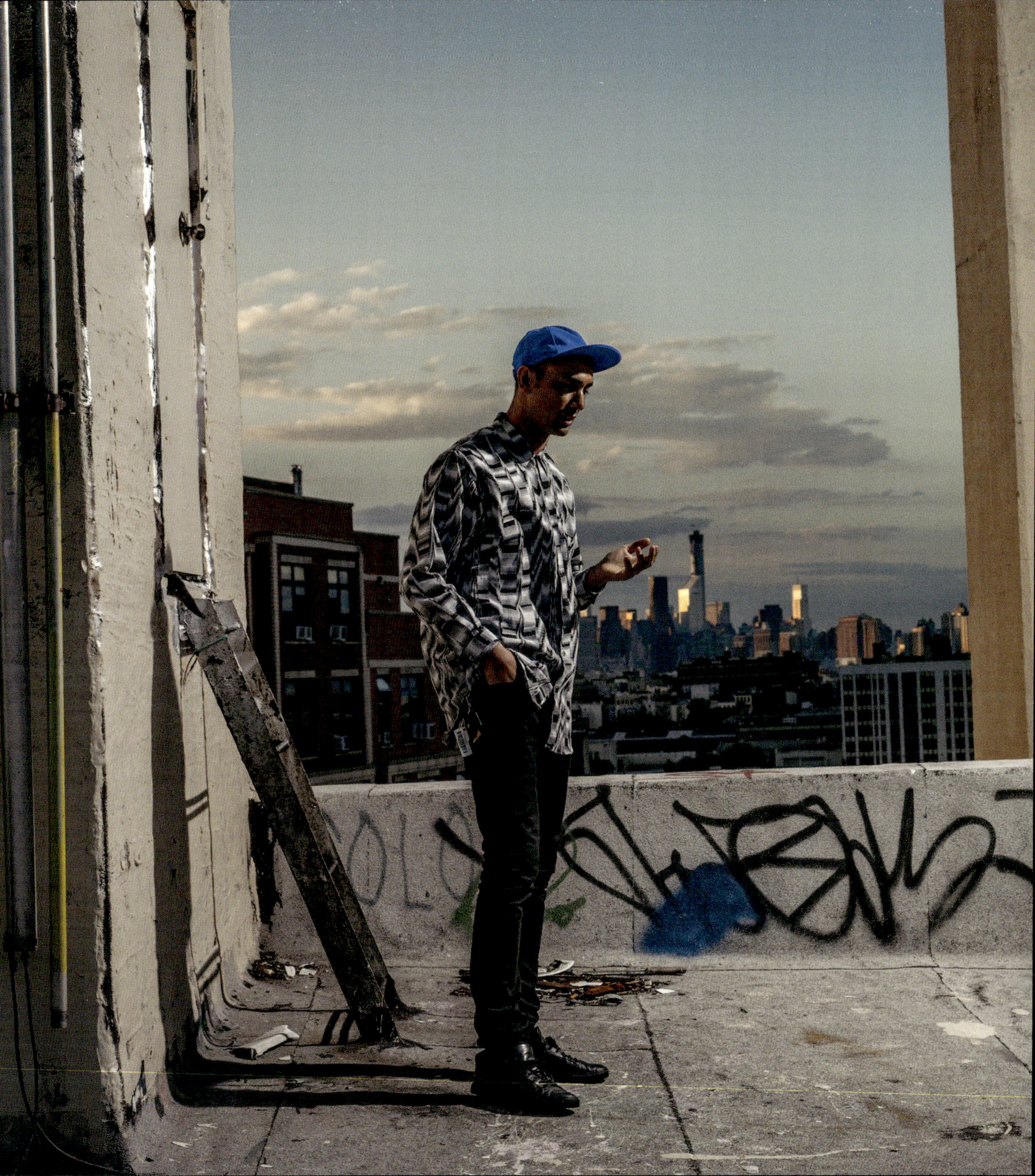

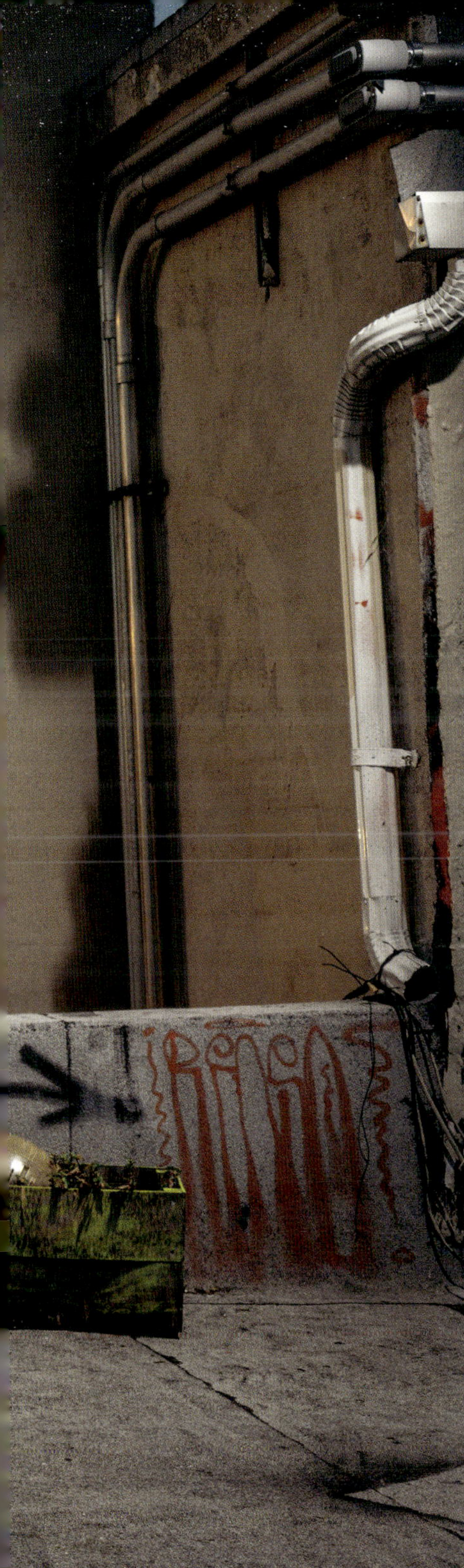

HISHAM BHAROOCHA

Soft Circle / Black Dice / Boredoms / Yokubari / Kill Alters. Photographed in New York

As a kid I was always excited about outsider art or art that came from people who didn't have an art education. Even though I have an art education, I still feel I tap into that instinctual creative mark-making. With music I think about it the way James Brown described it, where everything is a drum. Everything you're putting into the music has a space where it becomes a percussion instrument. The way every little sound makes you move, it should all fit in well together, and if you can pull it off in the most minimal way then actually that's the most rhythmic. Percussive music is all about creating a nice rhythm within the positive and negative space. Without that, it could just be mush and, even though a drummer is technically capable, it can be overplayed. That can drive any musician listening crazy. Like, you don't need to show off. It's all about trying to make good music, not show off your chops.

Improvising is something that just comes with experience. I know a lot of great players who cannot improvise at all. You can tell they just don't feel comfortable. The stage is such an honest place. If somebody is trying to be a pop star and they've created an image of themselves, or somebody else has created it or many people have created this image for them to emulate, that's fine. But if you're really collaborating onstage and really trying to make something that all the parties involved couldn't have imagined on their own, then you're constantly listening and feeling the space and the timing of things. It's a really fun place. When I do improvisation it feels like tapping into an old library in my mind. Sometimes I'll play guitar or bass for improvisation too, and I'll pay attention to the different timbres that each thing can create. Then I use that vocabulary and make sure that I'm spreading it out throughout the performance so I don't spill all the beans at once and risk the audience losing interest.

I've seen all kinds, from free jazz to experimental noise to whatever, where people are just letting their steam out onstage and you think, that's not a performance. You should, even if you haven't thought about it, be paying attention to the air in the room. I spent my teenage years in Japan. There's a phrase in Japanese that means 'to read the air', so that's what I always reference. You just need to pay attention to the vibe of the room. Not that that should always decide the choices you are making, but you can tell if something is not working for that audience.

I think about musical work like a piece of artwork. The more serious I get about my visual art practice, the more I'm able to apply that language to my music making. I can think about the marks I'm making with sound in a different way. I think about the context that I'm pulling from, the references that I'm pulling from and how I'm playing it, and how that will be perceived by an audience. But in the end that's totally out of your control. You can think about it till the cows come home, but all you can do is play how you're going to play. Perform how you're going to perform. I like that aspect of it, too.

MARK GUILIANA

Beat Music / David Bowie / Mark Guiliana Jazz Quartet / St. Vincent
Photographed in his studio, New Jersey

I've been a sideman for 95 per cent of my professional life and I love that. I'm lucky to be in some very inspiring situations and I play music I really like, but there's nothing quite like presenting my own music. As the drummer in someone else's group, I'm responsible for the drumming and supporting the music as best I can from the drums. When I'm playing my own music it's my melody and my chords and so it really changes the way I play. It gives me a much more meta way of thinking and presenting. I try to bring that to my sideman life too, that way of thinking.

We drummers are oftentimes responsible for keeping things organized. I think the music comes first and it would be unfair to the music to make decisions that get in the way of your responsibilities. Maybe everyone is relying on us for that. But it's those magic moments, especially when you're playing with people you trust – if the moment allows for those chances, then I think they should be taken. Even if you fail, being in the place where you can take those risks, you're opening yourself up to the possibility of the music reaching incredible heights. That's the drug for me, that's what keeps me coming back: improvising and taking those chances. And that's when the dopamine kicks in – because of that risk. It's like why people jump out of planes. I think my favourite musicians have all their tools really refined and sharpened but they are still taking chances right in front of you. That's why live music for me … a guy like Jim Black, or Dan Weiss – I used to stalk him, I would go to every gig!

My motives were never about getting the gig with somebody; it was always like, hey, I like this music. That's the beauty of New York, because you always have access. You could be walking down the street to get a sandwich and hear music coming out of a place and you're like, oh my god, who is that? And you poke your head in. It's like constant discovery.

I play a lot of music where improvisation is a very important element, so it's important for me to go back and listen to try to observe and learn from the decisions we made at the time and really assess what felt right. There's a fine line, because I don't want to listen back and get attached to any of the decisions, because you can really go down a dead-end road of trying to recreate them. So I try to avoid that. I try to just listen back to see if I remember a few very specific chances I took and see if they came out the way I intended, or see how it affected the other musicians around me.

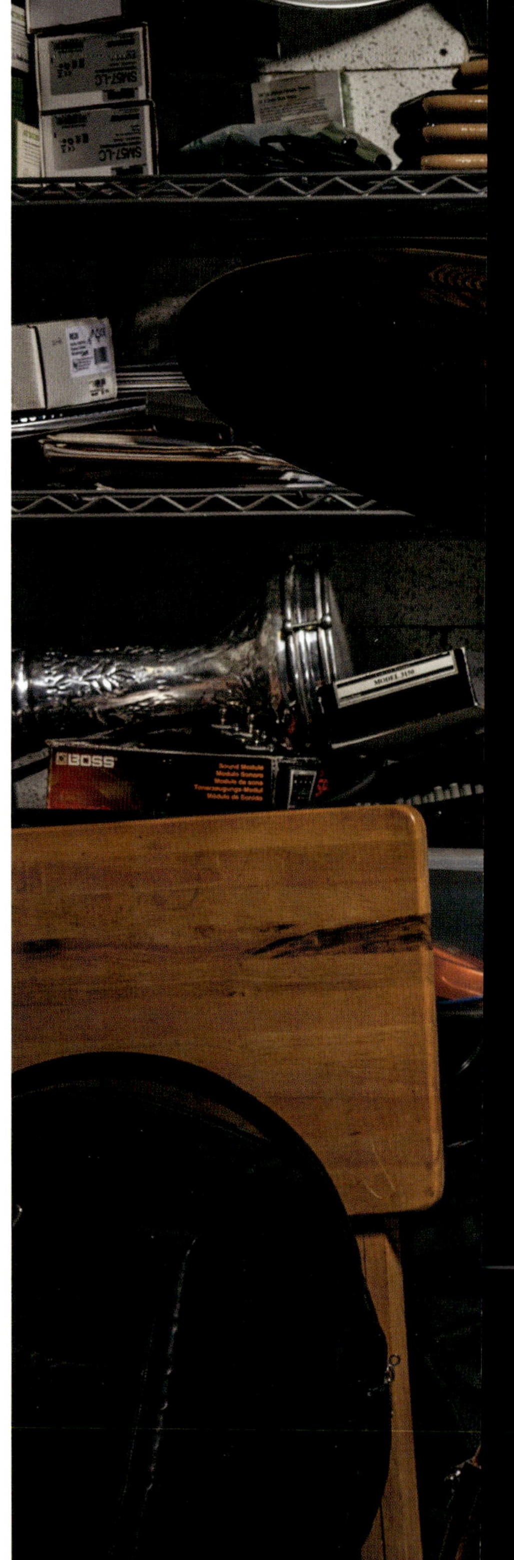

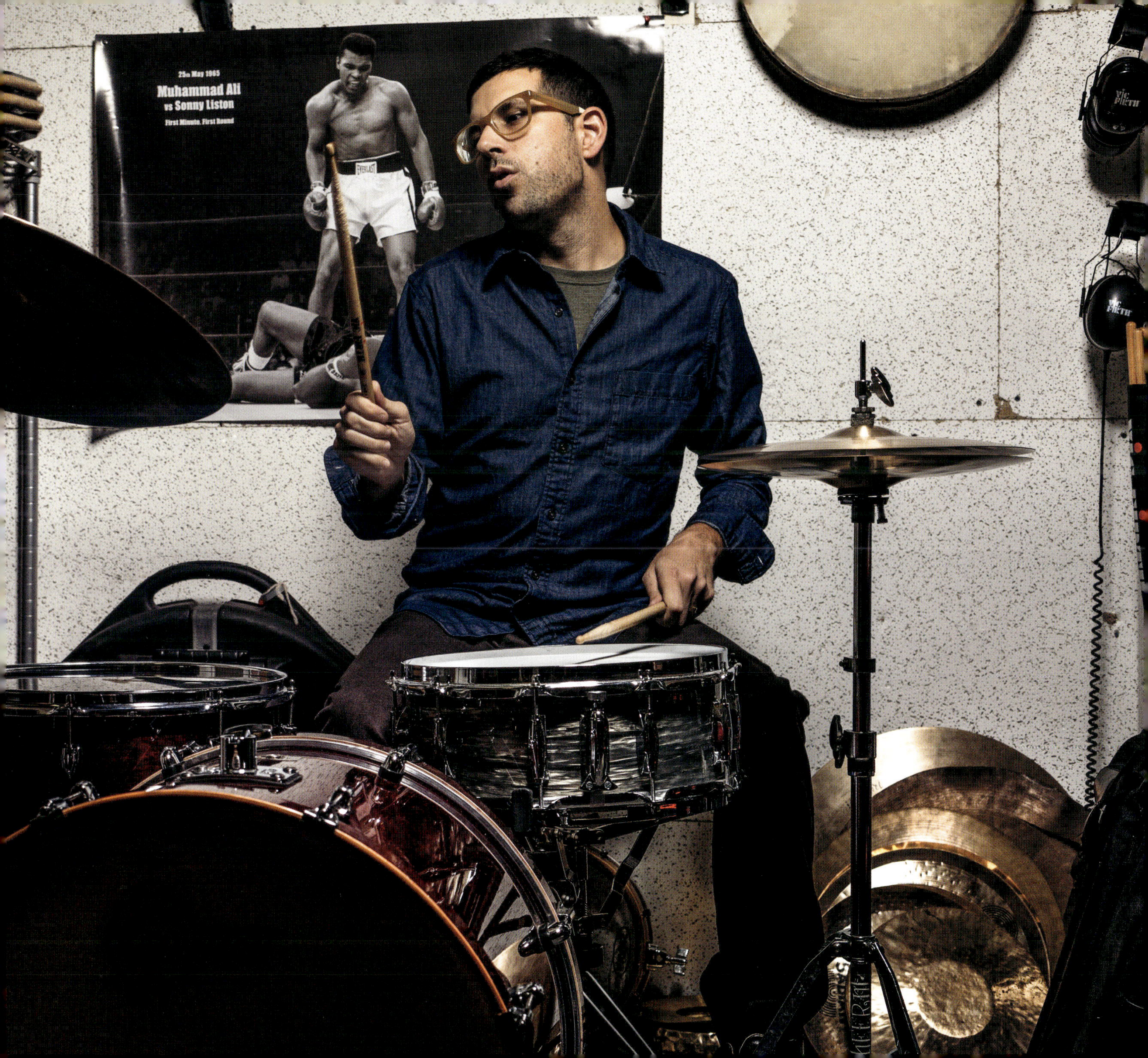
Muhammad Ali
vs Sonny Liston

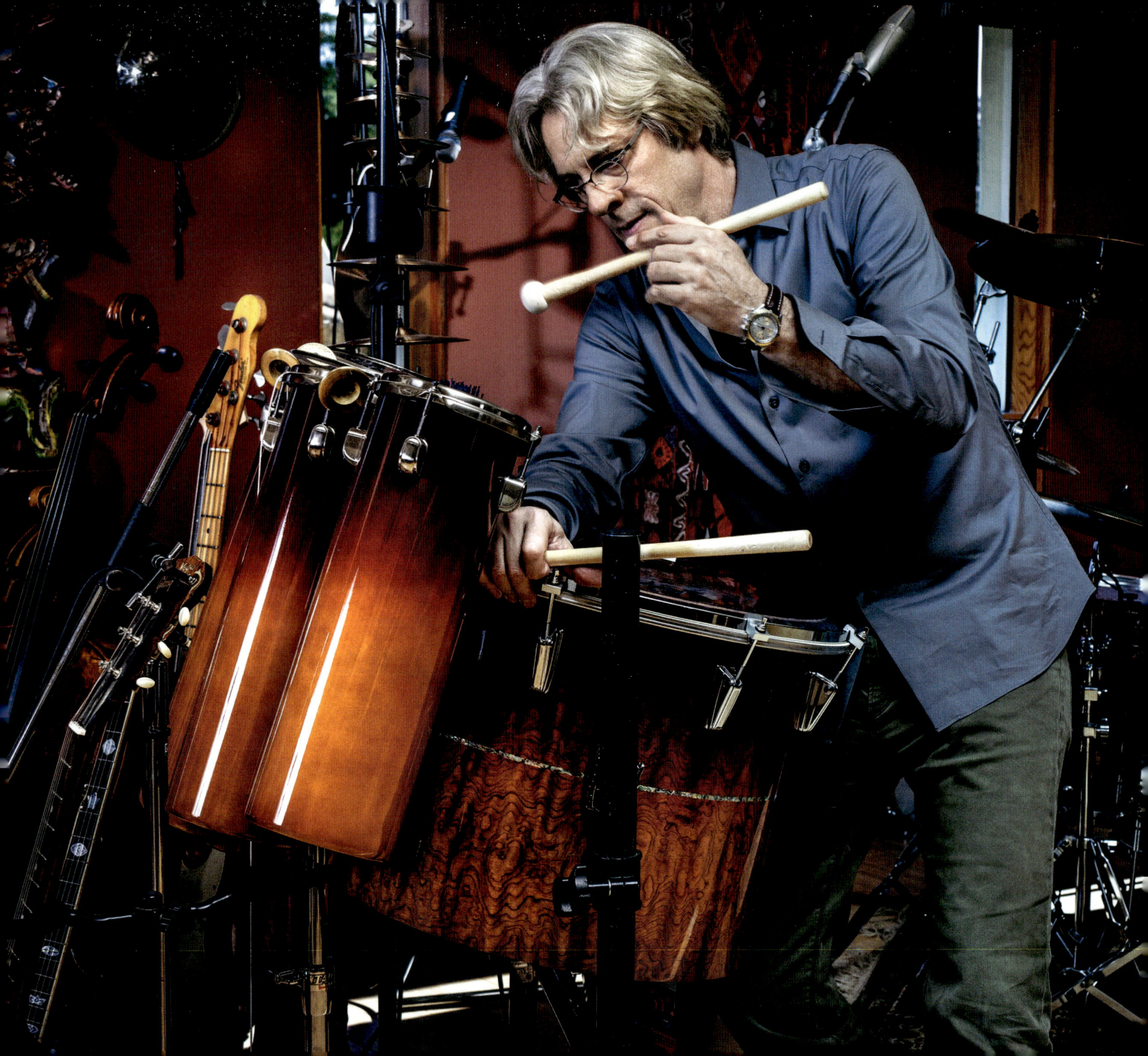

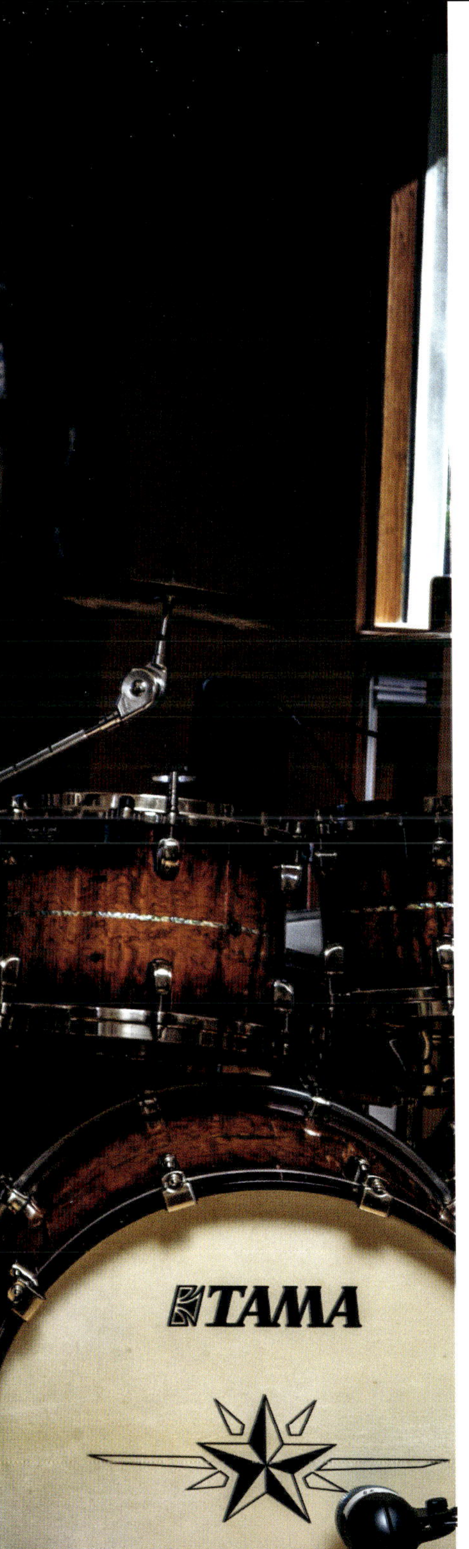

STEWART COPELAND

The Police. Photographed in his home studio, California

I was twelve when I played my first show. I remember it like it was yesterday; it was terrifying but it was life-changing. I was a late bloomer, a skinny kid with no hair on my chest, and my voice wasn't to break for another three or four years; and yet on that night I became an adult male silverback swinging through the trees, desired by the fifteen-year-olds with breasts. Actually, the prelude to this epiphany was in the afternoon, at the American Embassy beach club. This was in Beirut, Lebanon. I hear two of the aforementioned fifteen-year-old girls, so distant from my wildest dreams, talking about the Black Knights' new drummer, Ian Copeland, the coolest kid on campus in Beirut. But no, it's not Ian, it's actually his kid brother Stewart. 'Ian's got a brother? Wow! Is he as hip as Ian?' And I'm hearing these two girls talking about this guy Stewart Copeland in panting tones, and I'm thinking, my god, their young minds are pouring their imagination into this unknown vessel called Stewart – Ian's kid brother, the drummer in the band. This is very potent; it's a very important leg-up for a twelve-year-old.

After that Black Knights gig, the next big one was Wells Cathedral, Christmas service, Somerset, when I was at boarding school. A thousand voices raised in song, echoing around that building, floodlit from outside. Others might have seen God in it; I just heard the music. I felt the power of what music was for, the spiritual part of music. Not only is it for getting laid and for bringing those bosoms to my face, it is also for spiritual salvation. The power of it was magnified by the fact that I was a participant and that we played 'Little Drummer Boy'. For most of the service I had to be kept away from my drums because I'd be tipping and tapping. When it came time I'd get the nod to go and play, and in that cathedral, in the silence and the pews creaking in anticipation of the next dollop of shamanism, the next ladleful of spiritual power, there was little old me. To hit those drums to herald this piece of music and the voices raised, it was something very powerful. What's so powerful about it is that it takes an individual and makes him part of something huge. To be steering that ship, controlling the rhythm, is very potent.

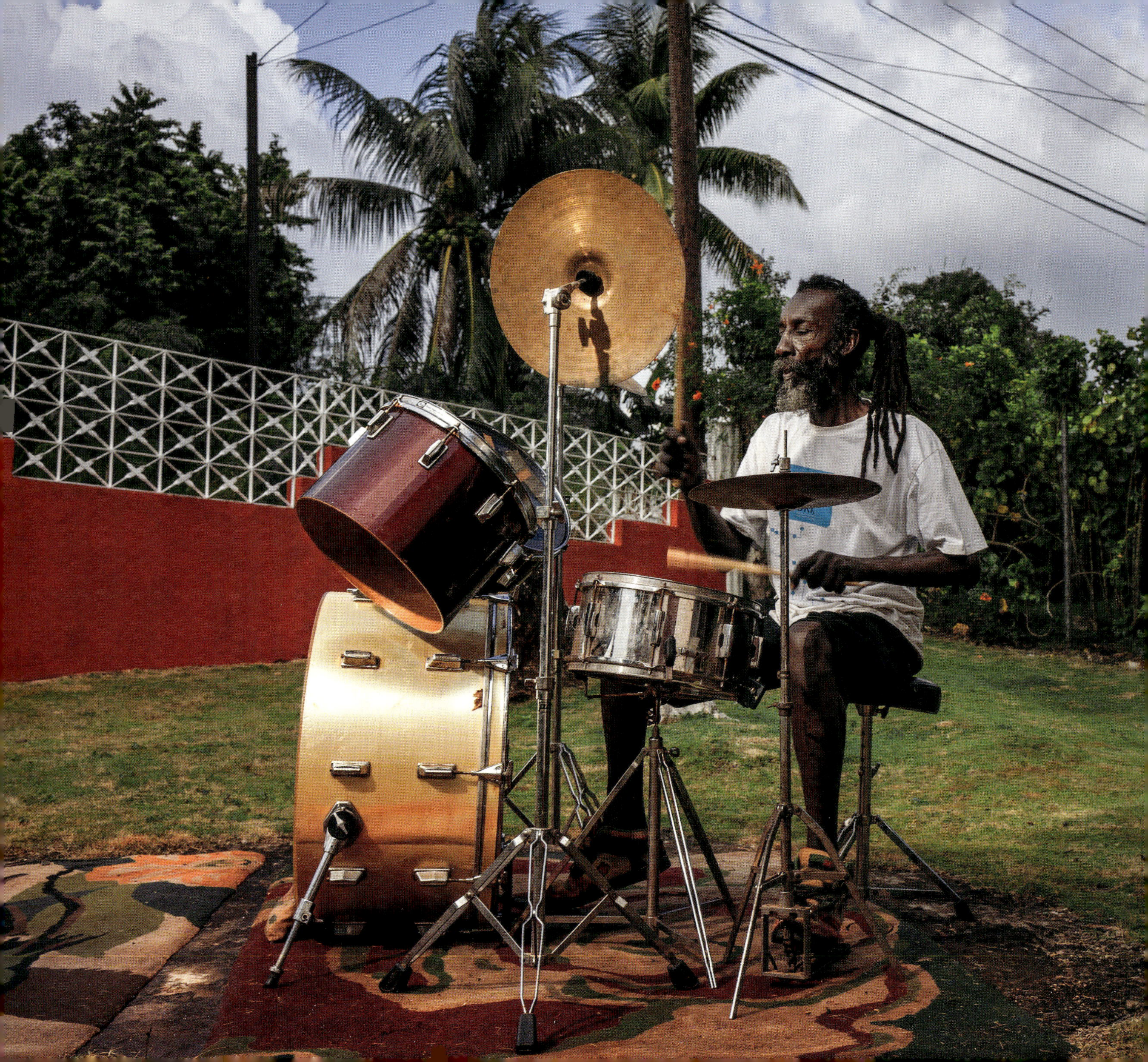

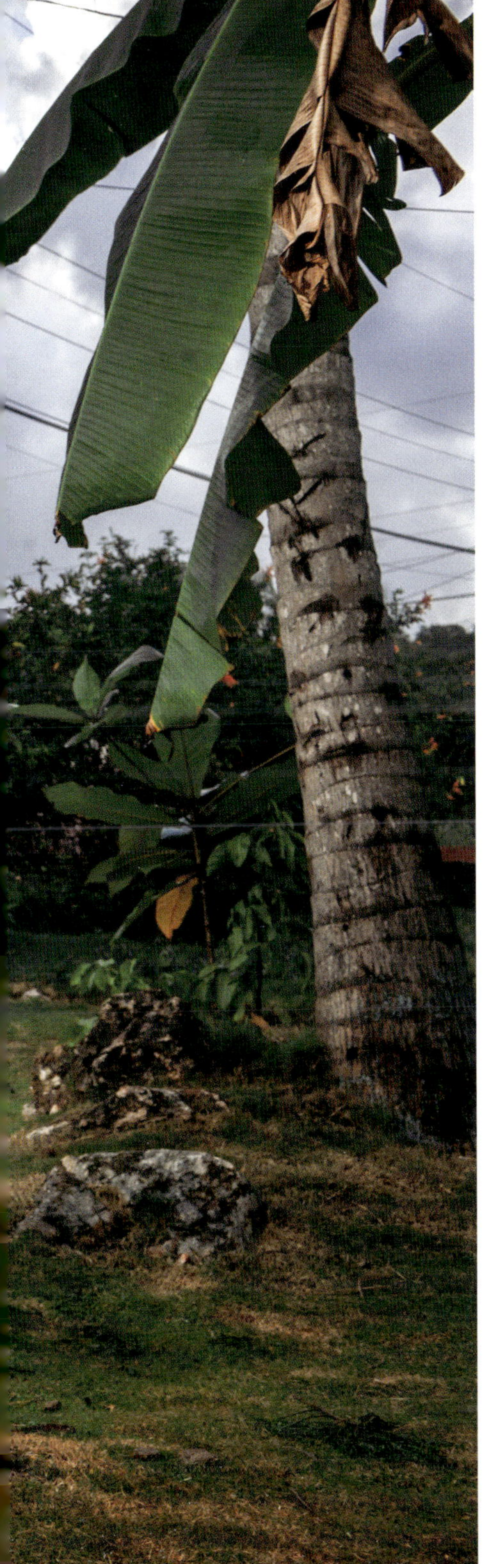

"A LOT OF DRUMMERS THEY PLAY TO BE HEARD. FOR ME, A DRUMMER MUST NOT BE HEARD, HE MUST BE FELT"

LEROY 'HORSEMOUTH' WALLACE

Burning Spear / Dennis Brown / Bob Marley / Peter Tosh / Gregory Isaacs / Studio One session drummer
Photographed at home, Jamaica

I still play music because, just like my friend Bob Marley, I have a dream. We talk every day, I still hear him in my ears. I hear Bob Marley speaking to me, he say, 'Horsemouth, go there and do it. You are there. Maybe you're the only one left.' It's like a revolutionary in a battle and we're going to be victorious.

You know those drumsticks you see me play with in the *Rockers* movie, wooden drumsticks? I'm looking for my drumsticks and I can't find them, and I take two chair posts from old chairs in the back of the Silver Sea Hotel and I go very fast, so you could never see it's not real drumsticks, it's just two chair posts. So it's not the drumsticks neither, it's you. That's the big difference; a lot of people don't understand, and a lot of drummers they play to be heard. For me, a drummer must not be heard, he must be felt. If you can't feel this drummer it makes no sense, I'm sorry.

A lot of drummers, they mark timing, they play for the timing of the song; they don't create. Like, timing is mathematics, right? A lot of people don't understand that music is second nature to God. Music is a very jealous thing. If you leave it out, it leave you out too. It says, 'That's what you want? Okay, go'. When I did *Rockers* the movie I said to myself, I'm going to play for nobody, I'm rich now. But the music leave you out too. The music, you can hear it talk to you, it say, 'Okay, that's what you want, okay, go ahead and sit here for the whole time and do nothing.' So I wake up, the music, wakes me up, and then I wait to see somebody that can play reggae music that great.

Most drummers, they keeping timing, and to make a roll they're waiting for some space, and it's not that. You have to be in the feel of the calculation, that mean you master the timing. That's why I love Elvin Jones – he mastered the timing, he played a solo right through the whole timing, he don't just keep on a specific timing. He keep a timing but he has about a million different timings he keep in that one timing. When you do that you master the timing, you master the beat you play. A lot of drummers they don't master the beat; you can see in their face they're dying for the song to be done. It's like a job.

You make your own space, you know. That mean you have to know the timing of what you're doing. A lot of people they don't know the timing, they make a space for the bass somewhere. But for me, you know, I make different spaces. I don't like to make spaces that people make, so it's all calculation. Maybe I think about a different space in a Rasta form. Thinking like a Rasta, what we do is we create things.

Reggae, it represent a lot of things, not just one beat. It's several beats in one. It's hip hop, Tchaikovsky … when I was a kid I used to play all the records and then I find out there's one jump in all of them … I don't care about how slow it go. And in everything you play, there's a reggae beat in it. Every music, there's a one-drop beat in it. It's all calculation, it's there. And if you play your music and say, 'Horsemouth, find a one drop in this beat,' don't care how funny the beat is going, I will find the one drop there for you.

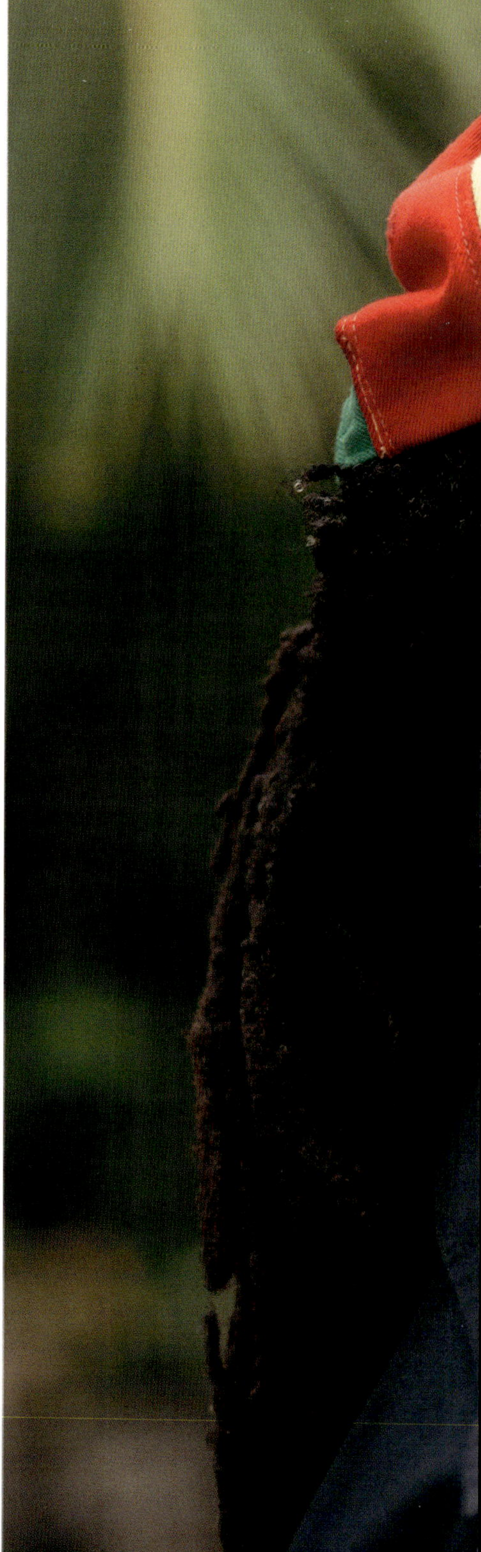

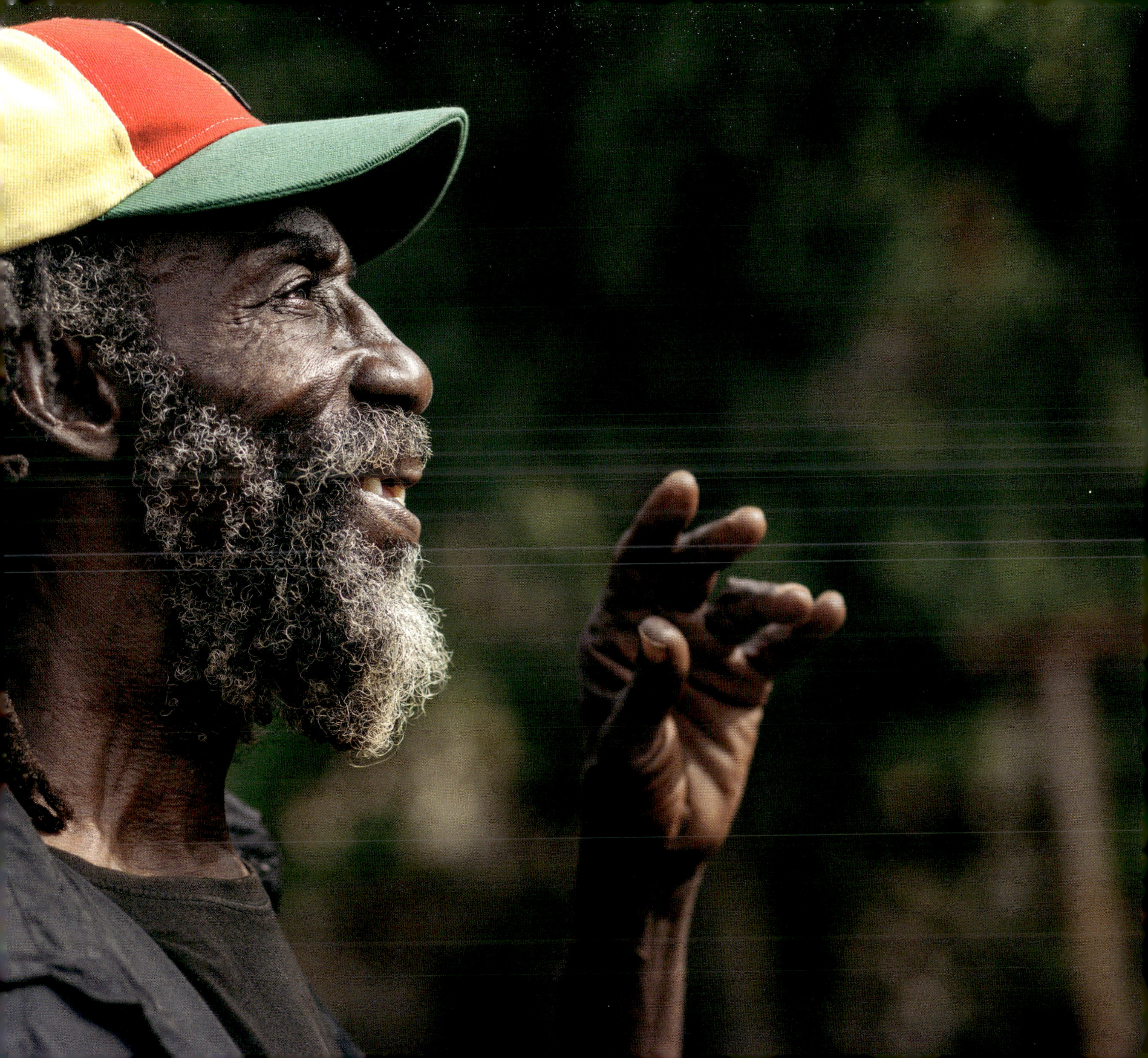

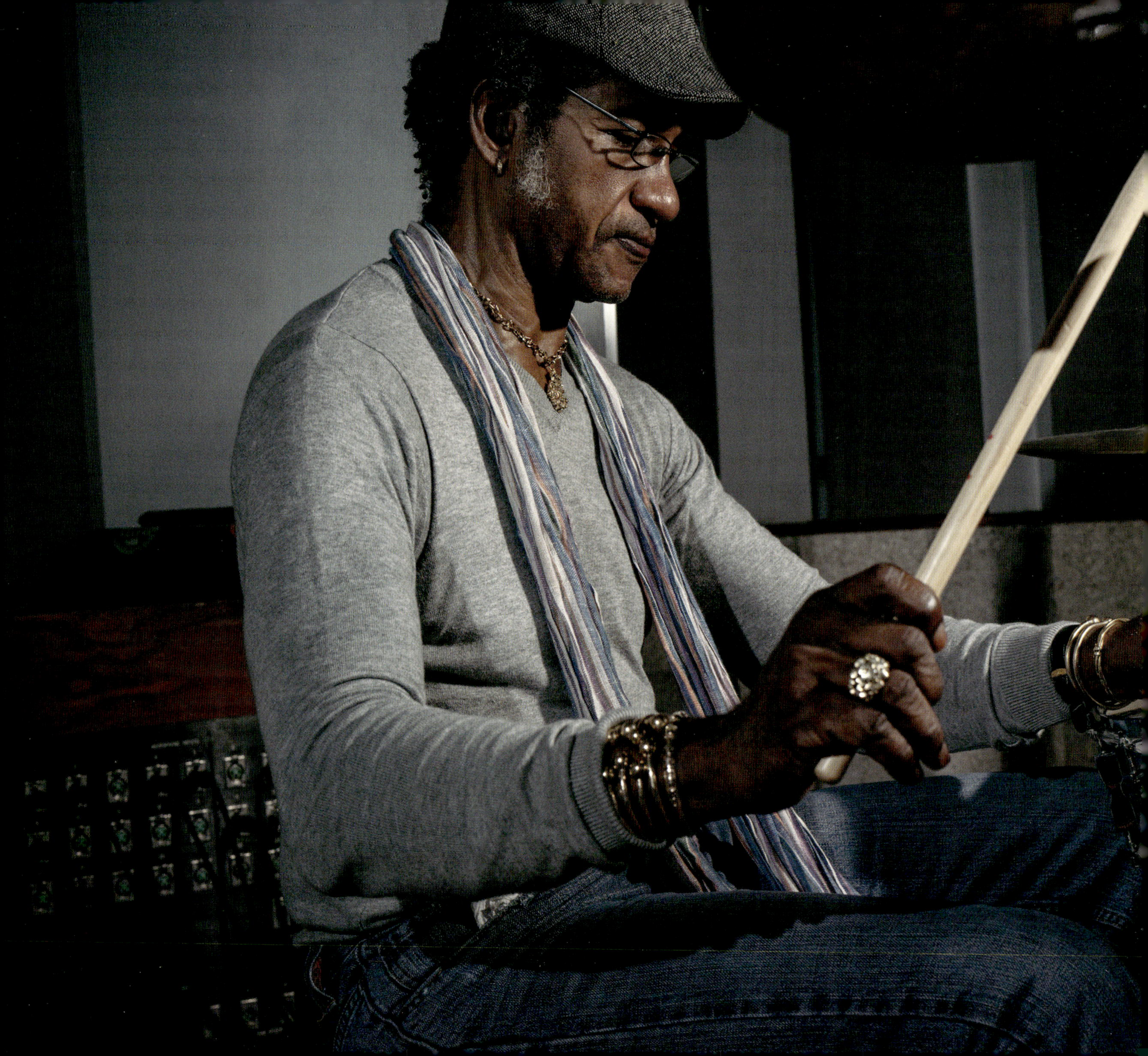

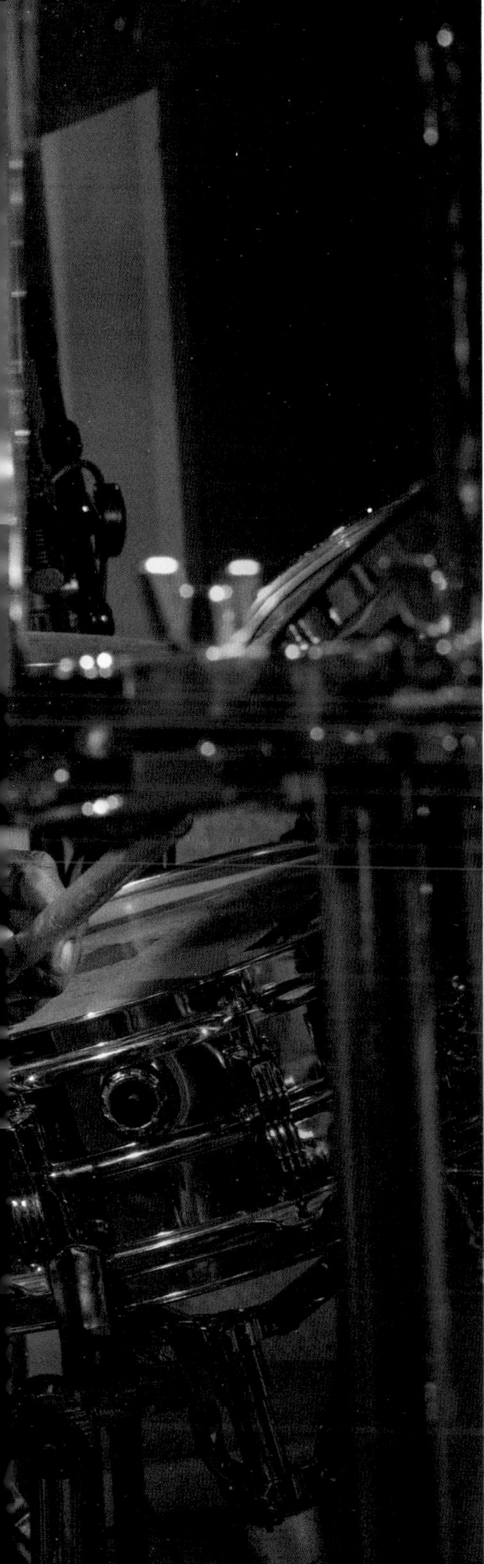

SLY DUNBAR

Sly & Robbie / Peter Tosh / Grace Jones / No-Maddz. Photographed at Anchor Studios, Jamaica

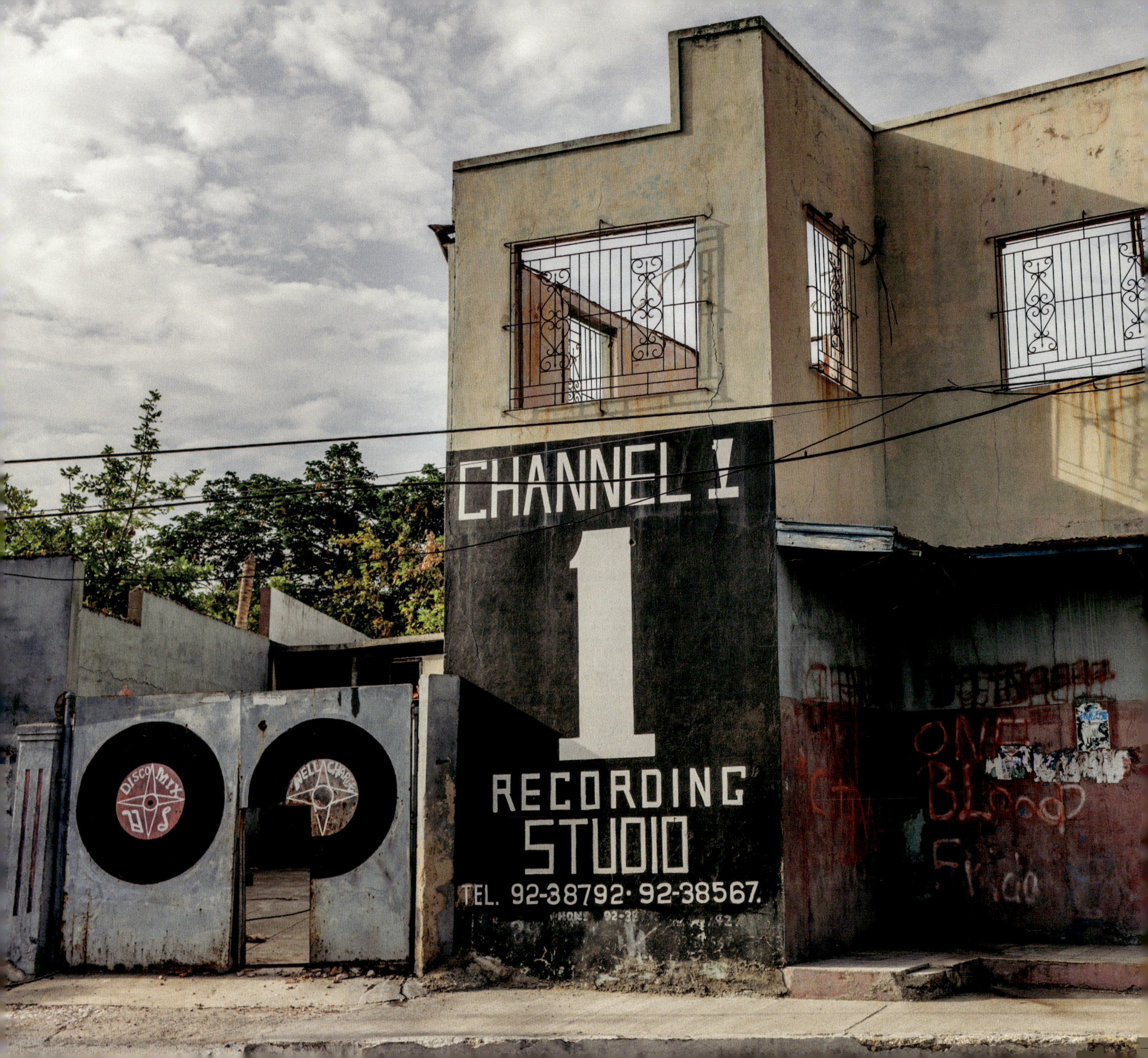
CHANNEL 1
1
RECORDING
STUDIO
TEL. 92-38792· 92-38567.
DISCO MIX

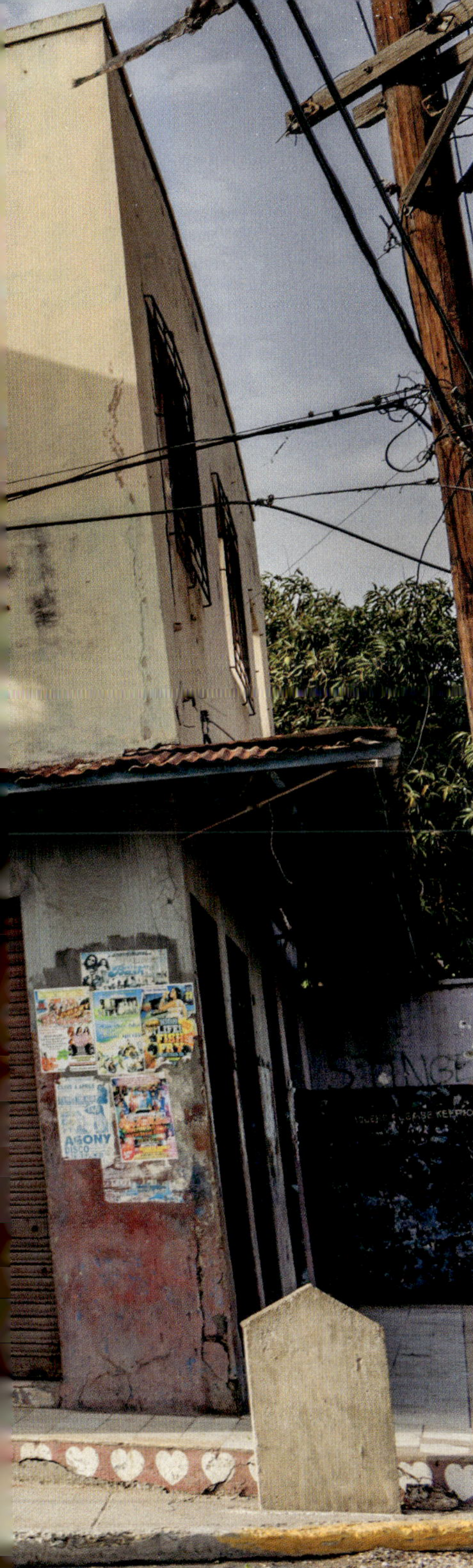

Earl Young is wicked, man. He's one of my favourites. I got a lot of ideas from him, just the way he plays and the way he approach his sound, very steady. I listen to him a lot because I listen to a lot of Philadelphia, because I like RnB. I listen to all these people and I learn from them – some of the other Jamaican drummers like Mikey Boo, Phil Callender, Horsemouth himself, Paul Douglas, Santa [Carlton 'Santa' Davis]. So with all these people around, because I was like the last drummer that came in to play, I was the little one. And also Carlton Barrett from the Wailers, we were youngest. I tried to listen to a lot of this music and then I realized that I had to create a style and a sound for myself, and I wondered, how am I going to go about it, because these are some great drummers. I didn't know if I could survive.

When the Philly sound came in, I started listening to what Earl Young was doing … But what really helped me is like, after I played on *Double Barrel* [by Dave and Ansel Collins], there was a lull and then we went to Channel One recording studio. We used to beg free time whenever we didn't have any money; we wanted to record ourselves. Ernest [Hoo Kim] would give us the time, and then in return I would make a track for Ernest and say, 'This is your track.' So the track I made for Ernest was 'When the Right Time Comes', which The Diamonds sang on, and he couldn't believe it. Eventually it became a big, big hit, and the drum style that I played on it, everybody was saying, 'No, this is a trick, he's a boy, he's not playing it like that live, man.' Nobody believe, and so people used to come to the studio and try and peep in to see what I was doing. After this, Joseph [Hoo Kim] and Ernest from Channel One, they gave me the go ahead – they said, 'Sly, it's all yours, do what you want in it.' So we used to listen to a lot of the Philadelphia records, and we used to try and get the same drum sound that Earl Young used to have. He's one of my mentors, I respect him very much.

Robbie and me used to go downtown and we used to do recording sessions. I used to play in a club called Tit for Tat; Robbie used to play in a club called Evil People. So when I get a break I would go over and listen to Robbie's band, when he get a break he'd come over and listen to my band. I was like maybe eighteen, nineteen, going on twenty. Robbie asked me to come and join him with Peter Tosh because Peter was looking for a drummer. This is really where we got the international exposure because there was Carlton Barrett and his brothers for Wailers, and there was Sly and Robbie for Peter Tosh. So at night-time Robbie and myself would think about what we were going to do with the show, and what crazy things we could put into it, and this is where all things are developing.

Working with Peter Tosh on 'Buk-in-Hamm Palace', there's a beat that Robbie and myself had created, and we said, let's try and put Peter in one of these beats. And we started grooving, and Peter would start playing to the beat, jamming, and he would start to sing. And sometimes that's a great idea, so I said, 'Let's take it from there.' Then other times we go in first and we make the rhythm for an artist like ... say Mighty Diamonds: the rhythm was made first and they came and sang in it, and then they wrote a song. Like with Black Uhuru now, they were in the studio while everything was being cut.

I always think of finding a beat or a pattern that will make the tune, the groove come alive. Sometimes you can't help it. For example, there was a song I played on for Culture, a song called 'Two Sevens Clash'. But the song was so slow and I was thinking, my god, how am I going to play this record today? Robbie didn't play in the session, but he was sitting on the step [nearby] and I say, 'I don't know what to play because he's so slow,' and Robbie said, 'Play this.' I say, wow, I never think of that – that tune was so slow. I was trying to find out how am I going to make this tune come alive, because that is the point of playing. It was good.

At the moment I'm recording in Jamaica, live recording; it's not as good as back then. We used to take pride and time in getting the drum sound right, and 80 per cent of the time the engineer would come and check it to get it just right. A lot of the new engineers never grew up on that sound. It's come with the age of the drum machine, but in those days we had to use a drum to create that tight sound working with the engineer. But today it's very hard to get that: if you compare the older reggae sound to now, it's not there.

With Peter Tosh, our music was a bit more musical. The other day I was looking at some Peter Tosh live, and I thought, oh my god, this is great, but you never get the chance to hear because I'm playing it. I'm listening back to that tape, and man, it's wicked.

GREG ERRICO

Sly & the Family Stone. Photographed in his home studio, California

Leon Patillo, who later on became a lead singer in Santana, had a group called Leon's Creation. He used to call me when his drummer couldn't make it for a gig. One night he called me saying, 'You got to help me out tonight. Joe can't make it, he's sick.' I went down and played. It was a good group and they were very popular in the Bay Area. He also had someone sitting in with him on guitar named Freddie Stewart – he was Sly Stone's brother. So we're talking, we kind of hit it off. I actually went to sit in again a second time and Freddie was there again and he said, 'Hey, I'm going to put something together. You want to do something with me musically?' So we put a group together called Freddie & the Stone Souls. We had that for about a year and from that we went into Sly & the Family Stone.

Sly was a local DJ at a couple of stations here and he had a very popular radio show. He had made a few attempts at putting a band together that didn't work and so he was taking one last shot at it. One day I showed up for rehearsal for the Stone Souls, which was at Sly's house where his folks lived – the two brothers lived there. I showed up and asked, 'Where is everyone in the band? Aren't we rehearsing tonight?' And he said, 'We're going to start something new tonight.' They had already talked, I didn't even know about this yet. We didn't play music that night, we just talked about what we were going to do. We rehearsed for the next seven days straight. Then our first manager, Richard, he owned a nightclub in the Peninsula down south of San Francisco. We started playing there that following week. Things moved fast then, because everything we did happened in five years. We started the group in December 1966 and I left the band in the middle of 1971.

Our first record came out in late '67 or early '68. It was right place, right time, really. At that time also there was a lot going on in San Francisco. That's when the whole psychedelic music explosion was happening here, the Grateful Dead and Jefferson Airplane, Moby Grape and all those groups.

We needed a big sound system and lights. Although we did small clubs, the festivals started happening, with Woodstock being the granddaddy of all festivals. There have been concerts and outdoor festivals since that time that were as big, or even bigger for that matter, but that was the first time half a million people just got together, assembled like that. The seed was planted and it happened. The intention wasn't to have this big, half-a-million-people festival; it was just supposed to be a relatively small music and art fair in the country in New York, and it turned out to be what it was. And actually a lot of the groups back then didn't like playing those big festivals because they were either hot and dusty and uncomfortable or it was raining and it was muddy. You'd get electrocuted onstage and there were no dressing rooms. It wasn't fun. So a lot of groups turned Woodstock festival down. Looking at the whole picture now, those were very unique, creative times; the music that came out of that period still lives.

Woodstock was very intense, amazing … the spirit of what was going on there was incredible. We were supposed to go on at 8 p.m. and we didn't go on until 3 a.m. This festival had already been going on for two days. These people had been there already now for two days, in tents and sleeping bags and what have you. Been sunned on, been rained on, hot, cold, day, night – had heard music for all those hours now. And then we're ready to go on at eight and they keep coming and saying it's going to be another hour or so. You get your adrenaline up, you're ready to go on … so it's up, down, up, down. And then when it's finally three in the morning you're thinking, what are we doing here? How are we going to go on and deal with this? Everyone was at a low ebb. People are just in their tents, they've had it, and you got to go on and play and try and get these people up. We just looked at each other before we went on and said, all we can do is go on, do what we do, and do it the best we can do it and not think about the rest. So that's what we did. Sure enough, by about the third song people start opening up their tents to check out what is going on. By the fourth, fifth song they are up and there's half a million people roaring. It was incredible.

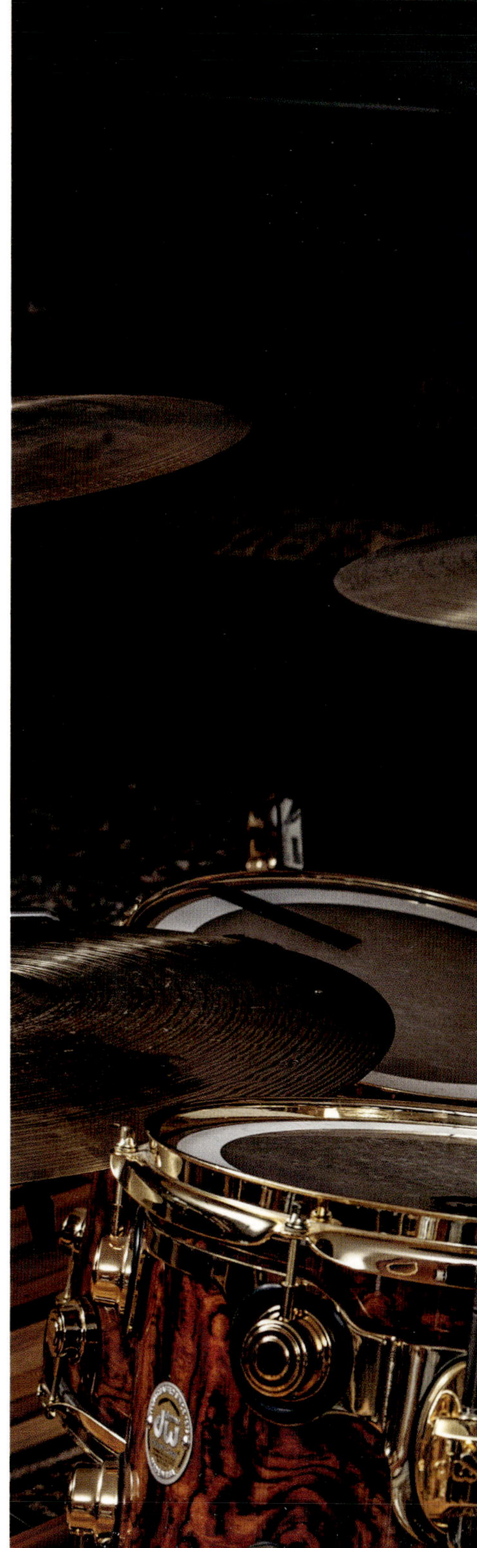

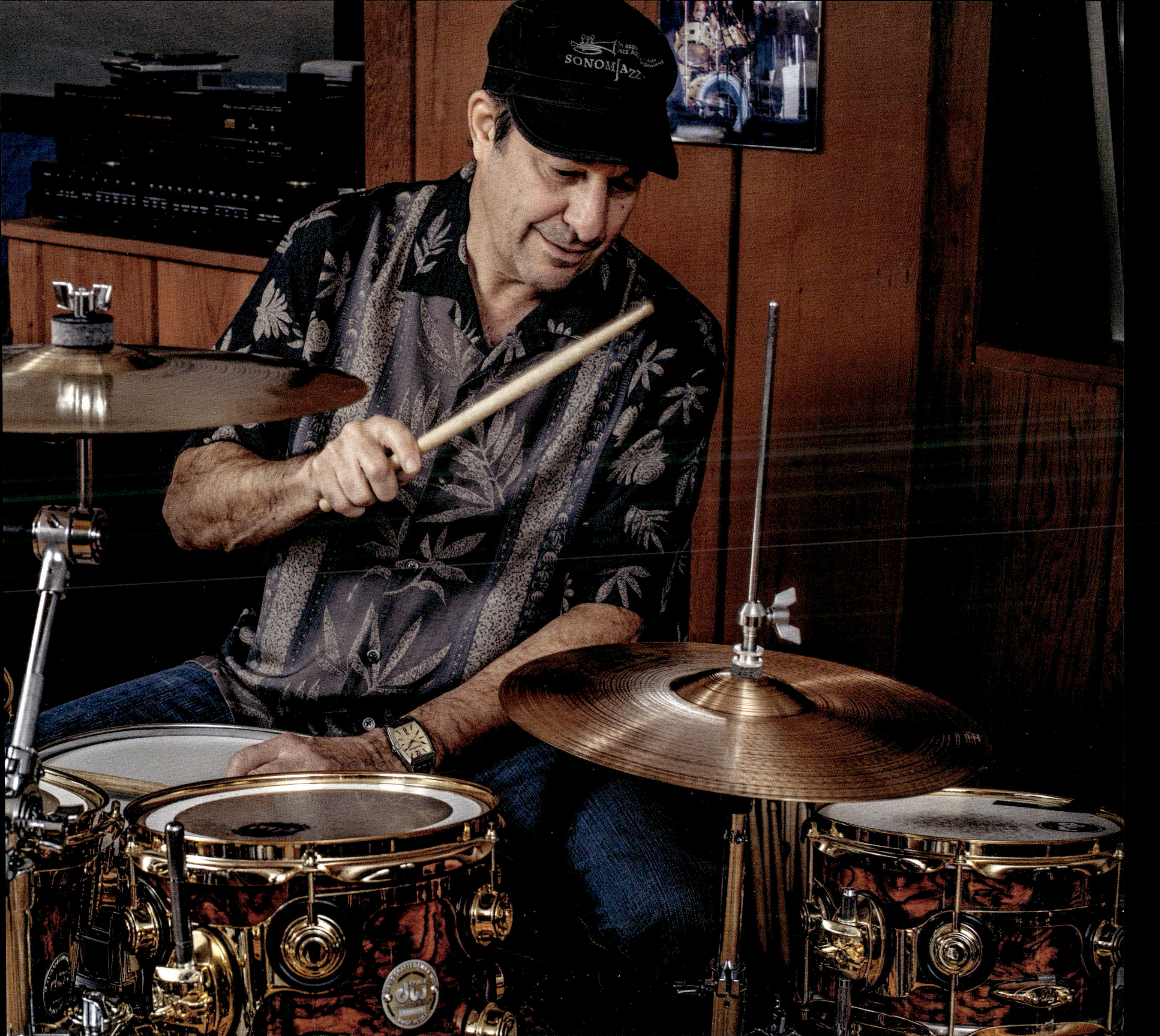

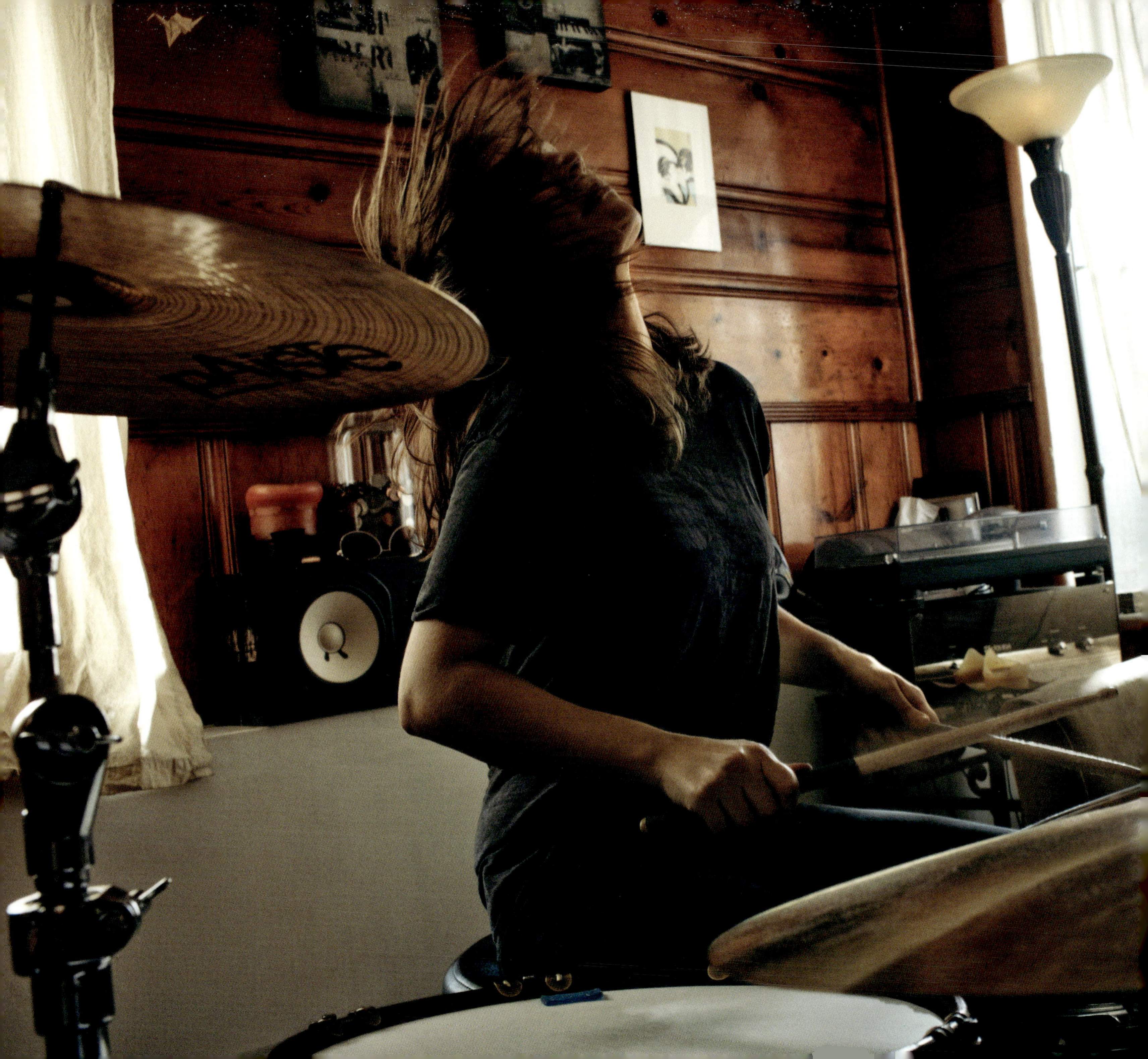

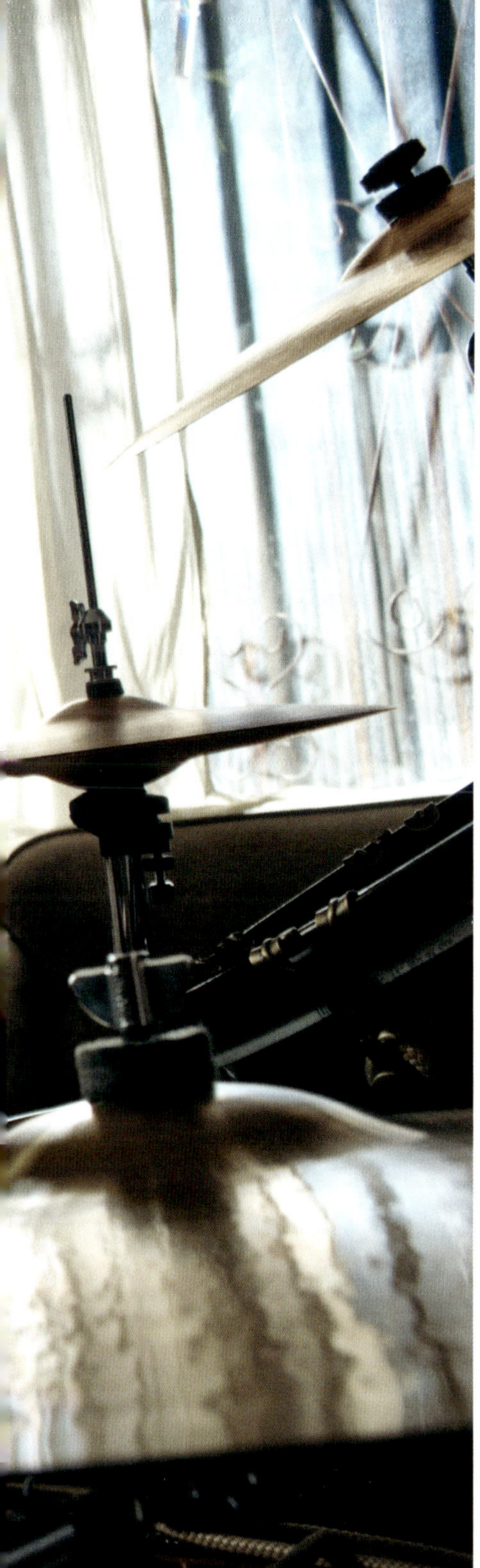

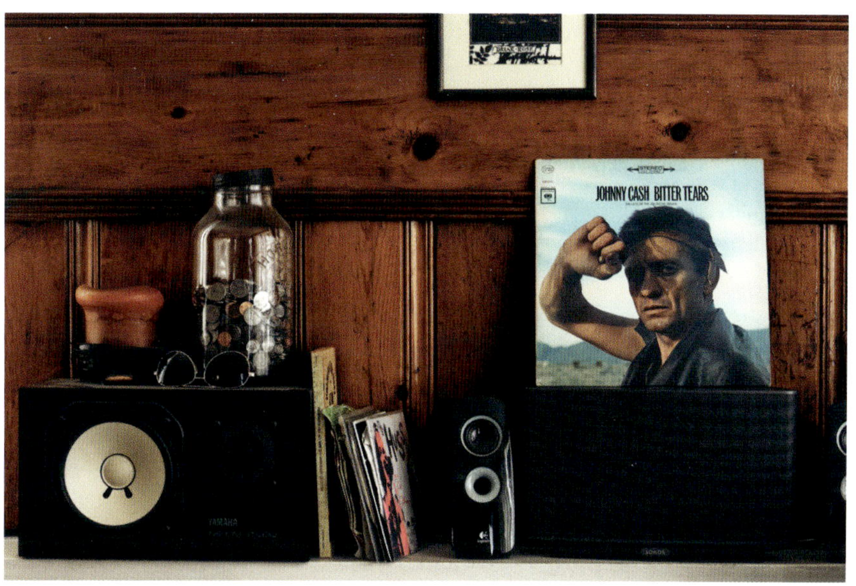

LEAH SHAPIRO

Black Rebel Motorcycle Club. Photographed at home, California

The best times are when I'm not thinking about technical perfection and not worrying about fucking up or things not being perfect. Imperfections are great. Sometimes mistakes end up being the coolest part. I've had plenty of fuck-ups that end up being part of the song because they are incredible moments that I would have never planned.

The best shows are when you turn off. I call it 'Dimension X': that zone where you're really in the music and it takes you outside yourself. It's very much like a meditation. That's when the more interesting stuff starts happening between the three of us when we're playing, because nothing is planned out and the music just leads the way it's supposed to go, wherever it wants to go. And hopefully that comes across as more interesting to the listener. Those moments don't happen every night. They're very special, those moments when it locks in like that. The playing changes completely. It becomes really free.

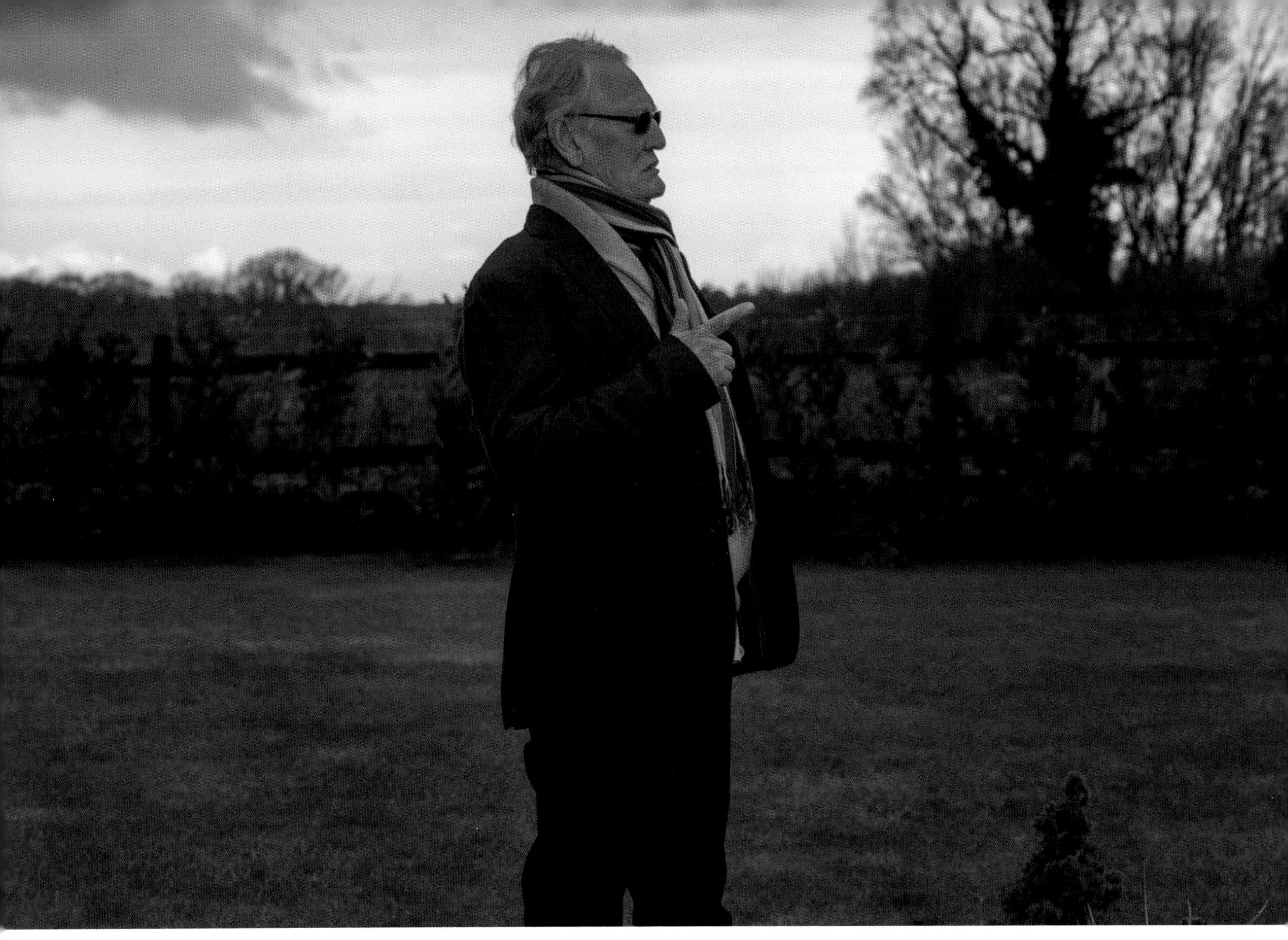

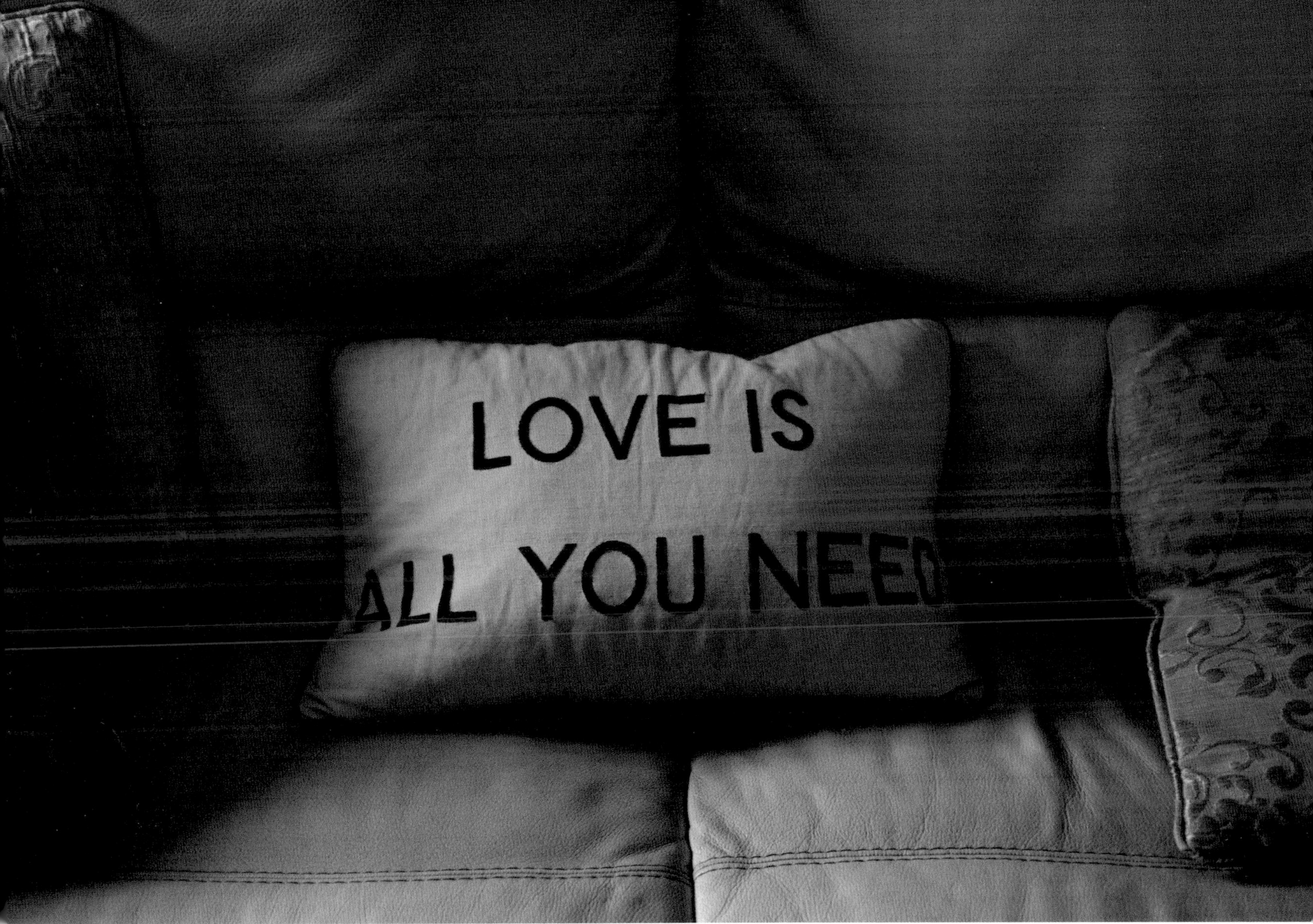

GINGER BAKER
Cream / Blind Faith / Ginger Baker's Air Force. Photographed at home in the UK

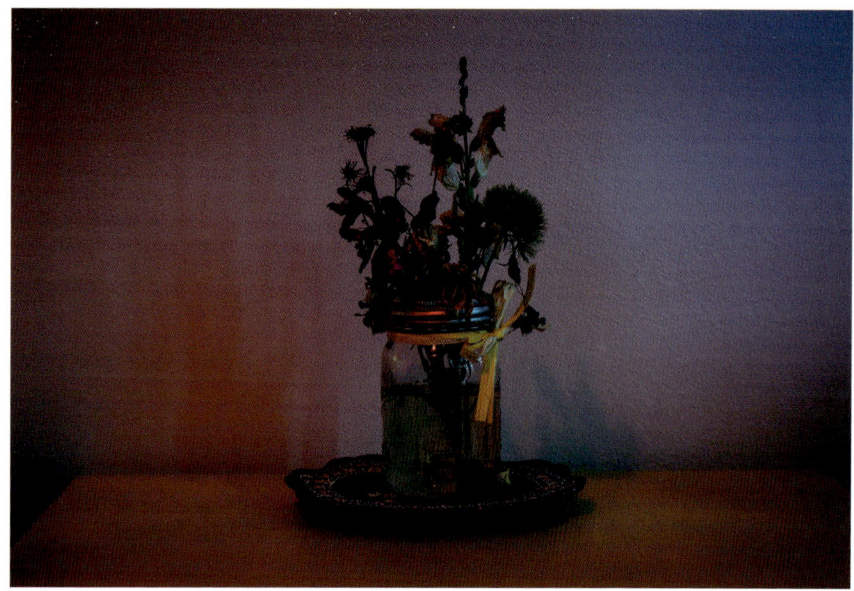

KIRAN GANDHI

M.I.A. / Thievery Corporation / Floating Points / Kehlani / Lizzo
Photographed at home, Massachusetts

I love listening to music and songs that make me feel good, analysing why they made me feel good, and then using that as inspiration. Before, I used to think only about the drum part, but now I think more holistically about the music and the parts that work together to create a certain emotional reaction.

From my position at the back, it's so powerful: you can see the audience vibing so hard off our dancers and the main singer – the whole event. You can feel a full crowd of people reacting to every hit on the drums. It makes you feel like you have a great responsibility and, quickly, you rise to the occasion.

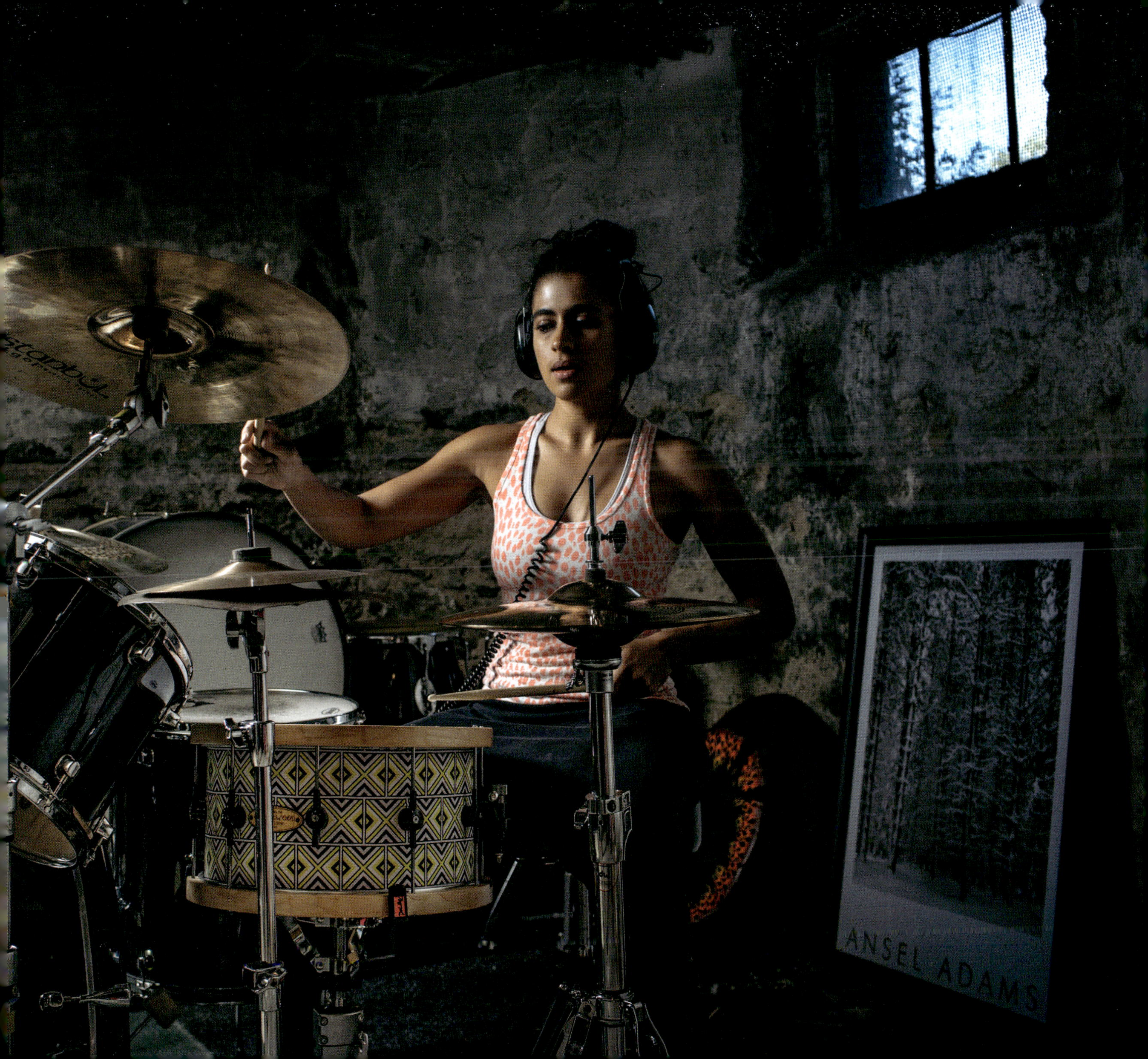
ANSEL ADAMS

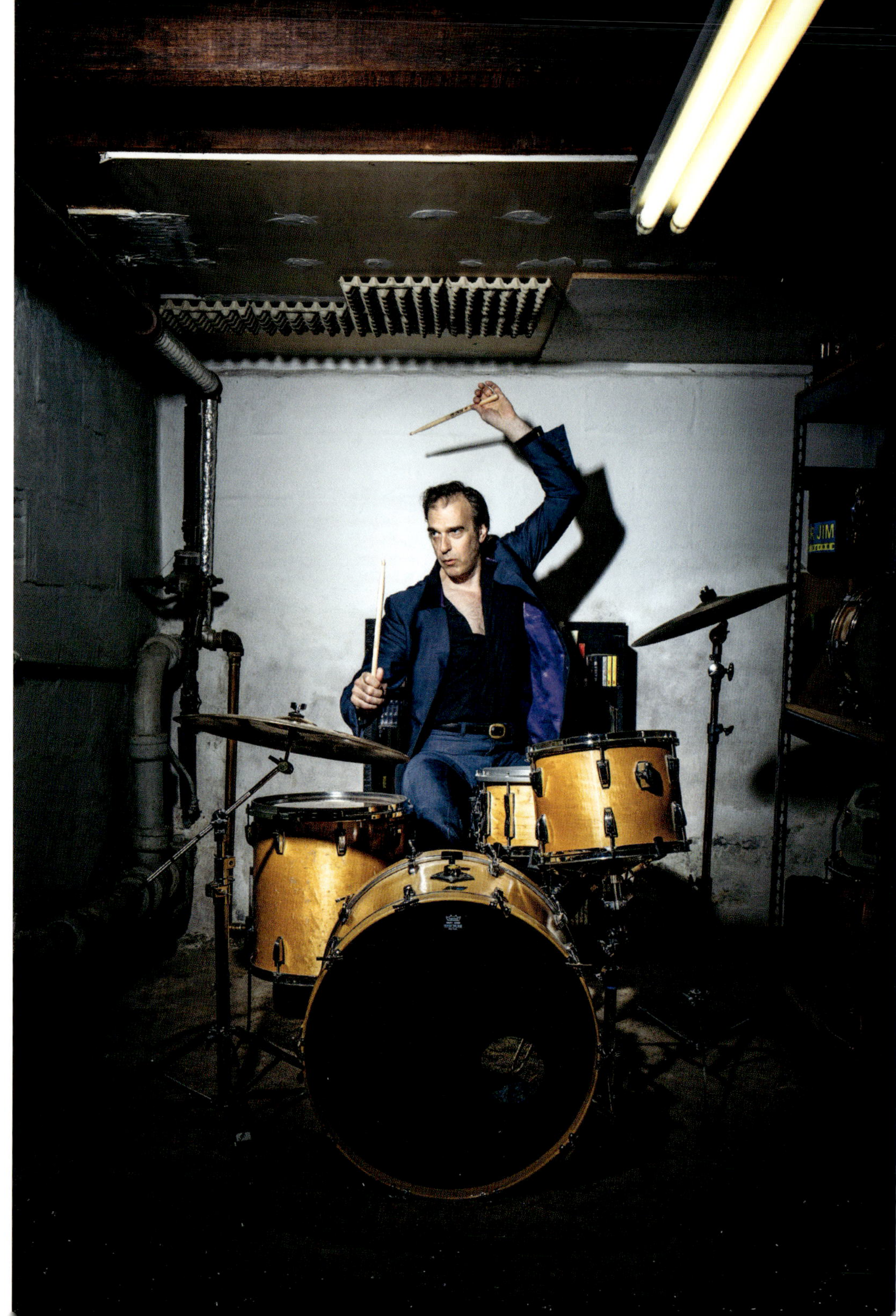

JIM SCLAVUNOS

Nick Cave & the Bad Seeds / Grinderman / Sonic Youth / The Cramps
Photographed at home, New York

It would be dishonest of me to try to state what inspires me as an artist. I find the actual moment and source of inspiration impossible to pinpoint. Typically, my creative process commences with a bit of procrastination. I endeavour to move on from that as quickly as possible, by trying different things. When I happen upon a path that promises to be the way forward, most of the time it only ends up being the long way around; but eventually, without quite knowing how or why I got there, I find myself creating something. I find any creative undertaking – a drum part, a song, writing lyrics, producing an artist, et cetera – a confounding quest guided by a contrary compass. For every posited intention, an unintended exciting possibility can spontaneously present itself, sublime or ridiculous. It takes open-mindedness to recognize the potential of something that wasn't planned, something that isn't a direct product of your conscious, controlled efforts to create.

I'm mostly self-taught, but luckily for a brief few weeks I took lessons from Jim Payne, an esteemed drummer and teacher. He taught me many things in that short period, and I truly wish I could have kept up the lessons, there was so very much more he could have taught me. One point of guidance that he bestowed upon me, which I believe he attributed originally to Bernard Purdie and which has stuck with me ever since, was the admonition that in order to drum properly, and be properly balanced on one's throne so that all limbs can move freely and independently, one must have a 'relaxed asshole'. These are harrowing but vitally important words of wisdom for any student of the instrument, it has to be said.

The key moment of my recording career happened very early on: I was listening to a playback of a song my band 8 Eyed Spy had just recorded and was deeply dismayed by the loud clicking sound that was meant to be the sonic representation of my kick drum. I told the producer it didn't sound the way my kick drum sounded in the studio; in fact, it didn't sound like a drum at all. The producer reassured me that it was the 'disco drum sound' and that, like it or not, even though we weren't a disco band, it was the sound I was going to get. I resolved from that session on to understand both more about the sound of drums, as well as more about producing. I can understand that in this instance the producer thought he was doing the right thing. On that particular occasion I disagreed – for that session, I had my own particular drum sound that I felt was unique, if raw, and much better suited to the band. But in the bigger picture there is surely much to be said for challenging musicians' (and producers') expectations and exploring what can be done in the studio, and that sometimes includes making instruments sound radically different than they do ordinarily.

I would like to be remembered as a humbly diligent devotee of the art of music. I would like to be known and ultimately remembered as a musician and producer who strove to make music that was not ordinary, who brought something uniquely his own to everything he worked on, and who was found worthy. And, I hope, whose music endures.

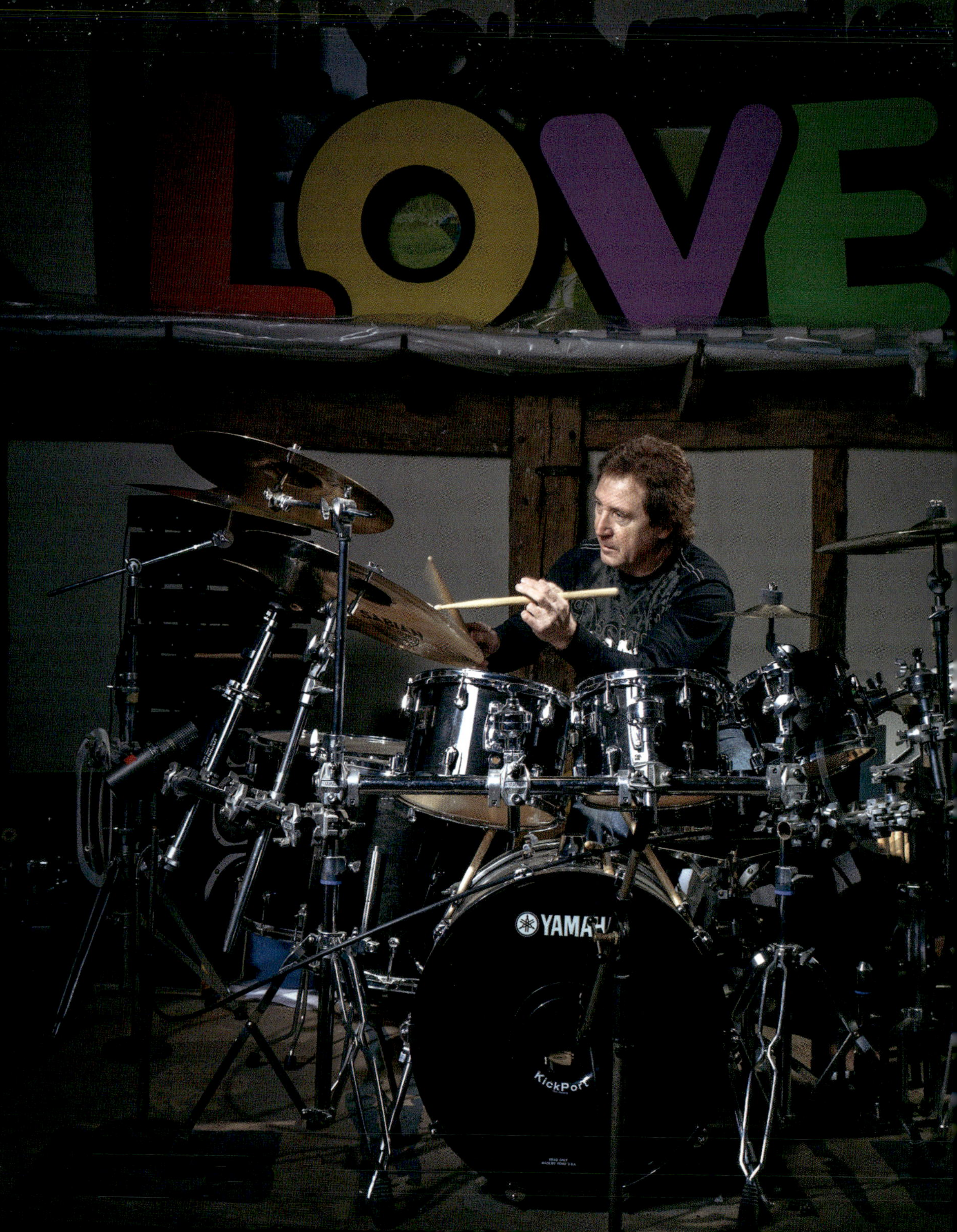
LOVE
YAMAHA
KickPort

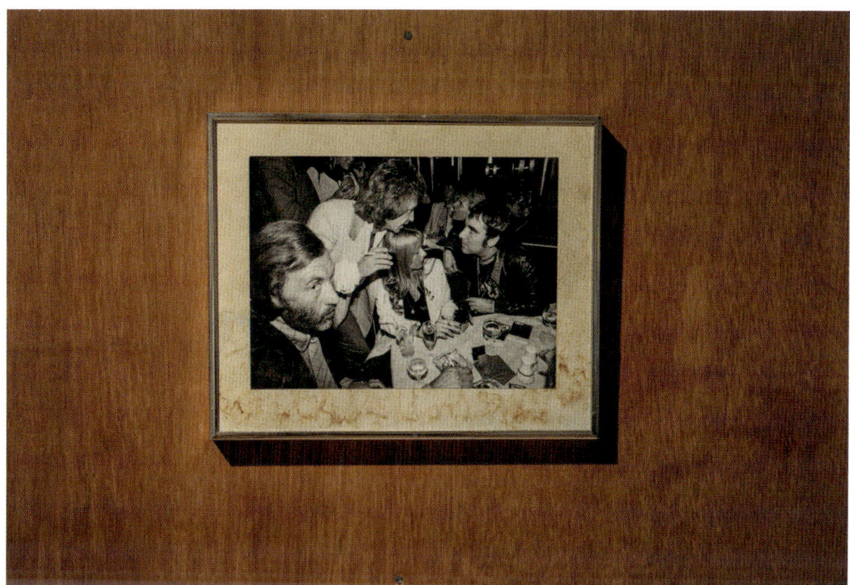

KENNEY JONES

Faces / Small Faces / The Who. Photographed at home in the UK

The first gig I ever did we played in the rectory for the church in Stepney in the East End [of London]. I went out and bought these big hobnail boots, bright red. They were the forerunner of the big boots, the Mod boots that Townshend used to wear. I didn't realize that you couldn't actually play your hi-hat properly or your bass drum with them.

I grew up in the East End and my playground was the bomb ruins. It was just after the war and rationing was still on. There were lots of factories in the East End, you really couldn't see your hand in front of your face, and I'm not kidding. Everyone wore black and grey. Nothing was clean. A white shirt was unbelievable, if you ever saw one of those. And so I grew up in black and white; and also TV, when it first came out, was black and white. So when I became a teenager, I was craving colour. I remember seeing a shirt – there weren't Mod shirts in those days, it was just like a normal jumper type of thing – and so I bought one of them. Then I bought pink trousers and I had my white Levi's instead of normal Levi's and stuff like that, and colourful socks ... and that was the forerunner of the Mod look.

Small Faces were very special. We never told each other what to do; the telepathy we had between us was remarkable. Everywhere we went, we couldn't walk down the street, couldn't do anything. If I walked from here to there, I'd have had one sleeve ripped off and all kinds of stuff like that. Playing, you couldn't hear yourself because the girls were screaming all over it. You get the ego trip out of the way and then it drives you nuts, because all you want to do is play.

I miss Keith [Moon] to this day. I was with him the night before he died at the Buddy Holly film that Paul McCartney put on. The reception beforehand was in a bar just across the road from Leicester Square. After, masses of us walked across the road to the Odeon, said hello to each other again and went up, watched the film, came back down, said goodbye to everyone, said goodbye to Keith, and that was it, went home. I turned on the TV when I woke up and just straight away it said, 'Rock star Keith Moon died last night of a drug overdose,' and I went, I can't believe it, this is a prank on his part. But it wasn't, it was true.

CLYDE STUBBLEFIELD

James Brown. Photographed in Michigan

We'd never mic instruments, just the voice. We were just used to playing behind the voice. That was great but eventually we got into amplifying the instruments, and it got fuller, and we said, wow, this is what we've been missing. Then we started performing a lot better, and it just kicked ass, actually, after that.

Shows were two hours all the time, but it would go sometimes two and a half hours. We'd play with the opening show for about maybe an hour; our opening act would come on say for fifteen, twenty minutes, and then we'd bring on another opening act, Bobby Byrd, and he'd come on and sing for fifteen, twenty minutes, half an hour. Then James Brown would come on, and nothing changed within the hardness of the hitting. It was just that we put James Brown pattern in the main show. His pattern was the one that people loved, so we hit that very hard, and never got tired. But before we got microphones for the drums, the horns and that, my hands used to bleed. I'd come out like somebody had cut me with something. Blood would be everywhere and I never paid any attention to it. I never thought, my hands are bleeding, I got to stop, or I need a Band Aid. No. We played until we couldn't play, but it didn't hurt. I learned how to control it.

I was with him forever, from '65 until '71, and I made his 'Cold Sweat', 'I Got the Feelin'', 'Give It Up or Turnit a Loose' – all those were my hits, but I never got credit for them with him. I went places I never would've thought of going. I didn't see no schedule but the manager came up and said, 'You got to go get a passport.' He preferred to have us, because if he had to switch us with someone else that don't know the show, he's in trouble.

Musically it was great. There wasn't a lot of rehearsing; there was a lot of thinking. You had to think more than play the music. You had to know where he was going, when he was going and how he was going, and we'd fit right in with him; simple. When he was standing up front singing a song, he might go, *zoom!* and we'd go to some other rhythm. So that was the whole idea of his show: technique, and doing those things right when he needed them. There wasn't no guessing. It was just *bop schtung!* and you're into the next song. So we played the truth on those songs. And he showed me so much in his musical career and his group.

I learned how he was so disrespectful, but I didn't let that interfere with my music. I knew things, but I didn't bring that out. When we even got into conversation, I never argued. I'd go, 'Hey whatever you want. You're the boss.' It was great. I learned a lot, and I'm still learning, and I try to teach people attitude. You've got to have a great attitude. Respect is number one and if you don't have that, fuck you. I'm serious.

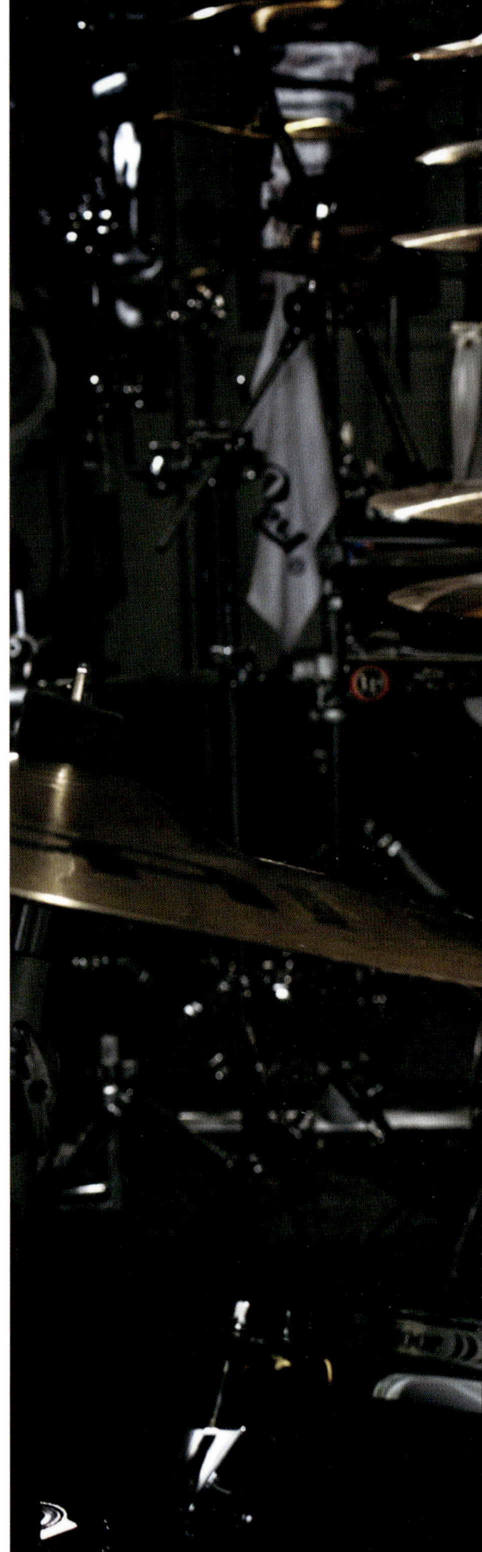

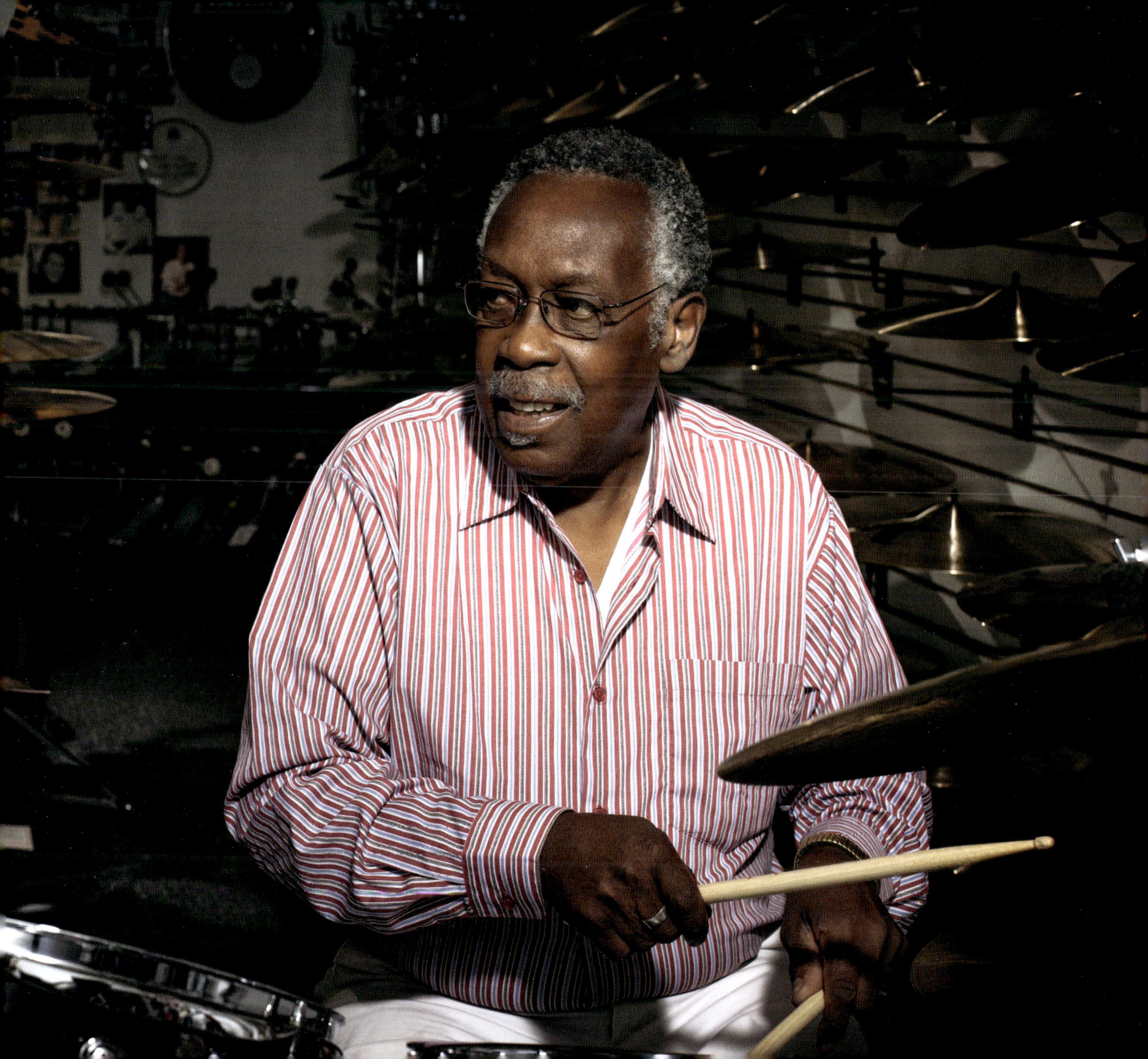

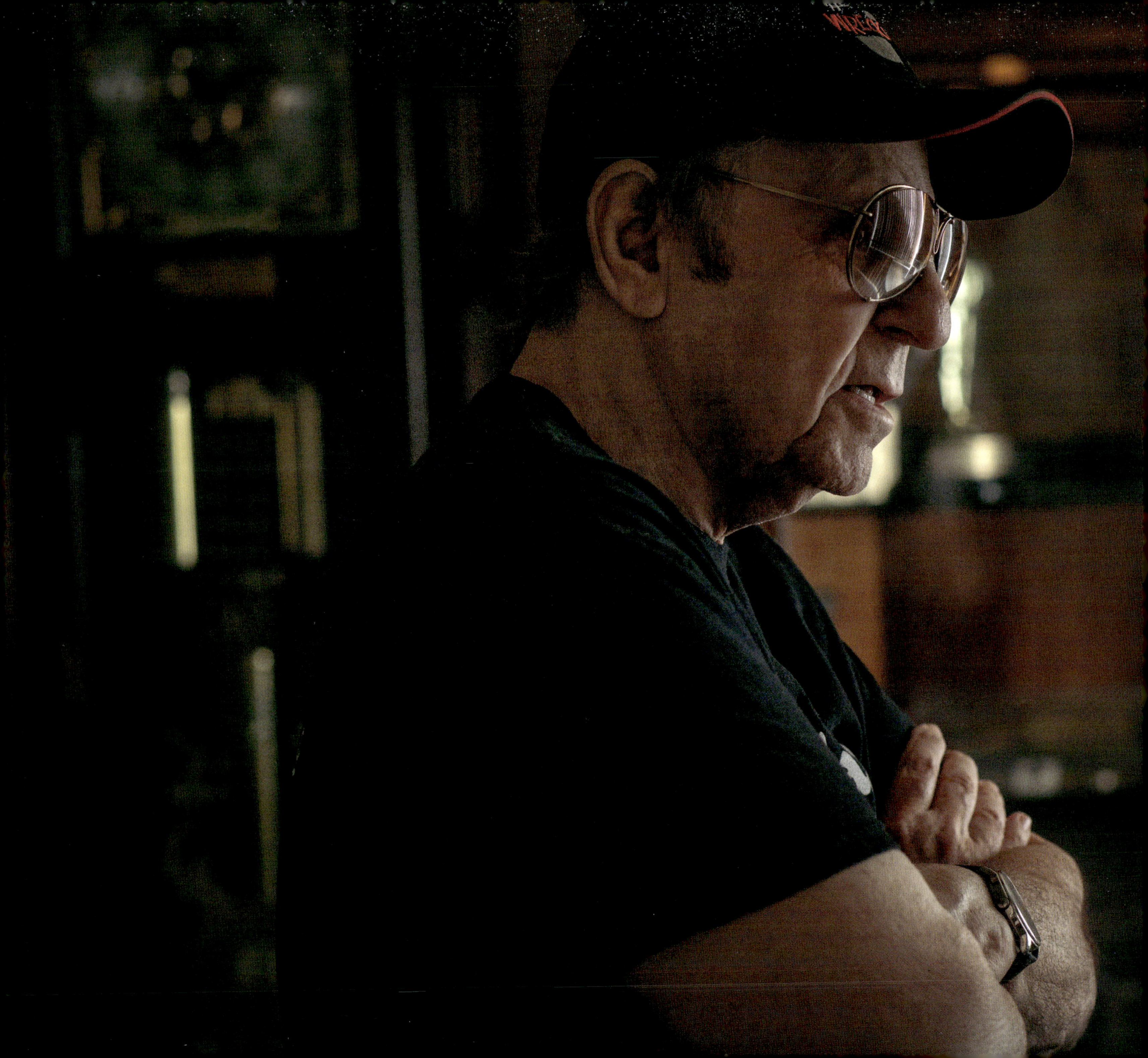

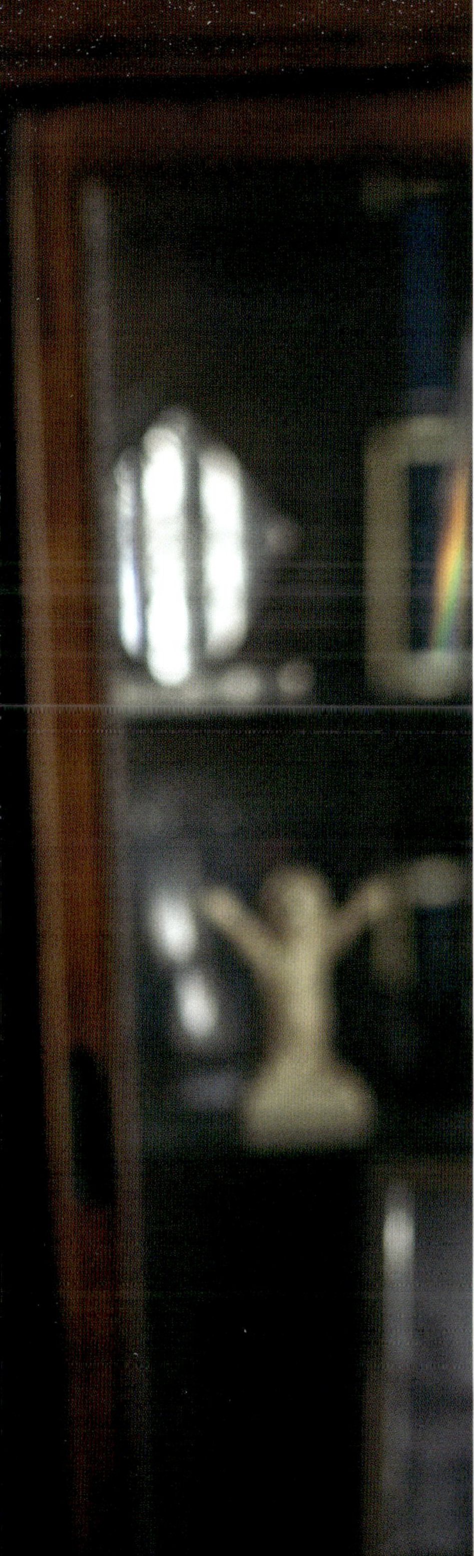

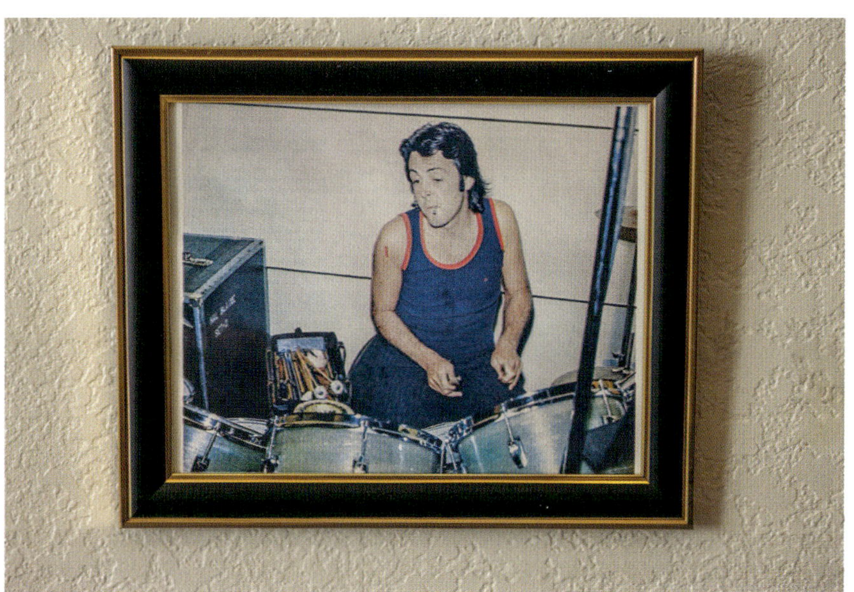

HAL BLAINE

The Wrecking Crew (The Beach Boys / The Byrds / Frank Sinatra / Nancy Sinatra / Sammy Davis Jr / Elvis Presley). Photographed at home, California

If you listen to the Carpenters – perfect example – you will hear the dynamics that I played: soft, quiet, loud, whatever. It doesn't happen today; engineers say, 'Just play, we'll fix it in the mix.' Kids play loud. I used these small sticks. If I needed something a little bit heavier during the session I'd turn the stick over, I'd use butt ends – what's the difference? These kids are using baseball bats today. When I studied drums every drum, every cymbal was right within reach.

The Wrecking Crew did the first Motown hits and we never knew what they were because this little guy used to come out from Detroit to the session. The songs were marked 'Song 1', 'Song 2', 'Song 3'. No titles. The courier would take the tapes first class on the plane back to Detroit and then Mr Berry would have each one of his groups – The Supremes and all these groups that he had – sing some of these songs to see who fit what. And then whatever was best for them, that's what they did. I mean, we know we did 'Baby Love'. There are certain drum sounds that I know the difference between, like mine and Benny Benjamin's sound, and he was a great funky drummer. We not only did Black stuff out here, we did every colour, from every country. Producers came from all over the world because we had so many hits. Our little band, six, seven, eight guys, we would record a song and we didn't know anything about it.

People were not stupid. They'd say, 'Who are these guys, the Wrecking Crew, making all these hits? We don't know who they are but we want 'em to do our records.' They were coming from France, from Germany, from England – everywhere. I had a mansion. It's ridiculous. A drummer with a mansion and a Rolls. I mean, the whole thing is unfathomable.

JON THEODORE

Queens of the Stone Age / One Day as a Lion / The Mars Volta / Bright Eyes / Golden
Photographed in his studio, California

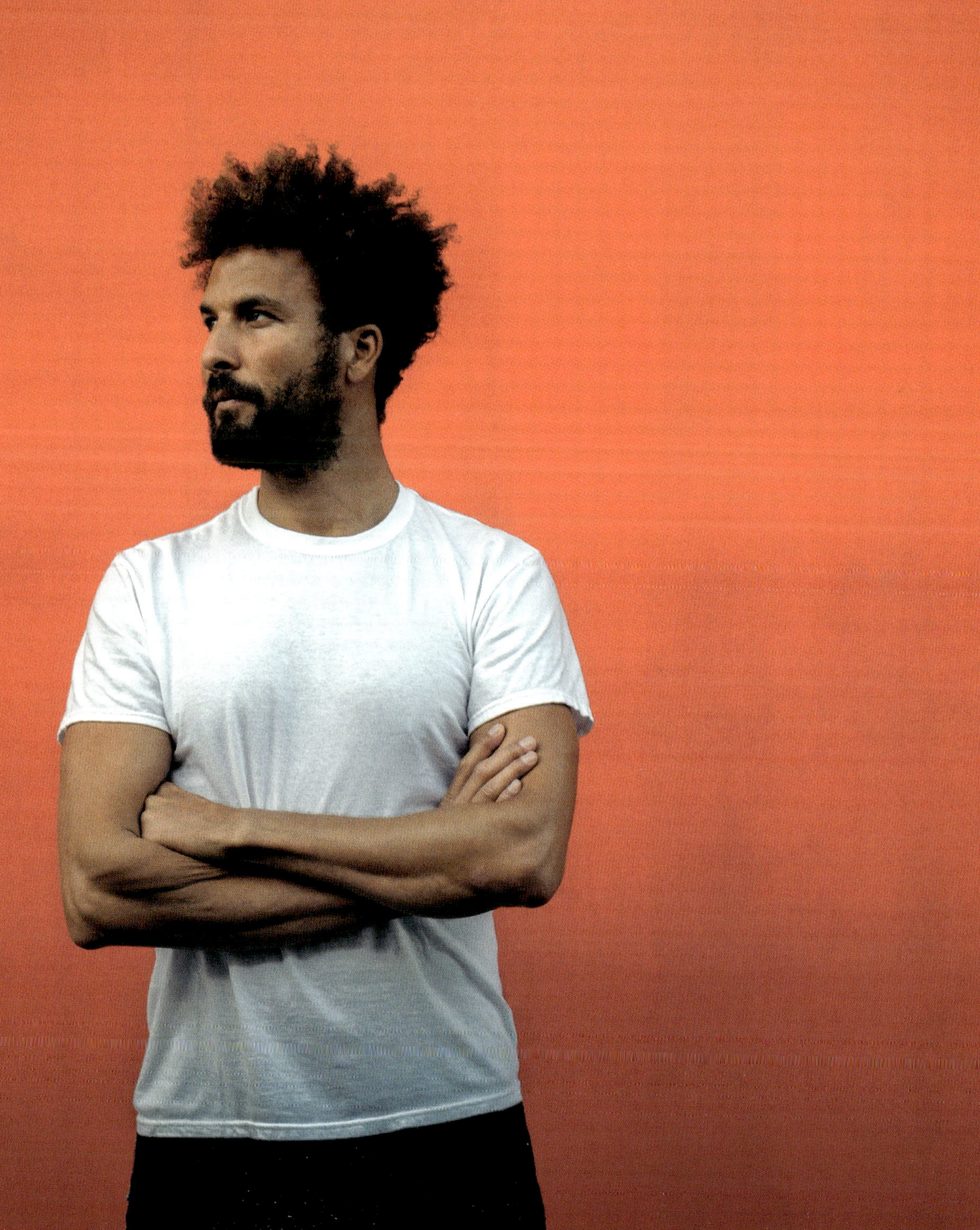

I started when I was fifteen or sixteen at a summer camp. There was this guy, Dean, a Deadhead who brought his gear. He was going to be the music department. He got bounced almost immediately because he got caught smoking weed. They sent his ass packing so fast that he left his gear. Then suddenly there I was with this big yellow drum set that looked like a Tony Williams set and I just played it every single day. I had the help of a really awesome neighbour and family friend. She worked at Johns Hopkins Hospital and she wrote my parents a letter on official letterhead calling all of [their] characters into question and questioning why they would keep art from a child and all this. She strong-armed them into considering it a beautiful opportunity. That year for my birthday it was like, okay, let's do this. Man, that was the beginning of something great.

Don Caballero, Helmet, Melvins, Big Black, Rapeman and The Jesus Lizard – it just all blew my mind. I remember specifically Damon [Che, drummer for Don Caballero] and John Stanier [then drummer for Helmet], I was scared for my life when I saw them play. Maybe it had to do with the acid, I don't know. Then you meet them and they turn out to be giant sweethearts. It really shocked me because … I don't know what I thought, that I was going to be vaporized by laser beams coming out of their eyes or something. I really found the beauty of that type of power. Watching Damon kick his drums over and completely crush an entire light rack and microphone rig and then blow a 151 fireball into the ceiling, it blew my young mind. That really turned me on.

The first time I ever played live was with my band in high school. I remember it being the most important thing in the world, but I can remember specifically being completely out of touch. I tried to play Neil Peart fills on a Neil Young song, but I still remember feeling like I needed to know that no one could say I wasn't trying as hard as I could. It was a very passionate kind of burning for it. I mean, I don't even pay that much attention when I drive my car or my motorcycle (which is probably not that smart). But when you're playing a show the focus is so singular, there isn't anything else. That is what I find so addictive, it feels like you're optimized. It feels like you're operating at your fullest potential because there isn't any brain space or intention left for anything else.

I don't normally listen back and think I nailed it. There's a couple of times when I'm like, man, I don't know if I could have done that any better, but that's about as close as I get to being happy with listening to it. It can be pretty challenging. I know that James Brown before shows would listen to James Brown, but I would too if I were him, because there is nothing that could be improved on his records, on any of them. So that makes sense. But until I reach James Brown's heights I'll be listening to other things. I'll be listening to James Brown.

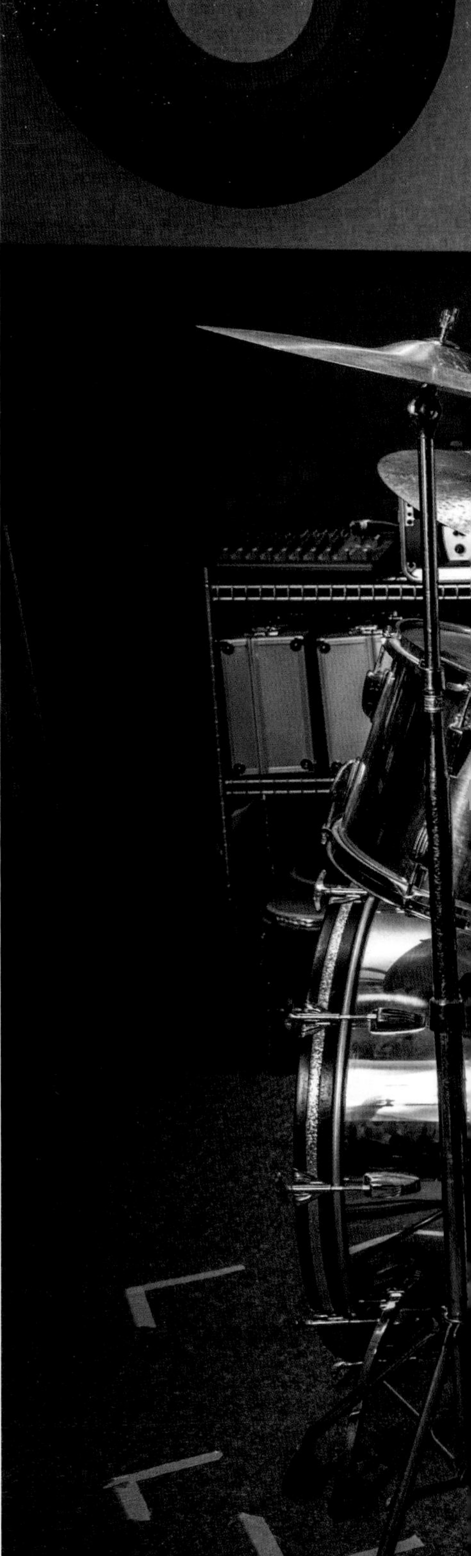

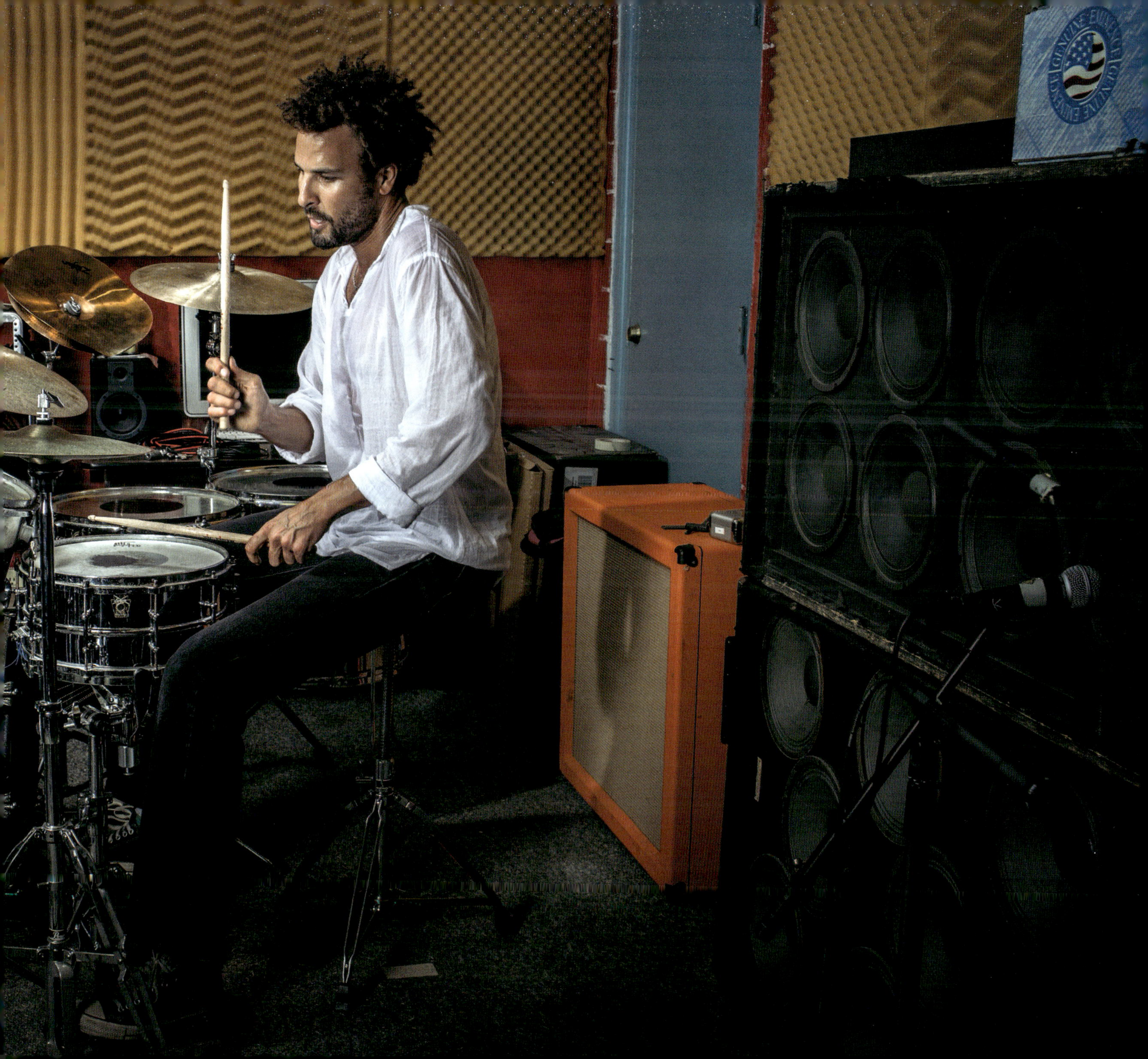

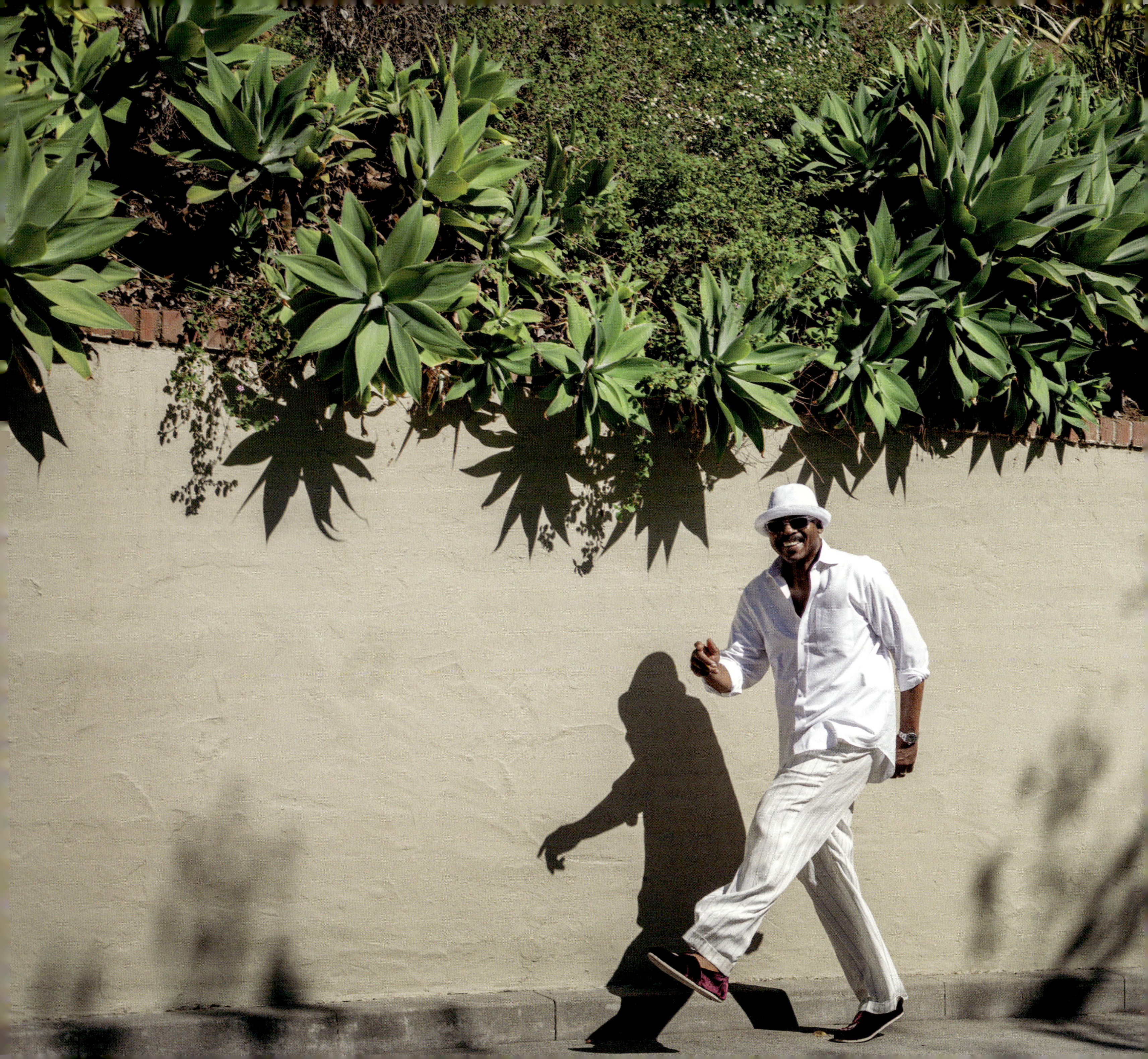

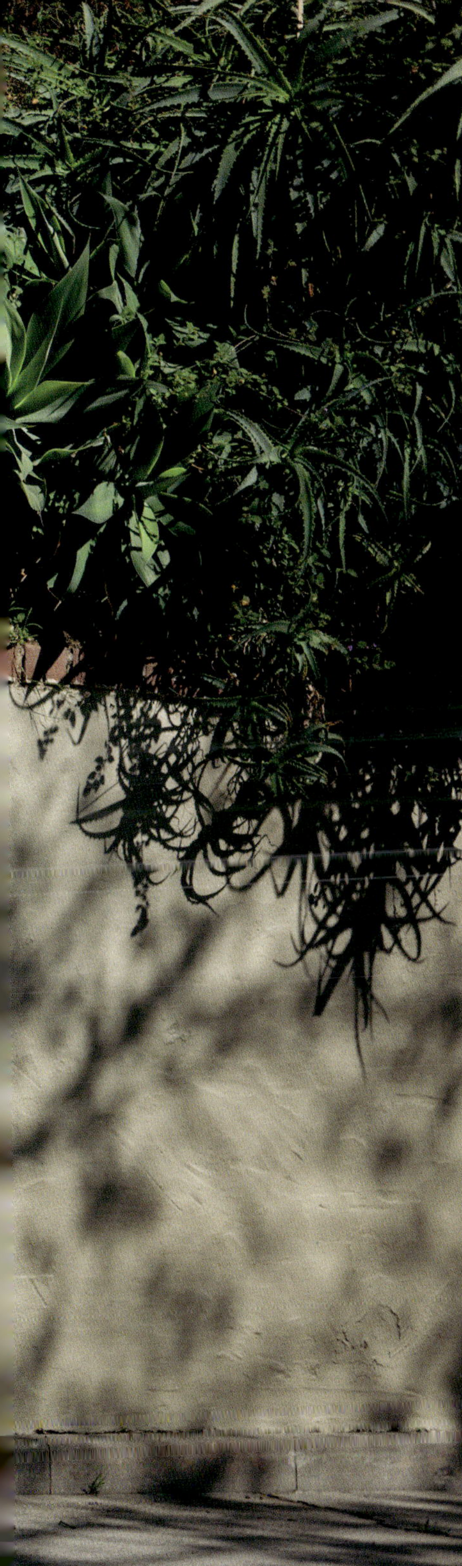

HARVEY MASON

Quincy Jones / Herbie Hancock / John Williams / John Legend / Fourplay
Photographed in California

I got my first drum set at about fourteen from Herb Shapiro, the guy who owned the local drum store. I'd begun to work in town and I was borrowing drum sets from different guys. Herb told me to take that Gretsch set and pay him when I had the money. He knew I was starting to work and could play. So he just told me to pay him as I could.

It was a very interesting early life. We were very poor, eight kids and my mom. My father wasn't there, but he had been kind of a musician in an army band. Not really great – more a frustrated musician. My mother was very supportive of me playing. She recognized I had talent and kind of pushed me in that direction. I was definitely motivated. At that age you're looking for something that you can do really well and stand out. It's funny, during my early years I found a drum book, a very advanced one, in a closet in my house and I knew it was my father's, so I wanted to learn to play that drum book to impress him, thinking that he might come back. I spent my early years getting as good as I could, hoping that one day he would recognize me for that. We didn't have any kind of relationship.

Church was a big part of keeping us together. My mother's biggest goal was that we would all care for each other, love each other and be together as a family. Music was a big part of it. My mother didn't play anything but she sang at church choir. She always had an ear. If you were practising she'd say, 'Wait a minute, that's wrong. Try that again.' She could be in the other room, [but] because the house was so small you could hear everything that was going on. Music has been a part of my life and I think from very early on I realized I had some gifts.

I used to listen to all kinds of music. I'd listen to the classical station and try and sing songs that I'd never heard before. I used to call it 'hearing around corners'. It really helped me later in life because, even today, if there's a song I have never heard, I can hear where it's going to go and whistle along with it or sing it. I like to compose; I compose a lot of songs. There's lot of music in my head, probably from the early days.

I became interested in piano. The church organist was teaching me and then she encouraged me to play for the choir. It was a stodgy kind of church, a Baptist church. Not like today's church with the drums. You couldn't have drums in there. I was in high school, playing in talent shows and listening to other stuff, so I was trying to play hipper chords than the chords with the hymns. The old ladies would say, 'Oh no, he's jazzing the music up.' It was kind of sacrilegious but the organist dug it. She understood, so she was always encouraging me to play. And my mother was saying, 'Ah! You're listening to that bumpy-bump music,' which was her word for popular music.

These days they have drums in all these churches and these guys are playing mad, mad stuff. Most of the drummers who have the big pop gigs now come out of the church. The younger guys all grew up in church. I've heard these young guys playing and then, all of a sudden, they try some crazy fill and come in on the wrong beat and the whole choir will shift to go right with them. If the kid can walk and hold drumsticks and he wants to play in church, they let him play.

It's all about working with people and getting along with people. You have to be instinctive. Too much talking can sometimes get in the way of what has to happen. You have to bond with people quickly, you have to feel people's vibe and energy real quickly, and obviously you have to feel the music very quickly and get inside it and just give your heart to it. You have to surrender to it. That's what it's about. I feel really happy that I can leave the planet at any time and I'll be remembered by someone, somewhere, at some point. I'm very happy that I came up in the golden age of recording and got a good twenty-something years in of that.

DAVE WECKL

Dave Weckl Band / Chick Corea Elektric and Akoustic bands / Mike Stern Band / Oz Noy Trio
Photographed in his home studio, California

I'm basically composing melody from rhythm in everything that I play. Sometimes I have to work that in with other musicians so that my composition relates to what's going on in the song.

Playing a solo, that's when the composition is total free-form. I'm not being stimulated or influenced by something else I'm hearing that causes a different spontaneous thought in my composition. It's a headspace of freedom. But honestly speaking, I find myself working too much to allow myself to go into that headspace, because when I'm working a lot I want to get into different headspace and not think about what I actually do for a living. I want to disengage. I want to go drive the car on a track. I want to watch a movie; I want to do something else. For me and the drum set, it's kind of easy at this stage to understand when I'm not doing something [right], or to do what I want to do. With the car, I'm just learning how to do that now, I'm just understanding. I'm not anywhere close to being where I think I could be. But being in that zone, and that type of concentration, is not unlike [drumming]. I think it's got something to do with why I've been able to adapt to track driving pretty quickly and get fairly good so quickly. I can see the correlations. It's all about balance. A lot of the same things are in play.

The way that I try to think about it is like a dance. It has to be something that I can move to while I'm doing it, if it's that kind of rhythm. My favourite types of rhythm to play are not so complex, actually, where it takes a compass and a calculator to figure out what's going on musically.

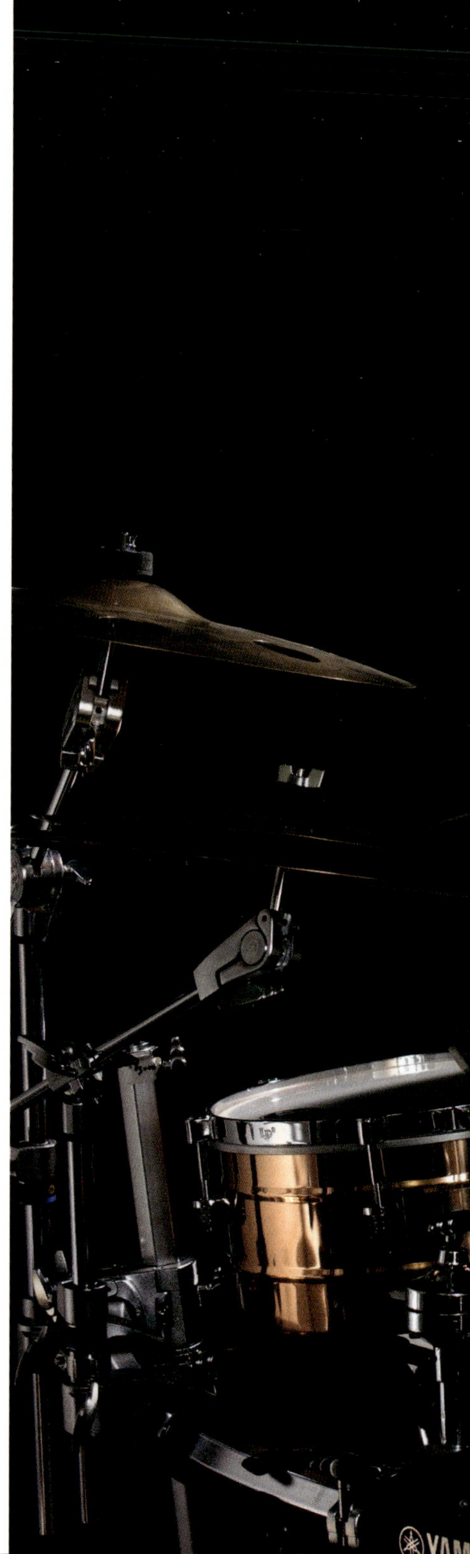

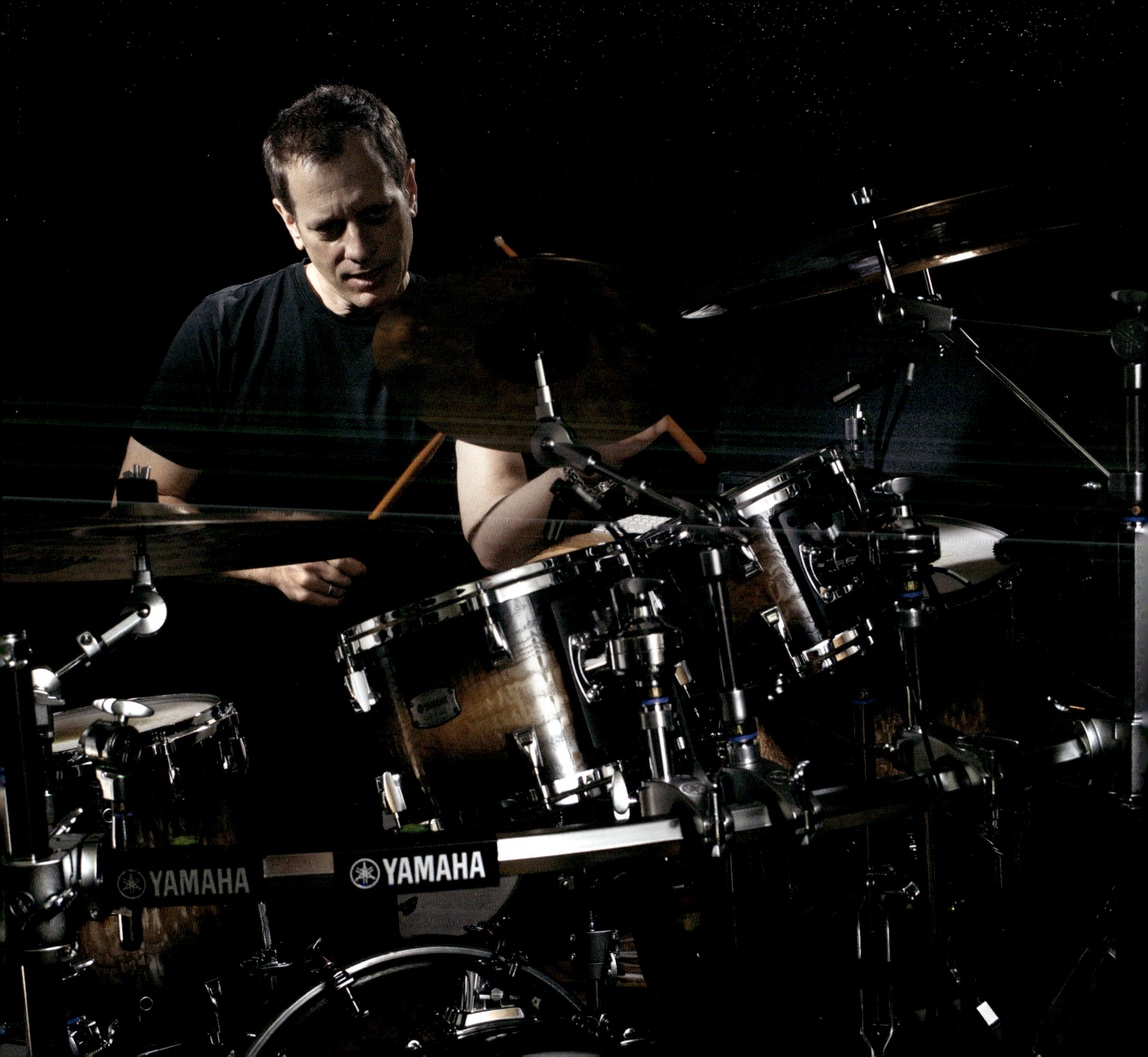
YAMAHA
YAMAHA

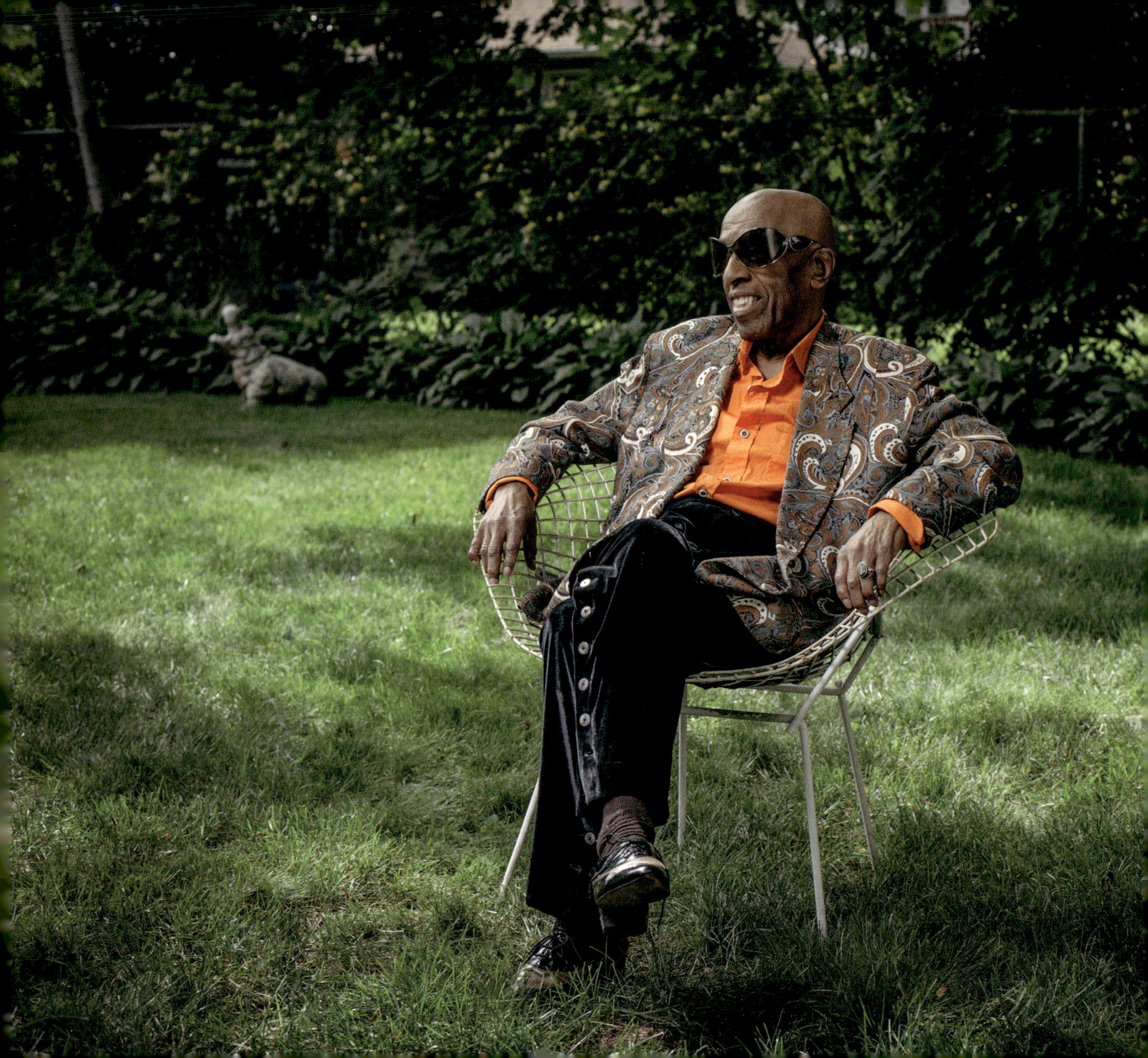

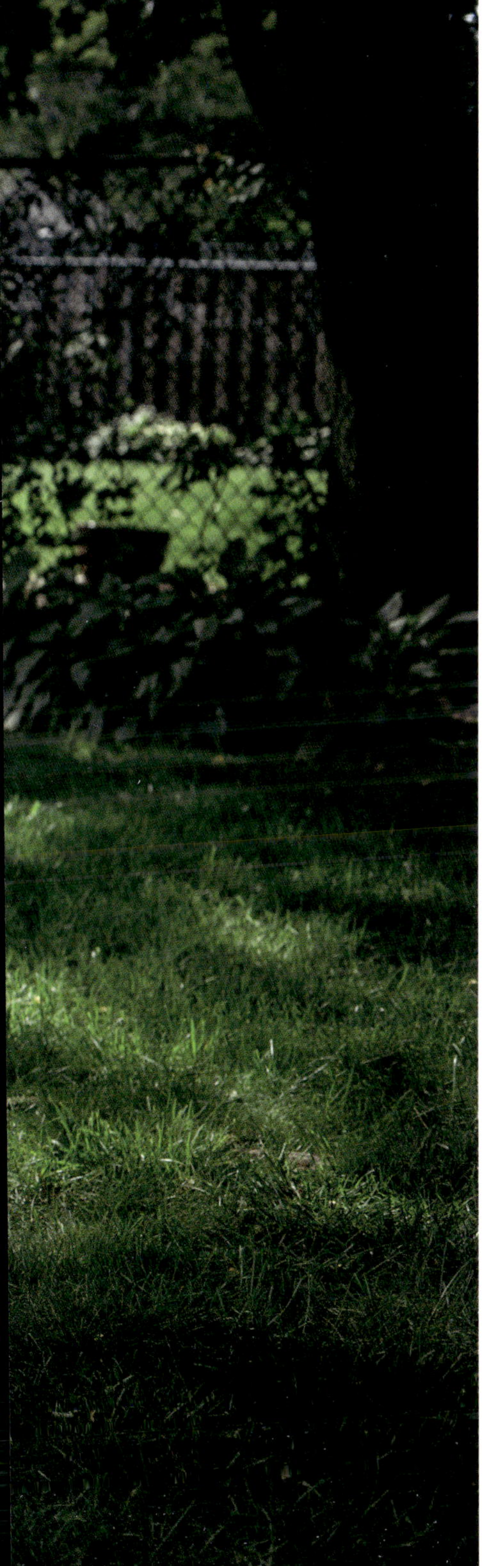

"ME AND MILES HAD SPORTS CARS, AND PEOPLE WOULD DRIVE UP NEXT TO YOU AND REV. I USED TO GET A LOT OF TICKETS"

ROY HAYNES

Charlie Parker / Sarah Vaughan / Thelonious Monk / John Coltrane / Chick Corea
Photographed at home, New York

STEVEN DROZD

The Flaming Lips. Photographed at home, Oklahoma

By the time I joined the Lips I really was trying to be a cross between Bill Ward and John Bonham meets, like, Mac McNeilly and Dale Crover all rolled into one drummer. I remember I went from just trying to copy John Bonham, like the funk part of John Bonham. People always talk about how heavy a hitter he was, which he was, but to me, I like the mid-'70s period where it was more feel and funky than just beating the shit out of the drums. I think it was when we were making *Clouds Taste Metallic* with The Flaming Lips where I really felt like I was doing my own trip on that record. I really felt like, on that record especially, that people could hear that it was me: 'That's Steven Drozd playing drums.'

It took me a while to get over the fact that I'd just joined one of my favourite bands on the planet. I took it for granted at the time, but it was really one of the best times of my life, because everything changed so fast. Just trying to find some people to play with, much less a band that was really great – I went from being frustrated playing with people that were kind of into it to joining this band that already had years of momentum and experience behind them. That was like icing on the cake.

I remember seeing The Jesus Lizard for the first time. It was spring of 1990 and I think they'd just got the line-up together with Mac playing drums. I'd taken some acid and we went to this place called the Pick and Pack. It was when I lived in Houston. And the place probably comfortably holds fifty people, but there was probably like two hundred people there. The place was just teeming with energy, and then I was on acid too. They came out and I couldn't believe what I was seeing. All of them, not just the drummer – they're all such good players and they played against David Yow's drunken abandon. He was shirtless and grabbing people in the crowd, and he's got people in headlocks and he's singing the whole time, and then you've got these three master musicians all playing this incredibly tight, funky, weird, psychotic rock and roll. That was a really crazy experience for me and I'll never forget that.

The kit I have at home to record with is a Rogers, a '63 or '64, I think. I bought it about five years ago. When the kids go to school or whatever, and I know they're going to be gone for five or six hours, I pull the drums out of the closet, set them up and I just bang on the drums for about two hours, sometimes longer, and record into Pro Tools. Then I pack the drums back in the closet. I listen and find beats that I think I like a lot, and I just start to work from there.

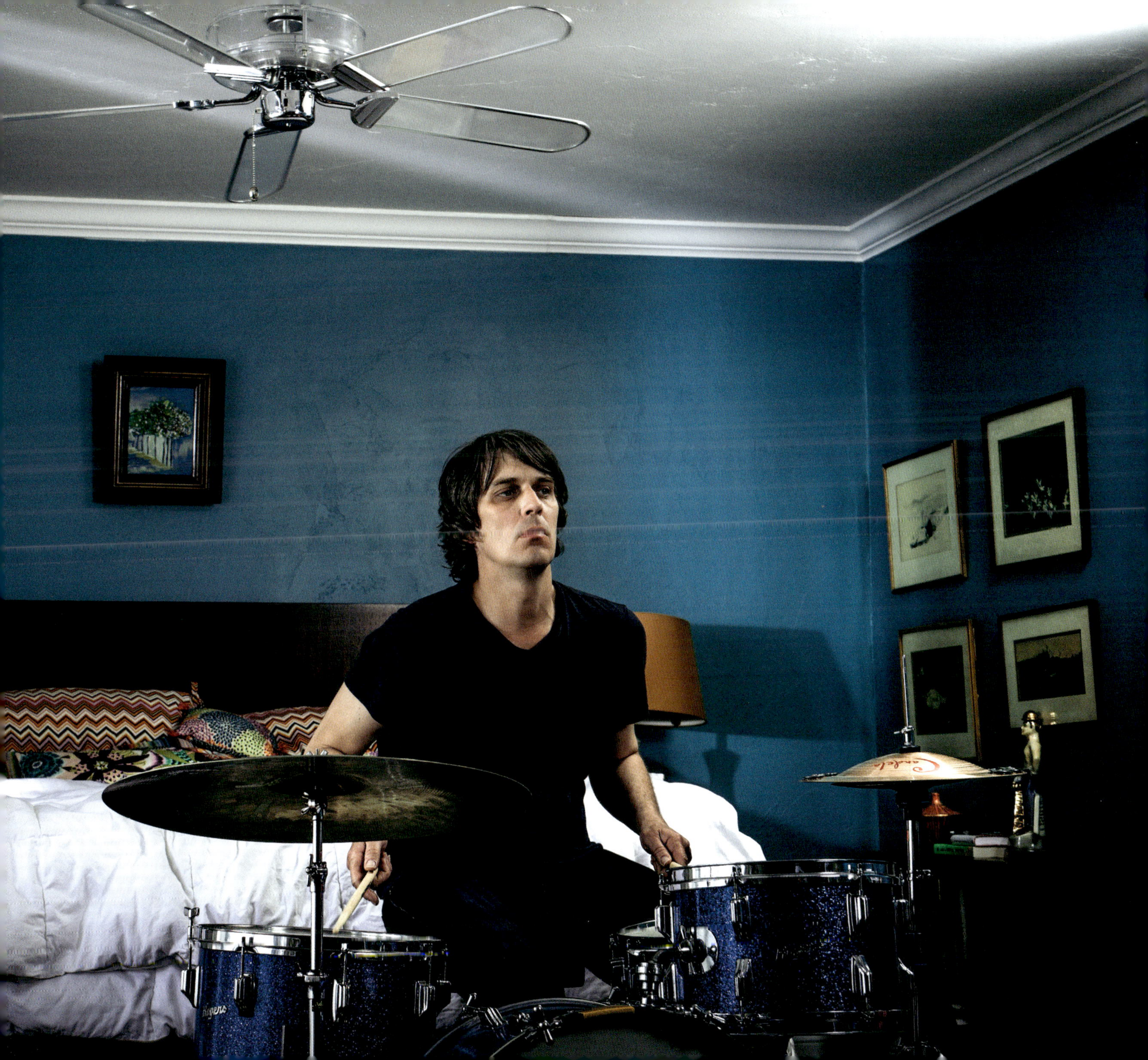

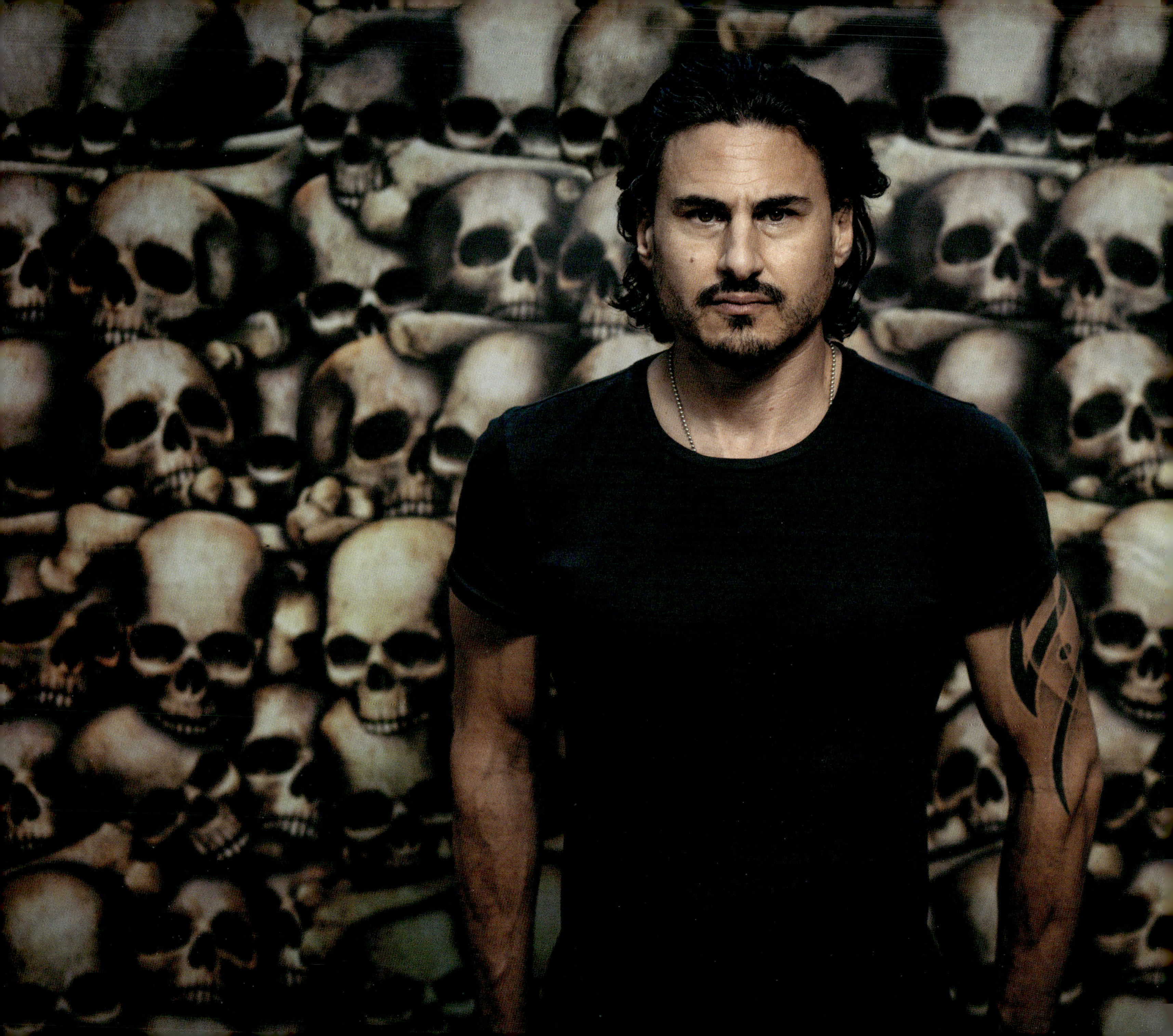

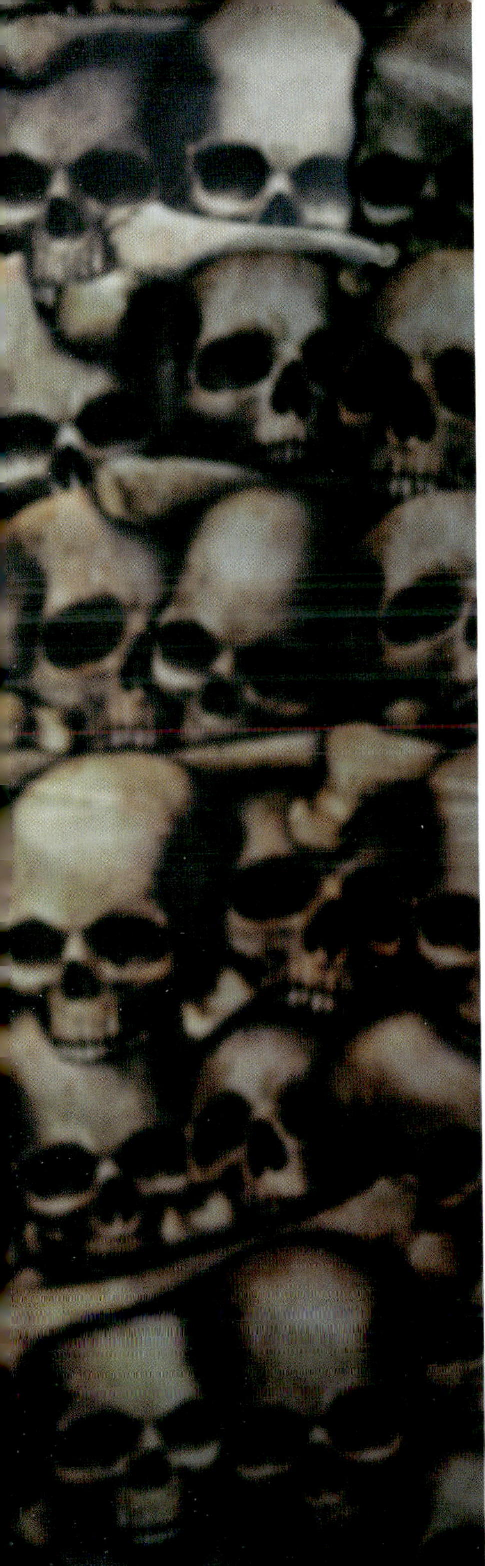

BRAD WILK

Rage Against the Machine / Audioslave / Prophets of Rage. Photographed at home, California

CARLA AZAR

Autolux. Photographed in her studio, California

I didn't remember the moment I decided to play drums until recently. The memory came completely out of the blue. When I was around four years old I went to a local football game with my parents in Huntsville, Alabama. Before the game, there was a drum line that marched up into the bleachers and was playing right behind us. In retrospect, they were probably not very good, but the emotional impact of that sound and volume behind me was so powerful that I remember turning around and being frozen and mesmerized by it. That feeling comes right back every time I think about that. I didn't start playing drums until years after that, but I'm sure that was the moment that made my decision.

The first time I was onstage was in the high school Christmas concert. I was in my junior year and was in the orchestra playing mallet instruments, snare drum and everybody's favourite, the triangle. I left Alabama and the South the day I graduated.

The most addictive thing to me is spontaneity, chaos and honesty in music – especially when playing live. I feel the most satisfaction when I finish playing and I don't understand how I played some of the things I played or where those things even came from, yet it all worked better than I'd planned. I just want things to be real. Recording is the same for me but the fact that I know I can do it again if I don't like it makes it less dangerous.

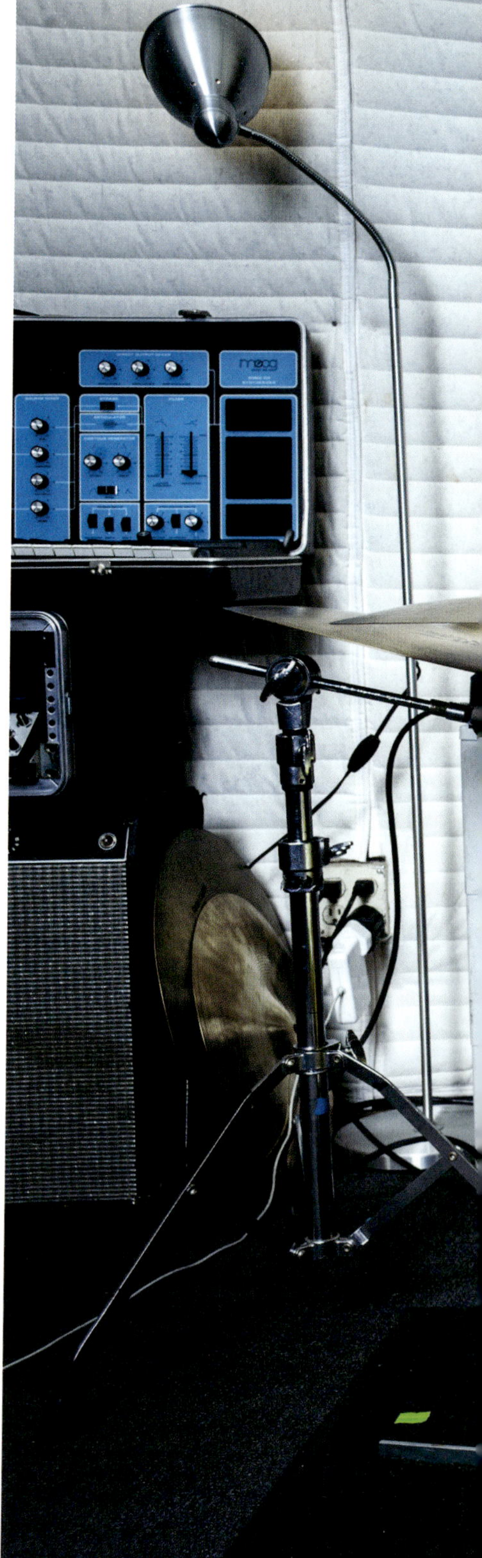

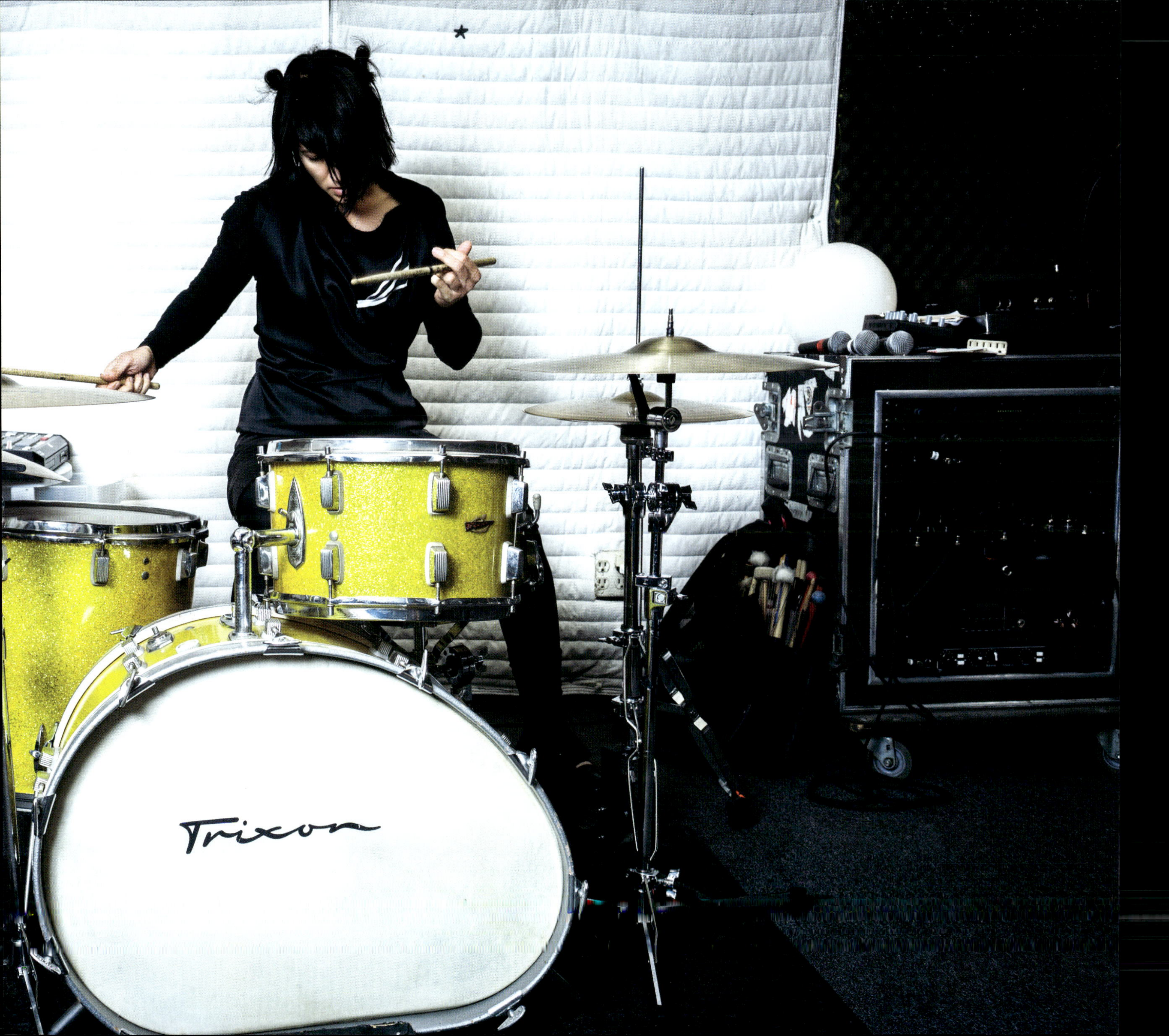
Trixon

NEIL PEART

Rush. Photographed at Drum Channel Studios, California

On a show day afternoon, I will arrive from somewhere-or-other on my motorcycle, do any necessary maintenance on it, then clean myself up. The day's first ritual is sound check with my bandmates at five o'clock – something we always do, even if we happen to be playing a second night in the same venue. At six o'clock we have dinner together in the dressing room, after which I will retreat to my bus for a call home, or a little quiet time.

A half-hour before the show, I sit down at my little warm-up kit in the 'Bubba Gump' room. (My drum tech's nickname is Gump, and one of mine is Bubba, and there is a chain of seafood restaurants in the United States called Bubba Gump, presumably inspired by the movie *Forrest Gump*. So that's why. Sort of.)

When I pick up the sticks and settle my feet on the pedals, I have a couple of favourite rhythmic foundations that I fall into every day – repeating patterns (ostinatos) that are both comfortable and inspiring. I nearly always begin by improvising over a 3/4 'waltz' lilt, and gradually build intensity, then modulate through a couple of Latin rhythms I like. I often try out new ideas that may well appear in my solo in that night's performance.

My wristwatch is placed carefully on the floor beside me, leaning on a floor tom leg, so I can keep an eye on the time (I need to stop after twenty minutes and get dressed for the show), but during that warm-up I feel a sense of peace and timelessness behind the drums. There is no audience, no responsibility to be 'good', and there are no consequences – no trainwreck or embarrassment – for a failed experiment, a bungled transition, a dropped stick. It is just me and my chosen instrument.

The word that occurs to me to describe my state of mind in that interval is 'self-possessed', and it is apt – because that performance belongs only to me. Such a mental and physical state feels like a complete reverse polarity to the way I will feel onstage, just a few minutes later. During the show, I am responsible to my bandmates, the songs and the audience to play 'correctly' – to control the tempo, remember the arrangement and execute the fills and transitions with as much strength and grace as I can muster (never enough).

Thus I feel a constant tension, a moment-by-moment pressure, and almost automatically slip into a mode of fierce concentration. (Actually, I guess it is only a different angle on the metaphor of being 'self-possessed' – in this instance, possessed by a desperate demon for whom time is slowed down to milliseconds, each of which is analysed and found wanting in one degree or another.) Naturally, with an audience in front of us who have spent their time and money to be there, I feel a further responsibility to play as well as I possibly can – giving everything I have in every song, sweating and pounding and thinking as hard as I can.

All of that hurts. Apart from the mental exertion and anguish, my muscles, joints and tendons are jolted and jangled by that ceaseless pounding on tightly tuned heads and metal pedals. Like the pistons in an internal combustion engine, no matter how fast my hands and feet are moving up and down, they have to come to a full stop at the end of each stroke. Mechanical engineers call those stops in a piston's stroke 'top dead centre' and 'bottom dead centre', and it is at bottom dead centre – where my hands and feet are striking an unyielding surface with as much force as they are able to exert – that the pain is born.

I hit those drums and cymbals as hard as I can almost constantly throughout the entire show, because I like the sound that can only be produced by such an impact. When struck that way, bass drum, low toms and the all-important snare drum have more attack as well as more body in their sound. In the higher toms, I hit them hard enough to stretch the heads and thus detune them slightly, giving not only a sharp, percussive attack but a thicker, throatier sound. So yeah, that hurts.

My mother has always complained that I don't smile enough onstage. Perhaps now the reader may understand why that might be true. So whenever a photographer happens to capture a transitory image of me actually smiling at something – most likely the madcap antics of our guitarist, Alex (known to my second bandmate, Geddy, and me as 'the funniest man in the world') – I will ask that photographer to please publish that image.

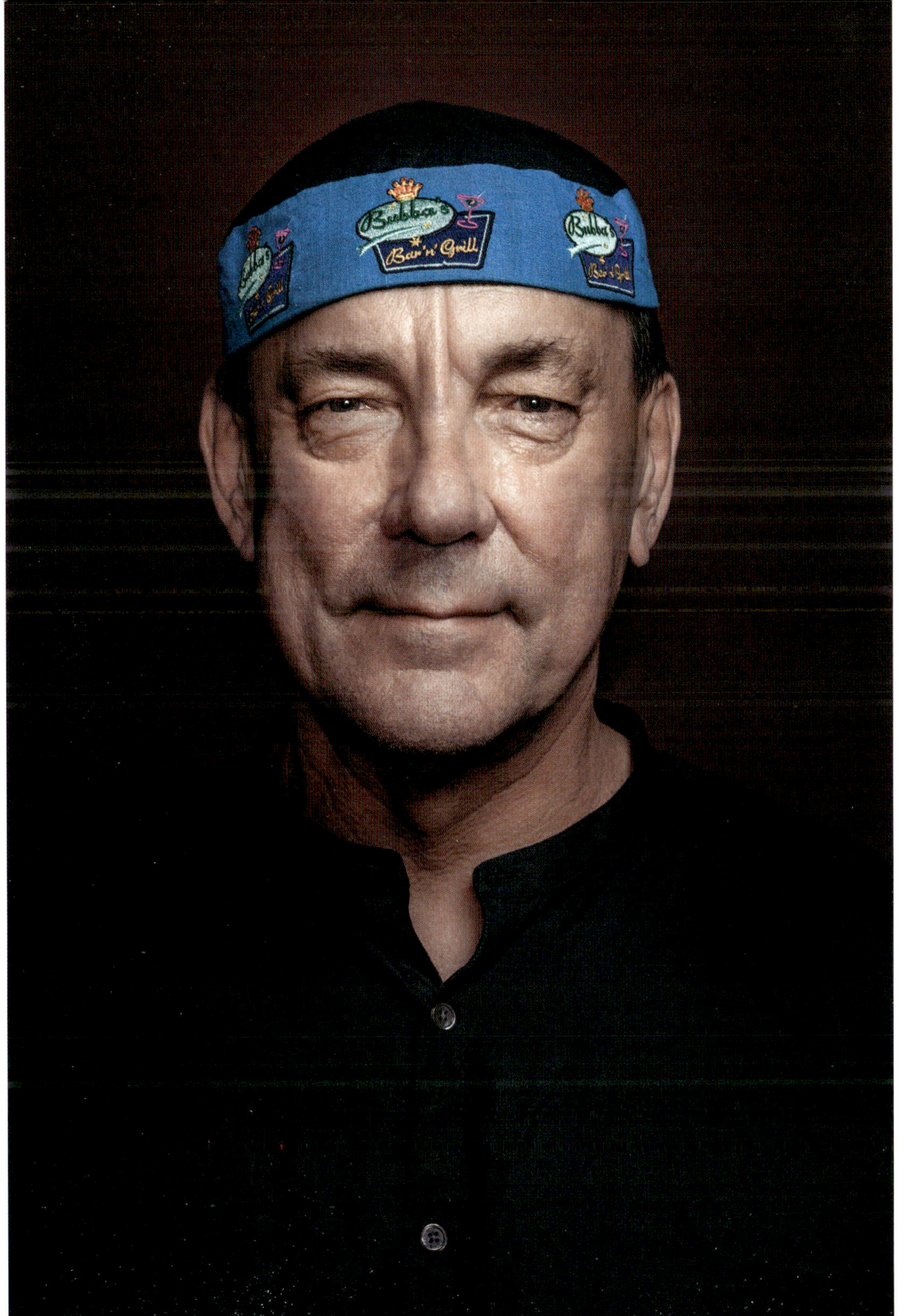
Bubba's
Bar'n' Grill

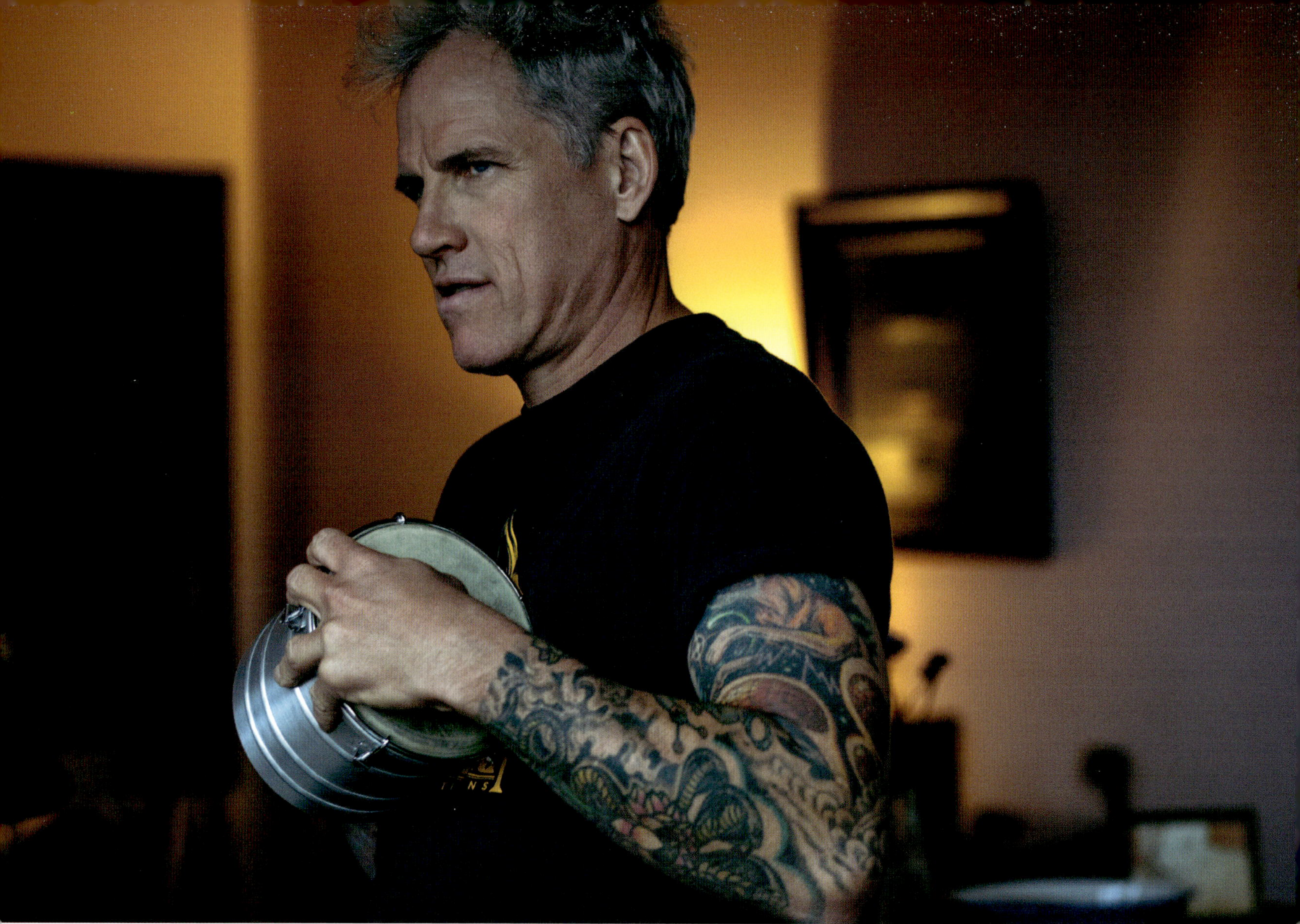

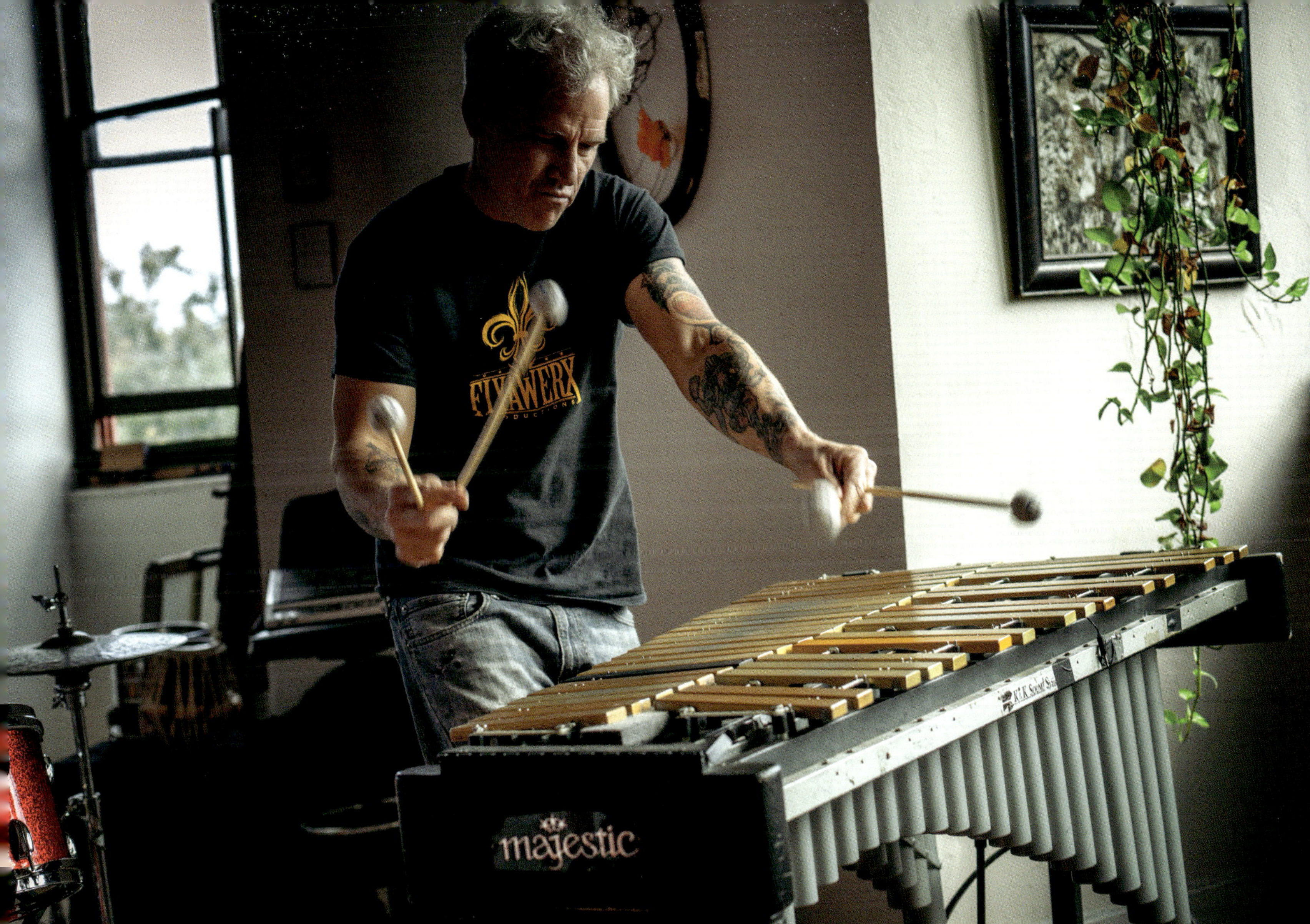

MIKE DILLON

Les Claypool's Fancy Band / Critters Buggin / The Mike Dillon Band / Punkadelick. Photographed at home, Louisiana

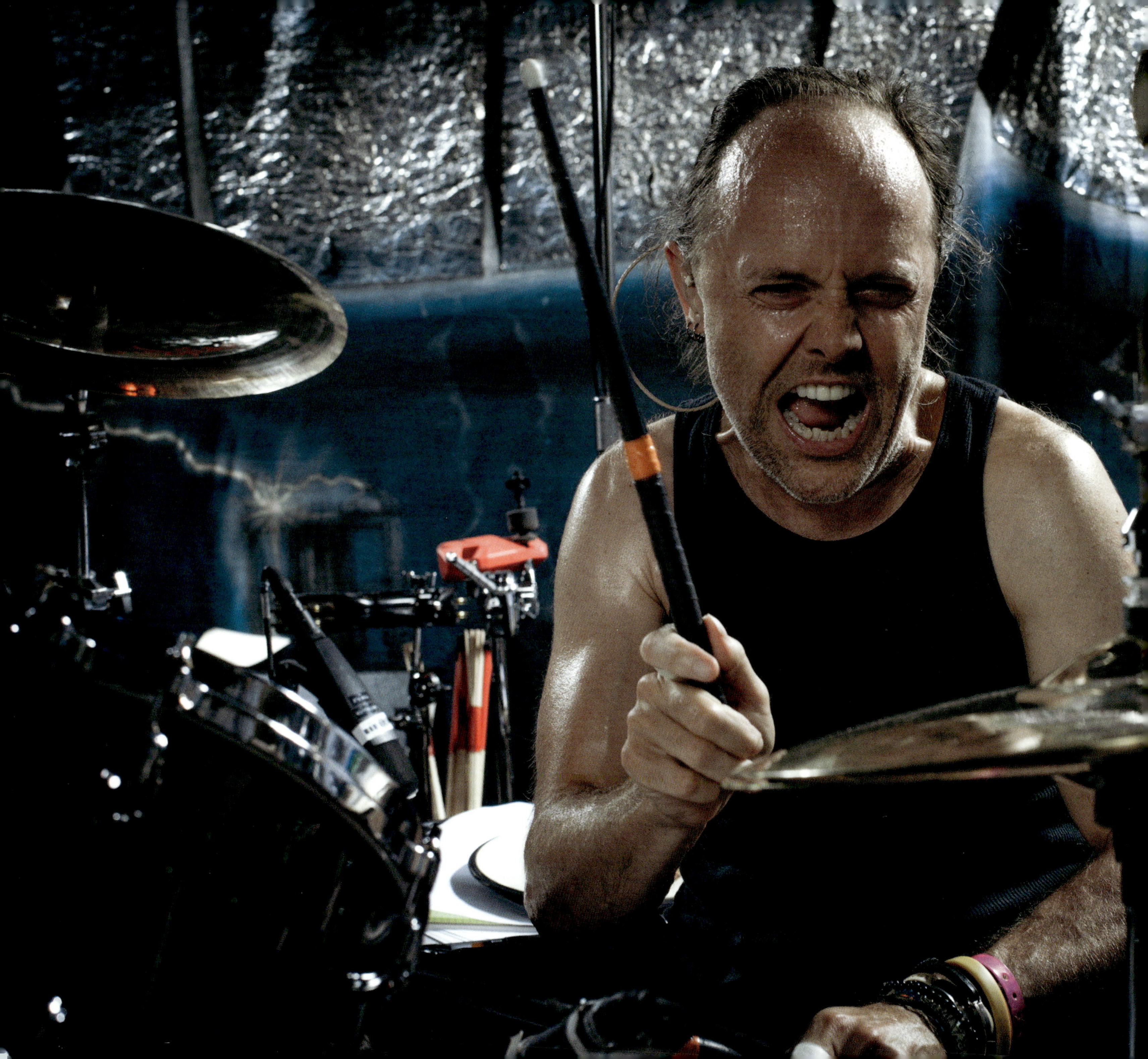

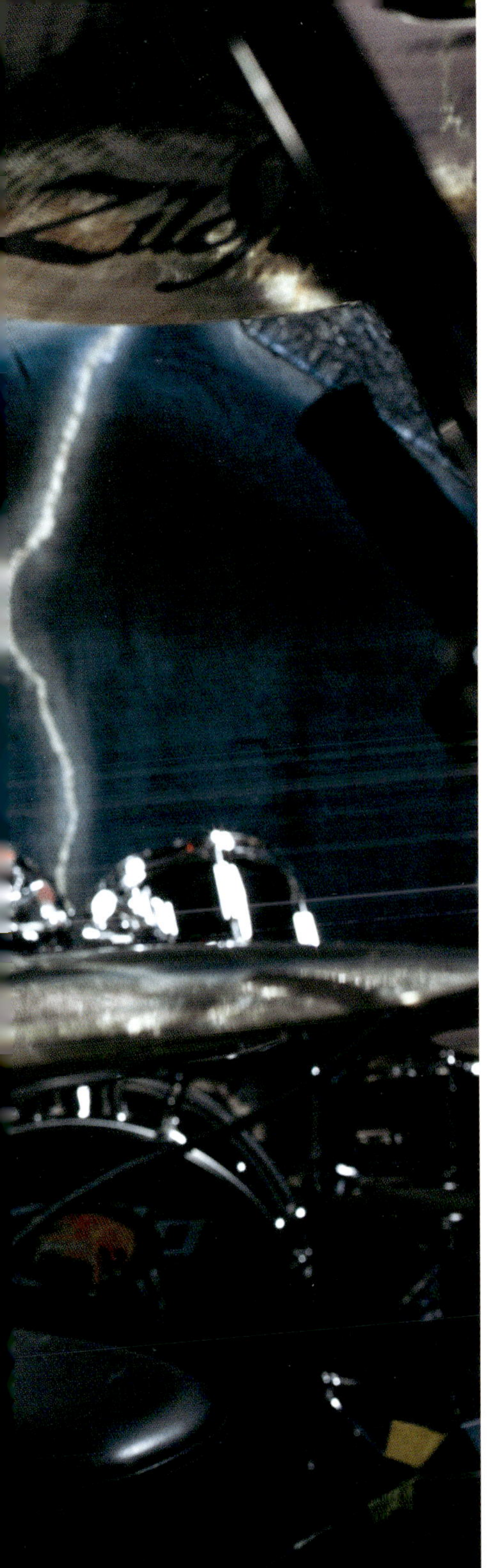

LARS ULRICH

Metallica. Photographed at Metallica HQ, California

We moved from Denmark to America in the summer of 1980. I'd just started finding my feet in terms of friends and turning into a pubescent teenager, hanging out and drinking a few beers and whatever else comes with being sixteen. So when I came to Newport Beach, I felt I was a bit of a loner. Also, at that time there were so many things happening in music in Europe, especially in England, with Iron Maiden and Motörhead and Saxon and all these bands that I was really into. So when I came to Los Angeles, there was a bit of a 'fuck me' moment because it was all about REO Speedwagon and Kansas and that kind of stuff. I felt far away from where the action was. There weren't really any kids in Newport Beach that were into Iron Maiden or Diamond Head in 1980, so I was just kind of doing my own thing – I wasn't particularly into hanging out with all these Lacoste-wearing sixteen-year-old Americans.

I think rhythm can be both natural and learned. I'm the first athletic fuck-up in the family. All the rest of them were Danish champion tennis players and footballers. I was going to be a tennis player but the whole tennis thing dissipated and music took over within six months of coming to America. Drumming has a lot to do with balance and coordination. I think balance is probably one of the most underrated elements of drumming, and playing tennis for the better part of fifteen years was very helpful. I've just always been more into feel and moods, and patterns and rhythms. To me it's never been so much about showcasing ability.

I've always been interested in the collective element of music rather than the solo element of music. If you want to get deeply psychological, I was probably always longing to be part of something with other people. And so I'm making up for my perceived loneliness, or my perceived autonomy or whatever. But I just wanted to be in a band. I wanted to be with other people, so I just never really looked at drums as a solo instrument and I've never really pursued that side of it. I've practised and I've learned but I always get fairly impatient sitting there by myself.

I was so anxious to play in a band, and I basically went straight into Metallica. It's the only band I've ever been in. When I formed Metallica, we started like twelve seconds later and we were playing gigs and playing cover songs. I wish I had spent a little more time learning rudiments and paradiddles. I wish I had taken marching band for a year or two, the kind of stuff which I never did. (I'm exaggerating for effect.) There was a very nice guy called Joe at the West Coast Drums at Santa Ana who thanklessly was trying to teach me some doubles and paradiddles and stuff. I had no patience for it. I just wanted to play with other people. But a few years later I took it more seriously and did some drum lessons up through the '80s while we were putting out records.

My first gig was Metallica's first gig. We played at a place called Radio City, which was a nightclub in Anaheim, California, in March 1982, so I was eighteen. It was a Sunday night. Dave Mustaine had just joined the band and he had been in a couple of bands before; he had a very magnetic personality. He had quite a lot of people hanging around him; there were lots of his friends there. We played seven or eight cover songs and I think one or two Metallica songs. Off we went with the first song, 'Hit the Lights', which was the first song we ever recorded, and in about a minute or two Dave broke a string on his guitar and he had to re-string his guitar in front of a hundred people, and I was sitting up there on stage trying to hide behind the drums. Trying to make myself invisible for what seemed like an eternity. It was probably five minutes but just went on forever. I was sitting there in front of a hundred drunk nightclub goers – it was terrifying. Now when I listen back to our early stuff, I just think, look at all that cool hair and what happened to it. Where did it go?

When I'm playing there are times when I catch myself not thinking. When you have a really good gig, and all the dots are connected, and all the planets are aligned and it's just your mood, the way you connect to the other guys in the band and the audience. When it's really working, you sit there and go, fuck, I was really lost there for two or three minutes. That's great – when it becomes physical rather than cerebral, when it moves from your head to your body, to your gut to your heart or whatever, to your balls, wherever it moves to – it's cool when it happens. It doesn't happen that often – and I'm not saying that to be cynical, I'm just being truthful – but when it does happen, it's really cool.

What separates the great from the good? Probably the ability to listen. To me the greatest turn-on is people who listen and pay attention. Whether it's to music or to conversation or to their environment, it's just being in the moment. I think the best musicians are the ones that really can listen and interpret – at least that's the stuff that interests me more, much more so than ability or showmanship. I love being around people who listen. I think it's probably the most underrated virtue.

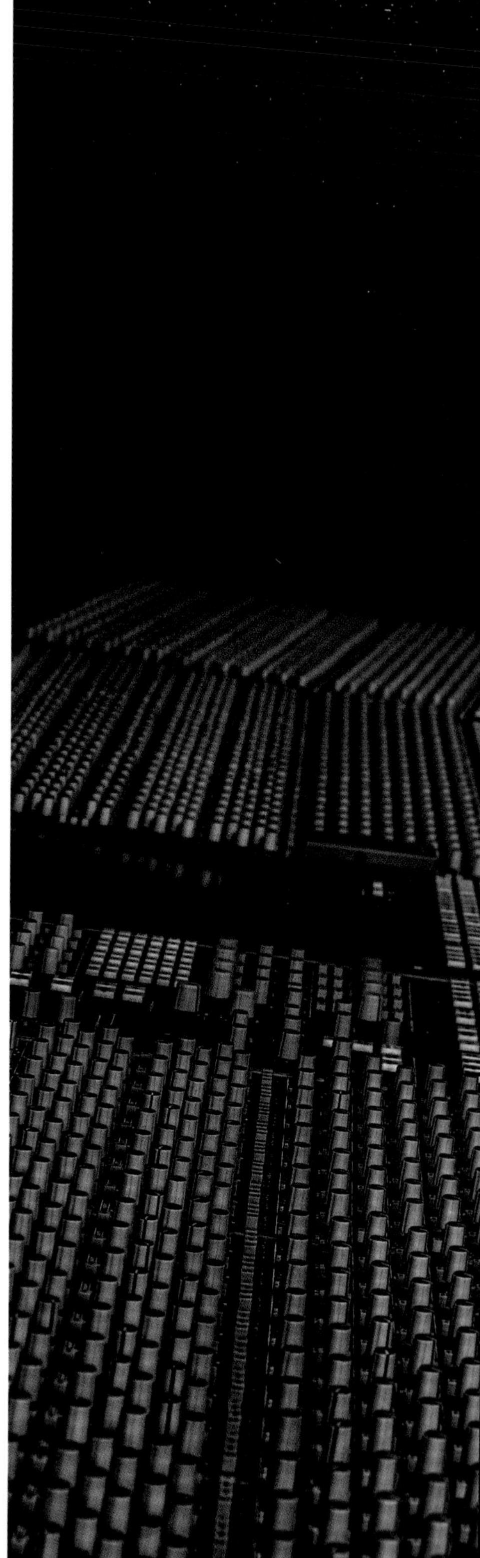

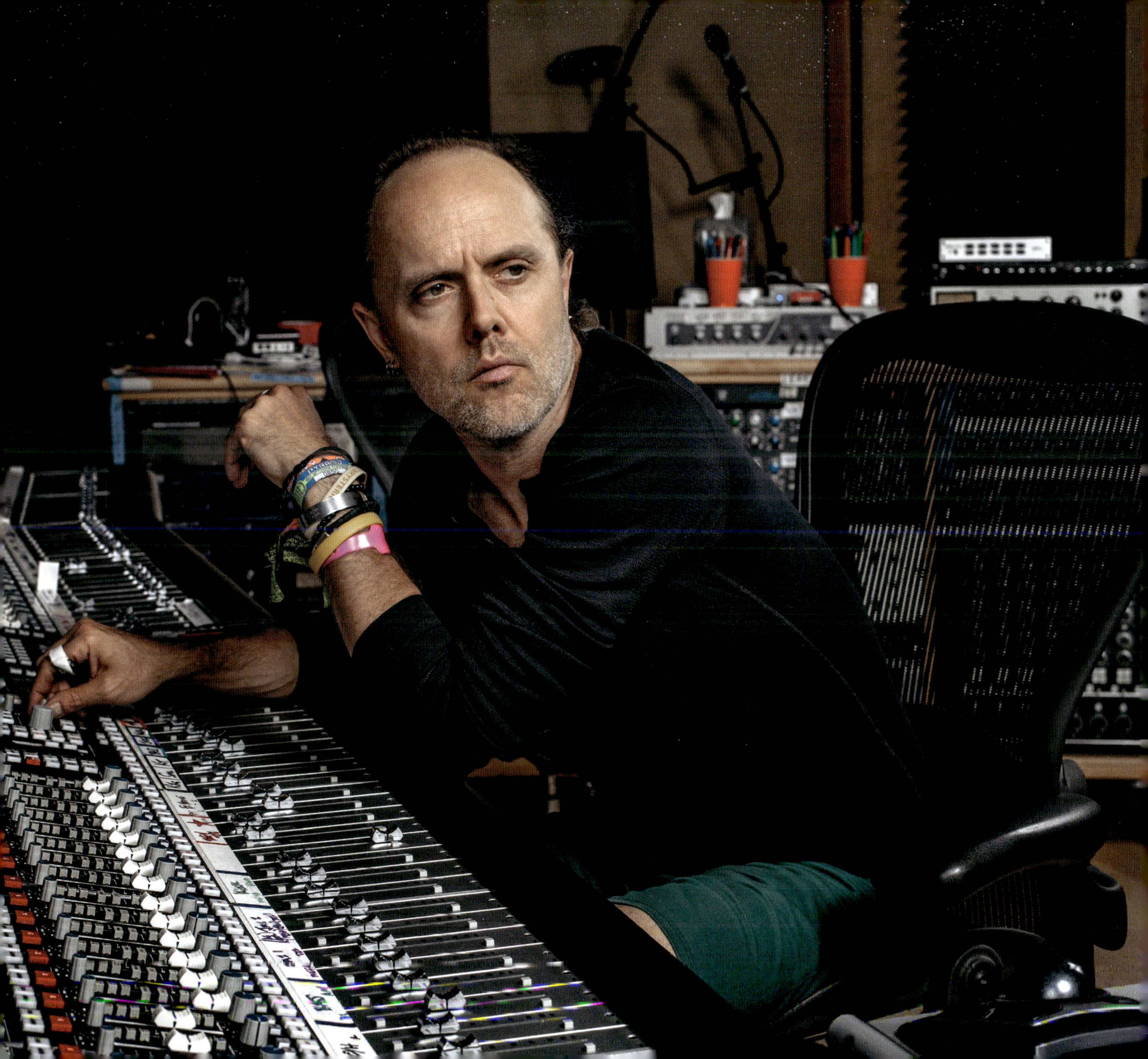

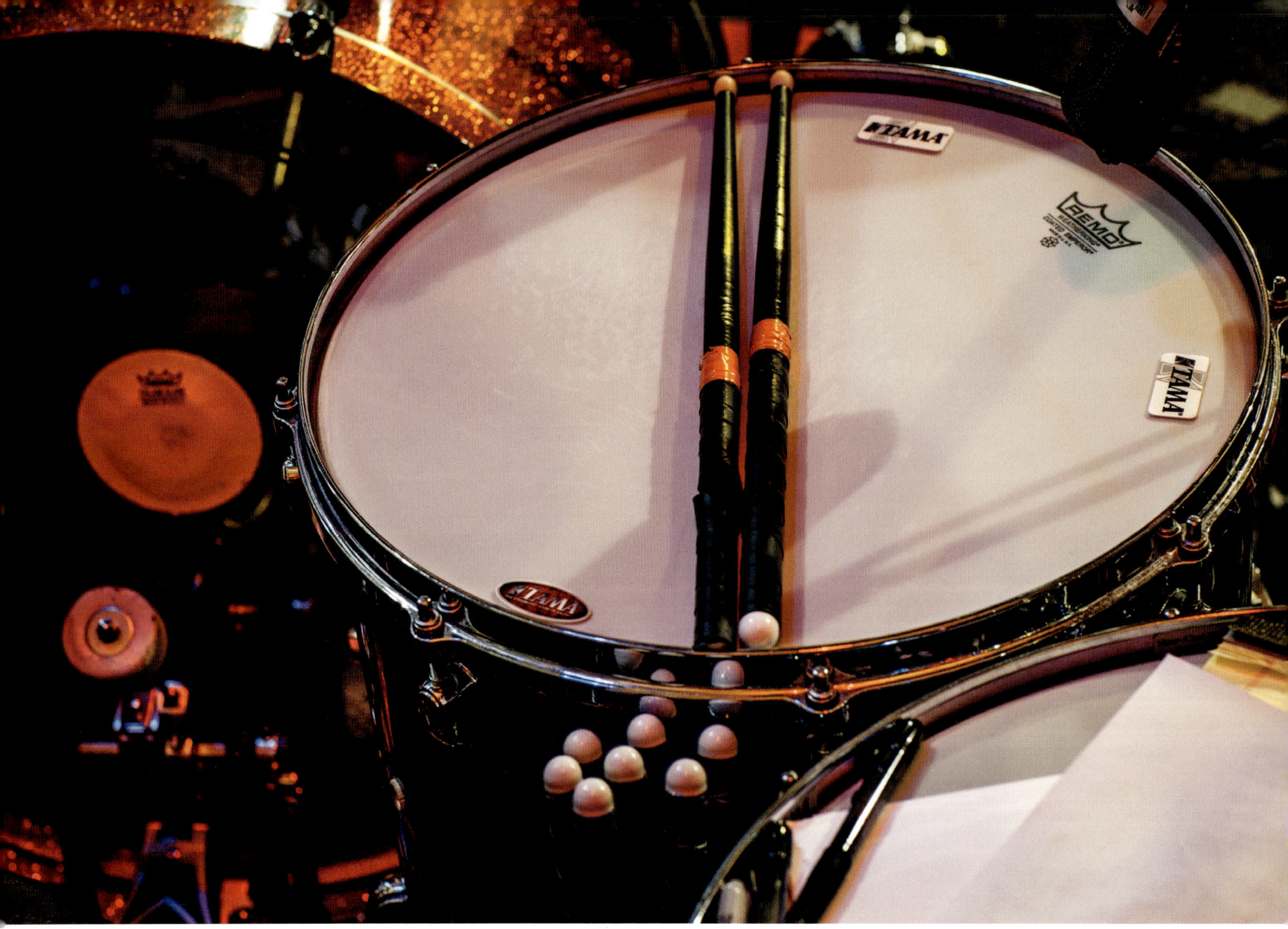
TAMA
REMO
TAMA
TAMA

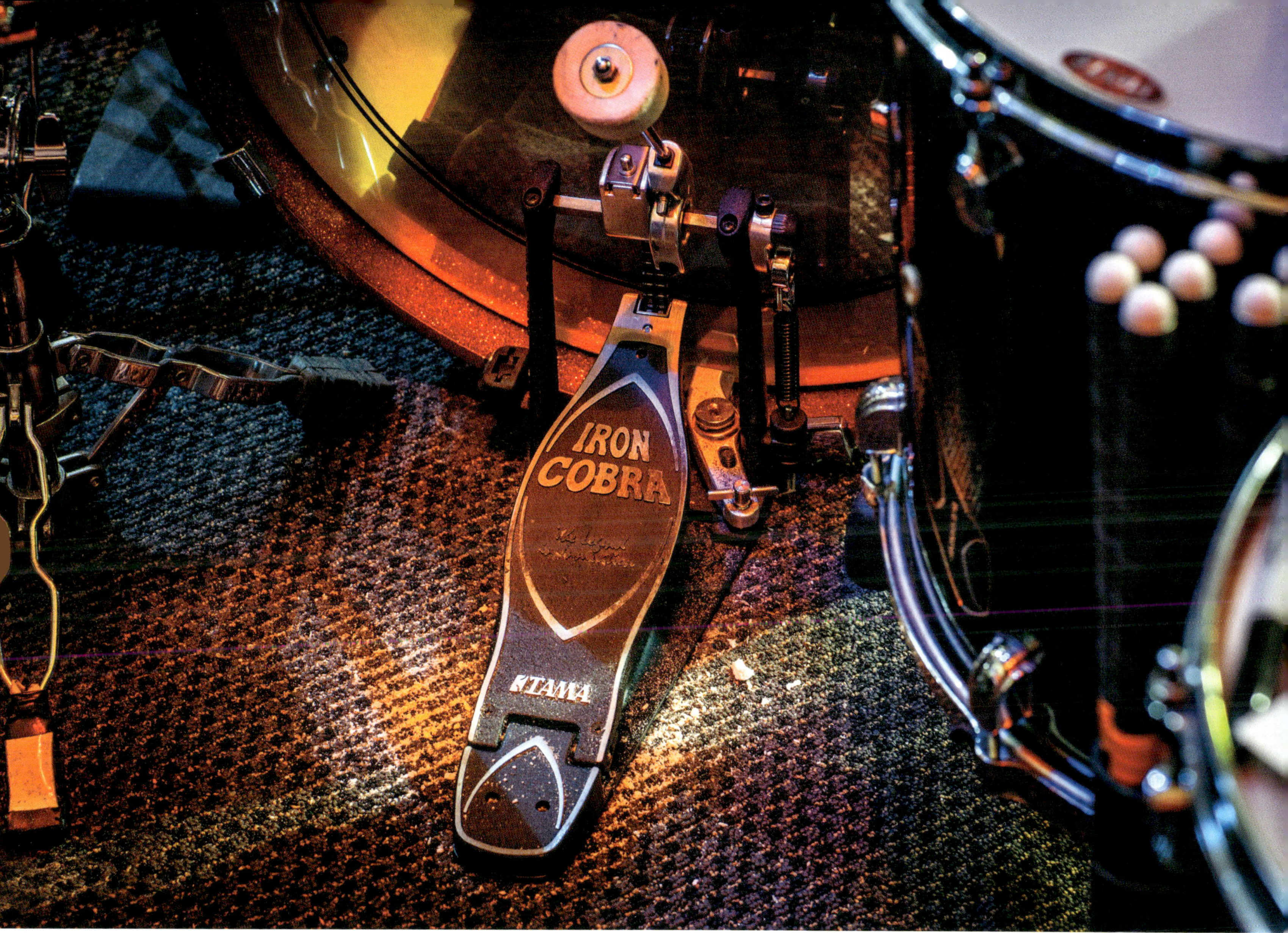
IRON
COBRA
TAMA

NICK MASON

Pink Floyd. Photographed in his studio in the UK

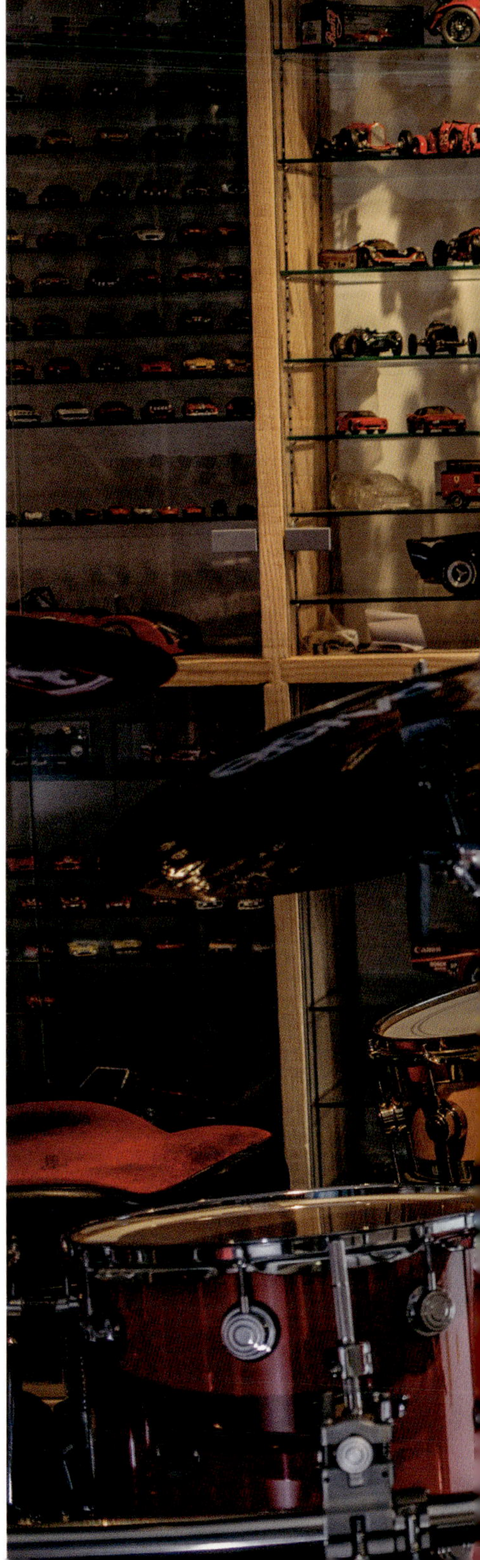

Going out to dinner with a lot of drummers and bass players is a fantastic thing. It's a bit like being in a train carriage, because the table's vibrating most of the time – they're always finding something to play along with.

The very first performance of *The Wall* was pretty chaotic, because we had two things going on. One was that there was a police chief in Los Angeles at the time who was making some sort of stand about young people and loud music and drugs, so there was a big police presence that made everyone very edgy. We also had various dramas with bits of set catching fire – you tend to remember that rather than the show itself.

A professor at one of the London colleges did some research into what he called the American School and the English School of playing, where the English tend just to be hanging back a little bit and pulling it, giving it a slightly different feel and dynamic. Terry Bozzio was talking about a player who said, 'What I do is, I'm a little bit earlier on the bass drum, because the bass will take longer to get to the ear.' It sounded a little far-fetched but really interesting, but it's probably correct that actually the sound waves are going to travel at different speeds.

When Pink Floyd were signed in 1967, we were given a lot of freedom by EMI, I think because our timing was fantastic, because we were very much the juniors to The Beatles. So when we were doing our first album, they were doing *Sgt. Pepper* – so that had established that the artists knew best, and that was a very new concept. Before that, the producers did everything, and the band came in, played a bit and went away again, and someone else mixed the record. We certainly were given studio time – we actually even renegotiated our record contract to take less money but have unlimited time.

We never doubted whether things would continue without Syd. It's really curious, because we should have done, but we didn't. I still look back on it and think, why did we think we could carry on without the guy who fronted the band and wrote all the songs? But we did, because I think by then we'd got the idea that we really liked what we were doing, and Syd was just holding us back … Looking at old videos with Dave miming Syd's songs, you think … But no, I think it was self-belief, probably. Roger had a lot of it, and even though Dave wasn't writing at all when he joined, we knew he was great – he played brilliantly and sang well.

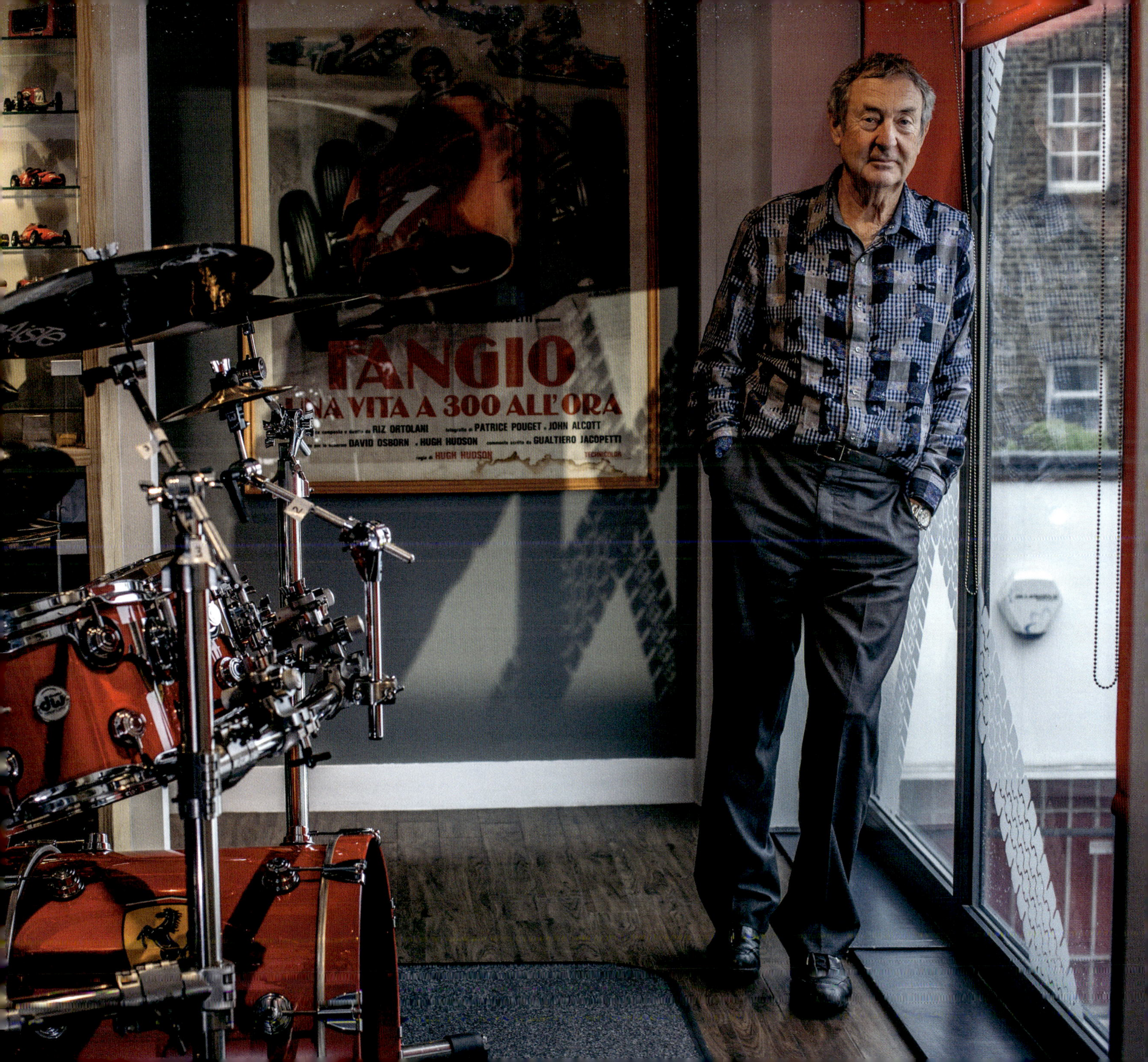
FANGIO
NA VITA A 300 ALL'ORA
RIZ ORTOLANI
PATRICE POUGET . JOHN ALCOTT
DAVID OSBORN . HUGH HUDSON
GUALTIERO JACOPETTI
HUGH HUDSON

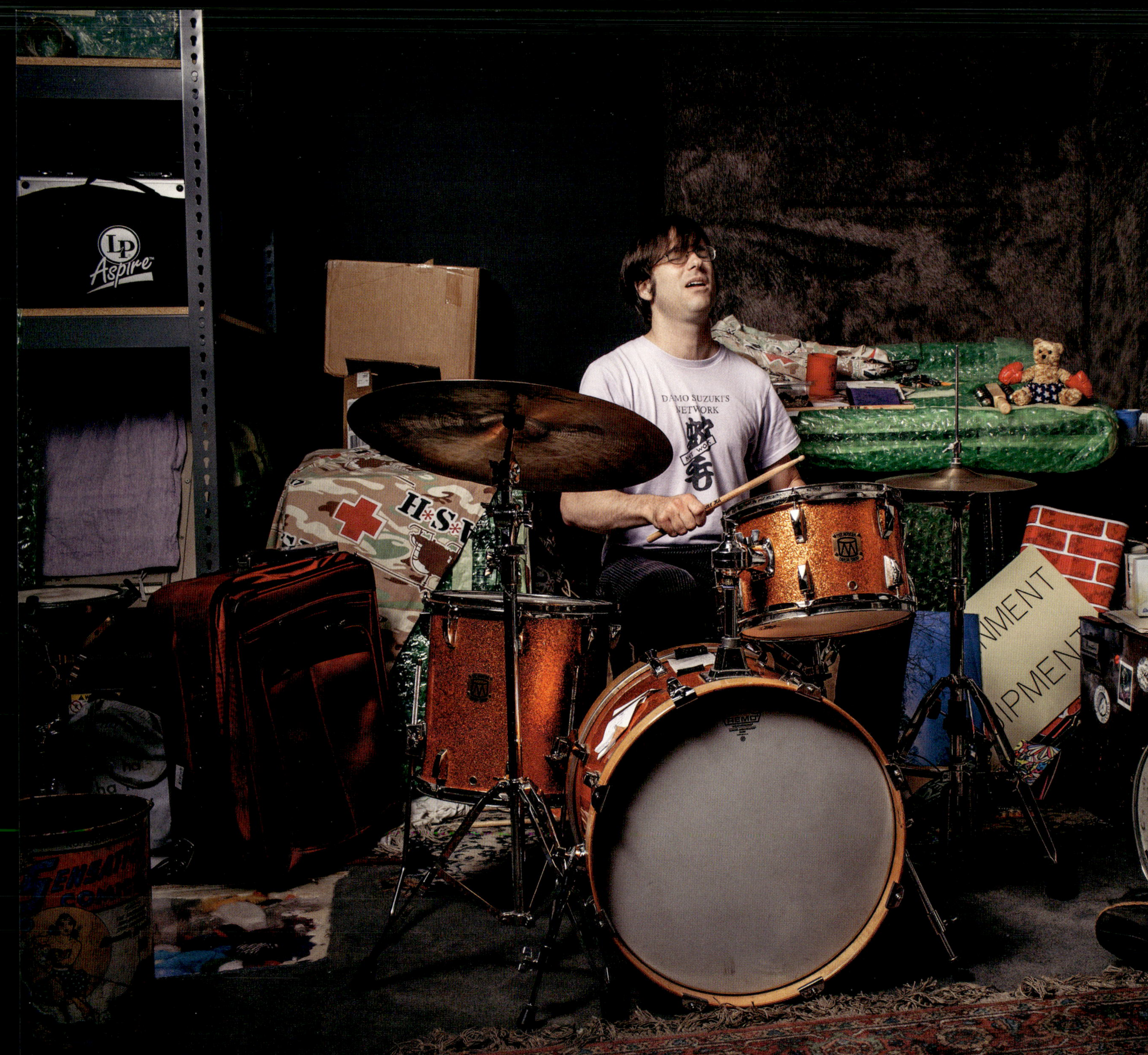
LP
Aspire
DAMO SUZUKI'S
NETWORK

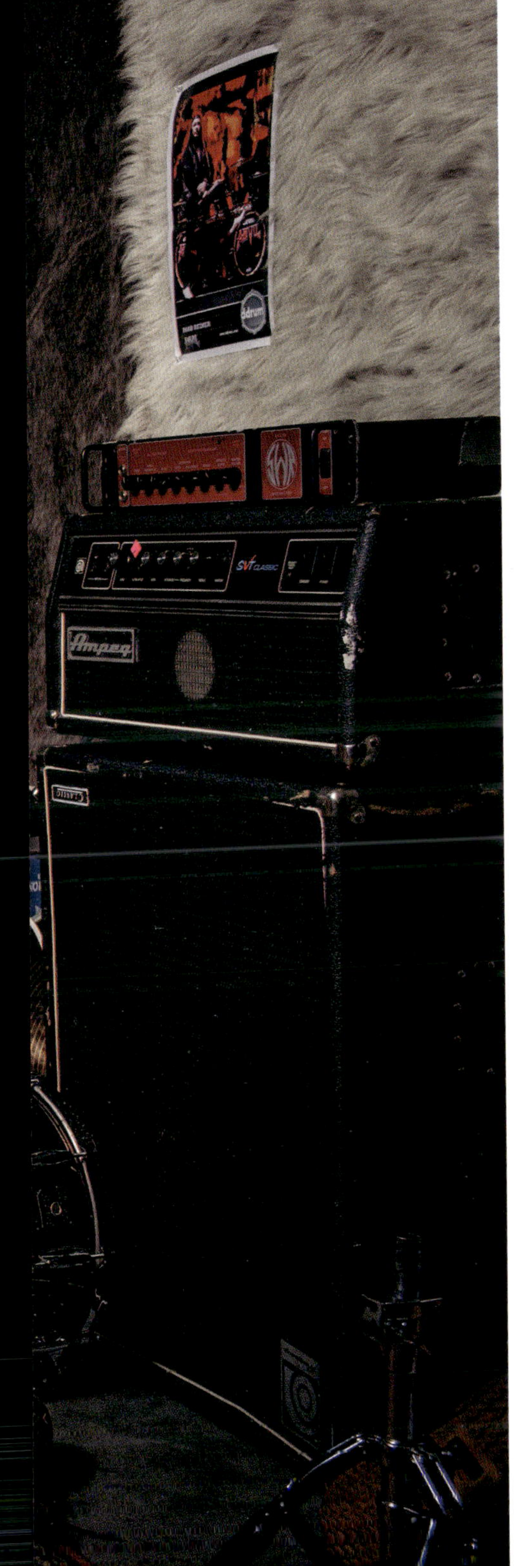

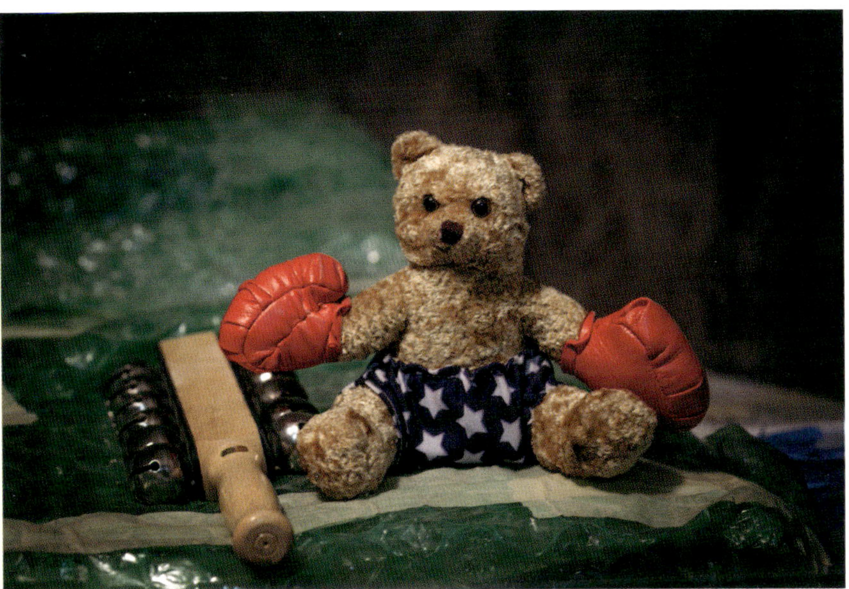

KID MILLIONS

Oneida / Man Forever. Photographed in his studio, New York

So much happens when you listen back to a recording. I can hear that day I took off last week, I can hear that, and it doesn't sound good! I think I can get too bogged down with technique, it's like a distraction, it's like an ego thing. It feeds into a certain part of my insecurity.

You have an energy before the performance that builds; it's like a preparatory energy that exists in opposition to the potential disorder of the space that you're playing in. It gets very concentrated and it is a bit of a battle, in a way, against that chaotic energy. There's an attention to the task at hand and just executing things clearly. There are a lot of distracting thoughts, though, so sometimes there's an inner dialogue. It's very much a meditative practice. For me it's about really clear and still focus.

My best recording experiences were the early Oneida recordings where we had this tape machine – we had bought this 8-track with an advance we got for our first couple of records. Those early recording experiences were so challenging but so exciting and interesting. It's like a lot of people say: the ignorance or the naivety is often what drives you to produce something. If you don't know you just do it. Knowing what it takes and the time it takes is daunting.

I played on the *77 Boadrum* performance with Boredoms, at a park in Dumbo. It was 77 drummers with Boredoms – I think there were fifteen of us – at the centre of it. That process was incredible because Boredoms were one of my favourite groups and I got this opportunity to play with them and work closely to present this piece of music that they had never done before, and nobody really knew what it would sound like. The process was this incredible organizational nightmare but it all fed into this one performance that made me feel, wow, this is the reason I did all this drumming in my life, it led to this moment.

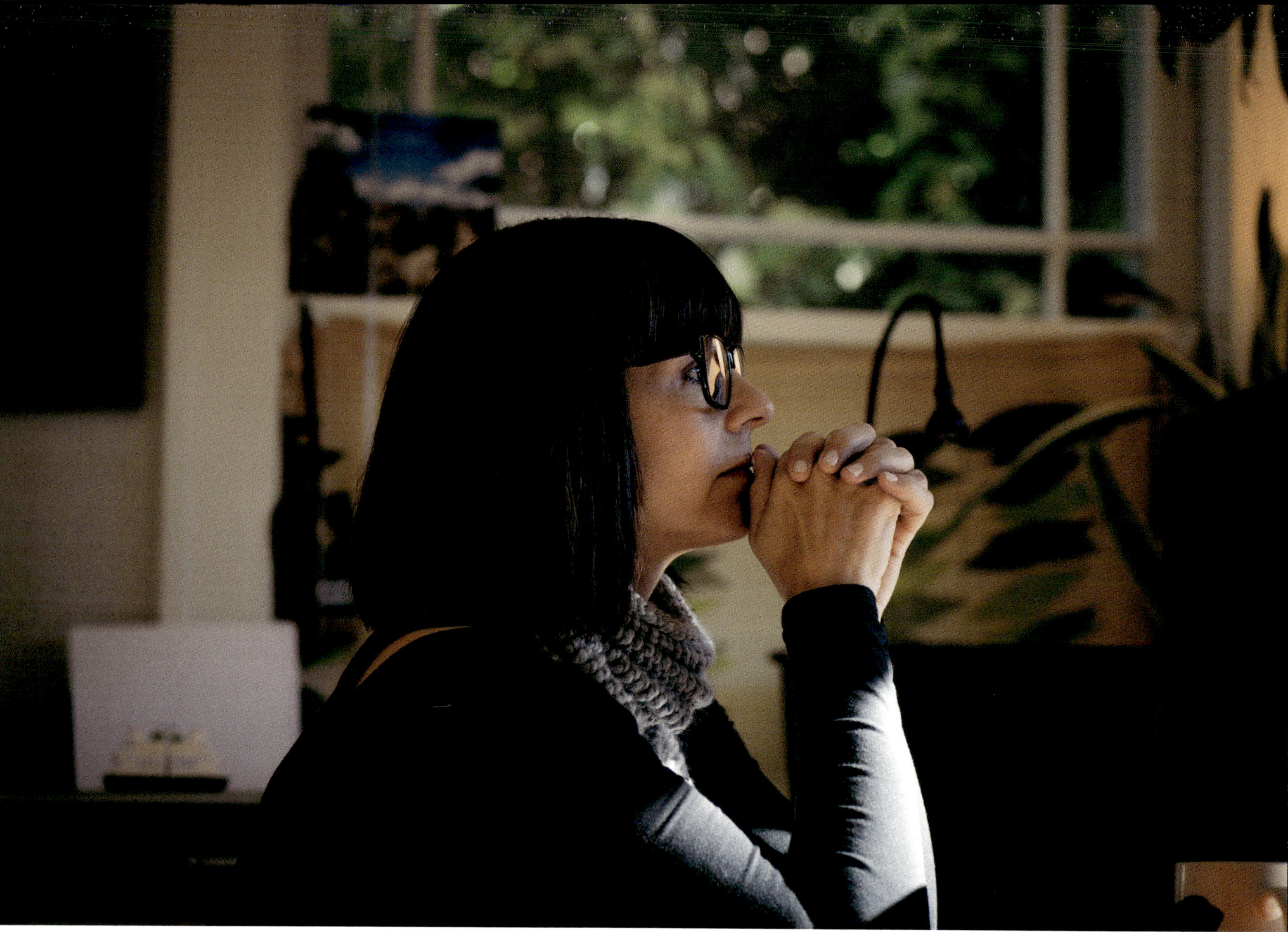

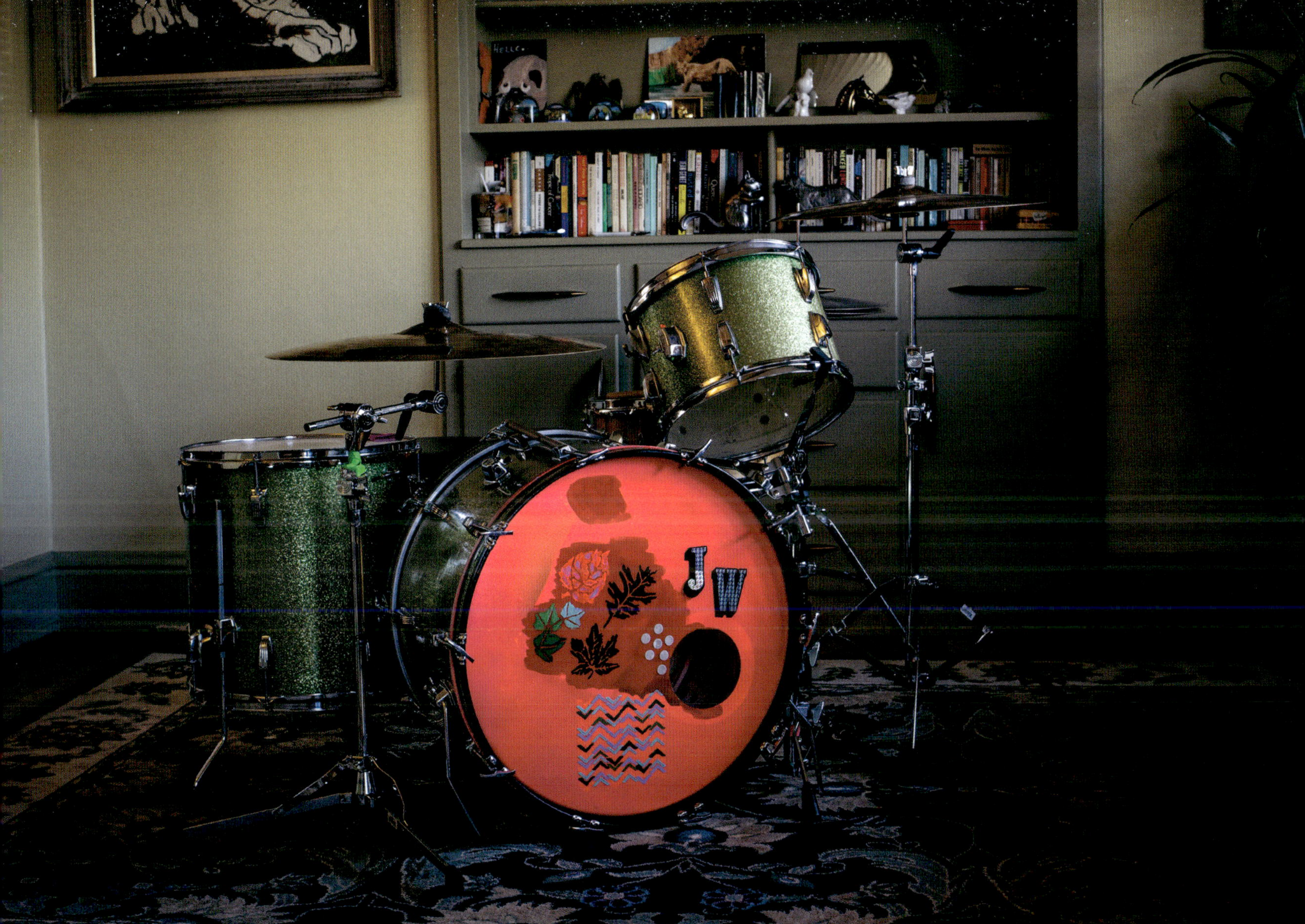

JANET WEISS

Sleater-Kinney / Quasi / Stephen Malkmus & The Jicks. Photographed at home, Oregon

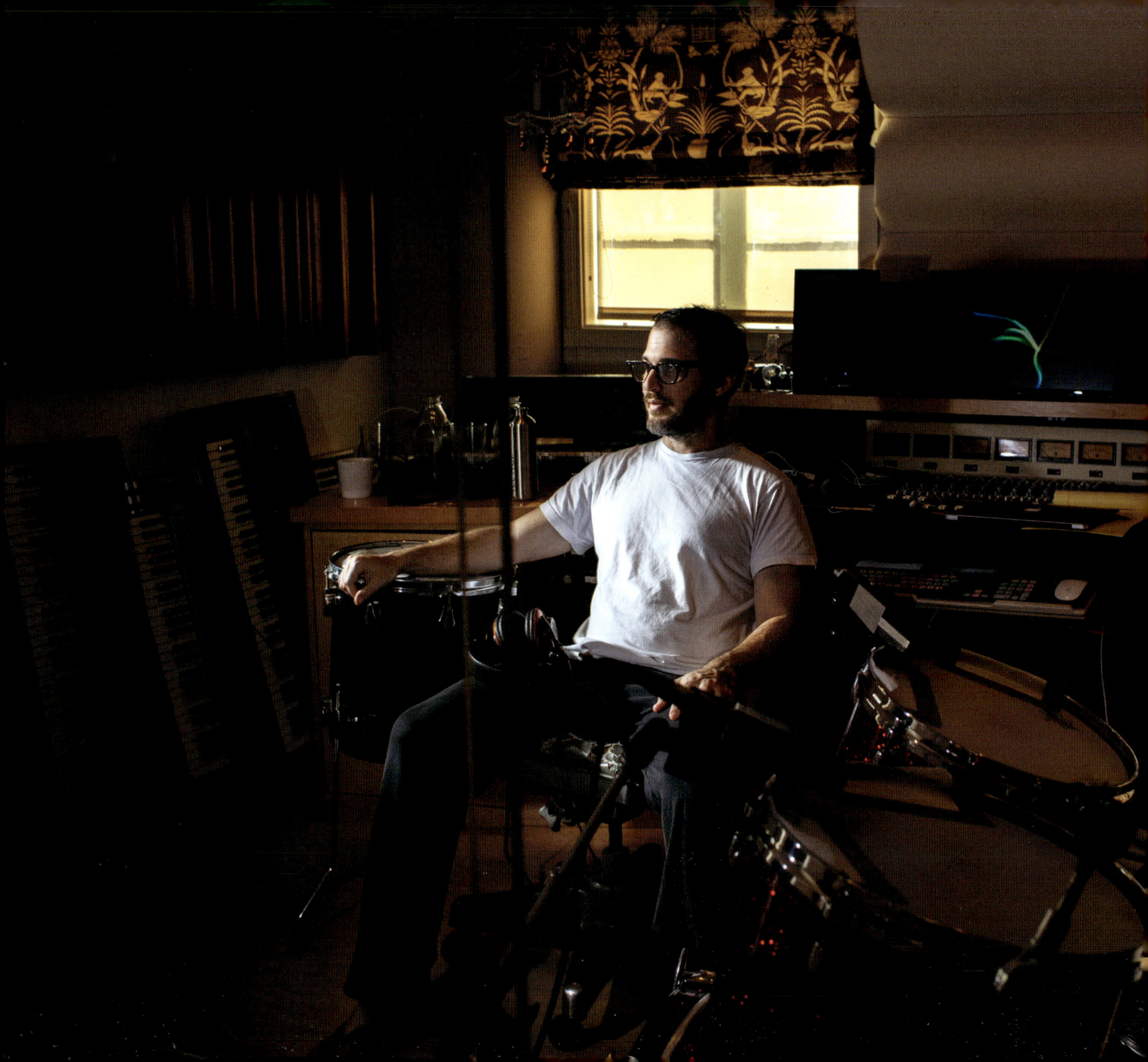

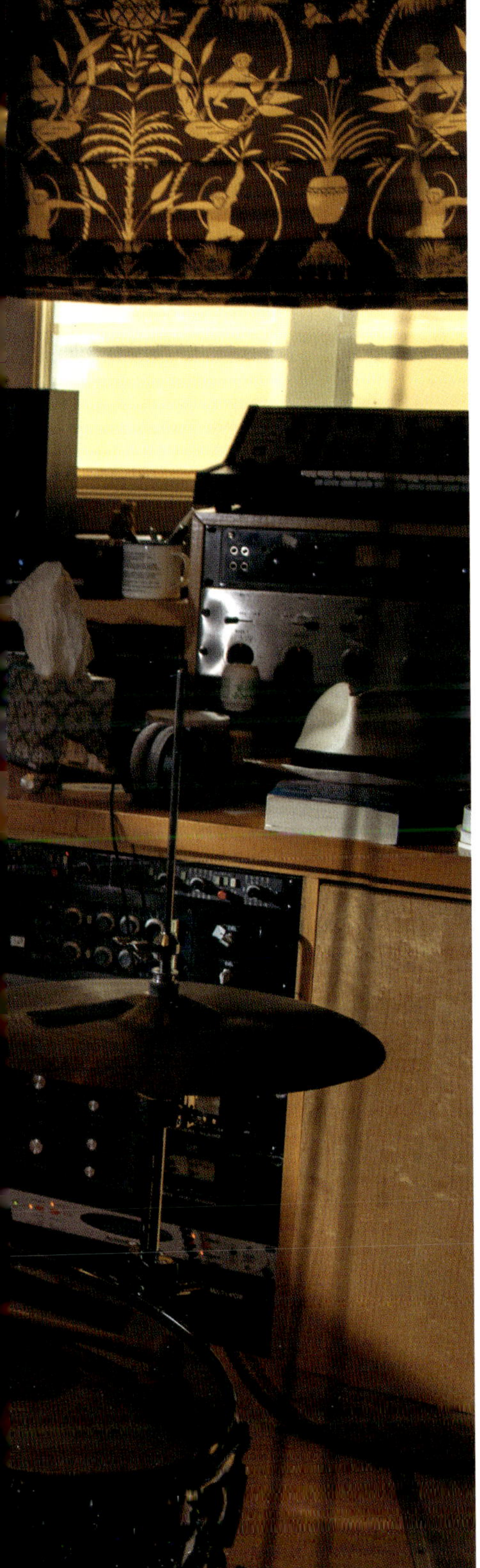

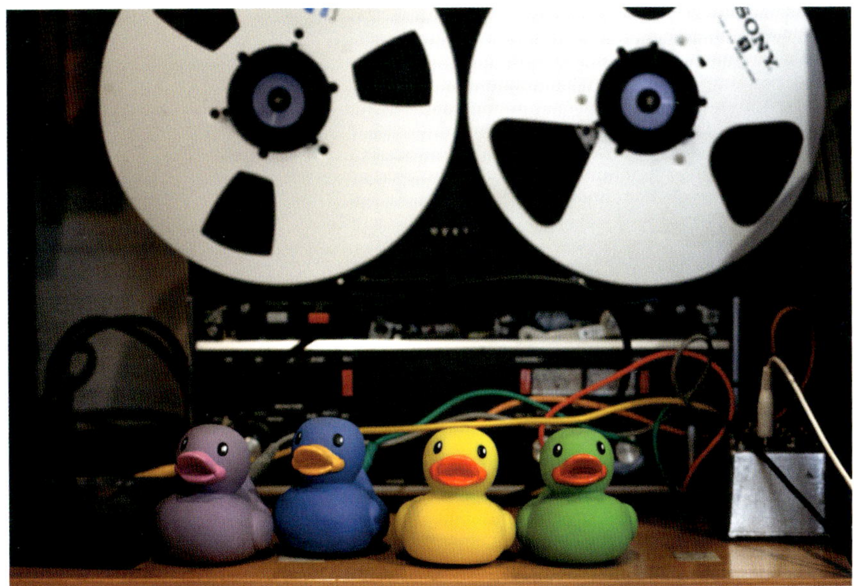

JOEY WARONKER

Beck / Atoms for Peace / R.E.M. / Roger Waters / Oasis. Photographed at home, California

My dad was a record producer at Warner Bros. As a little kid it was just normal, but when I was old enough I realized that it was pretty cool. He worked with Randy Newman – they were childhood best friends. Ry Cooder was another one. There were colourful characters around from that world. I went to gigs from a young age, but I think the big thing for me was I got taken to the studio a lot. One time there was a guy at the studio wearing traditional Chinese clothes, like the straw hat and red silk, and he had facial hair – but, you know, like an American guy, and I would play with him. Then I realized after that it was Captain Beefheart, and I was a huge fan of Captain Beefheart, oh my god. While he was recording *Clear Spot*, I think my dad was producing James Taylor at the time. I got exposed to a lot of drummers.

I love recording. I love producing too, but being a drummer in a band is the most natural thing for me. That's like being on vacation. I've played with Beck for years and I feel like that's where I've matured. We were touring so much and that repetition, that's the experience that it takes to develop a real style. In one set Beck was playing hip hop and folk and punk rock and arty stuff – it was all of the references that I was interested in. He had figured out a way to do it in a modern context – to fuse all that stuff. Those diverse skills came into play when R.E.M. got me in to broaden their horizons a little bit.

One of my favourite recording experiences was making the *Mutations* record with Beck. That's where I met Nigel Godrich and a lot happened. I started forging a style as a recording musician as opposed to as a live musician, and that was the first time I really had a chance to experiment to the point of accomplishing things that worked in the studio, under microphones. I knew that was a landmark thing for me but I still couldn't listen to it for maybe – and I hate that it's so many years ago – but I think it was ten years.

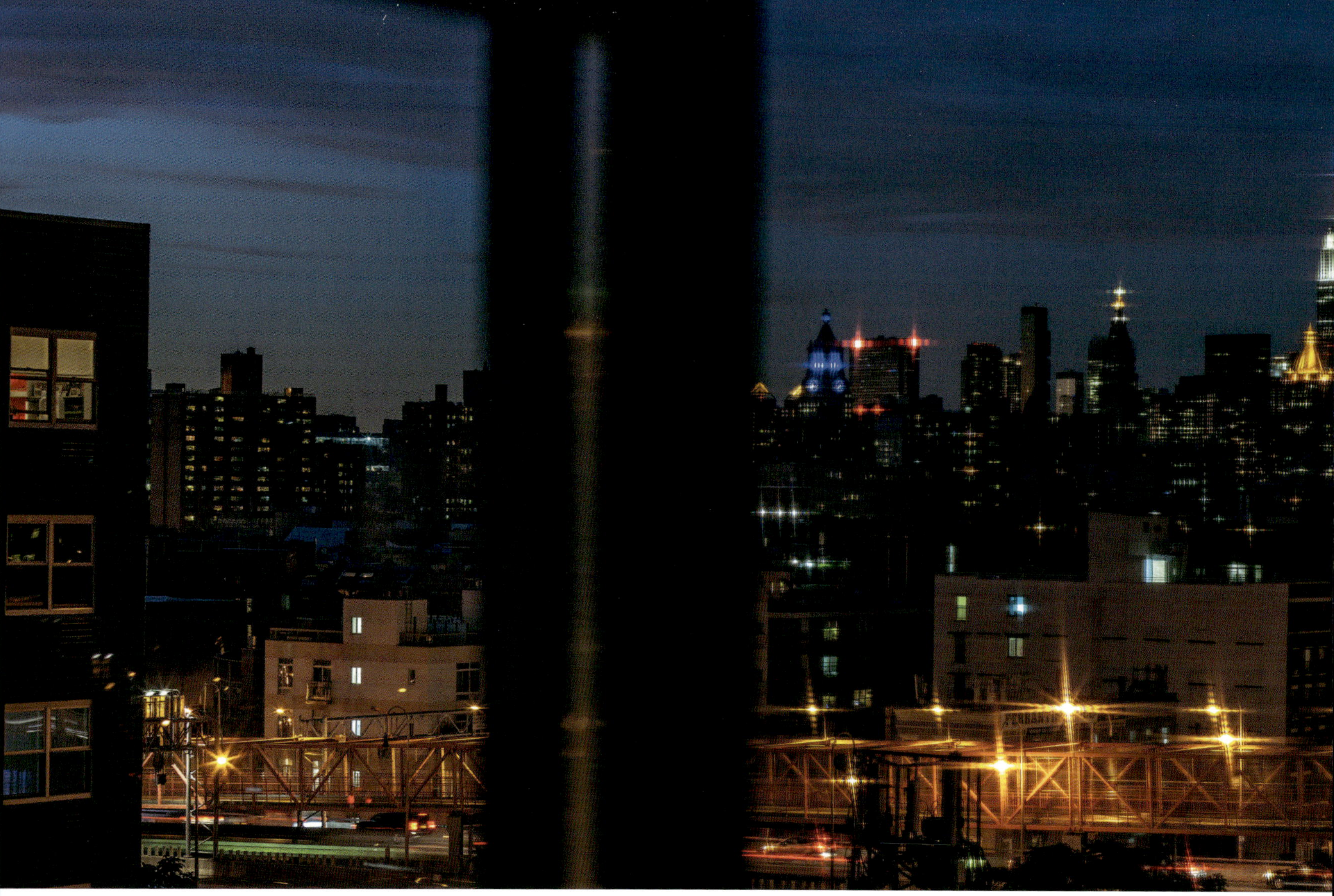

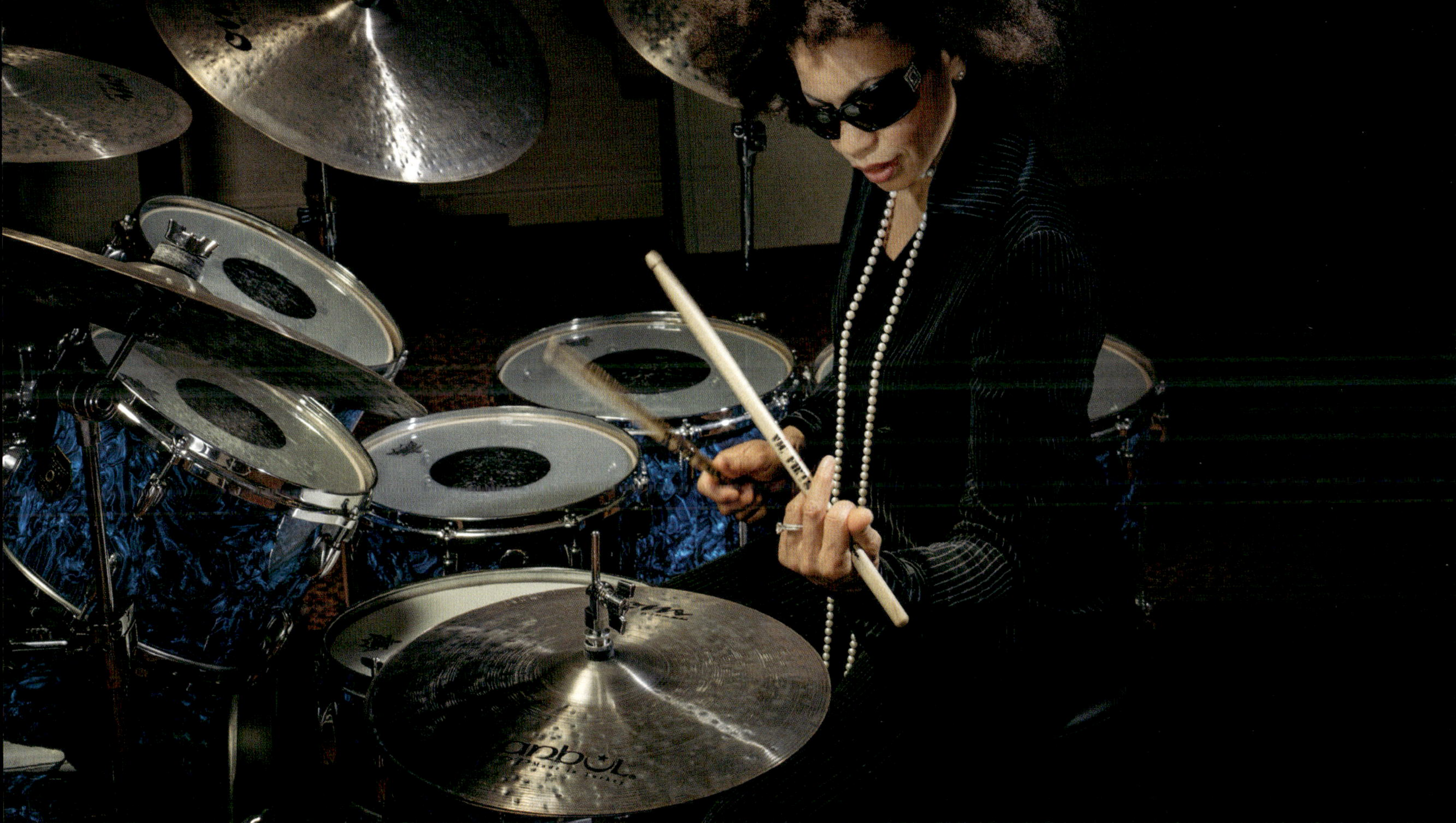

CINDY BLACKMAN

Lenny Kravitz / Carlos Santana / John McLaughlin / Jackie McLean / Don Pullen. Photographed in New York

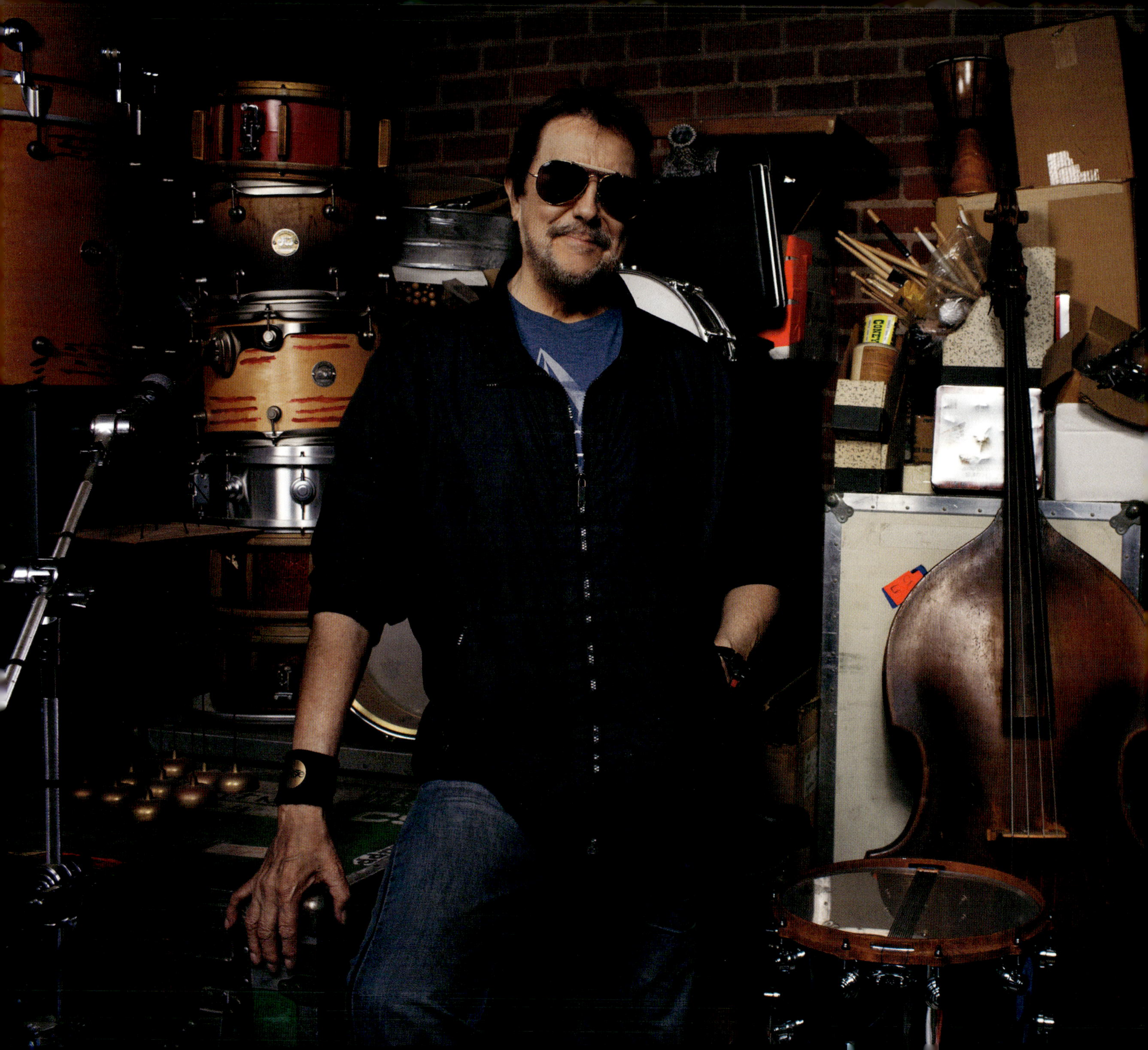

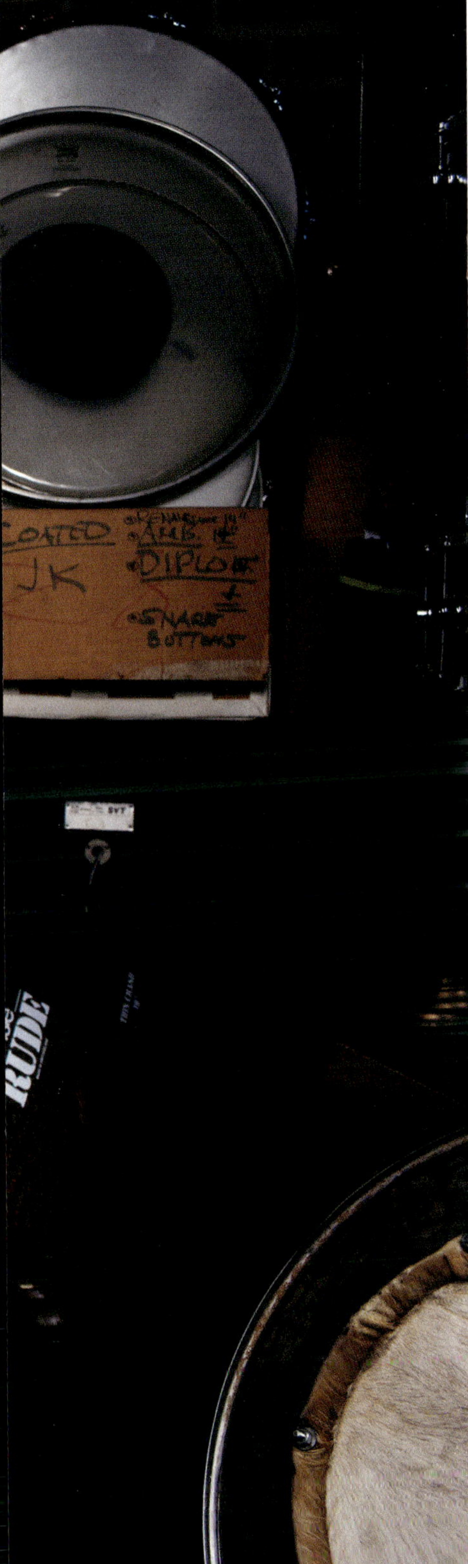

JIM KELTNER

John Lennon / George Harrison / Bob Dylan / Randy Newman / Ry Cooder
Photographed at Drum Doctors, California

The first real big record that I ever played on was in 1965. I got asked to be the drummer in Gary Lewis & the Playboys by Gary, who wanted to give up the drums and become the guy in the front. So I ended up playing on a record called *She's Just My Style*. Leon Russell was producing and he took note, there was something that I played that made him think. 'That's very cool,' he said, 'you're going to be a great rock drummer someday.' It felt good to hear that, but on the other hand I didn't really like rock and roll that much. I was a jazz player. And so it didn't mean quite as much at the time as it did later on. I've always considered Leon a musical guru of mine.

Making that record got me addicted immediately. In those days, you would make a record and, about three or four weeks later, you'd hear it on the radio. So I'm driving around in my car, 22 years old, in this band already, and it made me shave to look like a cute kid so that the girls would all get excited – that's what it was about in those days. The idea of making a record and hearing yourself playing on it, knowing it's you playing – it just was addictive. That was the way the door was opened for me.

Then, Hal Blaine had me sub for him. He threw me in the very deepest end of the pool because I had no clue what I was getting into. I showed up at TTG – a huge studio in LA – and it was a big day: all string sections, horn section, huge rhythm section. That was before the days when I had cartage: I carried my own drums up and I was late. I didn't realize time was money in the studio world. When I sat down and I played I remember feeling very confident. It was a big, long chart and I had no problem with it, and the groove was my groove and I rocked it. Then we went on a break and we were in the coffee room and there are all these guys – all these famous studio guys. And I'm standing there, I think at that time I was probably 24 or 25. Al Casey, who had played on every pop record ever done at that time, said, 'Who's the kid on drums?' And somebody else said, 'I don't know, Hal sent him.' And he says, 'He's good.' And I just sort of elevated a couple feet off the ground. I will never forget what that did to my confidence. Then we went back in and Jimmy – it was a Jimmy Webb day – he said, 'We need to do a thirty-second version of this. How can we change it up a little bit? I don't want to change the music or anything, just change the groove.' And Mike Dacy, the guitar player, said, 'Let's do it in 5/4, let's do it in 5.' And I froze, I thought, oh no, this is where I lose it. We started and it was just like the most natural thing in the world and I played the pee out of that thing. So that took me over the top: I knew I could do this.

My jazz background turned out to be the greatest thing. Now, every drummer has access to the jazz world, so everybody has some bit of jazz in their soul. But for me, I didn't know anything but that, so I came really pure, right out of Miles and Coltrane and Elvin and Philly Joe, Roy Haynes, and I brought as much of that as I could to the pop world when I played. But then I realized you have to be careful: when you're playing on a pop record it's really about being minimal and about feel and making sure the song is flattered by what you play rather than you being flattered by your little chit-chat. So I understood that and it was a good combination, because there's just a feel that you have when you come from the jazz world. You do have to temper it.

The older I get, the more I marvel at what I went through as a kid. I had some trauma, very bad trauma, losing my sister to a brain tumour, being with my aunt Connie when she was burned and almost died and the house burned down in the swamps in Louisiana … My mom and dad being children when they had me at seventeen and getting to the age 26, 27, that dangerous age where they were just fighting and threatening divorce, and all I did was pray every morning that they wouldn't. But the magical moments that I remember ... my uncle Willy Mendoza and my uncle Frank Mendoza lived in a duplex right across the street from the area where the Black population lived. In Tulsa, Oklahoma, at that time you had the Black folks' part of town and then you had the Mexicans in between that would buffer the white section. On those hot summer nights after dinner my uncle Willy would be sitting on this little swing out on the porch with his guitar, singing in Spanish and hearing the Black kids playing across the street, and I'm just this little white kid taking it all in. My world was in the white and the Mexican worlds because my mom was Mexican. So the richness of that experience is something that I just … I cherish it now.

CLAUDE COLEMAN JR

Ween / Eagles of Death Metal / Amandla. Photographed in New Jersey

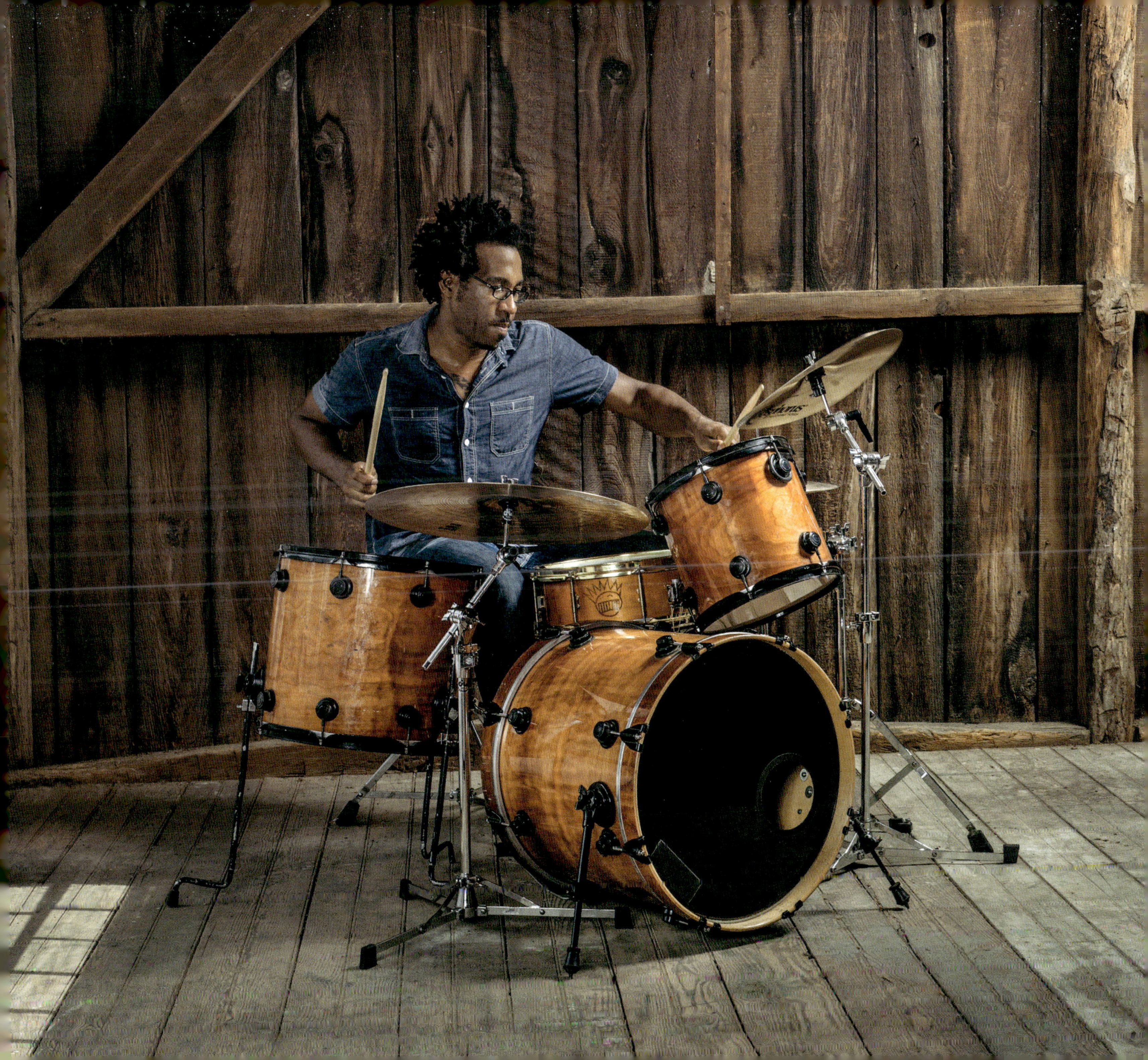

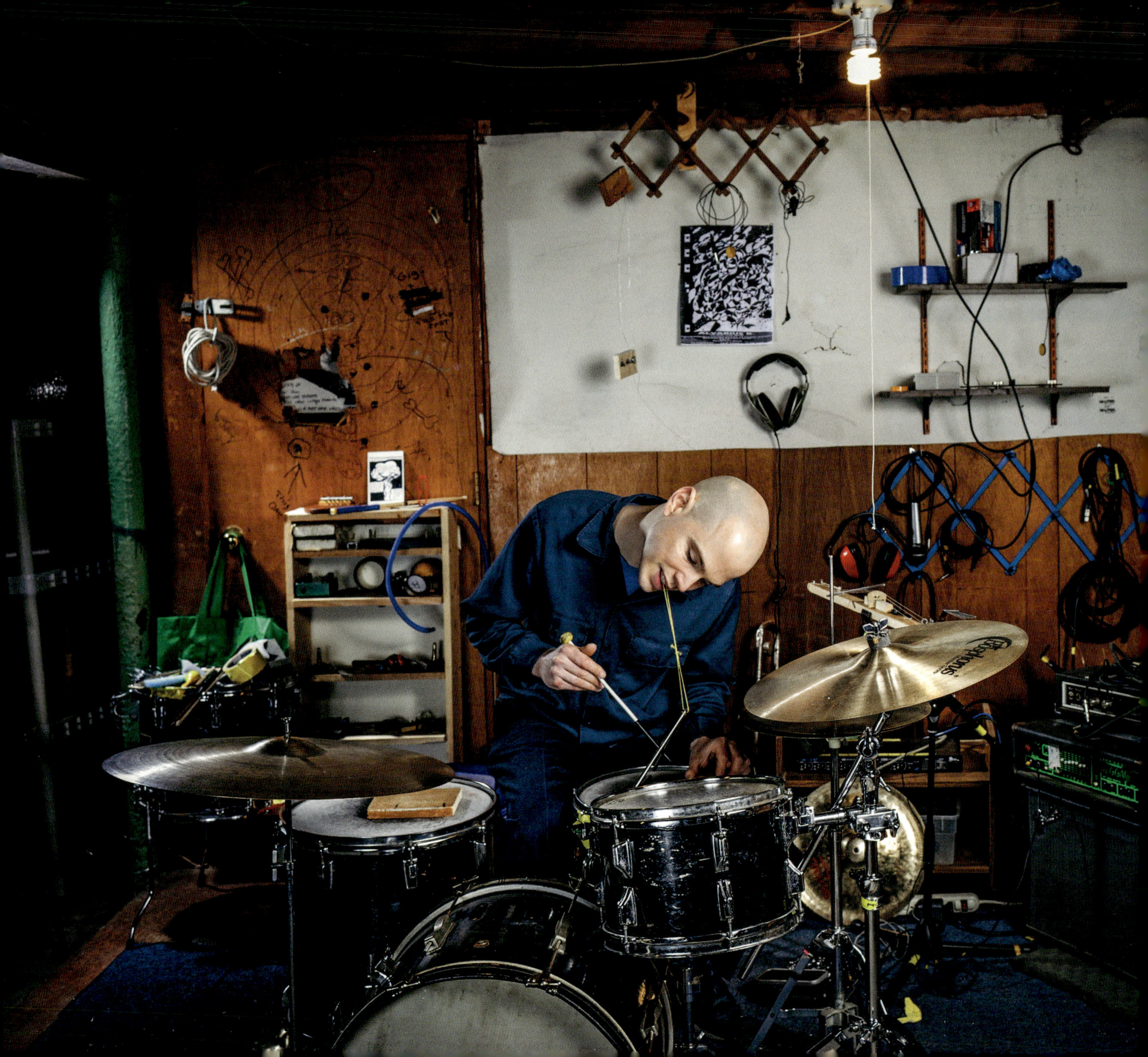

CHRIS CORSANO

Paul Flaherty / Flower-Corsano Duo / Vampire Belt / Björk / Joe McPhee
Photographed at home, Massachusetts

For a while I was really into kung fu and samurai flicks and the choreography of this pretty violent attack, and how it could be done so beautifully. Maybe there was a parallel in the movies, like all the different styles of when someone busts tiger style; that's totally applicable to drums, just the different ways of doing things. And not just the standard kind of thing, but to be good at anything you should be inventing something and putting your own spin on it. Maybe that's the one thing that's been in the back of my mind over the years just as something to play around with, for analogy's sake.

From the first time that I played live to the first time that I started playing free, that was a big change. A lot of the time, I think I was playing like I was taking a test. Whether I felt it was good or not was kind of like a pass/fail, like, did I mess up? Were there mistakes? You can lose a lot of perspective that way, because the rest of the audience really doesn't give a fuck if there are two mistakes. For argument's sake, say there's two performances that have two mistakes in them. They can be so different when you play note-for-note more or less the same thing, but the feel and all this other stuff going into it ... so I think when I started listening to free stuff, that pulled me in a lot more strongly because it got me out of this wrong way of thinking about what I was doing before. I think the first time that I played live in a more free, improvised context was definitely more interesting. It opens up a whole new world that you really want to explore.

A lot of basement shows are really memorable for me. I'm always kind of thinking back to being an audience member, because that's where I started, especially on the free thing. It was just feeling the power of what music can do and then hoping that I could do that. It strips away a lot of preconceptions that you have about music and authorship and who's really in charge of things. Some people want to attribute things to a creator – the person who created it or a religious entity … I don't know. Like when you have those moments when you're playing and there seems to be an audience even when there's not, but you kind of get outside yourself. It's not like a religious experience – that puts it in a whole context that I don't mean to put it in – but at least it isn't mundane and it's not day-to-day. Those are moments in music that really mean something.

If I'm playing, I want to get somebody out there to feel like I did when I saw those other bands, and that's at least a goal. There are those times when the audience is kind of getting into a group – and it's positive, too, a mob doesn't always have to be angry. To feel part of that – you don't feel like you're the only one driving the truck, because they're egging you on. It becomes this kind of great, great thing.

JAKI LIEBEZEIT

Can. Photographed in his studio, Germany

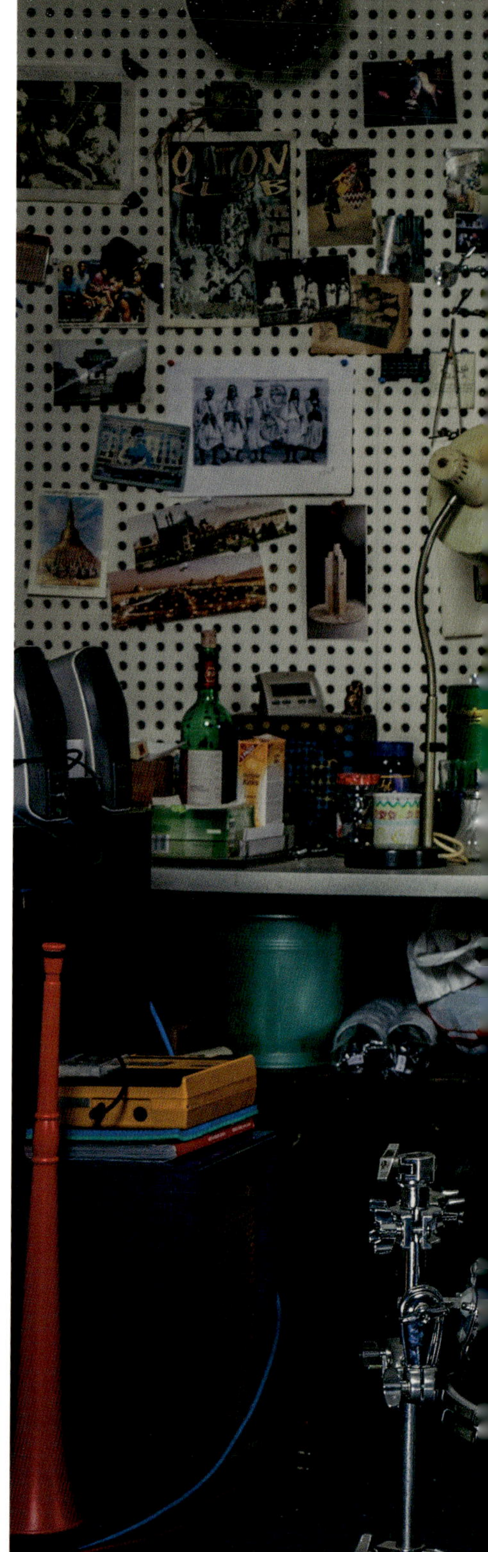

It was 1968; it was a year of revolution. That started with some student riots in Berlin and something happened in the mind, worldwide, I think, at that time. Also in music and in art and painting – Pop art came, and that's why we all had the idea to do something new. We were fed up with that old post-war thing. We came together, all of us had the same feeling, and I think that gave us the power to do something new.

Kraftwerk, we occasionally met them, or we played the same concerts. Otherwise there were not so many bands like that. We met some bands at festivals, but there was no real contact with them – and most of the bands at that time were imitating English bands. It was different with Can, it didn't sound English at all. So either people hated it or they loved it. I think most of the people who liked it liked it because they had the feeling that it wasn't just an English copy. It was something different. But we had problems in Germany in the beginning because we didn't sound English enough.

The studio was essential for us. No band had their own studio, because usually the bands would write a song, then rehearse it in their rehearsal room, and then go to a studio and record it. With Can, there was never anything written – we didn't want that. We thought we could go to a studio and play together and see what was happening, and if there were good ideas we'd work on them, without writing. We couldn't afford to go to a studio every day that cost a lot of money and stay there for four weeks and after that have maybe two tracks. The studio was very primitive, but was just enough for us. Years later we had multi-track machines, but that wasn't so good for the teamwork, because then we could separate the tracks and someone could do his track again, or play five guitar tracks, and then sort out the best – that destroyed the teamwork a little bit.

We were definitely a collective, or a team. We played every day together, and recorded and listened until we were satisfied. Because there was never one composer, no one was allowed to become boss and we split all the royalties. These ideas also came from 1968, there was that commune idea. Although we were not a commune living in one flat together, we shared the money in equal parts.

When I started with Can I had a lot of critics who said we were repeating all the time, and we didn't have ideas. But I think the repetition, you have to feel it. With Can, for every tune we played I designed a special rhythm, so each of the tunes had different rhythms. It's not like rock rhythm. I stopped with all that. I've given up that old style of – you can call it American drumming. American drumming, it was and still is normal, everybody plays American. So that's why I don't play what to me is normal. Like the typical drum set, with hi-hat, bass drum, snare drum, tom-tom, right cymbal – I've changed that.

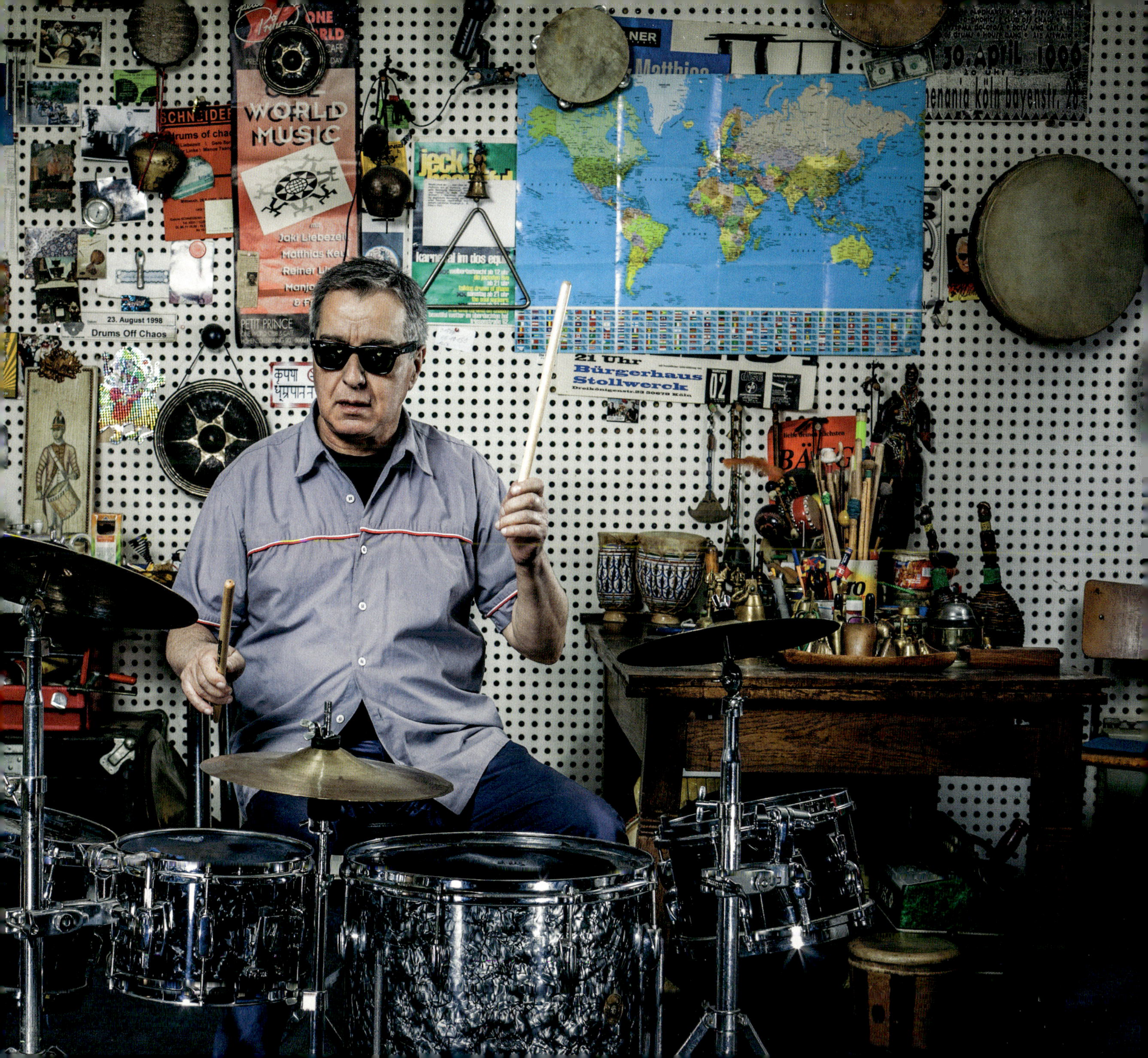
WORLD MUSIC
Jaki Liebezeit
SCHNEIDER
PETIT PRINCE
23. August 1998
Drums Off Chaos
21 Uhr
Bürgerhaus
Stollwerck
02

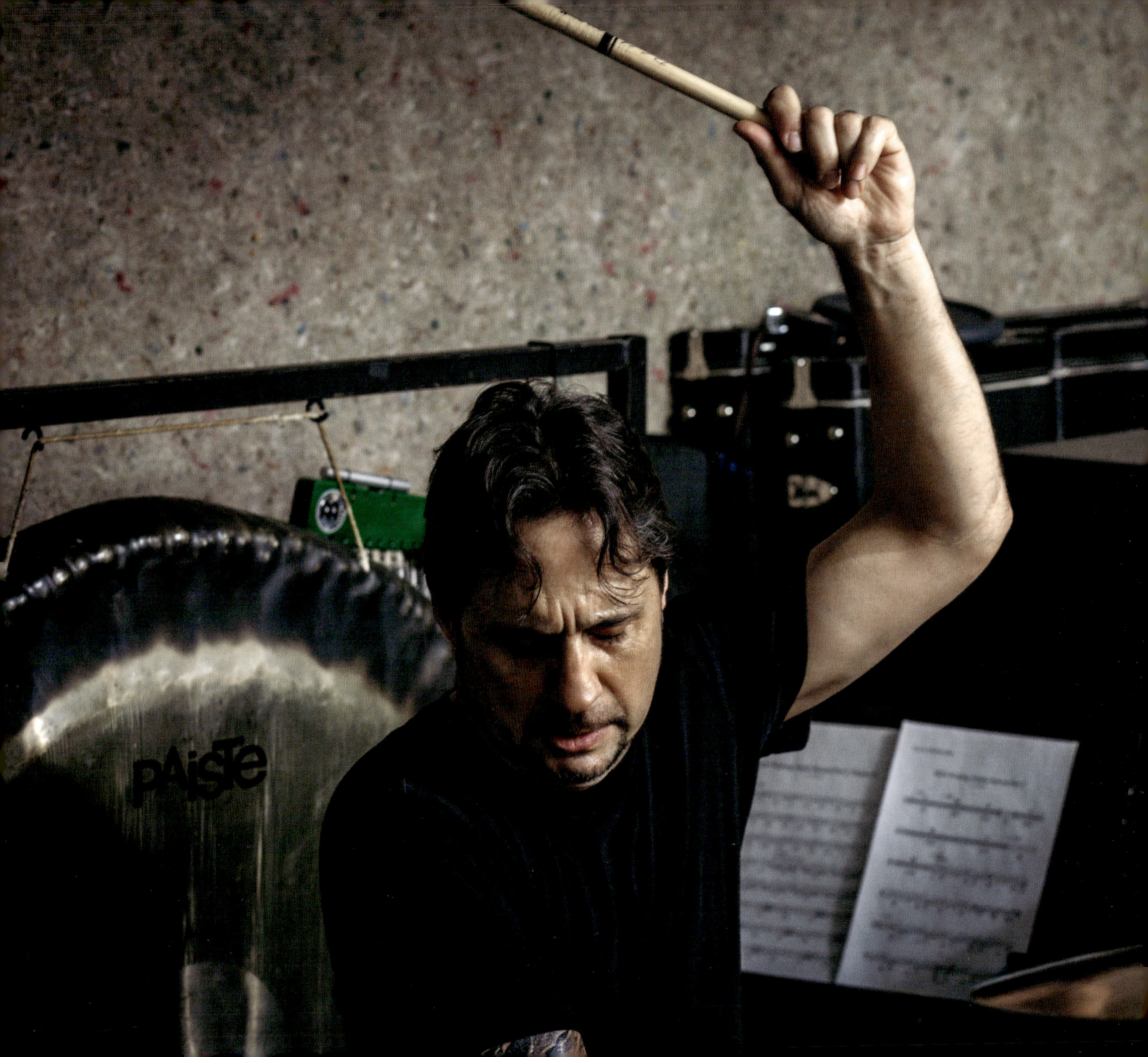
PAiSTe

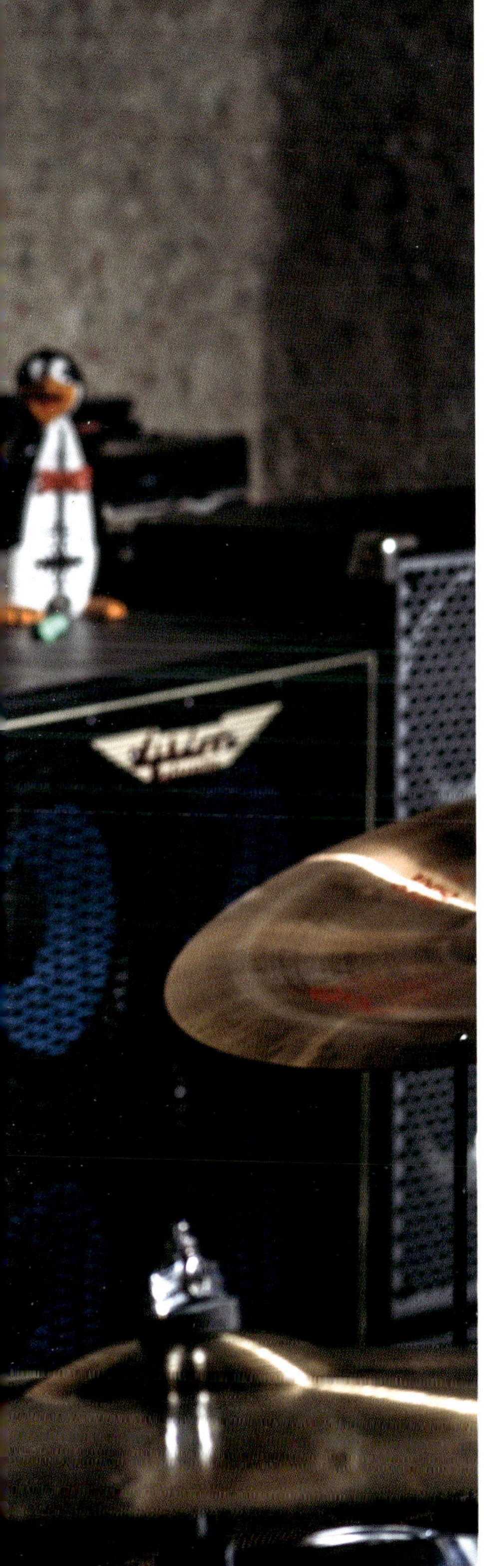

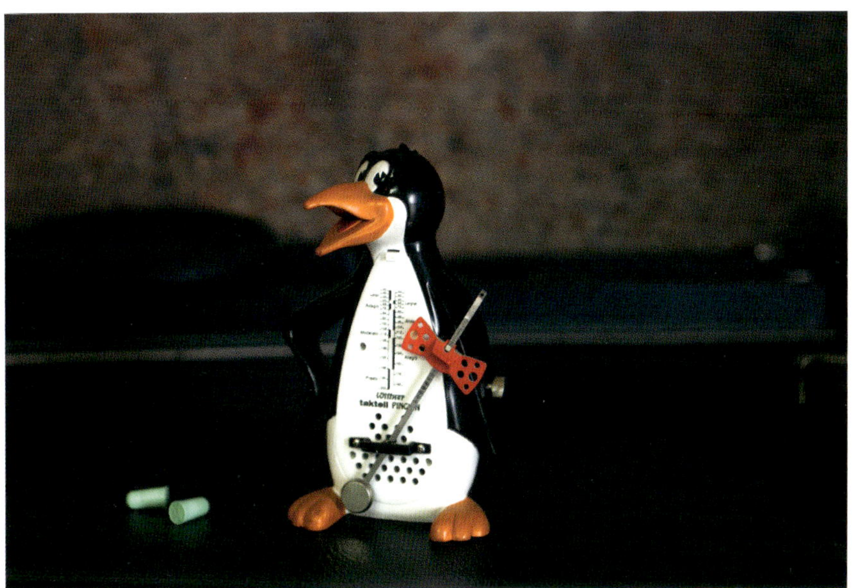

DAVE LOMBARDO

Slayer / Fantômas / Dead Cross / John Zorn / Mr. Bungle / Misfits. Photographed in his studio, California

My attorney once asked me what drumming is like. I told her it's like ballet. She looked at me kind of funny. I know the music so well and it is such a big part of me that, when I'm playing, it's a performance, it's a motion, it's a dance.

When I'm playing my drums what you're seeing is really fast, and what I'm playing is really fast, two hundred beats per minute. But in my mind, it's not really two hundred beats per minute – I'm in a whole different cycle. Although everything is going really fast, I'm breaking it down. If I was educated in music, I'd be able to explain it a little bit better – I cut everything down in time. What seems to be fast to you is actually a quarter of that to me. I was watching an old Slayer video and you can see I'm breathing very slow as everything is going really fast. My posture is straight up. Somebody brought that to my attention, telling me, 'You're just, like, at a slow tempo. Everything else is going fast but I just seem to lock in better when I break everything down.

When I watch myself sometimes I think, oh my god, what did I just do there? I'll get the chills and my palms start sweating. I start feeling what I felt at that moment and I hold my breath, and I kind of go with what I'm watching. For example, I was watching a video of this performance with Fantômas, Mike Patton's band. I had a broken leg and I was in bed watching it. My hands were sweating, my heart was palpating, just wanting to play.

It is humbling working around other musicians. I mean, John Zorn's discography – I can't believe the material that guy puts out. John called me to work with Bill Laswell, an amazing bass player. It's funny because when I go to the music store Amoeba, John Zorn, he's in the jazz section, Bill Laswell, he's in the electronica section, and I'm usually in with the metal. So you have these three genres of music but we all come together and we perform these amazing improv movements and it's amazing.

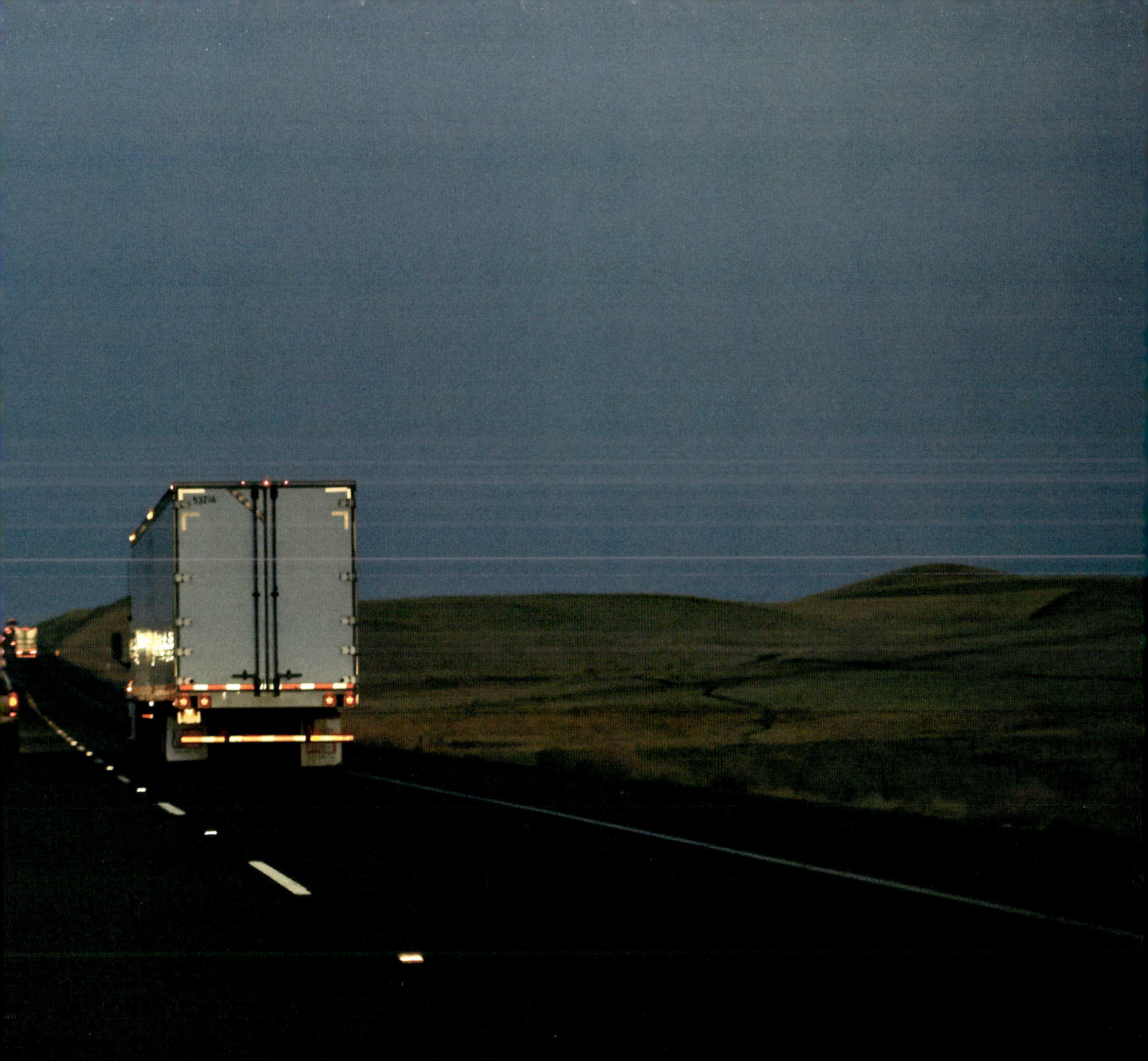

AUTHOR BIOGRAPHY

Part of the original team at *Dazed & Confused* magazine, Deirdre O'Callaghan has built a career uniting her passions for music and photography, shooting artwork and press for all the major record labels and collaborating with artists including Damon Albarn, Ezra Collective, De La Soul, Foo Fighters, Grinderman, Josh Homme, Laura Marling, Father John Misty, The National, Questlove and U2.

In addition to her commercial and editorial work, O'Callaghan has undertaken a number of independent photographic projects. Her first book, *Hide That Can*, is a culmination of four years spent photographing the men of Arlington House, a hostel in Camden, London. *Hide That Can* was awarded Book of the Year by both the International Center of Photography in New York and Les Rencontres de la Photographie in Arles. After moving to the US, O'Callaghan spent time photographing and interviewing the colourful residents of the infamous New York cultural landmark the Chelsea Hotel in the declining days of its original management. More recently, while living in Los Angeles, she worked on a photographic and short film project, *Winter In America*, about the homeless community living downtown on Skid Row.

ACKNOWLEDGEMENTS

Thanks to Mindy Abovitz, Ann Acheson, Billy Amendola at *Modern Drummer*, B+, Miura Band, Jae Barber at The JAE.B Group, Dawn Barger at Post Hoc Management, Geoff Barradale at Wildlife Entertainment, Scott Bomar at Electraphonic Recording, Scott Booker at Hellfire Enterprises, Guillaume Bougard at TABOU1Records, Rebecca Boulton at Prime Management, Alex Bramwell at William Morris Endeavor Entertainment, Gaylard Bravo, Aaron Budnik, Scott Byrne, Julie Calland at Courtyard Management, Jim Carroll, Clare at Naam, Dan Crowe at *Port*, Kirk Degiorgio, Debbie DeStefano, Mike Dolbear, Kate Edwards at *Guardian Weekend*, Bart Elliott at Drummer Cafe, Adam Fells at Santana Management, Deb Fenstermacher at Red Light Management, Josh Flaherty at Tenth Street Entertainment, Andrew Friedman at Monotone Inc., Chris Frith, Giolliosa Fuller, Kate Fuller, Natalie Fuller, Carol Gadd, Ross Garfield at Drum Doctors, Kate Gibb, James Gooding, Brie Greenberg at Metallica, Jo Greenwood, Jeff Gros, Laura Haber at Ciulla Management, Terri Hall at Turner Hall PR, Jodie Harkins at Wildlife Entertainment, Craig Haynes, Denis Henry Hennelly, Deborah Kee Higgins at ATP, Barry Hogan at ATP, Michael Holden, Julian Honer, Ro Hurley, Wendy Ide, Chris Ingram, Shahul Iqbal, Freddy Kabini, Tanya Kiang at Gallery of Photography, Carol LeFlufy at Eye Forward Inc., Jose Leon, Stephen Leslie, Lora at Naam, Dave Love at Montuno, Fui Yeang (Adrienne) Low, Mary McCartney, Andrew McDonagh, Callum McGeoch, Declan McGovern, Dan McNally, Keith McPhee at *The Tonight Show Starring Jimmy Fallon*, Karen McQuaid at The Photographers' Gallery, Colleen Maloney at Domino, Chris Marsh, Scott Martin, Laura Matula at Third Man Records, Lawrence 'Boo' Mitchell at Royal Studios, Paris Montoya at Rebel Waltz Inc., Mary Moyer at Sacks & Co., John Murphy at Leica, Nelly Neben at Axis Artist Management, Liz O'Riordan, Steve Orkin at Orkin Marketing, Sam O'Sullivan, Emma Petit, Steve Pereira, Sandra Podmore at Spoon Records, Derek Power at The Derek Power Company, Emma Reeves, Scott Robert Ritchie, David Ross, Kendra Ross, Andreas Schmid, Hildegard Schmidt at Spoon Records, Monica Seide-Evenson at Speakeasy PR, Sarah Seiler at Pearl Jam Inc., Diane Smyth, Jim Southwick, Kate Spicer, Petroc Trelawny, Eric Trosset at Comet Records, Steve Turner, Susie Turner, Vince Villard, Jenni Weinman at The Current Co., Jenny Wickens, Kathie Williams, Paula Willigar, Alex Wilshire and Zarah Zohlman.

Special thanks go to Ross Allen, Sandra Barron, Mary Pat Bentel, Tom Bird, Damian Bradfield, Matthias Clamer, Karen Downes, Allan Finamore at Epilogue Inc., Ali Esen, Ali Gitlow, Toni Greene, Zach Hill, Khai Le, Anna Lopriore, Sarah Lowe, Lily Moayeri, James Moriarty, Molly Murray, Willie Nedrow, Katy Niker, Lotte Ould, Rankin, Gerard Saint at Big Active, Mark Sanders, Jim Sclavunos, Aimee Selby, Michael Shields, Vanessa Soto, Jhett Thompson, Bradley Tuck, Susanne Waddell and Nick Waplington.

To my family: Mum, Dad, Conor, Ann Marie, Dermot and Peter.

Above all, I am grateful to the drummers who so generously gave me their time.

IN MEMORIAM

Tony Allen
Ginger Baker
Hal Blaine
Clem Burke
Jack DeJohnette
Milford Graves
Howard Grimes
Roger Hawkins
Roy Haynes
Jaki Liebezeit
Neil Peart
John 'Jab'o' Starks
Clyde Stubblefield

A member of Penguin Random House Verlagsgruppe GmbH, 2nd edition, 2026.
Originally published in 2016.

produktsicherheit@penguinrandomhouse.de
(The above information is mandatory according to GPSR and should be used for all queries relating to the safety of our books.)

A Library of Congress Control Number is available.

A CIP catalogue record for this book is available from the British Library.

Editorial direction: Ali Gitlow
Copyediting and proofreading: Aimee Selby
Design and layout: Gerard Saint and Ali Esen

Production: Luisa Klose
Origination: Schnieber Graphik, Munich
Printing and binding: TBB, a.s., Banská Bystrica

Penguin Random House Verlagsgruppe FSC® N001967

Printed in Slovakia

ISBN 978-3-7913-9413-8

www.prestel.com

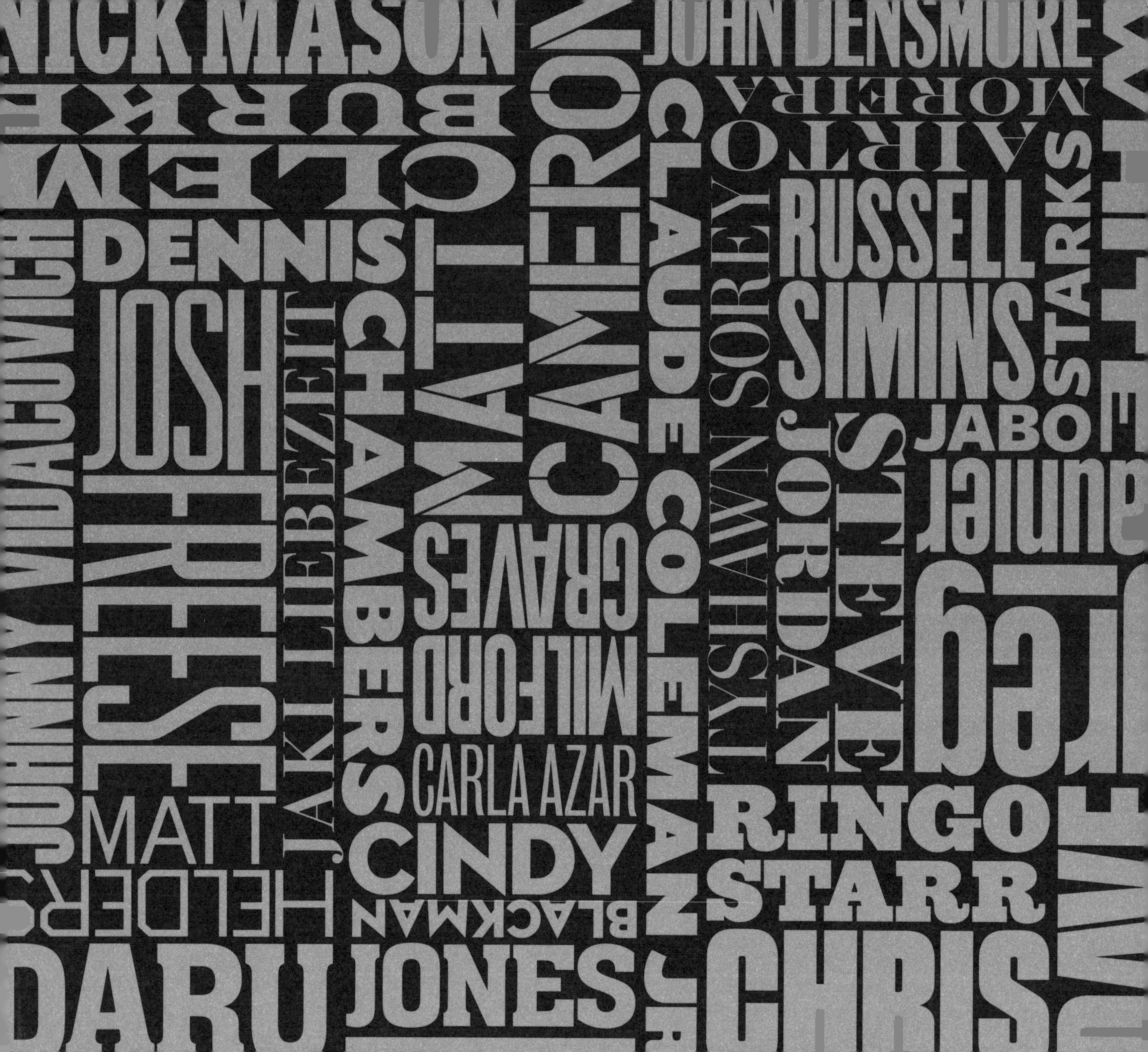

NICK MASON
JOHN DENSMORE
CLEM BURKE
AIRTO MOREIRA
DENNIS CHAMBERS
JOSH FREESE
JAKI LIEBEZEIT
MATT CAMERON
CLAUDE COLEMAN JR.
TYSHAWN SOREY
RUSSELL SIMINS
JABO STARKS
STEVE JORDAN
GREG SAUNIER
MILFORD GRAVES
CARLA AZAR
CINDY BLACKMAN
RINGO STARR
JOHNNY VIDACOVICH
MATT HELDER
DARU JONES
CHRIS DAVE